Diplomatic Dispute Settlement

The Use of Inter-State Conciliation

Dedicated to the memory of
Aart Koopmans and Henry Schermers

Diplomatic Dispute Settlement

The Use of Inter-State Conciliation

Sven M.G. Koopmans

T·M·C·Asser Press

Published by T·M·C·ASSER PRESS
P.O. Box 16163, 2500 BD The Hague, The Netherlands
<www.asserpress.nl>

T·M·C·ASSER PRESS' English language books are distributed exclusively by:

Cambridge University Press, The Edinburgh Building, Shaftesbury Road,
Cambridge CB2 2RU, UK,
or
for customers in the USA, Canada and Mexico:
Cambridge University Press, 100 Brook Hill Drive, West Nyack, NY 10994-2133, USA
<www.cambridge.org>

ISBN 978-90-6704-260-4

FOREWORD

Great advances have been made in the use of non-judicial dispute procedures – Alternative Dispute Resolution or ADR – in municipal contexts, and in their formal incorporation within the municipal legal systems. The practical importance of analogous procedures within the international system is at least as great, but they have attracted relatively little attention from international lawyers. With a few exceptions, such as the seminal studies by Cot and Kirgis, these procedures have not been made the subject of sustained analysis.

Dr Koopmans has, I think rightly, sensed that the time is ripe for a revival of non-judicial procedures in international dispute settlement. This careful analysis of one of the most flexible and responsive of those procedures, conciliation, is alive both to its advantages and its pitfalls, and also demonstrates the variety of forms that it may take. This monograph, a product of his doctoral research, is a substantial contribution to the literature on international dispute settlement and an important marker of the particular role of conciliation within international law. Dr Koopmans has not only championed its cause, but also invested a great deal of effort in the production of this valuable monograph; and for both, international lawyers are indebted to him.

Oxford, All Souls Day 2007 — Professor Vaughan LOWE

TABLE OF CONTENTS

LIST OF ABBREVIATIONS

ADB	Asian Development Bank
ADR	Alternative Dispute Resolution
AFDI	Annuaire Français de Droit International
AJIL	American Journal of International Law
APEC	Asia-Pacific Economic Co-operation
ASDI	Annuaire Suisse de Droit International
ASEAN	Association of South East Asian Nations
ASIL Proc.	Proceedings of the American Society of International Law
AU	African Union
BISD	Basic Instruments and Selected Documents (GATT)
BYIL	British Yearbook of International Law
CBD	Convention on Biological Diversity
CCSBT	Convention for the Conservation of the Southern Bluefin Tuna
CETS	Council of Europe Treaty Series
CIS	Commonwealth of Independent States
CITES	Convention on International Trade in Endangered Species of Wild Fauna and Flora
CJIL	Chinese Journal of International Law
COP	Conference of the Parties
Cot	J P Cot *International Conciliation* (tr 1972)
DSB	Dispute Settlement Body
DSU	Dispute Settlement Understanding
EAC	East African Community
EBRD	European Bank for Reconstruction and Development
ECHR	European Convention on Human Rights
ECJ	European Court of Justice
ECnHR	European Commission of Human Rights
ECOWAS	Economic Community of West African States
ECtHR	European Court of Human Rights
EEZ	Exclusive Economic Zone
EHRLR	European Human Rights Law Review
EJIL	European Journal of International Law
EU	European Union

GA	United Nations General Assembly
GATT	General Agreement on Tariffs and Trade
GYIL	German Yearbook of International Law
Habicht	M Habicht *Post-War Treaties for the Pacific Settlement of International Disputes* (1931)
IACnHR	Inter-American Commission of Human Rights
IACtHR	Inter-American Court of Human Rights
IADB	Inter-American Development Bank
IBRD	International Bank for Reconstruction and Development
ICC	International Chamber of Commerce
ICJ	International Court of Justice
ICLQ	International and Comparative Law Quarterly
ICSID	International Centre for the Settlement of Investment Disputes
IDA	International Development Association
IDI	Institut de Droit International
IFC	International Finance Corporation
IJIL	Indian Journal of International Law
ILC	International Law Commission
ILM	International Legal Materials
ILQ	International Law Quarterly
ILR	International Law Reports
IMF	International Monetary Fund
IOLR	International Organizations Law Review
ITLOS	International Tribunal for the Law of the Sea
ITO	International Trade Organisation
LJIL	Leiden Journal of International Law
LNOJ	League of Nations Official Journal
LOSC	United Nations Convention on the Law of the Sea
MIGA	Multilateral Investment Guarantee Agency
MLF	Montreal Protocol's Multilateral Fund
MOP	Meeting of the Parties
NAFTA	North American Free Trade Agreement
NATO	North Atlantic Treaty Organisation
NCP	Non-Compliance Procedure
NGO	Non-governmental Organisation
NILR	Netherlands International Law Review
NTIR	Nederlands Tijdschrift voor Internationaal Recht
NYIL	Netherlands Yearbook of International Law
NYUJILP	New York University Journal of International Law and Politics

OAS	Organisation of American States
OAU	Organisation of African Unity
OSCE	Organisation for Security and Cooperation in Europe
OSPAR	Convention for the Protection of the Marine Environment of the North-East Atlantic
PCA	Permanent Court of Arbitration
PCIJ	Permanent Court of International Justice
RADIC	Revue Africaine de Droit International et Comparé
RDILC	Revue de Droit International et de Législation Comparée
RECIEL	Review of European Community and International Environmental Law
Recueil des Cours	Academie de Droit International: Recueil des Cours
RGDIP	Revue Générale de Droit International Public
RIAA	United Nations Reports of International Arbitral Awards
SC	United Nations Security Council
UN	United Nations
UNCITRAL	United Nations Commission on International Trade Law
UNDP	United Nations Development Program
UNEP	United Nations Environmental Program
UNESCO	United Nations Education, Scientific and Cultural Organisation
UNGA	United Nations General Assembly
UNMOGIP	United Nations Military Observer Group in India and Pakistan
UNSC	United Nations Security Council
UNSCOM	United Nations Special Commission
UNTS	United Nations Treaty Series
WBIP	World Bank Inspection Panel
WIPO	World Intellectual Property Organisation
WTO	World Trade Organisation
WW	World War
ZfAÖRV	Zeitschrift für Ausländisches Öffentliches Recht und Völkerrecht

INTRODUCTION

1. The Use of Inter-State Conciliation

Inter-State conciliation is at the same time a common element in international dispute settlement and an unknown quantity. There are many provisions in international agreements naming conciliation as one of the options by which to settle disputes. Nevertheless, little is known about what conciliation is and what contributions it can make. The lack of knowledge is due largely to the rarity of its application. It is therefore also forgotten that at some time in the 20th century, conciliation was widely considered to be an outstanding method to resolve otherwise insoluble disputes, and thereby even to eradicate war:

> '... si, comme nous le croyons, les traités de conciliation et d'arbitrage vont se généralisant et si, comme nous l'espérons, une convention collective est élaborée un jour afin de consacrer universellement le principe de la conciliation préliminaire, la paix dans le monde sera assise sur des bases sérieuses, solides.'[1]

The lack of knowledge of conciliation is also partly due to international lawyers, who have traditionally focussed on international courts as the centre of international legal practice. While this limited view is increasingly broadened to include diplomacy, custom and legal and political thought, conciliation still remains little studied.[2] Further, it is to be assessed whether international lawyers may also have directly contributed to the neglect of conciliation by fre-

[1] C. Gorgé, 'L'évolution de la conciliation internationale', (1927) 54 *RDILC* 58, 106.

[2] There are some notable works on conciliation, but the most important ones are over thirty years old: J.P. Cot, *La Conciliation Internationale* (1968) and J.P. Cot, *International Conciliation* (tr 1972); H. von Mangoldt, 'Arbitration and Conciliation', in H. Mosler and R. Bernhardt (eds.), *Judicial Settlement of International Disputes* (1974) 417; further: U. Villani, *La Conciliazione nelle Controversie Internazionali* (1979). Other, more recent work considers conciliation usefully but succinctly amidst a wide range of methods of international dispute settlement: e.g., J.G. Merrills, *International Dispute Settlement* (4th edn. 2005); J.G. Collier and A.V. Lowe, *The Settlement of Disputes in International Law* (1999); United Nations *Handbook on the Peaceful Settlement of Disputes between States* (1992).

quently treating it, both in writings and in practice, as resembling adjudication, only without binding force. Following one such case, Suzanne Bastid wondered whether inter-State conciliation had yet found its distinctive and definitive form.[3] Fifty years later, the identity of conciliation remains in question.

1.1 The distinct identity of conciliation

The concept of international conciliation developed in the early 20th century out of the method of inquiry, which was itself just being formalised.[4] Many see a high profile inquiry case of 1905 as in fact the first exercise in conciliation,[5] even though the procedure did not assume its name until after the First World War. From 1919 onwards it was elaborated, promoted and put into practice by the Swiss government.[6] In 1922 it was embraced by the League of Nations.[7] Since then, conciliation has its own place in the classic enumeration of diplomatic dispute settlement methods of negotiation, inquiry, mediation and conciliation.[8] Hundreds of special bilateral conciliation treaties were concluded,[9] and a few dozen conciliation commissions convened.[10] Later, conciliation provisions would gain a matter-of-fact place in bilateral and multilateral agreements on substantive issues.[11] Nevertheless, it appears that over the years the distinct nature of conciliation was increasingly denied.

The problem of nomenclature is one both of lawyers and of laymen, rooted in everyday conversation. In 1994 the World Trade Organisation created the

---

3 S. Bastid, 'La commission de conciliation franco-suisse', (1956) 2 *AFDI* 436.

4 Hague Convention for the Pacific Settlement of International Disputes (29 July 1899) (1899 Hague Convention) Art. 5; Permanent Court of Arbitration *Basic Documents* (1998) 3.

5 The *Dogger Bank* Case (United Kingdom/Russia), where an inquiry commission recommended a solution to the dispute. See chapter II 1.3. For the report and the inquiry agreement: J.B. Scott, *The Hague Court Reports* (1916) 403.

6 Rapport du Conseil fédéral à l' Assemblée fédérale concernant les traités internationaux d'arbitrage' (1919) 71; Feuille Fédéral Suisse Vol. V 808.

7 Assembly Res (22 September 1922), League of Nations Official Journal (1922) (special No. 9) 6.

8 A fuller enumeration would usually comprise negotiation, consultation, good offices, inquiry, mediation, conciliation and the binding legal methods of arbitration and judicial settlement.

9 M. Habicht, *Post-War Treaties for the Pacific Settlement of International Disputes* (1931); United Nations *Systematic Survey of Treaties for the Pacific Settlement of International Disputes 1928-1948* (1948); United Nations *A Survey of Treaty Provisions for the Pacific Settlement of International Disputes 1949-1962* (1966).

10 See chapter II 1.

11 E.g., Framework Convention on Tobacco Control (21 May 2003), (2003) 42 *ILM* 520 Art. 27; Israel-Palestine Liberation Organisation Interim Agreement on the West Bank and the Gaza Strip (28 September 1995), (1997) 36 *ILM* 551.

official settlement method of mediation, conciliation and good offices,[12] which is in fact only one procedure, and one that international lawyers would recognise as a form of mediation.[13] It may also be related to the fact that in various national jurisdictions no distinction is made between mediation and conciliation.[14] Equally, in the press the peaceful settlement work of the United Nations Secretary-General is often called conciliation, whereas – as will be discussed in more detail – his activities in this field would often legally be classified as 'good offices' or 'mediation'.[15]

Here, however, in order to assess the use of inter-State conciliation as it originated in public international law early last century, it is necessary to return to the procedure as a distinct method. Concentrating on the distinct identity of inter-State conciliation will produce a better perspective on the special traits of mediation and of other conciliation-like methods. Lastly, a focus on the distinct nature of conciliation can help to assess whether the confusion over its identity was also reason for the relative lack of its application.

Looking back, conciliation can be associated with anti-war idealism prior to WWII,[16] but also with the legal and political culture clashes of the 1960s, when provisions for compulsory conciliation were found to be the ultimate compromise between two opposing camps on dispute settlement, one demanding binding adjudication, another insisting on non-legal amicable settlement.[17] One of the questions on conciliation is therefore how it could obtain such different connotations.

2. Questions on Conciliation

The aim of this work is to present the legal and practical reality of inter-State conciliation,[18] by addressing a range of questions about the method. Among

---

[12] Art. 5 Dispute Settlement Understanding, Annex 2 to the Marrakech Agreement Establishing the World Trade Organization, 15 April 1994, (1994) 33 *ILM* 1144.

[13] See chapter IV 4.

[14] E.g., UNCITRAL Model Law on International Commercial Conciliation (2002) UN Doc A/57/18 Art. 1(3) on <http://www.uncitral.org/uncitral/en/uncitral_texts/arbitration.html> (5 October 2007); H.J. Brown and A.L. Marriott, *ADR Principles and Practice* (2nd edn. 1999) 127; see chapter I 2.5, I 3.

[15] See chapter I 2.5, with exceptions such as the arbitration in the *Rainbow Warrior* Case (*France* v. *New Zealand*), (1987) 74 *ILR* 256.

[16] E.g., J. Efremoff, 'L'Organisation de la conciliation comme moyen de prevenir des guerres', (1937) 59 *Recueil des Cours* Vol. I 99.

[17] As in the negotiations on the Vienna Convention on the Law of Treaties ((23 May 1969), 115 *UNTS* 331): I. Sinclair, *The Vienna Convention on the Law of Treaties* (2nd edn. 1984) 226-233.

[18] Without denying the value of insights of legal philosophy and political science, to which references must be included.

those to be asked are: What ideas were at its root? How did conciliation develop? How is it used? What is the role of the dispute, the parties and the conciliators in its use? What forms of conciliation are possible? When should what form of conciliation be used? How can conciliation deal with the application of norms? What are viable alternatives? Is it useful to develop new procedures? These and other questions are placed in the broader perspective of non-binding third party dispute settlement, also known as diplomatic dispute settlement. To this end, other questions also need to be asked, such as: What is a dispute? Are there disputes that cannot be settled by adjudication? In view of the many questions, some limitations are necessary, such as that on inter-State disputes.

2.1 Inter-State disputes

Conciliation between States is special, among other things because in international law there is often no alternative of recourse to adjudication, such as is normally the case in domestic settings. Furthermore, States are a different kind of actor than individuals and private organisations, having interests, durability, power, decision-making processes and many other attributes of a different level. Further, in public international law conciliation developed specifically as an inter-State procedure. Therefore, this work has an essential focus on inter-State conciliation, to the relative exclusion of sub-State conciliation, and does not claim equal treatment of State/non-State practices. Nevertheless, there are various forms of non-inter-State settlement that have significance for inter-State practice, or that, due to a combination of shared characteristics and alien elements, provide useful analogies and lessons for inter-State conciliation. It is therefore occasionally necessary to take a broader view.

2.2 A broader view

Where appropriate, extrapolations must be made to other relevant forms of third party dispute settlement. Doctrinal separation, in particular that between private and public law, should not hinder the gathering of insights.[19] Many references are possible. In recent decades the United States and the United Kingdom, among others, have gained much experience in the use of 'alterna-

[19] J. Paulsson, 'Cross Enrichment of Public and Private Law Dispute Resolution Mechanisms in the International Arena', (1992) 9 *Journal of International Arbitration* 1, 59; R.B. Bilder, 'International Third Party Dispute Settlement', (1989) 17 *Denver Journal of International Law and Policy* 475, 500; J.K. Lelewer, 'International Commercial Arbitration as a Model for Resolving Treaty Disputes', (1989) 21 *NYUJILP* 379.

tive dispute resolution' (ADR), methods of settlement re-discovered or newly developed to avoid or alleviate the judicial system.[20] Other States, particularly in Asia,[21] have a long-standing tradition of forms of mediation and conciliation, often as an important part of the regular court process.[22] Further, several international organisations, such as the World Intellectual Property Organisation (WIPO),[23] the Multilateral Investment Guarantee Agency (MIGA)[24] or the International Chamber of Commerce (ICC), have developed their own mediation or conciliation practices for disputes between private parties or private parties and States.[25] Such developments should be taken into account. One should nevertheless be careful to concentrate on those additional conciliation-like mechanisms that have most linkages with the central focus of inter-State conciliation, and that thereby provide clear and relevant lessons to the core topic. To that end, a selection is made of what appear in this respect to be the most enlightening non-inter-State conciliation procedures and compliance mechanisms.

2.2.1 *Non-inter-State conciliation procedures and compliance mechanisms*

Among non-inter-State settlement mechanisms, the practice of the International Centre for the Settlement of Investment Disputes (ICSID) stands out as closely associated with public international law. Set-up by a multilateral convention,[26]

---

[20] R. Caller (ed.), *ADR and Commercial Disputes* (2002); L.A. Mistelis, 'ADR in England and Wales', in J. Bell (ed.), *Studies in UK Law* (2002) 197; H.J. Brown and A.L. Marriott, *ADR Principles and Practice* (2nd edn. 1999).

[21] Including the Middle East: G. Sayan, 'Arbitration, Conciliation and the Islamic Legal Tradition in Saudi Arabia', (1997) 9 *University of Pennsylvania Journal of International Business Law* 211.

[22] A. Ye, 'Commentary on Integrated Dispute Resolution Systems in the PRC', International Council for Commercial Arbitration *New Horizons in International Commercial Arbitration and Beyond* (2005) 478; J.D.M. Lew, 'Multi-Institutional Conciliation and the Reconciliation of Different Legal Cultures', idem, 421; J.K. Lee, 'Non-binding Dispute Resolution Process- Experience in Korea', idem, 430.

[23] The WIPO Arbitration and Mediation Center <http://arbiter.wipo.int/center/index.html> (25 July 2006) administers the 1995 WIPO Mediation Rules, (1995) 34 *ILM* 559.

[24] MIGA offers mediation and conciliation <http://www.miga.org/sitelevel2/level2.cfm?id=1061> (5 October 2007) and Art. 3 Annex II Convention Establishing the Multilateral Investment Guarantee Agency, (1985) 24 *ILM* 1598.

[25] The ICC offers Alternative Dispute Resolution Rules of the International Chamber of Commerce (ICC ADR Rules), see <http://www.iccwbo.org/index_court.asp> (5 October 2007) and 'The New ICC ADR Rules', (2001) 12 *World Arbitration and Mediation Report* 301, and also offers ICC Dispute Board Rules (idem, and D.J.A. Cairns and I. Madalena, 'The ICC Dispute Board Rules', (2005) 8 *International Arbitration Law Review* 41.

[26] Convention on the Settlement of Investment Disputes between States and the Nationals of Other States (18 March 1965) (ICSID Convention), (1965) 4 *ILM* 52.

the Centre administers a growing number of high profile international settlement procedures for disputes between States and private investors. Like ICSID arbitrations, its conciliation cases involve major governmental and economic interests.

The 1950 European Convention on Human Rights,[27] revised by successive Protocols, set-up a well-respected judicial and semi-judicial system. By means of the European Commission of Human Rights, a friendly settlement practice involving States and individuals evolved. In ingenious ways it aimed to reconcile the desire to avoid adjudication with the need to ensure respect for the Convention's norms. The Commission was abolished in 1999. A comparable situation existed under the 1947 General Agreement on Tariffs and Trade (GATT) for international trade disputes.[28] GATT provided various procedures in-between negotiation and adjudication. In 1994, with the creation of the World Trade Organisation (WTO), they were replaced by a more judicial structure.[29]

Around same time, the World Bank created its own Inspection Panel, to review the Bank's compliance with its internal policies and procedures. Though hardly a means of diplomatic dispute settlement, among other things because parties objecting to the World Bank's actions are not involved in the conduct of the proceedings, its rules and practices may give an indication of alternatives to inter-State conciliation in particular situations.

Lastly, bypassing other forms of international third party dispute settlement, in the 1990s States invented non-compliance procedures (NCPs) to address particular disputes arising under a range of treaties. With the leading example of the Montreal Protocol NCP,[30] a mechanism emerged that comprises elements of various settlement procedures, and thereby created new questions on the relationship between non-binding settlement and treaty norms, as well as between settlement methods themselves. The above-mentioned procedures therefore deserve their own place in a study with the essential focus on inter-State conciliation.

3. Planning

Following this Introduction, this work contains four substantive chapters, each in two related parts, with conclusions pulling the parts together. It concludes

[27] European Convention for the Protection of Human Rights and Fundamental Freedoms (4 November 1950), 213 *UNTS* 221.

[28] General Agreement on Tariffs and Trade (30 October 1947), 55 *UNTS* 194.

[29] The Marrakech Agreement Establishing the World Trade Organization (15 April 1994), (1994) 33 *ILM* 1144.

[30] The Montreal NCP, pursuant to the Montreal Protocol Art. 8 is contained in a decision by the Fourth Meeting of the Parties: UNEP/Ozl.Pro.4/15.

with a fifth chapter with conclusions on the use of inter-State conciliation. The first part of chapter I presents conciliation within the context of diplomatic dispute settlement. It investigates the concept of a dispute, and aims to present a fresh view on the differences between justiciable and non-justiciable disputes, and legal and political disputes. It then examines the variety of means of diplomatic dispute settlement, including old and new practice. The second part of chapter I discusses the constitutive elements of conciliation. It challenges some standard views on inter-State conciliation, and discusses basic features of conciliation commissions. Further, the practice, diversity and complexities of the method are illustrated in three brief case studies.

On the basis of the core understanding of conciliation provided by the first chapter, chapter II analyses the development of conciliation among means of diplomatic dispute settlement, with particular focus on its legislative and contemporary practical record. The first part of this chapter surveys the history and addresses past criticism of the method with the help of hindsight. The second part contains a critical discussion of model rules of conciliation as prepared in the 1990s by the United Nations and the Permanent Court of Arbitration.

Chapter III discusses the sensitive relationship between conciliation and law. In the first part, starting from the factors influencing the conduct of conciliation, two 'ideal types' of conciliation are distinguished: political and legal conciliation. This leads to a reassessment of the central debate on inter-State conciliation in the 20th century, and a review of alternatives to common conceptions. Part two of the chapter then considers various ways in which conciliation may involve legal problems, and addresses ways to manage such problems.

Having discussed the relationship between conciliation and general legal aspects in chapter III, chapter IV focuses on the relationship between conciliation and specific norms at issue in disputes, in particular the norms contained in multilateral agreements. These deserve special attention, especially because of the interest in respecting rules previously agreed between the disputants and other parties to the relevant agreement. Starting with the complex settlement system of the Law of the Sea Convention, the first part of this chapter reviews how international agreements may employ conciliation in a way that promotes respect for the treaty norms. Taking matters further, part two analyses distinct methods created to address compliance with particular international norms. It studies the systems that evolved in the European Convention on Human Rights and in GATT/WTO, and continues with a discussion of the special mechanism developed by the World Bank. It concludes with a discussion of the non-compliance procedure.

The concluding chapter V draws together the findings on the use of inter-State conciliation. Starting with an outline of the use of diplomatic dispute settlement generally, it proceeds to find a core identity of conciliation, pointing out, on the basis of practical usage, how the divergent ideas and concepts both limited and inspired the use of the method. Following an assessment of how conciliation can be used, the chapter closes with a discussion of remaining challenges and new options.

Chapter I
DIPLOMATIC DISPUTE SETTLEMENT AND INTER-STATE CONCILIATION

In order to assess the use of inter-State conciliation, the method should be placed in the context of diplomatic dispute settlement. There is a traditional distinction between diplomatic and binding means of settlement of disputes. Arbitration and adjudication are binding methods, in which independent experts apply the law to a dispute, resulting in a judgement that the parties are bound to respect. On this basis, binding means of international settlement are often also called legal methods of dispute settlement, even though other binding means are possible that are not based on law, such as judicial settlement *ex aequo et bono*.[1] Diplomatic dispute settlement, on the other hand, as a whole employed much more frequently than any form of binding settlement, comprises all forms of settlement in which each of the parties legally retains the last word in accepting a finding, ruling or compromise. The classification is irrespective of the pressures that may, in practice, compel a party to comply with the outcome of the settlement method. The outcome of diplomatic dispute settlement methods is not legally binding upon a State.

In the first part of this chapter, the essentials of diplomatic dispute settlement are examined. The first section assesses what counts as a dispute, and what importance this finding may have for the use of settlement methods. The second section examines a range of diplomatic dispute settlement options. The second part of this chapter analyses the elements of conciliation in section three, and its basic features in section four. Lastly, in section five, three case studies illustrate the many faces of inter-State conciliation.

[1] E.g., on the basis of ICJ Statute Art. 38(2).

PART ONE

THE ELEMENTS AND PRACTICE OF DIPLOMATIC DISPUTE SETTLEMENT

1. What is a Dispute

There is both legal and political importance to a shared understanding of the term 'dispute'. Certain dispute settlement mechanisms allow one party to put a matter to a third party body unilaterally, provided the matter constitutes a 'dispute'. Even if there is no such mechanism available, parties can be sensitive to the qualification of 'dispute'. To agree to call something a dispute may seem to some to imply recognition of a competing legal claim, or at least recognition of the status of an opponent to pursue a competing claim. Thus, the dispute arising out of the division of Cyprus, involving strongly divergent views on in the status of the Turkish Cypriot political representatives, is officially called 'the Cyprus problem.'[2]

1.1 Differences of opinion, conflicts and situations

In legal discourse, the term 'dispute' is normally used in relation to dispute settlement procedures. A useful understanding of the term should take account of that context. When a third party settlement mechanism allows for unilateral applications, it must have been envisaged that use of a third party shall only be made if there is a concrete problem between the two sides that may benefit from the efforts of that third party.

Therefore, a mere difference of opinion will not by itself qualify as a 'dispute'. This should not, however, be understood to imply that only disputes merit the involvement of outside parties. There may be reason for parties to submit also differences of opinion to a third party.[3] Such would have to happen on the basis of mutual agreement. The need for third party involvement would arise, for instance, if one of the parties is about to act on the basis of its opinion

---

[2] And not the Cyprus/Turkey dispute or the Greek Cypriots/Turkish Cypriots dispute. See generally: 'Report of the Secretary-General on his Mission of Good Offices', UN Doc S/2004/437.

[3] This is provided for in the Preamble of the 2001 Alternative Dispute Resolution Rules of the International Chamber of Commerce (ICC ADR Rules), which are created for consensual adoption by private parties. Under the ICC ADR Rules, also when there is merely an uncertainty over what a contractual provision means, an application under the Rules can be made. See <http://www.iccwbo.org/index_court.asp> (5 October 2007) and 'The New ICC ADR Rules' (2001), 12 *World Arbitration and Mediation Report* 301.

of its legal responsibilities toward the other, where if it so acts, this would indeed give rise to a dispute.

A 'dispute' is also to be distinguished from a 'conflict', which is used to signify a general state of hostility between the parties.[4] A 'situation' is a similar concept, more commonly used among francophone writers.[5] Charpentier describes a 'situation' as being more diffuse than a dispute, though it can be more dangerous, because it is harder to find a way to resolve it. He names the example of the Chinese invasion of Vietnam in 1979 in order to 'teach it a lesson', without a concrete underlying dispute.[6] The understanding of 'conflict' is different from that argued by Iran in a failed effort to have the 1980 *Hostages* Case brought to the ICJ by the United States declared inadmissible. Iran held that the dispute was only one dispute in a long series, which could not be addressed separately.[7] The difference lies therein that whereas a 'conflict' is not necessarily a combination of disputes, in the latter case there was indeed such combination. The Court could therefore rule on the particular dispute that was placed before it.

1.2 **Legal, non-legal and political disputes**

The elaboration in the 20th century of the dispute settlement method of conciliation arose in part as a consequence of the intentions of States to qualify certain disputes as suited only for diplomatic treatment. A primary point of contention was the definition of a 'legal dispute', to be distinguished from a 'political dispute'.[8] Political disputes were historically distinguished on subjective criteria, such as 'disputes involving the honour and essential interests'.[9] In recent times such overt subjectivity is uncommon. The seemingly logical dichotomy between legal and political disputes is the source of confusion, as in varying definitions a subset of disputes on legal claims is also classified as 'political

---

[4] J.G. Collier and A.V. Lowe, *The Settlement of Disputes in International Law* (1999) 1. Cf., H.J. Brown and A.L. Marriott, *ADR Principles and Practice* (2nd edn. 1999) 7.

[5] An alternative is 'tension', used for the same concept: C. de Visscher, *Théories et Réalités en Droit International Public* (4th edn. 1970) 371.

[6] J. Charpentier, 'Article 2 Paragraphe 3', in J.P. Cot and A. Pellet, *La Charte des Nations Unies; Commentaire Article par Article* (1985) 103, 108; C. Tomuschat, 'Article 2(3)', in B. Simma and others (eds.), *The Charter of the United Nations; A Commentary* (1994) 97, 102-103.

[7] *US Diplomatic and Consular Staff in Tehran* (*US* v. *Iran*) (*Judgement*), (1980) *ICJ Rep* 3 [35]-[38]; J.G. Merrills, *International Dispute Settlement* (4th edn. 2005) 168.

[8] S.R. Ratner, 'Land Feuds and their Solutions: Finding International Law beyond the Trial Chamber', (2006) 100 *AJIL* 808, 813.

[9] Such exceptions of 'honour and essential interests' were proposed by the meeting of *Institut de Droit International* (1873). V.D. Degan, 'International Conciliation: Its Past and Future', in P. Fischer, H.F. Köck and A. Verdross, *Völkerrecht und Rechtsfilosofie* (1980) 261, 262.

disputes': a dispute would then be a legal dispute and a political dispute at the same time.[10] Charles de Visscher held:

> 'Aucun critère ferme tiré de l'objet ou de la nature du différend ne permettant de ranger *a priori* les différends en différends politiques et différends juridiques, c'est l'attitude des parties qui, dans l'ordre procédural, est seule decisive.'[11]

The matter is further complicated by the ready assumption that the classification of a dispute as legal, non-legal or political also regards the way in which the dispute should be settled: a legal dispute by legal means, a political dispute by diplomatic means.[12] In 1968 Rosalyn Higgins turned this around, arguing that disputes are not inherently one or the other, but that the labelling of a dispute as legal or political should refer to the method by which it is to be resolved.[13] This would dismiss any *a priori* distinction between legal and political disputes. There is, nevertheless, a continuing question on whether two kinds of disputes may be distinguished, irrespective of the means of settlement that are in practice employed for them. While doctrine and practice should be interdependent, on the basis of their distinct roles an attempt is made here to separate the classification and the settlement suggestions.

The International Court of Justice and its predecessor the Permanent Court of International Justice have made several pronouncements on the understanding of 'dispute', in the sense of a 'legal dispute'.[14] It held that the existence of an international dispute is a matter for objective determination.[15] In the classic *Mavrommatis* Case the PCIJ held that a dispute is 'a disagreement on a point of law or fact, a conflict of legal views or of interests between two persons.'[16]

---

[10] 'No one questions the impossibility of drawing a satisfactory logical distinction between legal and political disputes or more specifically, between disputes which may appropriately be decided by a court and those which require a political solution possible by the decision of an international organ.' H.W. Mosler, 'The International Society as a Legal Community', (1974) 140 *Recueil des Cours* Vol. IV 1, 288-289. Nevertheless, a valuable attempt was made by Verzijl: J.H.W. Verzijl, *International Law in Historical Perspective* (1976) Vol. VIII ch 1. Orrego Vicuña believes the distinction 'will continue to fade, if it ever was clear': F. Orrego Vicuña, *International Dispute Settlement in an Evolving Global Society* (2004) 101.

[11] C. de Visscher, *Théories et Réalités en Droit International Public* (4th edn. 1970) 371.

[12] Ibid.

[13] R. Higgins, 'Policy Considerations and the International Judicial Process', (1968) 17 *ICLQ* 58, 74.

[14] Which must also be distinguished from the concept of a 'legal question', which does not necessarily involve a dispute. *Legal Consequences of the Construction of a Wall in the Occupied Palestinian Territory* (*Advisory Opinion*), (2004) *ICJ Rep* [36] [37].

[15] *Interpretation of Peace Treaties with Bulgaria, Hungary and Romania* (*Advisory Opinion*)(*First Phase*), (1950) *ICJ Rep* 65, 74.

[16] *Mavrommatis Palestine Concessions* Case (*Judgement No. 2*), (1924) *PCIJ Series A* No, 2, 11.

Conceptually, however, this is too broad. A disagreement about a point of fact or about what the law is, is not yet a dispute until the settlement of it is required by one State, that can argue that the matter affects its claims or rights. The ICJ moved closer to this position, though not yet sufficiently, in its pronouncement in the *South West Africa* Cases, which required that the claim of one party is positively opposed by the other.[17] In the *East Timor* Case, the Court said more boldly: 'Portugal has, rightly or wrongly, formulated complaints of fact and law against Australia which the latter has denied. By virtue of this denial, there is a legal dispute.'[18]

Consequently, a legal dispute exists when a relevant party formulates a claim that is denied by – and seeks validation from – another relevant party. The formulation chosen by the ICJ in the *East Timor* Case suggests that also the denial by one party of another's complaints of *facts* only can also be a *legal* dispute. This appears to be contradicted by the ICJ Statute, which determines in Article 36(2) that the Court can be granted jurisdiction 'in all legal disputes concerning: (...) the existence of any fact which, if established, would constitute a breach of an international obligation.' Slightly broader, then, it is suggested that a dispute on the existence or meaning of facts is a legal dispute, if these facts are relevant to the determination of rights.[19]

Verzijl defined non-legal disputes as 'disputes which originate in a collision of interests and which do not lend themselves to a juridical decision.'[20] This, however, appears to be a definition more appropriate for non-justiciable disputes. If there is clarity on what legal disputes are, as set out above, there must also be clarity on non-legal disputes, namely disputes that do not concern competing legal claims.[21] Non-legal disputes are thus controversies in which parties have claims, not based on an interpretation of the law, but on a conception

---

[17] *South West Africa* Cases (*Ethiopia, Liberia v South Africa*) (*Preliminary Objections*), (1962) *ICJ Rep* 319, 328. This has become a staple of case law: *Northern Cameroons* (*Cameroons* v. *United Kingdom*) (1963), *ICJ Rep* 15, 27; *Applicability of the Obligation to Arbitrate under Section 21 of the United Nations Headquarters Agreement* (26 June 1947) (*Advisory Opinion*), (1988) *ICJ Rep* 27 [34]-[44]; *Southern Bluefin Tuna* Case (*Australia and New Zealand* v. *Japan*) (*Provisional Measures*), ITLOS Order 27 August 1999 [44], (1999) 38 *ILM* 1624, 1632.

[18] *East Timor* Case (*Portugal* v. *Australia*), (1995) *ICJ Rep* [22]; confirmed in *Questions of Interpretation and Application of the 1971 Montreal Convention arising from the Aerial Incident at Lockerbie* (*Preliminary Objections*) (*Libya* v. *United Kingdom*), (1998) *ICJ Rep* 17 [22].

[19] Also: *Southern Bluefin Tuna* Case (*Australia and New Zealand* v. *Japan*) (*Provisional Measures*), ITLOS, (1999) 38 *ILM* 1624, 1632. On when legal claims are opposed, see *Case Concerning the Arrest Warrant of 11 April 2000* (*Democratic Republic of the Congo* v. *Belgium*) (2002) *ICJ Rep* [23]-[28].

[20] J.H.W. Verzijl, *International Law in Historical Perspective* (1976) Vol. VIII 18.

[21] F. Münch, 'Die Schweizerische Initiative zu zweiseitigen Abmachungen über die friedliche Beilegung von Streitigkeiten', (1966) 26 *ZfAŐVR* 705, 729.

of the good, or a belief in the existence of certain facts, provided these facts do not affect the other's rights.

1.2.1 *Legal disputes and the means of settlement*

The definition of legal disputes, and with that the definition of political disputes, is historically burdened by the legalist optimism of the late 19th, early 20th century. Many lawyers and politicians held that many important disputes were legal, and they had much faith in the ability of adjudication to further the cause of peace.[22] All legal disputes should be submitted to the courts: international courts and tribunals were instruments for the achievement of peace.[23] The 1899 Hague Convention for the Pacific Settlement of International Disputes identified questions of a legal nature and considered that for them, arbitration was 'the most, and at the same time the most equitable, means of settling disputes which diplomacy has failed to settle.'[24] The practice of tying legal disputes to adjudication was continued in the jurisdictional clauses of many,[25] though not all conciliation commissions.[26] Thereby, the kind of dispute became associated with a preferred means of settlement.

The link between the kind of dispute and the kind of settlement became less pronounced with Article 33 of the United Nations Charter. It recognises disputes 'the continuation of which is likely to endanger the maintenance of international peace and security.' The Security Council may call upon the parties to settle such disputes by various means of dispute settlement, including conciliation and judicial settlement. According to Article 36(1), the Council may itself recommend the appropriate procedure to deal with such a dispute. The Charter implies that peace-endangering disputes are not necessarily legal disputes, because in Article 36(3) the Security Council is told to consider that 'legal disputes should as a general rule be referred by the parties to the International Court of Justice.'

---

22 In the same spirit, Charles Rousseau in the late 1930s counselled against consultations between a weak State and a strong State, as this could lead to unfair results: L.B. Sohn, 'The Use of Consultations for Monitoring Compliance with Agreements Concluded Under the Auspices of International Organizations', in N. Blokker and S. Muller (eds.), *Towards More Effective Supervision by International Organizations* (1994) 65, 76.

23 Thus, the accommodation built for the Permanent Court of Arbitration was named 'The Peace Palace'.

24 Art. 16 Hague Convention for the Pacific Settlement of International Disputes (29 July 1899): Permanent Court of Arbitration *Basic Documents* (1998) 3.

25 Up to the Treaty for Conciliation, Judicial Settlement and Arbitration (United Kingdom/Switzerland) (7 July 1965), 605 *UNTS* 206; 'Schweizerische Bundesrat 'Botschaft'', (1966) 26 *ZfAÖRV* 723, 740-742.

26 The link did not exist in every case: R Donner 'The Procedure of International Conciliation: Some Historical Aspects', (1999) 1 *Journal of the History of International Law* 103, 118.

1.2.2 *Political disputes*

On the understanding that disputes threatening the peace are also political disputes, it follows from the UN Charter that legal disputes can at the same time be political disputes. It does not follow clearly, however, what disputes can be political disputes. The term 'political dispute' has no importance for current instruments creating jurisdiction. The ICJ has consistently rejected the argument that a case could not be considered because it was a political dispute.[27] Consequently, a definition should be found on the basis of its usefulness in other legal discourse.

One option is to build on the discussed terminology, and to consider as political disputes those disputes in which there are no competing legal claims: political disputes are then the same as non-legal disputes.[28] Such a narrow definition is however not in line with the practice of labelling disputes 'political': often this is done to argue that a matter is of the greatest importance. The definition could be widened, to consider as political disputes those in which application of the law would not be useful because of 'the conception of a higher general interest of the whole international community which will not necessarily be realized by the mere assertion of existing rights and disputes.'[29] This assumes that certain disputes are not capable of legal review. While this may be a valid view politically, it cannot serve as a definition in international law, considering among other things that the ICJ is of the view that the political nature of a dispute does not stand in the way of it being dealt with by the Court. By contrast, it is submitted that all disputes are political in the sense that they involve the opinionated stance of opposing parties. In line with this understanding, Verzijl held that political disputes are disputes 'of such a nature as to

[27] *Aegean Sea Continental Shelf* Case (*Greece* v. *Turkey*)(*Judgement*), (1978) *ICJ Rep* 3. Turkey claimed the dispute was highly political. Also *US Diplomatic and Consular Staff in Tehran* Case, (1980) *ICJ Rep* 3, [26]-[28]. The Court held in both cases that there was a dispute as to rights. Similarly, the Court does not decline to give an Advisory Opinion on the ground that a legal question also has political aspects: e.g., *Legal Consequences of the Construction of a Wall in the Occupied Palestinian Territory* (*Advisory Opinion*), (2004) *ICJ Rep* [41].

[28] '[L]egal disputes were meant to exclude moral, political, economic or purely commercial claims'. ICSID Tribunal *Fedax* v. *Venezuela* (*Objections to Jurisdiction*) ARB/96/3, (1998) 37 *ILM* 1378, 1381. Von Mangoldt juxtaposes legal and political disputes, thereby implicitly choosing the narrow definition of political disputes, but then goes on to equate political disputes with 'conflicts of interests'. For consistency, this should be understood to mean: 'disputes solely regarding a conflict of interests, and not legal claims': H. von Mangoldt, 'Arbitration and Conciliation', in H. Mosler and R. Bernhardt (eds.), *Judicial Settlement of International Disputes* (1974) 417, 516, 518-519.

[29] J. Fischer Williams, 'Justiciable and Other Disputes', (1932) 26 *AJIL* 31, 31.

arouse national political passions, irrespective of whether they are capable or not of settlement in conformity with international law.'[30]

1.3 Justiciable and non-justiciable disputes

Mixed with the controversy over legal and political disputes, and often using the same terminology, there is a long-standing debate over what are justiciable and non-justiciable disputes, and on whether the latter exist at all.[31] In this respect, the ICJ Statute is a good starting point.[32] The range of justiciable disputes is comprehensively identified in the provisions of the 'optional clause' of the ICJ Statute[33] holding that a State may *a priori* accept the jurisdiction of the Court for all legal disputes concerning: a) the interpretation of a treaty; b) any question of international law; c) the existence of any fact which, if established, would constitute a breach of an international obligation; d) the nature or extent of the reparation to be made for the breach of an international obligation. As regards the ICJ Statute, then, the category of non-justiciable disputes comprises any dispute not covered in the above enumeration. Justiciable disputes include all matters of opposing legal claims. Excluded are cases concerning the existence of a fact that, if established (or found to be absent), would not constitute a breach of an international obligation.

A remaining question is, however, whether there is a category of disputes that is not to be settled through adjudication. One of the rationales behind the development of conciliation was that some disputes were by their nature unfit for adjudication, and that conciliation would be the right alternative. Such was the underlying assumption of the very first conciliation treaty, and many to follow.[34] In 1921, Switzerland and Germany agreed that conciliation would be used for non-justiciable disputes: [35]

---

[30] J.H.W. Verzijl, *International Law in Historical Perspective* (1976) Vol. VIII 18; P.H. Kooijmans, 'International Arbitration in Historical Perspective: Past and Present', in A.H.A. Soons (ed.), *International Arbitration: Past and Prospects* (1990) 23, 28.

[31] J. Hostie, 'Différends justiciables et non-justiciables', (1928) 55 *RDILC* 263, 568, 580 arguing that no dispute is by its nature non-justiciable, but that it may not be opportune to apply the law to certain disputes, in which case a decision *ex aequo et bono* could be considered, understanding the latter as 'what the law should be'. Also: M. Habicht, *Post-War Treaties for the Pacific Settlement of International Disputes* (1931) 971-976

[32] The situation can in details differ for specialised courts and tribunals, as jurisdiction is tailor-made. Nevertheless, the ICJ Statute and its case law provide guidance for all.

[33] Art. 36(2) ICJ Statute.

[34] 40 bilateral dispute settlement treaties provided for judicial settlement of legal disputes and conciliation and arbitration of other disputes. 37 of these were concluded between 1928 and 1933: *Systematic Survey 1928-1948* 5.

> 'überzeugt, dass in Streitfällen, die ihrem Wesen nach sich zur Entscheidung durch Richterspruch nicht eignen, der Rat unparteiischer Vertrauensmänner in jedem Falle Gewahr fur eine friedliche Beilegung der Streitigkeiten bietet.'[36]

The continuing discussion on non-justiciability is partly rooted in the then-current view that there are gaps in international law.[37] The *Lotus* Case,[38] and the writings of Lauterpacht,[39] Kelsen[40] and – later – Dworkin,[41] have contributed to the now widely accepted notion that in any case there will be established principles and practices that could be interpreted to apply to the case,[42] and that therefore there are no gaps in the law.[43] In the absence of gaps in the law, a legal dispute cannot *inherently* be non-justiciable, in the sense that there is no legal function that a court can perform.[44]

There may however be disputes that a court would not be able to settle in a relevant sense.[45] In this respect, Kooijmans speaks of 'disputes which do not lend themselves to judicial settlement' regarding 'all those disputes where a settlement by application of rules of international law would *not settle the dis-*

---

[35] Treaty of Conciliation, Arbitration and Compulsory Adjudication (Germany-Switzerland) (3 December 1921, entered into force 25 May 1925), 12 *LNTS* 281; M. Habicht, *The Power of the International Judge to Give a Decision "Ex aequo et bono"* (1935) 79-80.

[36] 'convinced that, in differences which by their nature do not allow of a solution by arbitration, recourse to trustworthy persons of known impartiality offers in all cases a guarantee of a pacific settlement.'

[37] Still mentioned as a possible argument against adjudication in R. Lapidoth, 'Dispute Settlement under the 1997 Convention on the Law of the Non-navigational Uses of International Watercourses', in M.N. Schmitt (ed.), *International Law Across the Spectrum of Conflict* (2000) 231, 235. She further notes 'It is interesting that the reference to arbitration and adjudication has not been limited to conflicts of a legal nature', idem, 236.

[38] *S.S. Lotus* Case (*France* v. *Turkey*), (1927) *PCIJ Series A* No. 10, 18.

[39] H. Lauterpacht, *The Function of Law in the International Community* (1933).

[40] H. Kelsen, *Reine Rechtslehre* (1934).

[41] R.M. Dworkin, *Law's Empire* (1986).

[42] Though the indeterminacy of GATT/WTO law was controversially argued to be grounds for *non-liquet* rulings: L. Bartels, 'The Separation of Powers in the WTO: How to Avoid Judicial Activism', (2004) 53 *ICLQ* 861, 874.

[43] Nevertheless, recently one writer still argued that there may be cases where there are no legal rules applicable. T. Sugihara, 'The Judicial Function of the International Court of Justice with Respect to Disputes Involving Highly Political Issues', in A.S. Muller, D. Raic and J.M. Thuránszky (eds.), *The International Court of Justice* (1997) 117, 132, 138.

[44] Early writers on non-justiciability also refer to disputes in which one party wishes to change existing law, because it believes existing law is not just, e.g., M. Habicht, *The Power of the International Judge to Give a Decision "Ex aequo et bono"* (1935) 81; J. Fischer Williams, 'Justiciable and Other Disputes', (1932) 26 *AJIL* 31. This has become a rare view.

[45] Cf., *Legal Consequences of the Construction of a Wall in the Occupied Palestinian Territory* (*Advisory Opinion*), (2004) *ICJ Rep* 46-54.

pute itself or would solve only part of it.'[46] On this basis, it can be proposed that within the scope of non-justiciable disputes thus identified fall those disputes of which treatment by a court would not allow the court to fulfil its function as a court of *justice*. The scope of that category was identified by Hersch Lauterpacht, even while being the foe of a broad notion of non-justiciability. He argued that certain disputes *should* not be decided judicially, because practical reality does not allow for solution of the case through legal settlement.[47] Kunz succinctly said: 'While all international disputes can be judicially *decided*, it is not true that they can be judicially *settled.*'[48]

Depending on the function of a particular court, some additional disputes can also been identified as non-justiciable, or at least as disputes that 'do not lend themselves to judicial settlement' by that particular court. In practice, for particular courts such classifications are established politically. For instance, while drafting the dispute settlement mechanism of the OSCE, various States held that disputes relating to the use of force would be non-justiciable.[49] Furthermore, it follows from both this discussion as from the classification of legal and non-legal disputes, that non-legal disputes are non-justiciable: a court cannot apply a rule of law, because the dispute does not concern legal claims.

This must not be misunderstood to say that complicated or political disputes generally should not come before a Court.[50] Indeed, judicial decisions can be rendered on part of a composite dispute, and potentially become useful elements of further negotiations between the parties. Nevertheless, adjudication of only part of a wider dispute, especially when adjudication of the remainder of the dispute is barred, or when implementation of the decision would be impossible, could rightly or wrongly threaten negotiations, and could be detrimental to the stature of the relevant court. A court must be allowed to refuse cases on grounds of *judicial propriety*, as it was invoked, controversially, in the

---

[46] P.H. Kooijmans, 'International Arbitration in Historical Perspective: Past and Present', in A.H.A. Soons (ed.), *International Arbitration: Past and Prospects* (1990) 23, 30.

[47] H. Lauterpacht, 'Non Liquet and the Completeness of the Law', in F.M. van Asbeck (ed.), *Symbolae Verzijl* (1958) 196, 200. Also: I. Brownlie, 'The Justiciability of Disputes and Issues in International Relations', (1967) 42 *BYIL* 123, 141.

[48] J.L. Kunz, 'International Arbitration in Pan American Developments', (1948) 27 *Texas Law Review* 182, 201 op. cit. K. Zemanek, 'The Legal Foundations of the International System. General Course on Public International Law', (1997) 266 *Recueil des Cours* 285.

[49] G. Hafner, 'Bemühungen um ein gesamteuropäisches Streitbeilegungssystem im Rahmen der KSZE', in K. Böckstiegel and others, *Völkerrecht, Recht der Internationalen Organisationen, Weltwirtschaftsrecht* (1988) 147, 164-166.

[50] Also: M.N. Shaw, 'Peaceful Resolution of "Political Disputes": The Desirable Parameters of ICJ Jurisdiction', in J. Dahlitz (ed.), *Peaceful Resolution of Major International Disputes* (1999) 49.

Northern Cameroons Case, though on a different basis.[51] Judicial propriety has also been discussed regarding the discretion to render Advisory Opinions.[52] Disputes that are in practice non-justiciable, and disputes that cannot be settled judicially, may still be settled in another manner. They should be dealt with through other means, such as through diplomatic dispute settlement methods.

2. Diplomatic Dispute Settlement Methods

A great number of dispute settlement methods can be distinguished. Generalisations are required for the distinctions to hold, generalisations that by definition create some distance from the application in practice. Nevertheless, in practice too, such distinctions can be useful to facilitate discussion and comparison. It is noted that a dispute may be settled in many ways, and that in any attempt at settlement, various methods may be applied both sequentially and simultaneously. For proper assessment, though, they need to be separated. This section provides a brief examination of the main means of non-binding means of settlement. The UN Charter, in Article 33, enumerates negotiation, enquiry, mediation, conciliation, arbitration, judicial settlement and resort to regional agencies or arrangements.[53] The list is not exhaustive. Here, consultation and good offices are also introduced. A brief introduction is given of the settlement mechanisms of the United Nations and of the most important regional organisations involved in diplomatic dispute settlement.

2.1 Consultation

A State may choose to recognise the interest of another in a decision or situation pertaining to itself, without granting the other a definitive say in the matter.[54] Information exchange may lead to modification of the original plan, and

[51] *Northern Cameroons* Case (*Cameroon* v. *United Kingdom*), (1963) *ICJ Rep* 33-34; I. Brownlie, 'The Justiciability of Disputes and Issues in International Relations', (1967) 42 *BYIL* 123, 125-126. See also Separate Opinion [22] by Judge Kooijmans in *Case Concerning Legality of the Use of Force* (*Preliminary Objections*) (*Yugoslavia* v. *The Netherlands*), (2004) *ICJ Rep.*

[52] E.g., *Legal Consequences of the Construction of a Wall*, (2004) *ICJ Rep* [43] ff; *Status of Eastern Carelia* (*Advisory Opinion*), (1923) *PCIJ Series B* No 5.

[53] On the traditional order of discussion: J.G. Collier, 'The International Court of Justice and the Peaceful Settlement of Disputes', in A.V. Lowe and M. Fitzmaurice (ed.), *Fifty Years of the International Court of Justice* (1996) 364, 365.

[54] '[T]here is no across-the-board requirement in international law that governments must consult others whenever they contemplate taking or permitting any unilateral action that might adversely affect the interests of non-nationals or of the international community as a whole.' F.L. Kirgis, *Prior Consultation* (1983) 359.

thereby prevent disputes, by avoiding unnecessary disadvantages for an affected other.[55] Consultation may serve to co-ordinate behaviour, such as a joint approach to third parties, or may strengthen decision-making in international organisations.[56] Consultation therefore regards co-ordination or preventive diplomacy rather than settlement of disputes that have already arisen.[57] As the 'neglected Cinderella of dispute resolution methods',[58] its potential is rarely acknowledged.

Consultation may result in a more informed decision, and thereby increase the chance of success for the decision-maker, while also granting a sense of recognition to the State or organisation invited to express its views. Consultation is more than mere notification, which assumes one-way communication. At the same time, consultation does not require the consulted party's consent to the proposed action, merely the willingness to take its interests into account.[59] Even though in practice it may be difficult to sharply enforce the distinction between consultation and negotiation, when including the term 'consultation' in a dispute settlement provision the parties build on a conceptual distinction.[60] Many international agreements contain consultation clauses, but they do not set out how consultations should be conducted.[61] Many of these regard trade practices or the use of shared natural resources.[62] In some cases permanent

---

[55] For a broad overview: J.U. Kusumowidagdo, *Consultation Clauses as a Means of Providing for Treaty Obedience* (1981).

[56] L. Fuerle, 'Informal Consultation: A Mechanism in Security Council Decision Making', (1985) 18 *NYUJILP* 267. Consultations may be institutionalised, such as in the Group of 77 or, informally, between the permanent members of the UN Security Council.

[57] L.B. Sohn, 'The Use of Consultations for Monitoring Compliance with Agreements Concluded Under the Auspices of International Organizations', in N. Blokker and S. Muller (eds.), *Towards More Effective Supervision by International Organizations* (1994) 65.

[58] L.B. Sohn, 'Bipartite Consultative Commissions for Preventing and Resolving Disputes Relating to International Trade Treaties', in M. Rama-Montaldo (ed.), *El Derecho Internacional en un Mundo en Transformacion* (Vol. II) (1994) 1181.

[59] Contrast: C. Manga Fombad, 'Consultation and Negotiation in the Pacific Settlement of International Disputes', (1989) 1 *RADIC* 707, 709 who describes consultation as a form of negotiation for less contentious issues.

[60] Cf., J.G. Collier and A.V. Lowe, *Settlement of International Disputes* (1999) 20 who see consultation as part of the concept of negotiation.

[61] L.B. Sohn, 'The Use of Consultations for Monitoring Compliance with Agreements Concluded Under the Auspices of International Organizations', in N. Blokker and S. Muller (eds.), *Towards More Effective Supervision by International Organizations* (1994) 65, 80.

[62] E.g., Convention on the Law of the Non-navigational Uses of International Watercourses (8 July 1997), (1997) 36 *ILM* 700 Arts. 4(2), 6(2), 7 (R. Lapidoth, 'Dispute Settlement under the 1997 Convention on the Law of the Non-navigational Uses of International Watercourses', in M.N. Schmitt (ed.), *International Law Across the Spectrum of Conflict* (2000) 231, 233); North American Free Trade Agreement (NAFTA) (17 December 1992), (1993) 32 *ILM* 694 Art. 2006;. F.L. Kirgis, *Prior Consultation* (1983) and the book review concentrating on IMF practice by J. Gold, (1984) 24 *Virginia JIL* 729.

consultation bodies have been established.[63] Often, too, consultation is undertaken on an *ad hoc* basis.

While an obligation to consult has obvious advantages for the relations between the consultant and the consulted, such an obligation also carries with it the possibility that it itself becomes the object of a dispute.[64] The consulted State may find that its viewpoints have not been adequately considered, or that the consultation process was terminated prematurely. The difficulty, especially for concerned parties, to distinguish between consultation and negotiations creates the liability that a party entitled to be consulted can come to presume it has more rights, and lead it to adopt a negotiating position.

Sometimes treaties provide for an 'exchange of views' rather than consultation.[65] The International Tribunal for the Law of the Sea (ITLOS) has adopted a broad understanding of what amounts to such an exchange, so that the requirement to comply will quickly be met.[66] Nevertheless, the context of the creation of the obligation creates the presumption that the recipient will also take note of the other's viewpoints in taking his decision; its aim is therefore to be a reciprocal form of consultation.

2.2 Negotiation

Negotiation implies the discussion of an exchange of concessions or the creation of benefits. Robert Mnookin defined it as 'a joint decision-making process involving interactive communication in which parties that lack identical

---

[63] E.g., the Open Skies Consultative Commission, Treaty on Open Skies Art. 10 (24 March 1992) <http://www.osce.org/documents/doclib/1992/03/13764_en.pdf> (5 October 2007) (the Committee started meeting prior to the entry into force of the Treaty on 1 January 2002); OSCE *Handbook* (3rd edn. 1999) 130-131; and the classic model, the 1909 Canada-United States Boundary Waters Committee, resulting from the Canada-United States Treaty Relating to Boundary Waters and Questions Arising between the United States and Canada (United Kingdom-United States) (11 January 1909) [1910] US: 36 Stat. 2448.

[64] E.g., *Case Concerning Land Reclamation* (*Singapore* v. *Malaysia*) (*Provisional Measures*), (October 2003) ITLOS Order 8 October 2003 (on exchange of views); *Lac Lanoux* (*Spain* v. *France*), (1957) 24 *ILR* 101. See also the approach taken by arbitral tribunals, e.g., in the UNCLOS Annex VII Arbitral Tribunal Award in *Barbados* v. *Trinidad and Tobago* (11 April 2006) [200]-[206], holding that UNCLOS Art. 283(1) does not require an additional exchange of views following a negotiation process in accordance with UNCLOS Art. 74 and 83 on the same issue.

[65] E.g., Law of the Sea Convention Art. 283.

[66] *Case Concerning Land Reclamation* (*Singapore* v. *Malaysia*) (*Provisional Measures*), (2003) ITLOS Rep [47]-[48]; *MOX Plant* Case (*Ireland* v. *United Kingdom*) (*Provisional Measures*), ITLOS Order 3 December 2001, (2002) 41 *ILM* 405) [60]-[62]; *Southern Bluefin Tuna* Cases (*Australia and New Zealand* v. *Japan*) (*Provisional Measures*), ITLOS Order (27 August 1999) [60]-[61]

interests attempt to reach agreement.'[67] It is the most widely used method to prevent and solve disputes,[68] and the diplomatic method *par excellence*.[69] A resolution by the United Nations General Assembly of 1999, attempting to draw-up general rules for negotiation, unwittingly demonstrated that as international negotiations can cover everything, it is unfeasible to provide real guidance.[70] Negotiation, like consultation, is also used for matters not involving disputes, such as for co-ordinating foreign policy and for the conclusion of trade agreements. It is important to establish what amounts to a negotiation, because sometimes the conduct of negotiations is a precondition for submitting a dispute to another settlement method.[71] This was the case, for instance, in the *Mavrommatis* Case, in which the PCIJ stated:

> 'Negotiations do not of necessity always presuppose a more or less lengthy series of notes and despatches; it may suffice hat a discussion should have been commenced, and this discussion may have been very short; this will be the case if a dead lock is reached, or if finally a point is reached at which one of the Parties definitely declares himself unable, or refuses, to give way, and there can therefore be no doubt that the dispute cannot be settled by diplomatic negotiation. This will also be the case, in certain circumstances, if the conversations between the Gov-

---

67 R.H. Mnookin, 'When Not to Negotiate: A Negotiation Imperialist Reflects on Appropriate Limits', (2003) 74 *University of Colorado Law Review* 1077, 1080.

68 I. Brownlie, 'Why do States Take Disputes to the International Court?', in N. Ando and others (eds.), *Liber Amicorum Judge Shigeru Oda* (2002) 829.

69 Perhaps the latter makes that there is little legal writing on negotiations. J.G. Merrills, *International Dispute Settlement* (4th edn. 2005) ch 1; B.S. Murthy, 'Diplomacy and resolution of international disputes', in United Nations *International Law as a Language for International Relations* (1996) 161; M.A. Rogoff, 'The Obligation to Negotiate in International Law: Rules and Realities', (1994) 16 *Michigan JIL* 141; United Nations *Handbook on the Peaceful Settlement of Disputes between States* (1992) 9-24; N. Ghozali, 'La négociation diplomatique dans la jurisprudence Internationale', (1992) *Revue Belge de Droit International* 323; R.S. Lee, 'Multilateral Treaty-Making and Negotiation Techniques: An Appraisal', in B. Cheng and E.D. Brown (eds.), *Contemporary Problems of International* Law (1988) 157; G. Geamanu, 'Théorie et pratique des négociations en droit international', (1980) 166 *Receuil des Cours* 369; P.J.I.M. de Waart, *The Element of Negotiation in the Pacific Settlement of Disputes between States* (1973); H.G. Darwin, 'Negotiation', in C.H.M. Waldock and F. Vallat (eds.), *International Disputes: The Legal Aspects* (1972) 77; F.S. Northedge and M.D. Donelan, *International Disputes: The Political Aspects* (1971) ch 12; A.N. Talayev, 'Negotiations – Major Means of Peaceful Settlement of International Disputes', in International Law Association *Report on the Fifty-Third Conference* (1968) 57. Non-legal negotiation writing includes:V.A. Kremenyuk (ed.), *International Negotiation* (2nd edn) (2002); F.O. Hampson, *Multilateral Negotiations* (1995); A. Lall, *Modern International Negotiation* (1966); F.C. Iklé, *How Nations Negotiate* (1964); *Journal of International Negotiation: A Journal of Theory and Practice*.

70 UNGA Res 53/101 (1999).

71 Energy Charter Treaty (17 December 1994), 2080 *UNTS* 100 Art. 27(1) does not speak of negotiation but of settling disputes 'through diplomatic channels'.

ernments are only the continuation of previous negotiations between a private individual and a government.'[72]

The jurisdictional bar of a requirement to negotiate arose notably in the *Oil Platforms* Case.[73] Iran had brought a claim against the United States relating to the destruction by the US of two oil platforms, in response to alleged attacks on US ships by Iran. The US introduced a counter-claim against Iran relating to the attacks. Jurisdiction depended on the 1955 bilateral Treaty of Amity,[74] which provided that the ICJ had jurisdiction for disputes 'not satisfactorily adjusted by diplomacy'. The Court heard the counter-claim, stating that 'it is sufficient for the Court to satisfy itself that the dispute was not satisfactorily adjusted by diplomacy before being submitted to the Court.' This bold statement needs to be interpreted restrictively, so as not to completely nullify any requirement in the Treaty of Amity of negotiation before submission of a claim. It must be read to refer to the absence of any realistic chance that an opening of negotiations on the counter-claim would have a chance of success.[75]

The ICJ has adopted a liberal position on what may count as 'negotiation', including thereby plenary discussions on the floor of the UN General Assembly, though this position is disputed.[76] The Court recently ruled that mere protests, whether made on a bilateral level or in multilateral fora, do not qualify as a form of negotiation.[77] Exception was made for negotiations within a mediation process: negotiations taking place within a larger framework may not qualify

---

[72] *Mavrommatis Palestine Concessions* Case (*Greece* v. *United Kingdom*) (*Jurisdiction*), (1924) *PCIJ Series A* No. 2 p. 13. Emphasis omitted. See however Judge Moore's Dissenting Opinion 54, 62-63: 'negotiation is the legal and orderly administrative process by which governments, in the exercise of their unquestionable powers, conduct their relations one with another and discuss, adjust and settle, their differences.' This understanding led Moore to set higher standards in the identification of negotiations than the majority of the Court did.

[73] *Case Concerning Oil Platforms* (*Iran* v. *US*), (2003) *ICJ Rep* [106]-[107].

[74] Treaty of Amity, Economic Relations and Cultural Rights (Iran-United States) (15 August 1955), 284 *UNTS* 93.

[75] See *US Diplomatic and Consular Staff in Tehran* Case, (1980) *ICJ Rep* 3 [50]-[54]; *Military and Paramilitary Activities in and against Nicaragua* Case (*Jurisdiction and Admissibility*), (1984) *ICJ Rep* 392 [81-83].

[76] *South West Africa* Cases (*Ethiopia, Liberia* v. *South Africa*) (*Preliminary Objections*), (1962) *ICJ Rep* 319, 344-346 and critique by Judge Fitzmaurice and Judge Spender: ibid., 465, 561-2 and Judge Fitzmaurice's Separate Opinion in the *Northern Cameroons* Case (*Cameroon* v. *United Kingdom*), (1963) *ICJ Rep* 97, 123. The absence of negotiations may be irrelevant if the opposing party refuses to enter into any discussion at all, such as in the *US Diplomatic and Consular Staff in Tehran* Case, (1980) *ICJ Rep* 3 [51].

[77] *Case Concerning Armed Activities on the Territory of the Congo* (*Jurisdiction and Admissibiliaty*) (*DR Congo* v. *Rwanda*), (2006) *ICJ Rep* [91]. J.G. Merrills, 'The Mosaic of International Dispute Settlement Procedures: Complementary or Contradictory?', (2007) 54 *NILR* 361, 363.

as negotiations between the parties.[78] It is possible to argue, however, that the Court's interpretations in this particular case were inspired by a doctrine of negotiation as much as by a willingness to find jurisdiction.

Negotiations may consist of *ad hoc* communication between the parties, usually through their Foreign Ministries and embassies, but may also take place in institutional settings. This may consist of exchanges in a general forum such as the UN General Assembly, or in issue-specific organisations such as UNESCO or organisations with more limited membership, such as the OSCE. States may also set-up bilateral negotiation tools, which may be difficult to distinguish from the permanent consultation bodies referred to above. One such institutional negotiation body is the High-Level Technical Group (GTAN) set-up by Argentina and Uruguay in 2005 in an attempt to settle the dispute regarding the intended building of pulp mills on the Uruguayan side of the Uruguay River, the border between the two countries.[79] This also shows that negotiations need not exclusively consist of political exchanges, but may also comprise the use of expertise, research and other means to elucidate the dispute.

Negotiation is frequently part of other dispute settlement methods. Conciliation, for instance, is characterised by the neutral investigation of the facts by a third party, aiming at producing recommendations for consideration by the parties. Nevertheless, interaction between the disputants at various points in the procedure is essential for conciliation to be effective. The recommendations of the commission are normally geared towards their potential for a negotiated settlement between the parties. Negotiation can even be necessary when a dispute cannot be settled by negotiations: the parties can only through negotiations agree on a formulation of the dispute and on the other mechanism they should refer the matter to.

An advantage of negotiation is that it promotes direct contact between decision-makers, and thereby enhances the prospects for improved relations and conflict prevention. As negotiations are whatever the parties make of them, they also allow retention of control over the matter. A disadvantage from the vantage point of the law is that the outcome of negotiations usually reflects the relative power distribution of the parties rather than external normative standards. Weaker parties are therefore structurally disadvantaged, and results may deviate from previously or commonly accepted norms. Furthermore, starting

---

[78] The multi-party 'Contadora process' aiming to bring peace to Central America in the 1980s was distinguished from 'direct negotiations through the usual diplomatic channels' (as provided for in the Pact of Bogotá) in the *Border and Transborder Armed Actions* Case (*Honduras* v. *Nicaragua*) (*Jurisdiction and Admissibility*), (1988) *ICJ Rep* 69 [75].

[79] ICJ Press Release 2006/17 (4 May 2006); Application by Argentina, *Case Concerning Pulp Mills on the River Uruguay* (*Argentina* v. *Uruguay*) [4], [16], [17] on <www. icj-cij.org> (5 October 2007).

negotiations assumes that each party is willing to compromise to reach agreement.[80] If this is not the case in practice, initiating them may result in frustration. Declaring positions non-negotiable may therefore at times limit rather than aggravate a dispute.

In those cases where an agreement, customary law, general principles of law[81] or a decision by a court or tribunal gives rise to an obligation to negotiate, this is an obligation 'not only to enter into negotiations but also to pursue them as far as possible with a view to concluding agreements.'[82] Furthermore, the parties are:

> 'so to conduct themselves that the negotiations are meaningful, which will not be the case when either of them insists upon its own position without contemplating modification of it.'[83]

Elsewhere, the Court determined that negotiations demand that each 'must in good faith pay reasonable regard to the legal rights of the other.'[84] Examples of violations of good faith are the unjustified breaking off of the discussions, abnormal delays, disregard of the agreed procedures, systematic refusals to take into consideration adverse proposals or interests.[85] Nevertheless, an obligation to negotiate does not imply an obligation to reach an agreement: it is an obligation of conduct, not of result.[86] The Court saw an exception to this in its controversial advisory opinion on the threat and use of nuclear weapons. There, it was held that the legal import of the obligation to negotiate nuclear disarmament in good faith, as contained in Article 6 of the Treaty of Non-Proliferation, 'is an obligation to achieve a particular result – nuclear disarmament in all its aspects – by adopting a particular course of conduct, namely, the pursuit of

---

[80] R.H. Mnookin, 'When Not to Negotiate: A Negotiation Imperialist Reflects on Appropriate Limits', (2003) 74 *University of Colorado Law Review* 1077.

[81] In the *Fisheries Jurisdiction* Case (*UK* v. *Iceland*), (1974) *ICJ Rep* 3 [75], the Court stated 'the obligation to negotiate flows from the very nature of the respective rights of the parties' (i.e., preferential rights for one at the expense of those of the other).

[82] *Railway Traffic between Lithuania and Poland* (*Advisory Opinion*), (1931) *PCIJ Series A/B* No. 42, 116.

[83] *North Sea Continental Shelf* Cases (*Germany* v. *Denmark*) and (*Germany* v. *The Netherlands*) (*Judgements*), (1969) *ICJ Rep* 3, 47; UNGA Res 37/10 (1982) 'Manila Declaration' Art. 10 pt I.

[84] *Fisheries Jurisdiction* Case (*UK* v. *Iceland*), (1974) *ICJ Rep* 3 [78].

[85] *Lac Lanoux* (*Spain* v. *France*), (1957) 24 *ILR* 101, 128.

[86] *North Sea Continental Shelf* Cases (*Germany* v. *Denmark*) and (*Germany* v. *The Netherlands*) (*Judgements*), (1969) *ICJ Rep* 3, 47. Generally U. Beyerlin 'Pactum de Contrahendo und Pactum de Negotiando im Völkerrecht ?', (1976) 36 *ZfAÖRV* 407.

negotiations on the matter in good faith.'[87] This interpretation of a unique obligation to achieve a specific result is presumably due to the singular importance of the subject-matter for world security.

2.3 Good offices

Good offices, though often conflated with mediation,[88] and occasionally with conciliation,[89] can be distinguished as a third party method of enabling parties to settle their dispute without the third party taking upon itself an independent role as director of negotiations or a source of proposals.[90] The distinction between good offices and mediation was made by most 19th century writers, but was, under the influence of the first Hague Conference, more or less abandoned by those of the early 20th century.[91] The United Nations Charter does not mention good offices. Applying the distinction may however serve to make the initial phase of third party involvement more acceptable to parties in dispute, as it suggests a lesser degree of involvement in their affairs. This is so even though the operation of good offices in practice cannot always be distinguished from mediation.

Peaceful settlement treaties and other agreements do not regularly feature provisions on good offices.[92] This can be explained partially by the conflation with mediation, partially because if the parties are intent on settling their dispute, mediation will normally bring agreement closer. Good offices can help especially in precarious disputes in which the parties refuse to communicate directly, or refuse to acknowledge each other's status as opponent. This was the

---

[87] *Legality of the Threat or Use of Nuclear Weapons* (*Advisory Opinion*), (1996) *ICJ Rep* 226, 264. Treaty on the Non-Proliferation of Nuclear Weapons: (1968) 7 *ILM* 809.

[88] With a respectable historical basis: Vattel introduced mediation as 'La Médiation, dans laquelle un Ami commun interpose ses bons offices (...)', M. de Vattel, *Le Droit des Gens ou Principes de la Loi Naturelle* (1768) Vol. 1 book II ch XVIII, 219.

[89] Convention Against Torture and Other Cruel, Inhuman or Degrading Treatment or Punishment (10 December 1984, entered into force 26 June 1987), 1465 *UNTS* 85, Art. 21(5).

[90] N. Politis, 'L'Avenir de la Médiation', (1910) 17 *RGDIP* 136, 139-140. A more comprehensive definition is given in M.E. Dreher, *Die Institution der Guten Dienste im Völkerrecht* (1980) 114. Exceptionally, the Chile-US Agreement to settle the Letelier – Moffitt affair [9], (1990) 30 *ILM* 421 seems to refer to the good offices of the Inter-American Commission on Human Rights in a literal manner, expressing the desire to use its office facilities.

[91] 1899 Hague Convention Arts. 2-8 conflated the methods; W. Schücking, *Das Völkerrechtliche Institut der Vermittlung* (1923) 13-14.

[92] Exceptions include the American Treaty on Pacific Settlement (Pact of Bogotá) (20 April 1948), 449 *UNTS* 3 Art. 9, the Convention on the Law of the Non-navigational Uses of International Watercourses Art. 33(2) and the Convention on the Prohibition of the Development, Production, Stockpiling and Use of Chemical Weapons and on their Destruction, (13 January 1993) 32 *ILM* 800, Art. 14(3).

case, for instance, between Israel and the Palestinians,[93] and in the dispute on Cyprus.[94]

The *Cyprus* Case is a good example of how a mandate for good offices can evolve into very substantial third party involvement. After many months of shuttle diplomacy by Mr. De Soto, Special Advisor to the UN Secretary-General, the sides agreed to proximity talks. This refers to negotiations where the parties are close by, but not in the same room, with the intermediary moving between them.[95] Proximity talks were to be followed by direct negotiations. Even though the parties insisted that Mr. De Soto would only be present 'to take notes', their inability to fashion settlement proposals themselves led the United Nations in 2002 to submit its own draft for a Comprehensive Settlement for the Cyprus Problem, which both sides then accepted as a basis for negotiations.[96] In 2004 the parties further agreed that the revised document would be subject of separate simultaneous referenda, and that the Secretary-General would have the power to 'fill the gaps' that would remain in the document after the deadline for further negotiations.[97]

The provider of good offices is frequently called a 'facilitator'.[98] The essentially passive role of a facilitator makes that the role is often fulfilled by high officers of international organisations, and by others who can accept the required low profile without fearing criticism for appearing inactive. As in mediation, frequently it is left undetermined whether the provider of good offices is the individual or the State or organisation. Such uncertainty may sometimes be deliberate, in order to avoid wider political responsibility in case of failure.

---

93 W.J. Bien, 'The Oslo Channel: Benefits of a Neutral Facilitator to Secret Negotiations', in M.C. Greenberg, J.H. Barton and M.E. McGuiness (eds.), *Words over War* (2000) 109.

94 In extreme cases, the disputants may even be seated in adjoining rooms, with the provider of good offices walking in and out to relay their points of view – a form of 'proximity talks'. Further practical use of the method is described in United Nations *Handbook on the Peaceful Settlement of Disputes between States* (1992) 36-39.

95 Also practiced on occasion in the 1919 peace talks following the First World War. M. MacMillan, *Peacemakers* (2001) 310.

96 'Report of the Secretary-General on his Mission of Good Offices', (2003) UN Doc S/2003/398.

97 This power was indeed used. The referendum on the Greek Cypriot side failed: 'Report of the Secretary-General on his Mission of Good Offices', (2004) UN Doc S/2004/437.

98 E.g., UNSC Res 1286 (2000) regarding Nelson Mandela's role in the Arusha Peace Process and UNSC Res 1287 (2000) regarding the Russian Federation's role in the Georgian/Abkhaz discussions; J. Egeland, 'The Oslo Accord: Multiparty Facilitation through the Norwegian Channel', in C.A. Crocker, F. Osler Hampson and P. Aall (eds.), *Herding Cats: Multiparty Mediation in a Complex World* (1999) 527. Adopting the name of facilitator does not imply that good offices are offered: Belize and Guatemala, devised a mandate of conciliation, but named the conciliators 'facilitators': see chapter II 1.15.

2.4 Inquiry

The method of inquiry attempts to clarify controversial situations relevant to a dispute by means of an objective investigation, by an international commission, normally including members of third states, or by a single neutral investigator.[99] Investigators typically examine data, hear testimony and consider the relevant circumstances. Sometimes the terms of reference also allow them to make determinations regarding the possible violation of certain norms.[100] The method is an instrument rather than a procedure itself generating settlement, and therefore may also easily form part of wider negotiations or mediation.[101] Inquiry was included in the Hague Conventions of 1899 and 1907, and in the early 20th century provided the basis for the development of conciliation. Van Asbeck called conciliation the 'younger sister' of inquiry.[102]

The results of an inquiry are confidential and non-binding, except when the parties agree otherwise.[103] From the first application of the 1899 Hague Convention's inquiry provisions, it is clear that factual investigations are closely linked to legal determinations: if any implicit legal findings by an inquiry commission would be binding on the parties, inquiry could amount to an implicit form of judicial settlement. When in 1905 a Russian-English naval incident at Dogger Bank was investigated, the international commission of experts also pronounced on the question of responsibility, something actually requested by the parties.[104] Thereafter, bilateral agreements on the establishment of inquiry commissions for general peaceful settlement became very popular, fed by the belief that independent investigations could prevent wars by 'cooling down'

---

[99] T. Bensalah, *L'Enquête Internationale dans le Règlement des Conflits* (1976); N. Bar-Yaacov, *The Handling of International Disputes by Means of Inquiry* (1974); J.G. Merrills, *International Dispute Settlement* (4th edn. 2005) ch 3; United Nations *Handbook on the Peaceful Settlement of Disputes between States* (1992) 24-33; A.J.P. Tammes, *Internationaal Publiekrecht* (2nd edn. 1973) 301-307; H.G. Darwin, 'Fact-Finding and Commissions of Inquiry', in C.H.M. Waldock and F. Vallat (eds.), *International Disputes: The Legal Aspects* (1972) 159.

[100] T.M. Franck and H.S. Fairley, 'Procedural Due Process in Human Rights Fact-Finding by International Agencies', 74 *AJIL* (1980) 308.

[101] Nguyen Quoc Dinh, 'Les commissions de conciliation sont elles aussi des commissions d'enquête?', (1967) 71 *RGDIP* 565; D. Momtaz, 'Les Nations Unies et les commissions d'établissement des faits', in United Nations *International Law as a Language for International Relations* (1996) 450, 457.

[102] F.M. van Asbeck, 'La tâche et l'action d'une commission de conciliation', (1956) *NTIR* 1, 4

[103] E.g., the PCA Optional Rules for Fact-Finding Commissions of Inquiry Art. 14(2) in: Permanent Court of Arbitration *Basic Documents* (1998) 177. An exception: LOSC Annex VIII Art. 5(2) in which fact-finding is in principle binding.

[104] For the report and the inquiry agreement: J.B. Scott, *The Hague Court Reports* (1916) 403.

tense relations after controversial incidents. These agreements were however used only sparingly, mainly for technical aspects of maritime disputes.[105] From the 1920s onward, the role of inquiry commissions as dispute settlement mechanisms was to a significant extent taken over by conciliation commissions, which, unlike regular inquiry commissions, had the explicit competence to discuss all aspects of the matter.

2.4.1 *Fact-finding in international organisations*

The League of Nations created several inquiry commissions to investigate the sources of international crises, some with considerable success.[106] From 1949 onwards several attempts were made to facilitate inquiry in bilateral disputes through the United Nations by means of a permanent panel of investigators.[107] Inquiry is now increasingly used under auspices of international organisations, for the specific purposes of these international organisations.[108] A gradual distinction can be made on a continuum from pure fact-finding to compliance control.

If conducted by an international organisation, inquiry is generally known as fact-finding. Contested or unknown factual situations may be investigated by a commission appointed by the organisation.[109] Such fact-finding is used increasingly, often under the responsibility of the United Nations Secretary-General.[110]

---

[105] See chapter II 1.

[106] T.P. Conwell-Evans, *The League Council in Action* (1929) 135 ff; see chapter II 1.5.

[107] Following the abandoned 'Panel for Inquiry and Conciliation' established by UNGA Res 268 (III) (1949); UNGA Res 2329 (XXII) the UN Secretary-General was requested to set-up another register of experts to be used for fact-finding missions on request of member States. The register has, however, not functioned. Another initiative is found in the UN Declaration on Fact-Finding by the United Nations in the Field of the Maintenance of International Peace and Security UNGA Res 46/59 (1992) [14] that calls upon the Secretary-General to maintain lists of experts in various fields, available for fact-finding missions.

[108] The League of Nations Covenant Arts. 12 and 15 laid the basis for the active fact-finding practice of the Council and the Assembly: T.P. Conwell-Evans, *The League Council in Action* (1929) 133. For the current practice in the UN: D. Momtaz, 'Les Nations Unies et les commissions d'établissement des faits', in United Nations *International Law as a Language for International Relations* (1996) 450; M.C. Bourloyannis, 'Fact-Finding by the Secretary-General of the United Nations', (1990) 22 *NYUJILP* 641; 'Report of the Secretary-General on Methods of Fact-Finding' (1 May 1964) UN Doc A/5694 and the second 'Report' (22 April 1966) UN Doc A/6228; A.J.P. Tammes, *Internationaal Publiekrecht* (2nd edn. 1973) 303-306.

[109] E.g., the 1988 *Copper* dispute between the European Community and Japan, for which the GATT among others appointed a 'Group of Governmental Experts on Measures Affecting the World Market for Copper', BISD 36S/99.

[110] M.C. Bourloyannis, 'Fact-finding by the Secretary-General of the United Nations', (1990) 22 *NYUJILP* 641; A. Peters, 'International Dispute Settlement: A Network of Cooperational Du-

The purpose of an investigation may vary: it may be to settle a dispute,[111] but this is not necessarily so. An investigation can also be a negotiation tool or a goal in itself: the clarification of a matter may be the end of the affair. Furthermore, as one UN declaration states, sending a fact-finding mission may serve to signal the concern of the organisation.[112] This way, and by investigating an incident before a major controversy erupts, fact-finding can also contribute to dispute prevention.

Fact-finding may be compulsory, as in the Convention on the Law of the Non-navigational Uses of International Watercourses,[113] and when it is prescribed by the UN Security Council. It may also be on the request of the relevant party or parties, such as in the monitoring of elections, or in the observation of a cease-fire.[114] A major obstacle to fact-finding missions is normally obtaining the consent of the State in which the investigation is to take place. Israel, for example, would not allow a UN team to investigate the killing by Israeli forces of Palestinians in Jerusalem in 1990[115] and in Jenin in 2002.[116] Sanctions rarely follow such refusal; an extreme exception is the invasion of Iraq in 2003, which was motivated partially by alleged non-co-operation with fact-finding.[117]

---

ties', (2003) 14 *EJIL* 1, 5; Peters points out the 'International Commission of Inquiry Concerning the Assassination of the President of Burundi on 21 October 1993 and the Massacres that Followed' established by the Secretary-General pursuant to UNSC Res 1012 (1995); 'Report' UN Doc S/1996/682.

[111] A. Lenk, 'Fact-Finding as Peace Negotiation Tool – The Mitchell Report and the Israeli-Palestinian Peace Process', (2002) 24 *Loyola of Los Angeles International & Comparative Law Review* 289.

[112] UN Declaration on Fact-Finding by the United Nations in the Field of the Maintenance of International Peace and Security [5] UNGA Res 46/59 (1992). See also the terms of reference of the commission contained in 'Report of the Security Council Mission on the implementation of Security Council Resolution 1244 (1999) 27 to 29 April 2000' [2] (2000) UN Doc S/2000/363, relating to Kosovo.

[113] Art. 33(3-9). This arrangement is also notable in that fact-finding is prescribed, in the absence of agreement to an alternative, for the settlement of disputes 'concerning the interpretation or application' of the Convention Art. 33(1) thereby also for disputes in which facts are not disputed, but only the legal interpretation of the Convention. R. Lapidoth, 'Dispute Settlement under the 1997 Convention on the Law of the Non-navigational Uses of International Watercourses', in M.N. Schmitt (ed.), *International Law Across the Spectrum of Conflict* (2000) 231, 241.

[114] E.g., UNMOGIP (United Nations Military Observer Group in India and Pakistan), which, *inter alia*, has had to determine whether there was a breach of the cease-fire agreement, a highly controversial legal determination. A. Dholakia, *The Role of Mediation in Resolving India-Pakistan Conflict: Parameters and Possibilities* (2005) 41-46; N. Bar-Yaacov, *The Handling of International Disputes by Means of Inquiry* (1974) 248-258.

[115] UNSC Res 672 and 673 (1990); N.D. White, *Keeping the Peace* (2nd edn. 1997) 86.

[116] UNGA Res ES-10/10; UNSC Res 1405 (2002); 'Report of the Secretary-General' prepared pursuant to UNGA Res ES-10/10 (30 July 2002), (2002) 41 *ILM* 1444.

[117] H. Blix, *Disarming Iraq: The Search for Weapons of Mass Destruction* (2004).

Fact-finding by international organisations may form part of a previously accepted compliance procedure. Commissions are established to investigate compliance with specified international obligations. Bodies like these, such as the UN Special Commission (UNSCOM) charged with inspection missions on Iraqi weapons of mass destruction,[118] are instruments of supervision rather than of third party dispute settlement.[119] Unlike inquiry commissions under bilateral agreements, such fact-finding commissions do not normally include citizens from the concerned State. In these as in other cases, fact-finding mostly serves not to settle a dispute between two States, but to clarify a controversy between one State and the other Contracting Parties. A far-reaching example is found in the Convention on the Prohibition of Chemical Weapons, which grants any State party the right to request inspections in any other State, without its direct interests being involved.[120] Sometimes, inquiry for compliance is also a means to allow for the involvement of non-State actors. In these cases, inquiry can be treated as an alternative to giving individuals standing before an international court or tribunal.[121]

2.5 Mediation

Mediation is a method of international dispute settlement in which a third party advances its own proposals, based on information essentially provided by the parties, aimed at a mutually acceptable solution.[122] The conduct of mediation

[118] UNSC Res 687 (1991) and UNSC Res 1441 (2002).

[119] Another example is found in the Protocol Additional to the Geneva Convention Art. 90 (12 August 1949) and relating to the Protection of Victims of International Armed Conflicts Protocol I (8 June 1977).

[120] United Nations Convention on the Prohibition of the Development, Production, Stockpiling and Use of Chemical Weapons and on their Destruction Art. 9. See also the compulsory fact-finding system of the Convention on the Law of the Non-navigational Uses of International Watercourses Art. 33.

[121] E.g., before the Committee against Torture established by the Convention against Torture and Other Cruel, Inhuman or Degrading Treatment or Punishment, Art. 22.

[122] Cf., United Nations *Handbook on the Peaceful Settlement of Disputes between States* (1992) 40; J.G. Merrills, *International Dispute Settlement* (4th edn.) (2005) ch 2; H.G. Darwin, 'Mediation and Good Offices', in C.H.M. Waldock and F. Vallat (eds.), *International Disputes: The Legal Aspects* (1972) 83; F.S. Northedge and M.D. Donelan, *International Disputes: The Political Aspects* (1971) ch 13; J. Wilkenfeld and others (eds.), *Mediating International Crises* (2005); C.A. Crocker, F. Osler Hampson and P. Aall (eds.), *Herding Cats: Multiparty Mediation in a Complex World* (1999). There is also substantial literature from those involved in mediation: G. Mitchell, *Making Peace* (1999); R. Holbrooke, *To End a War* (1998); C.R. Hume, *Ending Mozambique's Civil War: The Role of Mediation and Good Offices* (1994); V.H. Umbricht, *Multilateral Mediation: Practical Experiences and Lessons* (1989). For a socio-psychological approach: T. Princen, *Intermediaries in International Conflict* (1992).

is usually confidential and frequently informal. The Pact of Bogotá even prescribes the latter explicitly.[123] In some situations, however, the acceptance, commencement and outcome of a mediation process is highly formalised in order to emphasise the political commitment of the parties.

In the 19th century mediation was frequently used as a means of the Great Powers to influence the smaller ones.[124] At the time it was also known as 'peaceful intervention'. It was therefore a significant development when the 1899 Hague Convention declared that the offer of mediation can never be considered an unfriendly act.[125] Mediation has since proven to be a very flexible method capable of affecting the attitudes, even if not always the positions of intransigent parties. This is one reason that the prediction Politis made in 1910 that with the development of international law eventually all differences between States would no longer be settled by mediation but by arbitration, has not held.[126]

Mediation provisions are included in many bilateral and multilateral agreements, though often without any further specification of the procedure to select a mediator or of the conduct of the mediation.[127] Such prior arrangements would be difficult in most cases, as the political character of most mediation efforts requires flexibility, including the liberty to choose a mediator suited for this specific case. A time limit may be given for the duration of mediation, though this is rare.[128] In such cases, a follow-up provision should be available to avoid unnecessary lapses in settlement.

In practice mediation is often undertaken on an *ad hoc* basis.[129] Mediators are often internationally respected political figures. It can be performed by an individual in his own name, but may also be conducted in the name of a State

---

[123] Pact of Bogotá Art. 12.

[124] N. Politis, 'L'Avenir de la médiation', (1910) 17 *RGDIP* 136, 142. Indirectly, another illustration is given by Hackworths review of US mediation in Central and South America early 20th century: G.H. Hackworth, *Digest of International Law* Vol. VI (1943) 24 ff.

[125] Hague Convention for the Pacific Settlement of International Disputes (29 July 1899) (1899 Hague Convention), Permanent Court of Arbitration *Basic Documents* (1998) 3, Art. 3(3). This statement remains relevant, considering its restatement in Art. 3(10) of the WTO 1994 Dispute Settlement Understanding, Annex 2 to The Marrakesh Agreement Establishing the World Trade Organization, 15 April 1994, (1994) 33 *ILM* 1144.

[126] N. Politis, 'L'Avenir de la médiation', (1910) 17 *RGDIP* 136, 141.

[127] E.g., Agreement on the Conservation of Ceteaceans of the Black Sea, Mediterranean Sea and Contiguous Atlantic Area (24 November 1996), (1997) 36 *ILM* 780, Art. 12; Treaty on the Southeast Asia Nuclear Weapon-Free Zone Art. 21, (1996) 35 *ILM* 639.

[128] E.g., Pact of Bogotá Art. 13.

[129] Overview in J. Bercovitch and J. Fretter, *Regional Guide to International Conflict Management from 1945 to 2003* (2004) 28ff. On the moment and method of entry into mediation: M.O. Maundi, et al., *Getting In* (2006).

or an international organisation,[130] or by an individual in the name of a Secretary-General, Head of State or government, in the form of a personal envoy.[131] Occasionally, a group of States can act as a joint mediator, though a recurring problem for a composite mediator is to speak with one voice. An example is the unsuccessful attempt at mediation by the European Communities regarding the war in the former Yugoslavia in the early 1990s,[132] and the effort by the Quartet (European Union, Russian Federation, United Nations, United States) in the Middle East.[133]

Mediation can also be performed by an international organisation as a whole, involving both the executive institutions and the representative ones, such as was occasionally practised by the League of Nations.[134] The representative bodies then perform the supporting function of providing explicit political backing for mediation initiatives, which need to be taken by a smaller and therefore more flexible unit within the organisation, such as the executive council or the presiding officer. More frequently, however, mediation is performed on an individual level by high officers of major international organisations, such as the Secretary-General of the United Nations[135] or the President of the World Bank.[136] The political backing of such efforts is often unarticulated, as the officer relies more on his stature than on power resources. The absence of supporting or guiding resolutions increases the room for manoeuvring and at the same time saves the member States from committing themselves politically.[137]

---

[130] For a list of instances of crisis mediation between 1918 and 2001, J. Wilkenfeld and others (eds.), *Mediating International Crises* (2005) 177 ff.

[131] M. Fullilove, 'All the Presidents' Men: The Role of Special Envoys in U.S. Foreign Policy', 84 *Foreign Affairs* (2005) (2) 12.

[132] K. Webb, V. Koutrakou and M. Walters, 'The Yugoslavian Conflict, European Mediation and the Contingency Model: A Critical Perspective', in J. Bercovitch (ed.), *Resolving International Conflicts* (1996) 171, 176-181. Other examples include the 1963 mediation by seven African States in a border conflict between Algeria and Morocco: T.O. Elias, 'The Commission of Mediation, Conciliation and Arbitration of the Organization of African Unity', (1964) 40 *BYIL* 336, 339.

[133] A press conference on behalf of the Quartet by six persons (4 May 2004) on <www.state.gov/r/pa/prs/ps/2004/32161pf.htm> (29 August 2004).

[134] E.g., in concerning the Mosul Vilayet, an area contested by the Turks and the British in Iraq in the early 1920s. T.P. Conwell-Evans, *The League Council in Action* (1929) 73-74. In its early days, the World Bank would also mediate as an institution: A. Dholakia, *The Role of Mediation in Resolving India-Pakistan Conflict: Parameters and Possibilities* (2005) 47; I.F.I. Shihata, *The World Bank in a Changing World* (Vol. III) (2000) 239.

[135] See chapter I 2.7.

[136] I. Shihata, 'Avoidance and Settlement of Disputes – the World Bank's Approach and Experience', (1999) 1 *International Law Forum* 90.

[137] E.g., the effort made by UN Secretary-General in 1998 to obtain an agreement between Iraq and the Security Council on inspection of Iraq's so-called 'presidential sites'. The unspecified brief of the Secretary-General on this mission benefited all parties: W. Shawcross, *Deliver Us From Evil* (2000) 238-241.

In certain cases the UN Secretary-General or his envoy acted in co-operation with particular States with an interest in resolving the dispute. Such a 'Group of Friends' proved beneficial in ending the civil war in El Salvador in 1992 but has a mixed record since.[138] International organisations can also facilitate the incorporation of inquiry into a mediation effort, such as when the views of the inhabitants needed to be consulted to agree on the status of Bahrain *vis-à-vis* Iran.[139]

Sometimes, mediation is also attempted by non-governmental organisations, or other 'unofficial intermediaries' such as politicians acting on their own initiative, without the support of a public institution.[140] While sometimes this can help to overcome political barriers, often the political backing of a mediation effort is essential for its success. Especially in disputes between less powerful States, the ability of a mediator to bring about rewards or sanctions has frequently proven instrumental.[141] Complete neutrality is therefore not a prerequisite for a mediator. When the parties are themselves very powerful, or if the *status quo* is too delicate, the disinterestedness of the mediator may however be more important.

Mediation can take many forms, and be combined with various other procedures. A notable example is the Cameroon-Nigeria Mixed Commission, established in December 2002 following the good offices of the UN Secretary-General.[142] The two States had earlier submitted their boundary dispute to the ICJ,[143] but following the judgement differences continued regarding its implementation, in particular in the important Bakassi peninsula.[144] Nigeria held that the Court had not considered 'fundamental facts'. The Mixed Commission, headed by the Secretary-General's Special Representative for West-Africa, and with high representatives from both sides, holds periodic meetings in

---

[138] T. Whitfield, 'Good Offices and "Groups of Friends"', in S. Chesterman, *Secretary or General? The UN Secretary-General in World Politics* (2007) 86.

[139] H. Al-Baharna, 'The Fact-finding Mission of the United Nations Secretary-General and the Settlement of the Bahrain-Iran Dispute, May 1970', (1973) 22 *ICLQ* 541.

[140] D. Chigas, 'Negotiating Intractable Conflicts: The Contributions of Unofficial Intermediaries', in C.A. Crocker, F. Osler Hampson and P. Aall (eds.), *Grasping the Nettle: Analyzing Cases of Intractable Conflict* (2005) 123.

[141] E.g., the Camp David mediation between Egypt and Israel, conducted by the United States. The US promised significant political and financial rewards: *Digest of United States Practice in International Law* (1979) 1686-1724.

[142] UNSG Statement 15 November 2002 <http://www.un.org/unowa/cnmc/preleas/sgstmts.htm#3> (5 October 2007).

[143] *Land and Maritime Boundary between Cameroon and Nigeria* (*Cameroon* v. *Nigeria: Equatorial Guinea intervening*), *ICJ Rep* (2002).

[144] Press Release UN Doc SG/SM/8495 AFR/515 (15 November 2002); 'Report of the Secretary-General on the Work of the Organisation', GAOR 58th sess. Supp. 1 UN Doc A/58/1. (2003) [29].

alternating locations, and established two sub-commissions, comprising experts from the parties and from the UN. One commission deals with land demarcation, one with affected populations.[145] In addition, the Secretary-General frequently meets with the governments of both States to promote progress.[146] The institutional set-up, in which the parties are closely involved in achieving progress in implementation, suggests that the work of the Mixed Commission is that of mediation, but the line between that and conciliation is occasionally a fine one.

2.5.1 *Mediation and conciliation*

The differences between mediation and conciliation are not self-evident:

> 'Mediation is a method of peaceful settlement of an international dispute where a third party intervenes to reconcile the claims of the contending parties and to advance his own proposals aimed at a mutually acceptable compromise solution.'[147]

Defining mediation in these broad terms as the United Nations Office of Legal Affairs does, there is no residual space for another active non-binding third party settlement method. Due to a similar broad concept of conciliation prevalent in international private law, mediation and conciliation are often considered interchangeable.[148] The WTO dispute settlement procedure speaks of

---

[145] G. Oduntan, 'The Demarcation of Straddling Villages in Accordance with the International Court of Justice Jurisprudence: The Cameroon-Nigeria Experience', (2006) 5 *CJIL* 79. Also: Press Release UNOWA/CNMC/2005/8 (29 November 2005).

[146] On 20 June 2006 Nigeria and Cameroon concluded the Agreement Concerning the Modalities of Withdrawal and Transfer of Authority in the Bakassi Peninsula <http://www.un.org/unowa/cnmc/preleas/cn_agreement.pdf> (5 October 2007).

[147] United Nations *Handbook on the Peaceful Settlement of Disputes between States* (1992) 40. Even broader: 'Mediation, as a method of peaceful settlement of international disputes, means the participation of a third State or a disinterested individual in negotiations between States in dispute.' H.G. Darwin, 'Mediation and Good Offices', in C.H.M. Waldock and F. Vallat (eds.), *International Disputes: The Legal Aspects* (1972) 83.

[148] E.g., the UNCITRAL Model Law on International Commercial Conciliation (2002) UN Doc A/57/18) Art. 1(3) on <http://www.uncitral.org/uncitral/en/uncitral_texts/arbitration.html> (5 October 2007); M. Rubino-Sammartano, *International Arbitration Law and Practice* (2001) 10-11; P. Sanders, *Quo Vadis Arbitration* (1999) 353; H.J. Brown and A.L. Marriott, *ADR Principles and Practice* (2nd edn. 1999) 127; H.M. Holtzmann, 'Dispute Resolution in Europe under the UNCITRAL Conciliation Rules', in D. Bardonnet (ed.), *Le Règlement Pacifique des Differends Internationaux en Europe: Perspectives d'Avenir* (1991) 293, 299. International relations scholars occasionally also see conciliation as part of mediation. E.g., K. Skjelsbaek, 'The UN Secretary-General and the Mediation of International Disputes', (1991) 28 *Journal of Peace Research* 99, 100.

'mediation, conciliation and good offices', but by that refers to one method of assisted dispute settlement.[149] Nevertheless, the UN Charter in Article 33 mentions mediation and conciliation separately, as do many other public international legal instruments[150] and public international lawyers.[151]

Certain elements of the normal usage of the terms in public international law discourse can be identified, which together distinguish the two methods from each other. Unlike conciliation, mediation is normally referred to as something that can be done by States, individuals or by international organisations. Mediation *commissions* are rare. Mediation is often *ad hoc*, and used in politically charged disputes.[152] Mediators can offer their services on their own initiative. Selection or acceptance is normally based on the political suitability and negotiation skills of the mediator, and less on subject-matter expertise.[153] Mediators are normally not expected to conduct a thorough investigation of the underlying situation that gave rise to the dispute, but rather to help the parties find a compromise. Mediators, especially when they are supported by the means of a major Power, occasionally apply pressure on the parties. Some even owe their status as mediator to their ability to do so.[154] These characteristics of mediation are not shared by conciliation, as is discussed further below.

On the basis of tradition arising out of the 1899 Convention, one may say that mediation nominally comprises all forms of non-binding dispute settlement in which a third party has an active role in bringing the parties together, and therefore formally encompasses conciliation. It is clear, however, that in normal parlance, at least in public international law, 'mediation' refers to a more specific method as described above. This core concept of mediation, however, itself refers to a wide variety of dispute settlement practices, ranging from

---

[149] R. Pratap, 'Trade and Environment: Trends in International Dispute Settlement', (2002) 42 *IJIL* 451, 485; N. Komuro, 'The WTO Dispute Settlement Mechanism – Coverage and Procedures of the WTO DSU', (1995) 29 *Journal of World Trade* 5, 47; E. Canal-Forgues and R. Ostrihansky, 'New Developments in the GATT Dispute Settlement Procedures', (1990) 24 *Journal of World Trade* 67, 70-71.

[150] E.g., OAU Charter (25 May 1963), (1964) 3 *ILM* 1116 Art. 3; UNGA Res 37/10 (1982) 'Manila Declaration on the Peaceful Settlement of International Disputes'.

[151] E.g., I. Brownlie, *Principles of Public International Law* (5th edn. 1998) 704; J.G. Merrills, *International Dispute Settlement* (4th edn. 2005) 28; C. Rousseau, *Droit International Public* (1983) Vol. V 266, 286; H. Lauterpacht, *Oppenheim's International Law* (7th edn. 1952) Vol. II 8, 12.

[152] United Nations *Handbook on the Peaceful Settlement of Disputes between States* (1992) 42.

[153] E.g., the mediation by Cardinal Antonia Samoré on behalf of the Pope in the Beagle Channel dispute between Argentina and Chile regarding in particular the contested implementation of an arbitration award regarding essentially maritime delimitation (Documents of the mediation: (1985) 24 *ILM* 1).

[154] Cf., R. Holbrooke, *To End a War* (1998).

an *ad hoc* political intervention by the UN Secretary-General to avert a war, using his prestige and international attention, to intervention by a convention chairman in the formulation of a draft paragraph. Building on long-standing tradition, it is argued here that a similar core concept of conciliation can be distinguished, usefully separate from the core concept of mediation.

2.6 Conciliation

Conciliation, as a method of international dispute settlement, can take on many forms. Generally, conciliation involves an independent commission, appointed by the parties, which investigates the dispute and proposes a solution to the parties to be presented in a report.[155] This implies a more in depth study of the dispute as compared to mediation, combined with the independence of the third party as it is found in adjudication, but aiming for amicable settlement in a non-binding manner instead of producing a binding finding of the law. A conciliation commission traditionally consist of five persons, of whom each party nominates one or two members of its own nationality, while the nationally appointed members agree on the remaining member(s).[156]

Conciliation arose out of the method of inquiry early in the 20th century. The success of the *Dogger Bank* inquiry, in which the commission not only investigated the facts but also submitted a report that upon adoption by the parties could constitute a solution,[157] led to the idea that the scope of the method of inquiry could be expanded. In 1919, with the guidance of Max Huber, the Swiss government adopted a policy statement advocating the conclusion of conciliation agreements.[158] The Swiss government saw conciliation as a means for the settlement of any international dispute. Conciliation could coexist with arbitration, to settle disputes for which one of the parties would not grant jurisdiction to an arbitral tribunal. In addition, conciliation could be a means to avoid the political costs of arbitration or judicial settlement.[159] Meanwhile, another rationale for conciliation found support in the Americas. US Secretary of State Bryan explored variations of conciliation with the specific purpose of preventing disputes from developing into war. The combination of the two sources of inspiration led in the 1920s and 1930s to the conclusion of hundreds of bilat-

155 See chapter I 3.

156 E.g., General Act of 1949 Art. 4 and the 1920s and 1930s bilateral treaties: see chapter II 1.6 and 1.7.

157 For the report and the inquiry agreement: J.B. Scott, *The Hague Court Reports* (1916) 403 ff.

158 'Rapport du Conseil fédéral à l'Assemblée fédérale concernant les traités internationaux d'arbitrage', (1919) 71 *Feuille Fédéral Suisse* Vol. V 808.

159 Ibid., 820.

eral and multilateral conciliation treaties, predominantly by European and American States.[160]

Despite its popularity, conciliation found application in smaller numbers than expected. It was nevertheless successful in most cases. Notably, in 1929 Bolivia and Paraguay eased the tensions, on an *ad hoc* basis, in the *Chaco* border dispute.[161] Various European States addressed mainly commercial disputes through conciliation, both before and after WWII.[162]

Conciliation enjoys an ambiguous relationship with the law, placed as it is in-between the largely political means of mediation, and the legal and binding alternative of adjudication.[163] In practice, many conciliators regarded it as their assignment to render a legal opinion.[164] The correctness of that interpretation, particularly on the question whether a conciliation commission should make pronouncements on the law, has been seriously debated.[165]

Despite the abandonment of bilateral treaties devoted especially to conciliation, the method continues to be commonly included in multilateral treaties on matters of substantive law.[166] Recent years have seen a renewed interest in conciliation. The OSCE designed a number of conciliation instruments, and set-up a Court of Conciliation and Arbitration.[167] Both the United Nations and

---

160 For the various treaties: M. Habicht, *Post-War Treaties for the Pacific Settlement of International Disputes* (1931); *Systematic Survey 1928-1948*. See chapter II 1.6, 1.7.

161 *Proceedings of the Commission of Inquiry and Conciliation, Bolivia and Paraguay, March 13, 1929–September 13, 1929* (1929); L. Woolsey, 'Bolivia – Paraguay Dispute', (1929) 23 *AJIL* 110 and (1930) 24 *AJIL* 122; H. Arbo, 'Le conflit entra la Bolivie et le Paraguay à propos du Chaco boréal', (1929) 36 *RGDIP* 528.

162 *Cot* 91; H. Wehberg, 'Die Vergleichskommissionen im modernen Völkerrecht', (1958) 19 *ZfAÖRV* 551, 568; D. Schindler, *Die Schiedsgerichtbarkeit seit 1914* (1938) 25; H. Fox, 'Conciliation', in C.H.M. Waldock and F. Vallat (eds.), *International Disputes; The Legal Aspects* (1972) 93; S. Bastid, 'La commission de conciliation franco-suisse', (1956) 2 *AFDI* 436; P. Guggenheim, 'Droit international public', (1954) 11 *ASDI* 173, 201; M. Breton-Jokl, 'La commission permanente de conciliation italo-suisse' (1957), 3 *AFDI* 210; (1958) 25 *ILR* Vol. I 313; See chapter II 1

163 In private law, mediation and conciliation are often considered to be two words for the same procedure: H.M. Holtzmann, 'Dispute Resolution in Europe under the UNCITRAL Conciliation Rules', in D. Bardonnet (ed.), *Le Règlement Pacifique des Differends Internationaux en Europe: Perspectives d'Avenir* (1991) 293, 299.

164 E.g., F.M. van Asbeck, 'La tâche et l'action d'une commission de conciliation', (1956) *NTIR* 1, 6. See chapter III 2.

165 E.g., (1961) 49 *Annuaire de l'Institut de Droit International* Vol. II 205, 252 ff. See chapter III 3.

166 E.g., the United Nations Convention to Combat Desertification in those Countries Experiencing Serious Drought and/or Desertification, Particularly in Africa (17 June 1994, entered into force 26 December 1996), (1994) 33 *ILM* 1328, Art. 29; Convention on the Prior Informed Consent Procedure for Certain Hazardous Chemicals and Pesticides in International Trade (11 September 1998), (1998) 38 *ILM* 1.

167 CSCE 'Decision on Peaceful Settlement' (15 December 1992), (1993) 32 *ILM* 556. See chapter III 3.4.2

the Permanent Court of Arbitration have adopted model rules for conciliation.[168] In addition, multilateral treaties, in particular those in matters of the environment, increasingly adopt non-compliance procedures, which borrow from conciliation and create new possibilities for its development.[169] Furthermore, conciliation and analogous methods continue to be used for sometimes highly contentious international disputes, such as the recent case between Belize and Guatemala.[170]

2.7 The United Nations

With the primary purpose of maintaining international peace and security, the United Nations provides a broad variety of means for the settlement of disputes, especially grave disputes.[171] The existence of the organisation itself facilitates international diplomacy by the fact that representatives of almost all States are permanently gathered and are able to conduct negotiations also when there is no other communication between the countries. The UN serves to internationalise disputes, and therefore to raise awareness of them. Disputes can be brought to the attention of the organisation by the States involved, but also by other States or by the UN organs themselves. The organisation has on occasion been described as the 'depository of lost causes', to which those matters are referred for which no other solution could be found.[172] It is often the

[168] The UN Model Rules of Conciliation for Disputes between States: UNGA Res 50/50 (11 December 1995) Annex 1; the PCA Optional Conciliation Rules (effective 1 July 1996): Permanent Court of Arbitration *Basic Documents* (1998) 161; see chapter II 2.

[169] E.g., the Montreal Protocol on Substances that Deplete the Ozone Layer (16 September 1997), (1987) 26 *ILM* 1550 to the Vienna Convention on the Ozone Layer (22 March 1985), 1513 *UNTS* 324. The Montreal Non-compliance procedure, pursuant to the Montreal Protocol Art. 8 is contained in a decision by the Fourth Meeting of the Parties UNEP/Ozl.Pro.4/15 on <http://ozone.unep.org/Meeting_Documents/mop/04mop/index.asp> (26 July 2006).

[170] 'Belize-Guatemala Territorial Differendum: Proposals from the Facilitators' (30 August 2002) II on <www.belize.gov.bz/features/proposals/belize_guatemala_differendum.html> (20 April 2003). See chapter II 1.15.

[171] 'Mechanisms Established by the General Assembly in the Context of Dispute Prevention and Settlement' (2000) UN Doc A/AC.182/2000/INF/2; United Nations Issue, (1998) 30 *NYUJILP* Vols. 3-4; United Nations *Handbook on the Peaceful Settlement of Disputes between States* (1992); N.D. White, *Keeping the Peace* (2nd edn. 1997); L.B. Sohn, *Broadening the Role of the United Nations in Preventing, Mitigating or Ending International or Internal Conflicts that Threaten International Peace and Security* (1997); C. Peck, *The United Nations as a Dispute Settlement System* (1996); A. Roberts and B. Kingsbury (eds.), *United Nations, Divided World* (2nd edn. 1993); United Nations *An Agenda for Peace* UN Doc A/47/277 (1992); *Supplement to An Agenda for Peace* UN Doc A/50/60 (1995); K. Venkata Raman (ed.), *Dispute Settlement through the United Nations* (1977).

[172] S. Northedge and M.D. Donelan, *International Disputes: The Political Aspects* (1971) 239.

least powerful party in any given dispute that requests involvement by the organisation. Apparently, in many cases States consider that the organisation diminishes power differences in international affairs.

The Secretary-General is the chief administrative officer of the organisation.[173] He is entitled to bring to the attention of the Security Council any matter which he considers threatens international peace and security.[174] Based on an increasingly extensive interpretation of their largely inherent rights, successive Secretaries-General have developed a well-respected role in dispute settlement and dispute prevention, especially in the fields of good offices and mediation.[175] This role is, with occasional exceptions, widely supported by the member States.[176] The Secretary-General may also appoint Special Representatives.[177] An overview of mediation successes given by former Secretary-General U Thant himself indicates that successes are frequently not publicly credited to the office holder.[178] It is notable, for instance, that he considered his involvement in the Cuban missile crisis of 1962 to have led to one of his most important successes,[179] while accounts by American and Soviet main actors hardly mention U Thant's involvement at all.[180] It may well be that a mediator overstates his importance, but in any case the involvement of the UN Secretary-General, bound not only by rules of confidentiality but also by a commit-

---

173 UN Charter Art. 97.

174 UN Charter Art. 99. On the various political aspects of the Secretary-General's work: S. Chesterman (ed.), *Secretary or General? The UN Secretary-General in World Politics* (2007).

175 An extensive interpretation is implicitly recognised in the Declaration on the Prevention and Removal of Disputes and Situations Which May Threaten International Peace and Security and on the Role of the United Nations in this Field Annex to UNGA Res 43/51 (1988) [8] [20] and [22]. A. Brehio, 'Good Offices of the Secretary-General as Preventive Measures', (1998) 30 *NYUJILP* 589; K. Skjelsbaek and G. Fermann, 'The UN Secretary-General and the Mediation of International Disputes', in J. Bercovitch, *Resolving International Conflict* (1996); C.S.R. Murthy, 'The Role of the UN Secretary-General since the End of the Cold War', (1995) 35 *Indian JIL* 181; T.M. Franck, *Fairness in International Law and Institutions* (1995) ch 6; H. Caminos and R. Lavalle, 'New Departures in the Exercise of Inherent Powers by the UN and OAS Secretaries General: The Central American Situation', (1989) 83 *AJIL* 395; U Thant *View from the UN* (1978) ch II; V. Pechota, 'The Quiet Approach: A Study of the Good Offices Exercised by the United Nations Secretary-General in the Cause of Peace', in K. Venkata Raman (ed.), *Dispute Settlement through the United Nations* (1977) 577; S.M. Schwebel, *The Secretary-General of the United Nations* (1952).

176 E.g., '2005 World Summit Outcome', UN Doc A/60/L.1 [76].

177 'The Peacemaker: An interview with UN Under-Secretary-General Alvaro de Soto', (2002) 26 *Fletcher Forum of World Affairs* 83.

178 U Thant, *View from the UN* (1978) 27.

179 Idem, 27, 191.

180 R.F. Kennedy, *Thirteen Days* (1971) 52, 56; N. Chroestjtsjov, *De Glasnost Tapes* (J.L. Schecter and V.V. Loetsjkov (eds.)) (Dutch trans) (1990) 180.

ment to the Organisation and to an enduring relationship with its disputing member States, can often be a thankless task.

The Secretary-General has also functioned as a quasi-arbitrator when, upon request of France and New Zealand, he delivered an almost unreasoned decision regarding the French sinking of the vessel *Rainbow Warrior* in Auckland.[181] Despite its label as depository of lost causes, the United Nations has made a significant contribution to the peaceful settlement of disputes.

2.8 Regional arrangements

As an alternative to submitting a dispute to the UN, States may also approach a regional organisation. The UN Charter accords significance to those organisations in the hope that they might be more suitable to deal with certain regional problems.[182] The UN nevertheless retains an overriding responsibility for any international disputes.[183] The spread and success of regional organisations is varied.[184] In Europe there are various relatively successful organisations such as the EU, the OSCE and the Council of Europe, while Asia has only few, mainly the Association of South East Asian Nations (ASEAN) and Asia-Pacific Economic Co-operation (APEC), with relatively little influence.[185] The role of the Commonwealth of Independent States (CIS), arising out of the dissolution of the Soviet Union, remains unclear.[186] Arab countries meet in the League of Arab States, and also in the broader Organisation of the Islamic Conference.[187] Africa had its relatively weak Organisation of African Unity,

---

[181] (1987) 26 *ILM* 1346.

[182] UN Charter ch VIII.

[183] This is an improvement upon the League of Nations Covenant, which in Art. 21 explicitly recognised the validity of 'regional understandings like the Monroe Doctrine', which entailed in practice that the US would have primary responsibility to deal with disputes in the Americas. Further: Declaration on the Enhancement of Cooperation between the United Nations and Regional Arrangements or Agencies in the Maintenance of International Peace and Security: UNGA Res 49/57 (1995). Manila Declaration [6] expresses preference for settlement through regional arrangements.

[184] L. Fawcett and A. Hurrell (eds.), *Regionalism in World Politics* (1995); P. Dallier and A. Pellet, *Droit International Public* (1999) 821 ff.

[185] T.C. Fisher, 'A Commentary on Regional Institutions in the Pacific Rim: Do APEC and ASEAN Still Matter?', (2003) 13 *Duke Journal of Comparative and International Law* 337. Cf., J. Rehman, 'Institutions of International Law and the Development of Regional Forum for Peaceful Dialogue in South Asia', (2006) 1 *Asian Journal of Comparative Law* Art. 16.

[186] The CIS has undertaken various peace-keeping missions, not endorsed by the UN Security Council because of concern about conformity with UN standards. Sipri/UNESCO *Handbook: Peace, Security and Conflict Prevention* (1998) 53-54.

[187] H. Moinuddin, *The Charter of the Islamic Conference* (1987) 69 ff.

which in 2002 was replaced by the African Union.[188] There is also the more active Economic Community of West African States (ECOWAS).[189] The Americas have a significant number of organisations, such as the Organisation of American States (OAS) and the Organisation of Eastern Caribbean States.[190]

One advantage of the existence of regional organisations is the increased contact among regional policy-makers, which in itself may serve to prevent disputes. Employing regional organisations in the settlement of disputes may however imply a move away from the United Nations to other organisations in which one of the disputants has greater influence. As such, the insistence of the United States to employ the OAS rather than the UN in many of the conflicts in Latin America signifies its preference to keep its regional involvement away from global scrutiny.[191]

Familiarity with and national interest in a local dispute can, however, bolster the regional effort at dispute settlement. From the perspective of the United Nations, the UN's actions may have more success if they are supported by the prestige of regional leaders.[192] Especially when the active involvement of third parties is required, such as in the form of observers, peace-keepers or peace-enforcers, the co-operation of a regional organisation has proven to be useful.[193] Higgins has however noted that the familiarity of the members of regional institutions with any given dispute often means that their positions are already fixed. Regional organs might therefore display the regional divisions rather than serve to alleviate them.[194] An additional problem lies in the proliferation of regional organisations, which can seriously hinder the development of a

---

[188] Constitutive Act of the African Union (11 July 2000), (2002) 8 *RADIC* 479 On the African Union's dispute settlement mechanism and the various recent initiatives in Africa: N.J. Udombana, 'The Unfinished Business: Conflicts, the African Union and the New Partnership for Africa's Development', (2003) 35 *George Washington International Law Review* 55.

[189] ECOWAS is essentially an economic organisation, but has also deployed forces for peace-keeping and peace enforcement, *inter alia*, in Liberia and Sierra Leone. A. Herkinson, 'Regionalism and the United Nations', in L. Fawcett and A. Hurrell (eds.), *Regionalism in World Politics* (1995) 122, 148-149; N.D. White, *The Law of International Institutions* (1996) 218.

[190] Treaty of the Organisation of Eastern Caribbean States (18 June 1981), (1981) 20 *ILM* 1166.

[191] Cf., F.S. Northedge and M.D. Donelan (eds.), *International Disputes: The Political Aspects* (1971) 225.

[192] E.g., in 1985 the UN Secretary-General and the Chairman of the OAU together encouraged Burkina-Faso and Mali to bring their frontier dispute to the ICJ. A. Brehio, 'Good Offices of the Secretary-General as Preventive Measures', (1998) 30 *NYUJILP* 589, 615.

[193] E.g., the ECOWAS involvement in Sierra Leone: (2000) UN Doc S/2000/186; the involvement of the OSCE in post-war Former Yugoslavia: OSCE *Handbook* (3rd edn. 1999) 45-58.

[194] R. Higgins, 'Presentation of the Topic', in United Nations *International Law as a Language for International Relations* (1996) 111, 113-114.

coherent conflict resolution strategy, as was demonstrated by the many simultaneous mediators during the years of fighting in the Former Yugoslavia.[195]

The potential contribution of a regional organisation is dependent not so much on its internal structure and legal competence as on the relative position of the disputants in the organisation, and the benefits it can offer to parties, in terms of economic assistance or political or military stability. When there is a dominant member, such as in the case of the OAS, the organisation will be incapable of dealing with those disputes in which that member has taken an adverse position.

The independent dispute settlement mechanisms set-up by political regional organisations have generally not been successful. The Commission of Mediation, Conciliation and Arbitration created by the OAU in 1964 never received the requisite appointments,[196] The Mechanism for Conflict Prevention, Management and Resolution, launched in 1993, remained inactive.[197] The intricate dispute settlement arrangements associated with the OAS have not seen more than incidental application.[198] The highly developed Court of Arbitration and Conciliation established by the OSCE in 1995 has not yet been seized.[199] The OSCE is however effective in the settlement and prevention of disputes, mainly through involvement of its High Commissioner on National Minorities in ethnic disputes in Eastern Europe.[200]

---

[195] The United Nations, the European Union, NATO, the OSCE and various *ad hoc* State groupings and other organisations were all involved.

[196] (1964) 3 *ILM* 1116 (OAU Protocol). For a discussion at the time of it inception: T.O. Elias, 'The Commission of Mediation, Conciliation and Arbitration of the Organization of African Unity', (1964) 40 *BYIL* 336.

[197] OAU 'Declaration of the Assembly of the Heads of State and Government' (28-30 June 1993), (1994) *RADIC* 158; D. Wembou, 'A propos du nouveau méchanisme de l'OAU sur les conflits', (1993) 6 *RADIC* 723. M. Wolfers, 'The Organisation of African Unity as Mediator', in S. Touval and I.W. Zartman (eds.), *International Mediation in Theory and Practice* (1985) 175.

[198] L.R. Scheman and J.W. Ford, 'The Organisation of American States as Mediator', in S. Touval and I.W. Zartman (eds.), *International Mediation in Theory and Practice* (1985) 197; G. Leoro, 'Peaceful Settlement of Disputes – An Overview', Inter-American Juridical Committee OAS Doc CJI/SO/II doc 34.94. Most if not all settlement activity in the OAS is done on an ad hoc basis, including the most recent conciliation of the Belize/Guatemala dispute (chapter II 1.13).

[199] OSCE Convention on Conciliation and Arbitration within the OSCE (1992) (OSCE Convention); Decision on Peaceful Settlement of Disputes (15 December 1992) Annex 2, (1993) 32 *ILM* 557. See chapter III 3.4.2

[200] J. Cohen, *Conflict Prevention in the OSCE: An Assessment of Capacities* (1999); R. Zaagman and H. Zaal, 'The CSCE High Commissioner on National Minorities: Prehistory and Negotiations', in A. Bloed (ed.), *The Challenges of Change* (1994) 95; R, Zaagman, 'The CSCE High Commissioner on National Minorities: An Analysis of the Mandate and the Institutional Context', in A. Bloed (ed.), *The Challenges of Change* (1994) 113. M.A. Martin Estebanez, 'The High Commission on National Minorities: Development of the Mandate', in M. Bothe and others (eds.), *The OSCE in the Maintenance of Peace and Security: Conflict Prevention, Crisis Management and Peaceful Settlement of Disputes* (1997) 123.

Ad hoc regional mediation initiatives outside of organisational frameworks appear more successful.[201] Noteworthy are the Contadora-process and the subsequent Contadora-Esquipulas II-process, aiming to resolve the fighting in various parts of Central America in the 1980s.[202] Shared cultural ties and interests of the mediators and the disputants, combined with opportune circumstances, facilitated substantial improvements. Similarly, though outside any regional organisation's setting, the mediation process in Northern Ireland, involving the Irish Republic, the United Kingdom and the United States, as well as the sub-State disputants, appears among the more successful attempts at resolution of the conflict, despite many difficulties and delays.[203]

In conclusion, there are many means of dispute settlement that may be used as an alternative to, or in combination with, the binding methods of arbitration and adjudication. Moreover, diplomatic dispute settlement methods are frequently adapted to practical situations *ad hoc*. There is no lack of means of diplomatic dispute settlement.

PART TWO

THE ELEMENTS AND PRACTICE OF CONCILIATION

3. Elements of Conciliation

The term 'conciliation' has many different meanings and is used in a great variety of instances. It conveys a notion of overcoming differences between actors, possibly including subduing animosity. It does not, however, carry the precondition that the parties were once in agreement, such as implied in 'reconciliation'. Also if restricted to legal matters, 'conciliation' has more than one meaning and is not necessarily related to the existence of disputes, nor to the involvement of a third party. It may for instance refer to the process of multi-party decision-making.[204] Specifically, conciliation is a common term in the

[201] Generally: T.A. Imobighe, *The OAU and the OAS in Regional Conflict Management: A Comparative Assessment* (2003).

[202] *Border and Transborder Armed Actions* Case (*Honduras* v. *Nicaragua*) (*Jurisdiction and Admissibility*), (1988) *ICJ Rep* 69, 99. A minor role was also accorded to the OAS Secretary-General and the UN Secretary-General.

[203] G. Mitchell, *Making Peace* (1999).

[204] UNGA Res 1995 (XIX) (30 December 1964) Art. 25 speaks of a 'process of conciliation to take place before voting and to provide an adequate basis for the adoption of recommendations with regard to proposals of a specific nature for action substantially affecting the economic or financial interests of particular countries.'

process of approving legislation by the various institutions involved.[205] Most often, however, in legal discourse the term refers to a method for the settlement of disputes by a third party.

Normally the term 'conciliation' is used in relation to non-binding dispute settlement.[206] Confusion arises because the naming of legal settlement procedures in particular instances is a political act, and terminology is therefore not always used accurately. Examples include the 'Conciliation Commissions' established by the Peace Treaty between Italy and the victorious powers of WWII.[207] Disputes arising out of specified articles of the Peace Treaties were to be brought before a commission, consisting only of representatives of the parties. If within three months no settlement was reached, a neutral person would be added to the commission, and the subsequent decision would be binding.[208] In practice, therefore, this was essentially an arbitration procedure. The insistence of one of the Powers to call it conciliation anyway was rewarded.[209] Similarly, the Organisation of Eastern Caribbean States created a 'conciliation procedure' that produces binding results.[210]

3.1 Elements of a definition of conciliation

Many definitions of international conciliation have been given over the years, though none is generally accepted. The task here is to identify the elements that

---

205 E.g., P. Craig and G. de Búrca, *EU Law: Text, Cases and Materials* (2nd edn. 1998) 135-137. Similarly, Villani described the official 'conciliation' procedure used in UNCTAD to reach consensus on Resolutions: U. Villani 'Conciliation and Consensus in UNCTAD', (1976) 2 *Italian Yearbook of International Law* 61.

206 F.M. van Asbeck, 'La tâche et l'action d'une commission de conciliation', (1956) *NTIR* 1, 3. Hazel Fox distinguishes 'compulsory conciliation', by which she means binding conciliation, from 'true conciliation': H. Fox, 'Conciliation', in C.H.M. Waldock and F. Vallat (eds.), *International Disputes: The Legal Aspects* (1972) 93, 93.

207 Treaty of Peace with Italy (10 February 1947), 49 *UNTS* 147 Art. 83.

208 E.g., the decision of the Dutch/Italian conciliation commission of 17 August 1963 in the *Gold Stolen from The Netherlands* Case, (1963) 20 *ASDI* 135. For an overview of cases: A.M. Stuyt, *Survey of International Arbitrations 1794-1989* (1990) 578-581; P. Bolla, 'Quelques considérations sur les commissions de conciliation prévues par l'article 83 du traité de paix avec l'Italie', in *Symbolae Verzijl* (1958) 67; I. Seidl-Hohenfelder, 'Die Vergleichungskommission gemäss Art. 83 des Friedenvertrages mit Italien von 1947', (1961) *Archiv des Völkerrechts* 278; A. Martin, 'Private Property, Rights and Interests in the Paris Peace Treaties', (1947) 24 *BYIL* 273.

209 D.H. Vignes, 'La Commission de Conciliation Franco-Italienne', (1955) 1 *AFDI* 212, 216. I. Seidl-Hohenfelder, 'General Principles of Law as Applied by the Conciliation Commissions Established under the Peace Treaty with Italy of 1947', (1959) 53 *AJIL* 853, 854; C. Rousseau, *Droit International Public* (1983) Vol. V 294-295 mentions other examples of conciliation commissions with binding powers.

210 Treaty of the Organisation of Eastern Caribbean States (18 June 1981), (1981) 20 *ILM* 1166 Art. 14(3) and Annex A.

together set conciliation apart from other methods. The basis of conciliation can be found in a definition given by Vulcan in 1932:

> 'la conciliation est une moyen de régler pacifiquement les différends internationaux, consistent dans l'examen du différend, *sous tous les aspects,* par un organe jouissant de la confiance commune des parties contendates qui dirige leurs négociations et qui, *sans leur participation directe,* leur *propose une solution,* fondée sur des concessions réciproques, *que les parties sont libres d'accepter ou de rejeter*.'[211]

Conciliation is on this basis (1) a method for the settlement of disputes, which is (2) not binding. There is (3) a commission that (4) has the confidence of the parties. The commission is (5) independent of the parties, (6) investigates the dispute and (7) proposes a solution to the parties to settle the conflict.[212] Vulcan demands too much, however, in requiring an examination of *all* aspects of the case, as well as *reciprocal* concessions. To reach a settlement surely the investigation may be limited if this would improve the chances of success. Further, the solution proposed is probably, but not necessarily dependent on both sides giving in to some extent. Building on experience gained by some of its members in the 1950s, the Institut de Droit International discussed the method at length in 1961, and adopted an influential model procedure, the IDI Conciliation Rules.[213] According to this model, conciliation is:

> 'a method for the settlement of international disputes of any nature according to which a Commission set up by the Parties, either on a permanent basis or an ad hoc basis to deal with a dispute, proceeds to the impartial examination of the dispute and attempts to define the terms of a settlement susceptible of being accepted by them or of affording the Parties, with a view to its settlement, such aid as they may have requested.'[214]

This definition is adopted by a number of writers.[215] While avoiding the problems identified in Vulcan's description, the Institute's definition implies the

---

211 C. Vulcan, *La conciliation dans le droit international actuel* (1932) 8.

212 A. Peters holds that conciliators are not to recommend a solution: 'International Dispute Settlement: A Network of Cooperational Duties', (2003) 14 *EJIL* 1, 6.

213 Based on a report by H. Rolin, *Annuaire de l'Institut de Droit International* (1959) Vol. I 5-130 published in *Annuaire de l'Institut de Droit International 1961* (1961) Vol. II 193-271. For the IDI Conciliation Rules: ibid., 374-380 (French) 385-391 (English). The Institute had discussed conciliation previously in 1927: *Annuaire de l'Institut de Droit International* (1927) Vols. II 835-873, III 299-317, 339-342.

214 IDI Conciliation Rules Art. 1.

215 J.G. Merrills, *International Dispute Settlement* (4th edn. 2005) 64; H. Fox, 'Conciliation', in C.H.M. Waldock and F. Vallat (eds.), *International Disputes: The Legal Aspects* (1972) 93, 95-

generally accepted condition (8) that the commission works towards a report. It also stipulates that the confidence the commission requires derives from it being appointed by the parties (4), and adds that the commission may provide such aid as the parties may have requested. Although providing additional aid can be useful, this should not be a defining element of conciliation.

Another element is mentioned by Cot, who emphasises the lack of political authority of the commission, and who incidentally revives Vulcan's requests that *every* aspect of the dispute be investigated:

> 'International conciliation may be defined as intervention in the settlement of an international dispute by a body having no political authority of its own, but enjoying the confidence of the parties to the dispute and entrusted with the task of investigating every aspect of the dispute and of proposing a solution which is not binding on the parties.'[216]

The authority of most conciliators derives from their acceptance by the parties, which in turn is often based on their expertise in legal or technical matters. The absence of political authority does, however, not seem to be a necessary condition. By the sole fact of its establishment the commission will generate some political power. Moreover, if a commission comprising influential third persons is set-up, this is not likely to alter either the character or the characterisation of the undertaking. On this basis, then, eight constitutive elements of international conciliation can be enumerated:

(1) a method of settlement of international disputes,
(2) which is not binding,
(3) involving a commission,
(4) appointed by the parties,

---

96. A similar definition is given by H. von Mangoldt, *Die Schiedsgerichtbarkeit als Mittel internationaler Streitschlichtung* (1974) 19-20, 'Drei Hauptelemente zeichnen das Vergleichsverfahren danach aus: Erstens vollzieht es sich vor einer von den Parteien eingesetzten ständigen oder *ad hoc* gebildeten Kommission, zweitens beinhaltet es eine in die Einzelheiten gehende Untersuchung der Tätsachlichen und sonstigen Elemente des Streites und drittens wird es abgeschlossen durch einen Bericht der Kommission, der Vorschläge zur Lösung der Streitigkeit enthält, aber nicht verbindlich ist.' A more general definition is given by H. Lauterpacht, *Oppenheim's International Law* (7th edn. 1952) Vol. II 12 'Conciliation is the process of settling a dispute by referring it to a commission of persons whose task it is to elucidate the facts and (usually after hearing the parties and endeavouring to bring them to an agreement) to make a report containing proposals for a settlement, but which does not have the binding character of an award or judgment.'

[216] *Cot* 9; Also J.G. Collier and A.V. Lowe, *The Settlement of Disputes in International Law* (1999) 29.

(5) which is independent,
(6) investigates the dispute,
(7) and proposes a solution to the parties,
(8) to be presented in a report.

Unless stated otherwise, whenever hereinafter the term 'conciliation' is used, the indicated procedure will comprise the above elements. Inter-State conciliation then refers to the use of conciliation in disputes between States.

3.2 Mediation and conciliation revisited

Without displaying a clear divide, core concepts of mediation and conciliation can thus be distinguished by degrees. Conciliators investigate the dispute and propose a solution. This indicates a relatively formal procedure, in which the conciliators take-up an independent role, which also involves substantial work independently from the parties.[217] Mediation tends to be more informal, with relatively more time spent in discussions with the parties. Conciliators are therefore more frequently selected on the basis of their expertise,[218] whereas mediators are more likely to be politically appointed diplomats,[219] or third parties that nominated themselves.[220] Unlike mediators, conciliators never nominate themselves, and will have less leverage with the disputants. Lastly, conciliators aim for settlement by working towards a formal report, while mediators only prepare a report if they consider this useful for their work towards a settlement.

Distinctions between forms of dispute settlement are sometimes hard to draw, and unless it serves a practical purpose it is better not to do it. It is preferable to indicate – rather than define – a middle form between conciliation and mediation. One such instance occurs when a mediator is dealing with a dispute that requires subject-matter expertise, and finds it necessary to make an in-depth study of the facts, history, accounting, legal and political positions or other matters, subsequently draws up a report presenting his findings, and assists the parties in negotiating a settlement. It may not fully amount to conciliation be-

---

[217] The importance of the investigative work in conciliation as opposed to mediation is emphasised by C.C. Hyde, 'The Place of Commissions of Inquiry and Conciliation Treaties in the Peaceful Settlement of Disputes', (1929) 10 *BYIL* 96, 101-102.

[218] E.g., the conciliators in the *Jan Mayen* Case on maritime delimitation who had all headed their respective delegations to the Conference on the Law of the Sea: J. Evensen, 'La délimitation du plateau continental entre la Norvège et l'Islande dans le secteur de Jan Mayen', (1980) 26 *AFDI* 711; E.L. Richardson, 'Jan Mayen in Perspective', (1988) 82 *AJIL* 443.

[219] Such as the personal envoys of Presidents or Secretary-Generals to conflict areas.

[220] Such as a powerful or neighbouring State interested in seeing a dispute between two foreign entities resolved.

cause there is no commission, and no final proposal is submitted to the parties in the form of a report. Nevertheless the third party takes more initiative than in standard mediation, and it may be hard to distinguish between a report on factual matters and a report on possible solutions to the dispute.

An important example of such a mixed process is that which in 1986 brought a solution to the distribution of the assets and liabilities of the East African Community (EAC), and which is discussed as a conciliation case study below.[221] Another example was the effort to settle State succession problems among the States emerging from the Former Yugoslavia.[222] In 1996 the High Representative for Yugoslavia appointed a Special Negotiator for Succession Issues, Sir Arthur Watts.[223] Major interests were at stake, such as the division of Yugoslav public property abroad, and the shares in membership of international financial institutions. The parties agreed to reach a settlement on the basis of international law. Watts provided drafts of a framework of settlement for negotiation by the parties, and saw himself as a mediator. Nevertheless, considering that he was an expert in the field, investigated the issue in detail and elaborated proposals for a solution, his functions may also be considered those of a conciliator. The elements of conciliation lacking in the process appear to be the existence of a *commission* and the appointment *by the parties*. Further, though arguably less determinative for the classification, he developed various proposals for settlement to the parties throughout the process, rather than working towards a single report for their consideration. Following the revolution in Belgrade in 2000, a settlement was reached early 2001.[224]

Both examples concern problems of succession under public international law. Considering the implications for finances and for sovereignty, it is understandable that the parties want to maintain as much control over the settlement process as they can. The complex nature of the subject-matter however requires special expertise. Especially in multiparty-disputes such as the ones discussed here, it will be hard to settle the issue by relying on the research and negotiation skills of the various national authorities involved. An expert mediator or conciliator is then required, who is subject to the parties' will, but has the authority and knowledge to perform in-depth studies and to make proposals. In such instances, the distinction between mediation and conciliation is a

---

[221] V.H. Umbricht, *Multilateral Mediation: Practical Experiences and Lessons* (1989). See chapter I 4.3.

[222] A. Watts, 'State Succession: Some Recent Practical Legal Problems', in V. Götzand and others (eds.), *Liber Amicorum Günther Jaenicke – Zum 85. Geburtstag* (1998) 397, 405 ff.

[223] A. Watts, 'Introductory Note to Agreement on Succession Issues between the Five Successor States of the Former State of Yugoslavia', (2002) 41 *ILM* 1.

[224] Agreement on Succession Issues between the Five Successor States of the Former State of Yugoslavia (29 June 2001), (2002) 41 *ILM* 3.

matter of degree. Nevertheless, where in the case of Yugoslavia the expert was not chosen by the parties but by an outside authority, this instance tends more towards mediation. In the EAC case, where this did not occur, it is more appropriate to speak of conciliation.

The main object of this study is to investigate the distinct characteristics and contributions of conciliation, separate from mediation. Mediation, distinguished as above, is therefore not the primary object of this study. Nevertheless, reference to mixed examples such as those discussed here will be included as a matter of course, also to demonstrate that in dispute settlement, as elsewhere, distinctions require nuances.

3.3 **Kinds of conciliation commissions**

For clarity of discussion, several further distinctions internal to conciliation can be made. These distinctions are between conciliation commissions and forms of conciliation. Commissions can be permanent or *ad hoc*. Occasionally plans are also formed universal permanent commissions. Conciliation can be optional or compulsory, while compulsory conciliation needs to be distinguished from the obligation to conciliate. In chapter III a further distinction is made between conciliation concepts, in terms of the norms that any conciliation commission can base its work on.

3.3.1 *Permanent commissions*

Most of the bilateral treaties that in the 1920s pioneered conciliation established permanent commissions. These bodies are permanent in so far as that a commission always has members, and may be called upon at any time. The alternative is an *ad hoc* commission, to which appointments are only made when a dispute is to be submitted to it. At the beginning of the 20th century there was a widespread belief that peace and international justice would be advanced by the establishment of permanent institutions. The Permanent Court of Arbitration and the Permanent Court of International Justice are testimony to that thinking.[225] The same optimism was reflected in the assumption that the conciliation commissions would be called upon frequently, and would therefore require a degree of continuity.

In the case of the Bryan treaties, the bilateral inquiry treaties initiated by the United States early in the 20th century, the permanent character of the commis-

---

225 On the name of the PCIJ: A. Eyffinger, *The International Court of Justice 1946-1996* (1996) 75.

sions made it possible to invest them with the power to offer their services on their own initiative. In later conciliation treaties, some commissions could even start conciliatory proceedings themselves and commence advising the parties in dispute, though this did not occur in practice.[226] These powers remained exceptional: most commissions can only be seized by one of the parties. None of the permanent commissions was established to be permanently in session in the sense that national courts are.[227] Most of the permanent commissions actually never met.

Permanent commissions can also exist as part of an international organisation, such as the UNESCO Conciliation and Good Offices Commission on Discrimination in Education.[228] This commission, composed of State representatives, has never seen a dispute since its creation in 1962. In 2005 an attempt was made to revive it.[229] Another form of a permanent commission can be seen in standing treaty bodies that count conciliation-like practices among their broader responsibilities. Examples include the former European Commission on Human Rights[230] and the Implementation Committee of the Montreal Protocol non-compliance procedure.[231]

3.3.2 Ad hoc *commissions*

Permanent conciliation commissions of the first kind seem to belong to the past. Unlike the early treaties that dealt exclusively with the settlement of disputes, contemporary treaties referring to conciliation primarily regulate specific political or economic relations, and conclude with a stipulation of dispute settlement methods for the cases arising there under.[232] In those agreements, conciliation is often one of a series of settlement options.[233] There is therefore

[226] Also these treaties were mostly concluded by the United States. *United Nations Systematic Survey of Treaties for the Pacific Settlement of International Disputes 1928-1948* (1948) 202-203.

[227] Those appointed to the permanent commissions were normally judges, law professors and diplomats who, because of the nature of their positions, could practice their professions while being available on short notice to act as commissioner. The composition of the commissions established between 1921 and 1928 is given at the end of each treaty reproduced in M. Habicht, *Post-War Treaties for the Pacific Settlement of International Disputes* (1931).

[228] Protocol Instituting a Conciliation and Good Offices Commission to be Responsible for Seeking the Settlement of Any Disputes Which May Arise between States Parties to the Convention Against Discrimination in Education (10 December 1962), 651 *UNTS* 362.

[229] <http://portal.unesco.org/en/file_download.php/7c7208f1c2c1c1ec4eaea00a2ffe932bCCBO+Report.pdf> (29 July 2006)

[230] See chapter IV 3.

[231] See chapter IV 6.2.

[232] See chapter IV 1.

[233] E.g., Convention for the Conservation of the Southern Bluefin Tuna (signed 10 May 1993, entered into force 20 May 1994), 1819 *UNTS* 359 Art. 16.

little need to keep a number of conciliators ready and waiting, as the likelihood that they will be called upon is low. Moreover, disputes arising under area-specific treaties will often require experts to be selected when it is known what kind of problem needs to be solved.[234] In addition, it is important for the parties at all times to have confidence in the conciliators, something that cannot be assured when appointments were made in the distant past. For these reasons, a commission established *ad hoc* has significant advantages over a permanent one.

A disadvantage of constitution *ad hoc* can be the delay involved in finding the appropriate persons, more particularly to agree on those conciliators to be appointed by the parties jointly. To alleviate this difficulty, a number of multilateral treaties, as for instance the 1969 Vienna Convention on the Law of Treaties and the 1982 Convention on the Law of the Sea, provide for a list of conciliators to be maintained by the depository institution.[235] It is the purpose of the lists to facilitate selection rather than to restrict choice. In addition, the General Assembly of the United Nations in 1949 created a panel of persons available for inquiry and conciliation,[236] which was however never used. It may be noted that when commissions are composed on the basis of such lists, the permanent character of the commission is the same as that of the arbitration tribunals for the settlement of inter-State disputes within the Permanent Court of Arbitration.[237]

An interesting mixture between a permanent and an *ad hoc* institution is attempted by the OSCE, which in 1992 agreed upon the establishment of a Court of Conciliation and Arbitration.[238] The OSCE Court, based in Geneva, consists essentially of a list of persons appointed by their State, who may be called upon on an *ad hoc* basis.[239] The permanence of the OSCE Court is reflected in the exclusive nature of the list: no other persons can be appointed. In addition, the conciliators who are not nationals of the disputants are chosen by

---

[234] Following the general standard, the members of permanent commissions could however also be replaced within fifteen days from the time the dispute was brought before the commission; e.g., 1928 General Act for the Pacific Settlement of International Disputes Art. 8.

[235] E.g., Vienna Convention on the Law of Treaties (23 May 1969), 115 *UNTS* 331 Annex Art. 1; Convention on the Law of the Sea Annex V Art. 2.

[236] UNGA Res 268 D (III) (28 April 1949).

[237] 1899 Hague Convention Arts. 23, 24; 1907 Hague Convention Arts. 44, 45.

[238] The Decision on Peaceful Settlement Annex 2 (15 December 1992), (1993) 32 *ILM* 551, 557 (the OSCE Convention) (entered into force 5 December 1994). The Court was established in May 1995. See chapter II 1.14.

[239] On the OSCE Court: various contributions in M. Bothe and others (eds.), *The OSCE in the Maintenance of Peace and Security* (1997); L. Caflish (ed.), *The Peaceful Settlement of Disputes between States: Universal and European Perspectives* (1998); R. Badinter, 'La Cour de Conciliation et d'Arbitrage au sein de l'OSCE', (1999) 1 *International Law Forum* 99.

the Bureau of the OSCE Court rather than by the conflicting parties.[240] The restriction of options makes choosing easier, but in the case of conciliation may also prevent States from making any choice at all.

3.3.3 *Permanent universal commissions*

Occasionally proposals are made for a permanent universal conciliation commission, available to deal with any international dispute brought to its attention. In 1989 Von Bar made a pioneering proposal,[241] on which others would build further ideas. Most notably, Walter Schücking and Jean Efremoff each proposed to attach a permanent commission to the League of Nations, to be an alternative to recourse to the League's Security Council.[242] Camille Gorgé, Legal Advisor of Japan, suggested instead the creation of a Conciliation Chamber within the PCIJ.[243]

In the 1950s and 1960s Grenville Clark and Louis Sohn advocated the establishment of two permanent commissions. One would be the World Equity Tribunal, which would deal with disputes not exclusively of a legal character. The tribunal would make recommendations, which, when supported by a large majority in the UN General Assembly, would become binding on the parties.[244] In addition, a World Conciliation Board would be established, which could be seized by the parties or by the General Assembly with respect to any international dispute or situation likely to threaten the peace.[245] The Board would consist of five persons elected by the General Assembly, to be supplemented by representatives from the parties in dispute. In 1968, following on a report submitted by Louis Sohn, the International Law Association adopted a resolution calling upon the General Assembly to create a permanent conciliation commission out of the panel for inquiry and conciliation already in existence at the UN.[246] Sohn further suggested that this permanent commission would be made

240 OSCE Convention Arts. 21(1) and (5)

241 Von Bar recommended the creation of a 'Permanent International Academy' composed of eminent personalities to which international disputes could be submitted. In 1912 this idea was elaborated by Efremoff at the Interparliamentary Union. Cf., *Cot* 60; C. de Visscher, 'Les commissions de conciliation et la Societé des Nations', (1922) 19 *RGDIP* 410, 413

242 J. Efremoff, 'La conciliation internationale', (1927) *Recueil des Cours* Vol. III 18, 1, 98, 104; criticism by G. Scelle, *Théorie Juridique de la Révision des Traités* (1936) 71-72.

243 C. Gorgé, 'L'évolution de la conciliation internationale', (1927) 54 *RDILC* 58, 105.

244 G. Clark and L.B. Sohn, *World Peace through World Law* (3rd edn. 1960) xxxiv-xxxv, 338-340.

245 Ibid., xxxv-xxxvii, 335-336, 340-341.

246 *Report of the International Law Association* (1968) 16-17, 32, 34. For the Panel: UNGA Res 268 D (III) (28 April 1949).

competent to hear the disputes that, in the existing bilateral treaties, are referred to the hundreds bilateral commissions leading a sleeping existence.[247]

As recent as 2001 Lucius Caflisch, President of the OSCE Court, suggested a global agreement on a procedure of compulsory conciliation, which States can opt into, similar to the Statute of the International Court of Justice.[248] In 1999 Francisco Orrego Vicuña and Christopher Pinto advocated a Permanent Conciliation Committee, as a subsidiary organ of the United Nations General Assembly.[249] The Committee, which would have the PCA as its executive agency, would comprise some twenty States from all regions of the world, with membership rotating every six months. Any UN member State, or the Secretary-General, could then refer a dispute to it, after which about five Members of the Committee would be selected to form a conciliation commission for that particular conflict.

The ideas of Orrego Vicuña, Pinto and Caflisch appear, however, to disregard some essential aspects of conciliation. The parties in dispute need to have confidence in the impartiality and expertise of the commission.[250] It is unlikely that States would agree to refer their dispute to persons selected by others, and who have no special knowledge of the matter, especially if these persons represent other States. Moreover, it seems improbable that States would agree to a conciliation if not they but the UN Secretary-General initiates the proceedings.[251]

---

[247] Ibid., 16. In 1994 Sohn also proposed the creation of a permanent consultation commission to deal with trade matters between the major economic powers: L.B. Sohn, 'Bipartite Consultative Commissions for Preventing and Resolving Disputes Relating to International Trade Treaties', in M. Rama-Montaldo (ed.), *El Derecho Internacional en un Mundo en Transformacion* Vol. II (1994) 1181, 1196-1200.

[248] L. Caflisch, 'Cent ans de règlement pacifique des différends interétatiques', (2001) 288 *Receuil des Cours* 245, 460.

[249] F. Orrego Vicuña and C. Pinto, *The Peaceful Settlement of Disputes: Prospects for the Twenty-First Century* (1999) [106]-[108], [257]-[259].

[250] A similar miscalculation appears to be at the basis of the 'International Court of Environmental Arbitration and Conciliation', an institution in Spain set-up by international group of environmentalist and lawyers as a civil association under Mexican law, which is available for arbitration and conciliation but in fact renders 'consultative opinions' on private unilateral application. Cf., X. Ezeizaberrana, 'The Role of the International Court of Environmental Arbitration and Conciliation', in M.-C. Cordonier Seggar and C.G. Weeramantry (eds.), *Sustainable Justice: Reconciling Economic, Social and Environmental Law* (2005) 506; E. Rehbinder and D. Loperena, 'Legal Protection of Environmental Rights: The Role and Experience of the International Court of Environmental Arbitration and Conciliation', (2001) 31 *Environmental Policy and Law* 282.

[251] Cf., C. Peck, *The United Nations as a Dispute Settlement System* (1996) 150.

3.4 Optional and compulsory conciliation

Optional conciliation refers to a system in which parties have laid down a conciliation procedure, but reserve the right in each particular case to determine each for themselves whether or not they will use it. When parties are in dispute, conciliation is naturally always an available option. The gain of pre-establishing an optional conciliation framework is, however, that if a relevant dispute arises, the procedure to deal with it is already available.

Compulsory conciliation, on the other hand, means that jurisdiction is granted in the original agreement, and that therefore a commission can unilaterally be seized. When the relevant commission is not permanent, this implies an obligation on the respondent to appoint its conciliator(s). This may not always be easy: in some cases the assistance of a third party may be called in to appoint the members that should be appointed by common agreement,[252] if necessary even against the will of the parties.[253] The appointment of the national members remains in the hands of the parties. In the field of arbitration, the *Interpretation of Peace Treaties* Case has shown that by refusing to appoint members to a tribunal, a State will incur legal responsibility, but may nevertheless effectively block the constitution of the body.[254] This is also what occurred in the *Vitianu* conciliation case, in which Romania refused to appoint conciliators, despite a treaty obligation to do so.[255] Switzerland, which had made the application, saw its efforts at conciliation effectively frustrated.

Compulsory conciliation entails that the other party is obliged to participate in the proceedings *in good faith*.[256] This not only means that it should produce the documents and statements as required, but also that it should actively co-operate to find a basis for settlement. Considering that in the end the procedure does not have any binding consequences and is therefore dependent on the goodwill of the parties, the relativity of the compulsory character is clear. The respondent may be opposed to third party intervention, or favour binding settlement instead. A reluctant yet meticulous party may appoint its members, co-operate in the procedure, but be determined from the start not to agree to any proposal. Compulsory conciliation, if applied to the letter but without good faith, can therefore turn into a time-consuming formality. The potential dam-

---

[252] E.g., the1949 General Act for the Pacific Settlement of International Disputes Art. 6.

[253] E.g., the Locarno Treaties common Art. 5.

[254] (*Advisory Opinion*) (*First Phase*), (1950) *ICJ Rep* 65.

[255] R. Probst, 'Die Schweiz und die internationale Schiedsgerischtbarkeit', (1960) 17 *Schweizerisches Jahrbuch für internationales Recht* 99, 131-132.

[256] E.g., explicitly in Convention on Biological Diversity Annex II pt 2 Art. 5; Framework Convention on Climate Change (1992) Art. 14(6); Norway/Iceland Agreement concerning fishery and continental shelf questions (28 May 1980), (1981) 20 *ILM* 797, 799 Art. 9.

age can be limited, however, by judicious use of the conciliators' discretion to propose termination of the proceedings.[257]

There is, nevertheless, an obvious advantage to a compulsory procedure. The initial agreement over the use of the procedure and the possibility to seize a commission without renewed consent will serve to create political pressure that may bring reluctant states to the negotiation – or conciliation – table. It is sometimes even argued that the existence of a compulsory procedure may keep the parties from conflict-provoking behaviour.[258] However, without a widespread practice of unilaterally seizing settlement bodies, there seems little reason to assume that this is the case. Only the *France/Portugal* Case provides an example of the unilateral seizure of a commission followed by a settlement before the convening of the commission.[259]

Another potential contribution of compulsory conciliation is that, provided the parties participate in the proceedings in good faith and the conciliators are in the position to issue their recommendations in the form or a report, this report will become a political factor in itself.[260] Even though it is purely of a recommendatory nature and therefore has no legally binding status, any side or position supported by the commission will gain political weight. How much weight is added depends not only on the clarity of the terms of the report, but also on the standing of the commission itself. Obviously the recommendations of highly regarded personalities resonate more than those of unknown functionaries. Similarly, a report clearly based on principles accepted by either side may more easily sway sceptics than one perceived to be based on partial reasoning. This political weight can be further increased if the report can be made public, and the support of populations or of third parties can be enlisted on its basis. This way, irrespective of the legal status of the report as non-binding, the result of an exercise of compulsory conciliation can significantly influence the settlement of a dispute.

Bilateral treaties normally provide for compulsory conciliation,[261] as do a number of multilateral treaties ranging from the Vienna Convention on the

---

[257] There is no known practice in this regard, though in the *F.OABV* Case (*France* v. *Morocco*) the commission had to terminate its work when the conciliators appointed by Morocco resigned: C. Rousseau, 'Echec de la procedure d'enquête et de conciliation dans l'affaire du deroutement de l'avion transportant de Rabat a Tunis les chefs nationalistes algériens le 22 octobre 1956', (1958) 62 *RGDIP* 691.

[258] E.g., C.P.R. Romano, *The Peaceful Settlement of Environmental Disputes* (2000) 44.

[259] H. Wehberg, 'Die Vergleichskommissionen im modernen Völkerrecht', (1958) 19 *ZfAŐRV* 551. See chapter II 1.9.

[260] Cf., N. Klein, *Dispute Settlement in the Law of the Sea Convention* (2005) 121, 188.

[261] E.g., Chile-Argentina Treaty of Peace and Friendship (29 November 1984), (1985) 24 *ILM* 11 Annex 1 Art. 2.

Law of Treaties[262] to the Agreement for the Establishment of the Indian Ocean Tuna Commission.[263] By contrast, the use of the Conciliation Rules established within the International Centre for the Settlement of Investment Disputes (ICSID) is completely voluntary: any proceedings must be based on explicit agreement between the parties. Such agreement may however be contained in a bilateral investment treaty, the usual basis for application of the ICSID Convention. Such a treaty provision can make conciliation compulsory. The ICSID conciliation commission will decide on any objections to its jurisdiction.[264] It is implied, therefore, that the commission can decide to continue in the face of a party that persists in its denial that the commission is competent to deal with a case. As a consequence, parties cannot legally terminate the proceedings by refusing to participate,[265] even though their absence will in practice force the commission to terminate the proceedings.

3.5 The obligation to conciliate

Compulsory conciliation is distinguished from the obligation to resort to conciliation before other methods of settlement are applied. Various treaties make conciliation an obligatory step before an application may be made for adjudication.[266] In the event, parties can by common agreement ignore such obliga-

[262] Vienna Convention on the Law of Treaties Art. 66(b).

[263] Agreement for the Establishment of the Indian Ocean Tuna Commission (25 November 1993), 1927 *UNTS* 330 Art. 23. Further examples include OSCE Convention Art. 18(1); the Vienna Convention on the Representation of States in their Relations with International Organizations of a Universal Character (UN GOAR 30th Sess. 2 UN Doc A/Conf/67/16 (1975); the Vienna Convention on the Succession of States in Respect to Treaties (23 August 1978) UN Doc A/Conf.80/31 Art. 42; the United Nations Framework Convention on Climate Change (12 June 1992), 1171 *UNTS* 107 Art. 14(5); the United Nations Convention on Biological Diversity Art. 27(4), (1992) 31 *ILM* 818; the United Nations Convention to Combat Desertification in those Countries Experiencing Serious Drought and/or Desertification, Particularly in Africa Art. 28(6); (1994) UN Doc A/AC.241/15/Rev.7.

[264] ICSID Conciliation Rules Art. 29.

[265] ICSID Conciliation Rules Art. 30(3). Under UNCITRAL Conciliation Rules Art. 15, proceedings are, *inter alia*, terminated by a written declaration by any party that the proceedings are (thereby) terminated.

[266] This is the Swiss model of treaties as laid down in the treaty with Italy: Treaty of Conciliation and Compulsory Adjudication (Italy-Switzerland) (20 September 1924, entered into force 29 January 1925), 33 *LNTS* 93; the Pact of Bogotá Art. 32 and the optional exception of Law of the Sea Convention Art. 298(1)ii. The ICJ found no such precondition to conciliate in the Optional Protocols concerning the Compulsory Settlement of Disputes connected to the Vienna Conventions on Diplomatic Relations (1961) and on Consular Relations (1963) as they arose in the *US Diplomatic and Consular Staff in Tehran* Case (*US* v. *Iran*), (1980) *ICJ Rep* 3 [48]. P. Pazartzis, *Les Engagements Internationaux en Matière de Règlement Pacifique des Différends entre Etats* (1992) 106-109.

tion, and immediately move on to binding settlement. This happened in the *Letelier and Moffitt* dispute between Chile and the US.[267] The treaty in force between the parties, the only Bryan treaty ever invoked,[268] prescribes a procedure of non-binding settlement. Only in advanced stages of escalation, arbitration was envisaged. Desirous of a speedy and definitive solution, the parties nonetheless agreed to give the settlement commission binding powers.

If one party insists on application of the conciliation clause, the consequence is a restricting effect on the jurisdiction of international courts and tribunals. Conciliation clauses may thereby contribute to the maintenance of amicable relations, by preventing the immediate recourse to the bolder means of adjudication. On the other hand, by making the use of a non-binding method a precondition for the jurisdiction of a court, a reluctant State is given the possibility to delay a final settlement by insisting on and drawing out fruitless attempts at amicable resolution. The issue arose before the ICJ in the *Border and Transborder Armed Actions* Case,[269] in which Nicaragua sought to find jurisdiction for its case against Honduras in the Pact of Bogotá, which includes acceptance of the jurisdiction of the ICJ.[270] The Pact also contains the provision that when a settlement procedure is initiated, no other procedure may be started before the first one is concluded.[271] It was disputed whether the diplomatic initiative of the 'Contadora process', considered by the ICJ 'primarily a mediation, in which third States, on their own initiative, endeavoured to bring together the viewpoints of the States concerned by making specific proposals to them',[272] amounted to such a procedure. The Court would have had to determine this, had it not come to the conclusion that the process had in any case ended by the time the application was lodged.[273]

More recently the issue of the obligation to conciliate, and the relevance of the old bilateral dispute settlement treaties, arose in the *Case Concerning the Legality of the Use of Force* (*Provisional Measures*) (*Yugoslavia* v. *The Netherlands*).[274] In 1999 Yugoslavia brought a case against various NATO coun-

[267] (1992) 88 *ILR* 727; (1991) 30 *ILM* 422.

[268] The Treaty for the Settlement of Disputes that May Occur Between the United States and Chile (19 January 1916).

[269] *Border and Transborder Armed Actions* Case (*Nicaragua* v. *Honduras*) (*Jurisdiction and Admissibility*), (1988) *ICJ Rep* 69.

[270] Pact of Bogotá Art. 31. Nicaragua did not rely on Art. 32 of the same, that provides for compulsory jurisdiction in case a conciliation procedure was unsuccessful, (1988) *ICJ Rep* 90 [48].

[271] Pact of Bogotá Art. 4.

[272] (1988) *ICJ Rep* 99 [75].

[273] Ibid., 105 [93].

[274] (1999) *ICJ Rep* [42]. A similar development in *Case Concerning the Legality of the Use of Force* (*Provisional Measures*) (*Yugoslavia* v. *Belgium*), (1999) *ICJ Rep* [42].

tries, including the Netherlands, concerning the bombing of Yugoslavia as part of the NATO military action in relation to Kosovo. An additional basis for jurisdiction, Yugoslavia pleaded, was found in a bilateral dispute settlement treaty concluded by the Netherlands and the pre-WWII Kingdom of Yugoslavia.[275] All disputes 'which it may not have been possible to settle amicably by the normal methods of diplomacy' shall be submitted to the (then) PCIJ. The treaty also provides for a permanent conciliation commission, to which the parties may – by a further special agreement – submit any dispute.[276] If no such special agreement is reached, and if no other special agreement is reached regarding a binding settlement method, either party may seize the PCIJ, 'after giving one month's notice'.[277] In this case, no such notice had been given. The Court would thus among other things[278] have to determine whether the claim by Yugoslavia 'may not have been possible to settle amicably by the normal methods of diplomacy', and whether Yugoslavia should have given one month's notice before submitting the dispute to the Court.

As it turned out in 2004, following a change of argument and legal position by the applicant (which had become Serbia and Montenegro and was admitted as a new member to the United Nations in 2000), the Court found it had no jurisdiction as the applicant was at the material time not a party to the Statute of the Court.[279] This finding left undecided the question whether, if this status had not been an issue, the 1931 treaty would have been a basis for jurisdiction. The curious turn of events nevertheless provides a demonstration that that the bilateral dispute settlement treaties of the early 20th century should not be forgotten.

4. Case Studies

On the basis of identification of the context and a discussion of the various elements of conciliation, this chapter has attempted to present a substantive understanding of the essence of conciliation in inter-State disputes. Adopting a

---

[275] Treaty of Judicial Settlement, Arbitration and Conciliation (Netherlands-Yugoslavia) (11 March 1931), 129 *LNTS* 89.

[276] The treaty provides in Art. 3 that before any recourse is had to procedure before the PCIJ or to any arbitral procedure, the dispute may 'by agreement between the Parties' be submitted to a conciliation commission.

[277] Ibid., Art. 4.

[278] Such as whether the treaty is still in force, and whether the reference to the PCIJ may in this case be read to include reference to the ICJ.

[279] *Case Concerning the Legality of the Use of Force* (*Preliminary Objections*) (*Serbia and Montenegro* v. *The Netherlands*) [2004] [90] and [124-125].

uniform concept of conciliation does, however, still allow for a wide variety of practices in the application and conduct of conciliation, as the following three case studies demonstrate. The first case is that of conciliation as it was envisaged in the bilateral dispute settlement treaties concluded between the 1920s and the 1960s; settlement by means of a permanent conciliation commission. The second case is that of conciliation as part of a range of dispute settlement methods (negotiation, conciliation, arbitration), in a procedure devised *ad hoc*, using a subdivision of an arbitral tribunal. The third case is that of conciliation mixed with mediation between multiple parties, in an *ad hoc* procedure, by an individual conciliator/mediator. The brief case studies address the set-up, process and result of the conciliation efforts, and aim to draw conclusions about the nature and use of conciliation in like circumstances.

4.1 Classic: the *Gorm and Svava* Case

Rare among conciliation cases, the *Gorm and Svava* Case of 1952, successfully settling a dispute by Belgium and Denmark, is known in some detail through commentary by members of the conciliation commission, and through publication of the commission's recommendation and *procès-verbal*.[280] It is an instance of conciliation in the traditional sense, by a permanent conciliation commission applying the procedural model laid down in one of the early conciliation treaties, concluded in 1927.[281]

The issue was the legal responsibility for the loss of two Danish ships during the outbreak of WWII. Following the German invasion of Denmark in April 1940, the Belgian authorities prevented the *S.S. Gorm* and the *S.S. Svava*, with cargo and crew, from leaving the port of Antwerp. Following the German invasion of Belgium one month later, the ships were commissioned by the Belgian authorities. The *S.S. Gorm* ran on a German mine and sunk, the *S.S. Svava* made it to Britain, where it was seized by the British Government. After the war, in 1952, the Belgian and Danish Governments, unable to settle the issue of compensation through negotiations, jointly called on the permanent conciliation commission. Presided over by Swedish Supreme Court Justice Sandström, the commission further comprised four jurists: the Brit Le Quesne, the Dutchman François, the Belgian Rolin and the Dane Cohn. It would be the commission's only case.

---

280 H. Rolin, 'Une conciliation belgo-danoise', (1953) 57 *RGDIP* 353 (contains the *procès-verbal* and the recommendations); N.V. Boeg, 'Le différend dano-belge au sujet des navires danois 'Gorm' et 'Svava'', (1953) 23 *Acta Scandinavica Juris Gentium* 48.

281 Treaty of Conciliation, Arbitration and Compulsory Adjudication (Belgium-Denmark) (3 March 1927), 67 *LNTS* 119.

As agreed *ad hoc* by the parties, over a period of some months they exchanged written conclusions, in a process supervised by the commission's president. He then invited them to a hearing in Stockholm before the full commission. There, the parties pleaded their case as they would in arbitration. The commission, however, set about differently. According to both Rolin and François, the commission assumed a role:

> 'non d'un juge, mais d'un conseil, avocat ou avoué, interrogé par un client sur les chances de succès d'une action judiciaire et l'opportunité d'une transaction, avec cette difference que la consultation lui etait demandée par les deux parties.'[282]

In its deliberations, it first made an inventory of all reasonable legal interpretations of the facts of the dispute. By consensus, it then discarded the least acceptable of these, leaving those legal readings accepted by some, but not by other conciliators. It had thereby identified the area of doctrinal legal dispute that it felt it should not enter. The conciliators then debated the chances of success the various arguments would have in a court of law. Once in agreement on such chances, they accorded relative weight to the respective claims. On that basis, the commission unanimously arrived at an allocation of financial liability for the various events in dispute.

Reconvening the parties, the commission presented them verbally with its understanding of the historical events, and then set out the various possible legal interpretations of these events, including the relative support they obtained in the commission. Finally, the commission indicated the outline of a settlement. The parties had earlier requested the commission not to propose any particular amounts. Within several weeks, they notified the commission that they accepted the outline. The governments agreed between themselves on the specific amounts, and thus settled the dispute.

There is no additional information on why the respective governments decided to commence conciliation, or what further considerations led them to accept the commission's recommendations in their entirety. It is clear, however, that the dispute involved two governments enjoying friendly relations, and that the events in dispute were isolated incidents. Conciliation proved to be an efficient settlement mechanism, with the proceedings opened and closed within nine months, with only one week of hearings.

The *Gorm and Svava* Case turned out to be an important exception to the general practice of non-use of conciliation provisions. Twenty-five years after concluding the treaty setting-up the conciliation commission, the body was

---

[282] H. Rolin, 'Une conciliation belgo-danoise', (1953) 57 *RGDIP* 353, 358; J.P.A. François, 'La Cour Permanente d'arbitrage', (1955) 87 *Recueil des Cours* Vol. I 456, 537.

called into action. The commission members had very little precedent to build on. Rolin mentions that initially there was some confusion in the commission as to its role and responsibility. The treaty provided only a general outline of the mandate:

> '... to elucidate questions in dispute, to collect with that object all necessary information by means of enquiry or otherwise, and to endeavour to bring the Parties to an agreement. It may, after the case has been examined, inform the Parties of the terms of settlement which seem suitable to it, and lay down a period within which they are to make a decision.'[283]

Though some commission members also had a political or diplomatic background, they were all lawyers, the president being a senior judge. Moreover, the parties had agreed to start the proceedings with an exchange of their argumentation. It should be no surprise, therefore, that the commission decided to assume a quasi-judicial role.

It is remarkable, however, that at the commission managed at the same time not to make legal pronouncements and to give a comprehensive, principle-based settlement proposal. According to Rolin and François, the commission acted as if it were a legal counsel, advising both parties simultaneously of the chance of success of their claims. In fact, however, the commission went beyond that. On those points where opinions could diverge, the commission weighed the various assessments. Therefore, if there was thought to be a 10% chance that one party would obtain 100% of a particular claimed amount, the proposal was that the party would get 10% of such amount.

The proceedings of the *Gorm and Svava* Case became the centre piece of a grand debate held by the Institut de Droit International in 1961, which found commission members Rolin and François drawing opposing conclusions for the future of conciliation. This debate is discussed in more detail in chapter III.[284] Also through that debate, the experiences of the *Gorm and Svava* conciliation have indirectly influenced the procedures embodied in multilateral conciliation instruments,[285] and directly influenced the one ICSID conciliation case reported in any detail.[286]

---

[283] Treaty of Conciliation (Belgium-Denmark) Art. 7.

[284] See chapter III 3.

[285] The 1961 IDI Conciliation Rules resulted from the debate at the IDI, which itself followed a report by Rolin on among others the *Gorm and Svava* example.

[286] See chapter II 1.13.1; L. Nurick and S.J. Schnably, 'The First ICSID Conciliation', (1986) 1 *ICSID Rev Foreign Investment Law Journal* 340, 348.

4.2 Conflated: the *Taba* Case

A substantially different conciliation was undertaken in the mid 1980s between Egypt and Israel. The Camp David accords of 1979, which brought peace between Egypt and Israel, required the two countries to demarcate the boundary between them.[287] There were disagreements on the location of the border in the Sinai desert, largely resulting from unclear demarcation exercises in the early 20th century, when the border divided English- and Turkish- controlled areas. In 1986, the parties agreed to put the dispute to an arbitration tribunal, consisting of five members, including one national of each party. The mandate of the tribunal was limited: it would have to chose from among the border pillar positions put forward by the parties. At the same time, the president of the tribunal had to select some of his fellow arbitrators to form a separate body, to attempt conciliation *during* the arbitration proceedings. The terms of reference provided:

> 'After the submission of counter-memorials, this chamber shall give thorough consideration to the suggestions made by any member of the chamber for a proposed recommendation concerning a settlement of the dispute. Suggestions based upon the memorials, the counter-memorials, and other relevant submissions shall be presented to the chamber commencing from the month immediately preceding the counter-memorials. The chamber shall thereafter consider these suggestions, and the counter-memorials, during the period after submission of the counter-memorials until the completion of the written pleadings. Any proposed recommendation concerning a settlement of the dispute which obtains the approval of the three members of the chamber will be reported as a recommendation to the parties not later than the completion of the exchange of written pleadings. The parties shall hold the report in strictest confidence. The arbitration process shall terminate in the event the parties jointly inform the Tribunal in writing that they have decided to accept a recommendation of the chamber and that they have decided that the arbitration process should cease. Otherwise, the arbitration process shall continue in accordance with this Compromis. All work pursuant to the above paragraphs absolutely shall not delay the arbitration process or prejudice the arbitral award, and shall be held in the strictest confidence. No position, suggestion, or recommendation, not otherwise part of the presentation of a party's case on the merits, shall be brought to the attention of the other members of the Tribunal, or be taken

---

[287] G. Lagergren, 'The Taba Tribunal, 1986-89', (1989) 1 *RADIC* 525; P. Weil, 'Some Observations on the Arbitral Award in the Taba Case', (1989) 23 *Israel Law Review* 1; R. Lapidoth, 'Some Reflections on the Taba Award', (1992) 35 *GYIL* 224; P.D. Trooboff, H. Ding and S. Koenig, 'Boundary Dispute Concerning the Taba Area', (1989) 83 *AJIL* 590; D.W. Bowett, 'The Taba Award of 29 September 1988', (1989) 23 *Israel Law Review* 429; E. Lauterpacht, 'The Taba Case; Some Recollections and Reflections', (1989) 23 *Israel Law Review* 443.

into account in any manner by any of the members of the Tribunal in reaching their arbitral decision.'[288]

Judge Bellet was chosen as chairman of the conciliation chamber, of which the respective Egyptian and Israeli arbitrators, Sultan and Lapidoth, were also members. It appears that the conciliators assumed functions resembling those of a mediator rather than a conciliator, in that they did not present the parties with a report of the issues in dispute. Nevertheless, as the conciliation phase took place towards the end of the written stage of the proceedings, the conciliatory work was necessarily based on a thorough investigation of the dispute.

The Compromis provided that the conciliation mandate expired at completion of the written proceedings. The conciliators decided, however, that they wished to take into consideration the arguments contained in the final written submissions. Therefore, bending the rules somewhat, it was agreed that the deadline for these submissions in the arbitral proceedings was extended with one month, while they would nevertheless be 'informally submitted' to the conciliators at the original date. The commission did however only meet once, two days after the 'informal submission'. Further work was done by Judge Bellet, acting alone. Four weeks later, at the expiry of the commission's mandate, Judge Bellet reported that the Chamber had not been able to make any recommendation for settlement. [289]

Insiders have given sparse comments on the precise reasons for the conciliation's failure.[290] Israel's arbitrator/conciliator Lapidoth considered it preferable that the conciliation and arbitration stage would not have been concurrent, but did not see this as the reason for the failure. On the other hand, Bowett, counsel to Egypt, recommends the option for future occasions.[291] It is noted that a concurrent mediation conducted by a US State Department official was also unsuccessful. Israel's counsel Elihu Lauterpacht reasons that in the light of the pending arbitration neither side was prepared to give the impression that it was willing to concede any points. The basis of the failure may of course have essentially been intransigence of the parties, and the fact that, unlike Belgium and Denmark in the *Gorm and Svava* Case, Egypt and Israel were not on equally friendly footing, and that the issue of demarcating Israel's bor-

---

[288] Agreement to Arbitrate the Boundary Dispute concerning the Taba Beachfront (Egypt-Israel) (11 September 1986), (1987) 26 *ILM* 1 Annex Art. 9.

[289] Ibid., Art. 10; G. Lagergren, 'The Taba Tribunal, 1986-89', (1989) 1 *RADIC* 525, 528.

[290] E. Lauterpacht, 'The Taba Case; Some Recollections and Reflections', (1989) 23 *Israel Law Review* 443; D.W. Bowett, 'The Taba Award of 29 September 1988', 23 *Israel Law Review* 429; R. Lapidoth, 'Some Reflections on the Taba Award', (1992) 35 *GYIL* 224, 237-240.

[291] D.W. Bowett, 'The Taba Award of 29 September 1988', (1989) 23 *Israel Law Review* 429.

ders was not an isolated matter. Lapidoth hints that over time the positions of the parties became more entrenched, and that in the advanced stages of arbitration, acceptance of a compromise may be seen by the national audiences as an admission of failure.

There were in any case fundamental problems in the conciliation commission's set-up and mandate. Bending the rules of the Compromis to allow for 'informal submission' of the statement of rejoinder, and leaving the conciliation work only to the non-national member, are only the beginning. All members of the conciliation commission were at the same time arbitrators, with a duty to assess the issues independently, from a legal perspective. In their discussions with their fellow arbitrators, they would develop a view of the likely outcome of the arbitration. The apparent requirement to take into account also the statement of rejoinder submitted by each of the parties points out that the legal merits of the case were a significant element also of the conciliation proceedings. Nevertheless, the conciliators were not allowed to hint to the parties what would likely be the outcome of the case. For the parties, on the other hand, it would be the likely outcome of the arbitration that would be paramount in any decision to settle the dispute before delivery of the award. In practice, the parties would understandably try to read as much as possible in what the conciliators (or, in practice, the single conciliator) said. For the conciliation effort, it would precisely be the ability to give off indications of a likely award that would enhance a settlement opportunity.

Therefore, the *Taba* conciliation effort was quite the opposite of the *Gorm and Svava* Case. In the latter instance, conciliation was a separate exercise, in which the commission had assumed the role of discussing possible outcomes of a legal case, and weighing the prospects in order to come to a recommendation. Had Belgium and Denmark not reached a settlement through conciliation, they would probably have had to initiate time-consuming arbitration or litigation proceedings later. In the *Taba* Case, the commission acted under pressure of ongoing arbitral proceedings. Moreover, while the *Taba* conciliators knew better than the *Gorm and Svava* conciliators what the actual litigation prospects were, unlike the latter they were prevented from indicating to the parties what their respective chances of success were. Furthermore, whereas in a separate conciliation exercise the parties could have freely demonstrated a willingness to concede certain points, and to argue some points but not others, in this combined procedure the agents could fear that any display of readiness to concede an issue could be perceived by the arbitrators/conciliators as making it easier on that point to decide in favour of the other party. This concern was embedded in the provision cited above, certainly also inspired by the requirements of due process: the conciliator/arbitrators were not entitled to communicate anything arising out of the conciliation proceedings to the other members of the arbitral tribunal.

With the failure of the conciliation exercise, the success of the procedure depended on the arbitration. The award turned out to be a controversial decision,[292] but was nevertheless implemented by the parties. The proceedings should however serve as a warning against *ad hoc* procedural rules, particularly against the simultaneous conduct of conciliation and arbitration.

4.3 Complex: the East African Community Case

A very different conciliation was undertaken by one man, working over a period of more than seven years, in a dispute involving three states. Following the successful conclusion, mediator/conciliator Umbricht wrote a full-length account of his involvement, allowing a rare view into such process.[293]

In 1977 the East African Community (EAC) broke down. The end of this economic and political co-operation between Kenya, Tanzania and Uganda caused many financial, organisational and logistical problems, and also heightened the already existing animosity between the parties. After some time, with assistance from the World Bank and UNDP, the three States appointed a 'mediator', the Swiss UN Under-Secretary-General Victor Umbricht, to assist in finding a settlement. His terms of reference were deliberately broadly formulated. He was to:

> 'recommend to the Partner States proposals for the permanent and equitable division of the assets and liabilities of EAC Corporations and the General Fund Services (GFS). Thereafter, [he] would assist the Partner States in reaching a definitive settlement on the basis of these recommendations.'[294]

The broad nature of these terms allowed Umbricht to vary the procedural approach to the settlement. Throughout his mandate, he made and commissioned various in-depth studies into the factual situation. He employed consultants and experts, and appointed an Advisory Board to assist him in elucidation of technical issues.[295] He also called on the assistance of various international organisations. Halfway through the process he obtained the creation of a Committee of High Officials, charged with comparing their respective country's findings and working out joint recommendations to their ministers.[296] Consid-

---

[292] Arbitral Award (29 September 1988), 80 *ILR* 224.

[293] V.H. Umbricht, *Multilateral Mediation: Practical Experiences and Lessons* (1989).

[294] Art. 1 Terms of Reference, ibid., 267.

[295] Ibid., 34.

[296] Ibid., 132-133.

ering the Committee's helpful role in committing the parties to assisting the fact finding process and developing settlement options, Umbricht later regretted that this body had not been set-up earlier.

Umbricht held that his task was to suggest terms of settlement and to explain the underlying reasons for them.[297] He issued his first draft proposals after two years. In reaching his recommendations regarding the distribution of assets, he notes that he regarded a variety of alternative criteria, some suggested by history, some by logic, some by analogy, and some by governments.[298] In the end, he concluded that there was no single criterion 'whose logic, simplicity and aptness make it the one and only choice.'[299] His solution, a 50/50 combination of geographical location and economic need, he called:

> 'inspired by profound exploration of alternatives, by thorough knowledge of the facts by counsel of advisors, by reflection, by the benefit of experience – and by some nuance of the arbitrary.'[300]

Umbricht backed up his recommendations with detailed data and considerations. Following the strong reactions of the parties, another four years were required to do additional fact-finding and to reassess and negotiate the final proposals, leading to an agreement signed by the Heads of State in 1984. Having apparently been impressed by the emphatic responses to his earliest proposals, Umbricht urged future third parties to be extremely cautious in suggesting a compromise, because a party could conceive this as demanding an unwarranted concession. Umbricht would therefore only bring proposals on joint request, preferring to offer suggestions from which the parties could choose.[301] Such approach is however not fully borne out by his description of his work, as he at times judged submissions by the parties to be unacceptable, and continued to table single formula he himself had devised.[302]

It is apparent that Umbricht was uneasy about the lack of necessity of the particular formula chosen by him for the distribution of assets, as well as of those adopted for his other recommendations. Nevertheless, he made a point of avoiding any detailed use of law, stating that he had to 'solve problems by equity and fairness, not by applying strict legal rules.'[303] He set out only the broadest of principles of international law as guidance in diplomatic dispute

[297] Ibid., 24.
[298] Ibid., 101-102.
[299] Ibid., 102.
[300] Ibid., 103.
[301] Ibid., 239.
[302] E.g., ibid., 118-121, 129-130.
[303] Ibid., 246.

settlement.[304] Similarly, he counselled against reliance on a single expert on a particular question.[305] Umbricht clearly felt he required sufficient freedom of action to develop settlement options which would not have emerged from a straightforward adoption of a rule or a non-political finding. This need for room to manoeuvre is striking, in view of the fact that he took such pains and time to establish as comprehensive as possible a factual overview of a situation that, due to local administration and accounting, hardly allowed for precise assessment. He must have been of the view that in order to create the possibility of success, he should transfer as many of the elements in dispute as possible beyond controversy, but that the move from establishing the facts to drafting a successful settlement could not be constrained or objectified. Most importantly, his method was successful, leading to a comprehensive settlement of the outstanding issues.[306]

Classification of this episode as mediation or conciliation is contested. Umbricht himself named it mediation, applying a broad understanding of the term, and stressing that conciliation is more formal, and involves a commission.[307] Nevertheless, considering that Umbricht, an independent actor, was appointed by the parties, investigated the dispute in much detail and produced reports including recommendations for settlement, the effort encompasses all defined elements of conciliation, except for the presence of a commission.[308]

The episode is noteworthy not only because one man managed to settle such a seemingly intractable dispute, even continuing when two of the three parties briefly were at war, but also because of the procedure followed. Umbricht combined elaborate fact-finding with lengthy political discussions, but refused to let fact-finding become a political exercise.[309] He engaged a body of advisers, but did not involve them in the proceedings. He obtained the establishment of a separate committee of representatives for further fact-finding, and to serve as a source and sounding board for settlement proposals. By this and other means, Umbricht moved from higher to lower political levels in the parties' ranks, depending on the importance of the issue and the state of the negotiations. He dealt with a complex multi-party dispute with complex procedural means, while

---

304 Ibid., 219-221.

305 Ibid., 253-254.

306 The co-operation is currently experiencing a revival: Treaty Establishing the East African Community (30 November 1999, entry into force 7 July 2002) <http://www.eac.int/documents/EAC%20Treaty.pdf> (25 July 2006). T.O. Ojienda, 'The East-African Court of Justice in the Reestablished East African Community: Institutional Structure and Function in the Integration Process', (2005) 11 *East African Journal of Peace and Human Rights* 220.

307 Ibid., 24-26. Merrills considers it an exercise in conciliation: J.G. Merrills, *International Dispute Settlement* (4th edn. 2005) 70-71.

308 See chapter I 3.1.

309 V.H. Umbricht, *Multilateral Mediation: Practical Experiences and Lessons* (1989) 223.

going into greatest factual detail, but at the same time avoiding the detail of rules and principles.

5. Conclusions: Diplomatic Dispute Settlement and Inter-State Conciliation

The case studies illustrate that conciliation can take on many forms, but also that there are certain common threads in the application. In all three cases the conciliators acted on the basis of detailed data and argumentation submitted by the parties, which was assessed independently by the conciliators. The conciliators reflected on the relationship between the facts, the norms and their own proposals. In all cases, they felt the need to develop their own approach to the proceedings, undoubtedly because of a lack of guiding documentation or precedent, but also because of the particular situation or the desires expressed by the parties.

Whether technical disputes between friendly nations, contested demarcation between former enemies or a political *and* technical dispute between multiple parties, no dispute is *a priori* unfit for conciliation. The results may differ, however, as will the types of conciliators required and the particular procedural means adopted. It is particularly notable that the procedure follows the desires of the parties, but that – as happened in all three case studies – the conciliators themselves reinterpret their terms of reference to reflect their views on how the procedure should be applied to the particular dispute. It is the adaptability of conciliation that stands out, and that has also historically led to confusion over its identity.

Despite the many forms which conciliation can take both in provisions and in practice, essential elements of the method were identified as: (1) a method of settlement of international disputes, (2) which is not binding, (3) involving a commission, (4) appointed by the parties, (5) which is independent, (6) investigates the dispute, (7) and proposes a solution (8) to be presented in a report. However, even when conciliation is clearly defined, many forms of conciliation available. For instance, note that the case studies include one permanent commission, one *ad hoc* commission and – exceptionally – one sole conciliator. The elements of a definition should help to identify the core understanding of conciliation, as also adopted throughout this work, but should not restrict the view on the alternative possibilities. Nevertheless, conciliation is distinguished from mediation.

Conciliation has its own place amidst other dispute settlement methods, which all are distinct but not separate. They can be combined in one single case, and the application of one method can evolve into the use of another. In this respect it is also important that in the early 20th century it was common to distinguish classes of disputes, such as legal and political disputes and justiciable and non-justiciable disputes, and that these distinctions were often connected to distinct settlement methods. Nevertheless the definition of a particular dispute no longer necessarily leads to the suggestion that it should be submitted to a particular settlement method. This implies that in settling inter-State disputes parties have a wide range of choices. On this basis, the next chapter assesses how decisions of States and developments in legal thought led to the adoption of inter-State conciliation in provisions and practice.

Chapter II
THE DEVELOPMENT OF INTER-STATE CONCILIATION

Conciliation has greatly developed over time. This means that historical roots may fade. The history of inter-State conciliation is however not just interesting in itself, but also relevant to the understanding of its contemporary use and disuse. The ideas and practices of the past did not always survive, but conciliation did. The question is how and why it did. To this end, the first part of this chapter analyses the emergence of conciliation among the other means of diplomatic dispute settlement. It addresses strong criticism by Hersch Lauterpacht written in the 1930s, and in view of later experiences assesses to what extent he is vindicated. Particular attention is given to recent developments and to conciliation practices rarely addressed at length. In this light also, the second part of this chapter contains a critical discussion of model rules of conciliation as prepared in the 1990s by the United Nations and the Permanent Court of Arbitration. The rules put forward are investigated and compared, assessing also their value for future practice.

PART ONE
THE DEVELOPMENT OF CONCILIATION

1. The Development of Conciliation

The history of the foundations of conciliation is rooted in that of non-binding third party dispute settlement generally, and can be traced to ancient times.

1.1 Pre-Modern History

Not only were arbitration and mediation known to the ancient Greeks, they believed that these methods were practised by the Gods themselves.[1] The Greeks

[1] J.H. Ralston, *International Arbitration from Athens to Locarno* (1929) 153; E. Wyler, 'Le médiateur, tiers impartial au coeur du droit', in M.G. Kohen (ed.), *Promoting Justice, Human Rights and Conflict Resolution through International Law* (2007) 973, 974.

frequently referred disputes, especially frontier disputes, to individual foreign rulers for binding settlement. For instance, around 600 B.C., Athens and Mytilene brought their dispute over the town of Sigeon on the Hellespont to Periandros, tyrant of Corinth, to act as sole arbitrator.[2] The Romans, however, had little experience with arbitration. Nevertheless, it was well-known to the barbarians who overthrew them, and became quite common again in the European Middle Ages.[3] A peace treaty concluded between many German principalities in 1254 even created a number of mixed arbitration committees, consisting of representatives of the parties, presided over by a neutral umpire.[4] Arbitration also became common as a means to end wars.[5]

Greek arbitrators of the later period, and arbitrators throughout the Middle Ages, often had the primary task of attempting amicable settlement. The umpire could try for a friendly compromise even after the full hearing of the parties, while he maintained authority to decide on a binding settlement himself. Arbitrators were often foreign Sovereigns or the Pope. The awards were often unreasoned.[6] Mediation itself has been normal practice throughout the ages and throughout the world.[7] Many examples are known of mediation between the Kings and Princes of mediaeval Europe by their equals or by the Pope.[8] It is often difficult, sometimes impossible, to distinguish between mediation and arbitration as practiced in that period. This may be due to inaccurate terminology, equivocal expressions, or simply because the distinction was not appreciated. For instance, Ralston mentions that in 1334 Philip of Valois declared himself 'judge, bargainer and *amiable compositeur*' between the King of Bohemia, the Princes of Germany and the Duke of Brabant.[9] Moreover, rejection of a mediator's proposals could be made impossible simply because of his

---

[2] J.H.W. Verzijl, *International Law in Historical Perspective* (1968) Vol. I 423-424, 472; H.T. King and M.A. Le Forestier, 'Arbitration in Ancient Greece', (1994) 38 *Dispute Resolution Journal* 49.

[3] J.H. Ralston, *International Arbitration from Athens to Locarno* (1929) 174 ff; W. Schücking, *Das Völkerrechtliche Institut der Vermittlung* (1923) 1, 4.

[4] J.H. Ralston, *International Arbitration from Athens to Locarno* (1929) 180.

[5] Ibid., 181. Notably, the constitution of Andorra is the result of an arbitral decision of the 13th century: J.H.W. Verzijl, 'La base des jugements internationaux au cours de l'histoire', (1955) 59 *RGDIP* 370, 391.

[6] H.T. King and M.A. Le Forestier, 'Papal arbitration', (1997) 52 *Dispute Resolution Journal* 74; J.H.W. Verzijl, *International Law in Historical Perspective* (1976) Vol. VIII 72 ff. This still occurs, as in the arbitration by the UN Secretary-General in the *Rainbow Warrior* Case (*France* v. *New Zealand*), (1987) 74 *ILR* 256.

[7] 'The are societies in the world (...) without formal procedures for judgement, but there are none without legitimate procedures for mediation.' W. Davies and P. Fouracre (eds.), *The Settlement of Disputes in Early Mediaeval Europe* (1986) 237.

[8] J.H.W. Verzijl, *Historical Perspective* (1976) Vol. VIII 52 ff.

[9] J.H. Ralston, *International Arbitration from Athens to Locarno* (1929) 179.

willingness to use persuasive force. In 1512 Denmark and Sweden concluded a treaty providing for a mixed arbitral commission, with mediation under the threat of war in case of failure.[10]

In the 16th and 17th centuries arbitration gradually lost much of its importance. The development of the idea of sovereignty did not sit well with submission of disputes to foreigners. Nevertheless, in 1625 Grotius advocated the use of arbitration and other means of dispute settlement.[11]

Throughout the ages, individuals, organisations and states have aspired to the creation of institutionalised diplomacy and internationally organised peaceful dispute settlement.[12] One remarkable initiative was that of the Bohemian King George Podebrad, who around 1460 developed a detailed proposal for a kind of federation of European Sovereigns, including a Parliament of plenipotentiaries and a Council of Kings, with compulsory peaceful settlement of disputes, and an international court. Despite a welcome reception in various Courts, the project foundered largely because of the exclusion of – and opposition by – the Pope.[13]

The historical examples are important in establishing the antecedents of present day methods of third party settlement, but direct lineage cannot be assumed.[14] As for their value as historical analogies, especially with regard to binding settlement through arbitration, account should be taken of the differences between the close cultural ties between the Greek cities and the binding ties of religion in the Middle Ages on the one hand, and the global cultural divergence and the frequent insistence on sovereignty in modern times.[15] The importance of sharing culture, religion and a conception of authority is still occasionally demonstrated, for instance in the successful Papal mediation in the Beagle Channel dispute.[16]

---

[10] In the Armistice Treaty of 1512 the two States agreed to submit their disputes to a board comprising twelve councillors of each party. In case of deadlock, the Wendish merchant cities should mediate, and if they were unsuccessful, they should join the treaty-abiding party in war. H. Rydberg, *Sveriges Traktater* (*Stockholm 1877 – 1896*) Vol. III 570 referred to in C.E. Hill, *Danish Sound Dues* (1926) 43-44.

[11] H. Grotius, *De Jure Belli ac Pacis* (1625) Lib II cap XXIII [VI]-[X].

[12] An informative study of thoughts and projects throughout the ages: J. ter Meulen, *Der Gedanke der Internationalen Organisation in seiner Entwicklung 1300-1800* (1917); J. ter Meulen, *Der Gedanke der Internationalen Organisation in seiner Entwicklung 1789-1889* (1929).

[13] J. ter Meulen, *Der Gedanke der Internationalen Organisation in seiner Entwicklung 1300-1800* (1917) 108-123; J. Žourek, 'Le Projet du Roi Tchèque George Podiebrad', (1964) 10 *AFDI* 14.

[14] J.H.W. Verzijl, *International Law in Historical Perspective* (1968) Vol. I 443 ff.

[15] J.H.W. Verzijl, *International Law in Historical Perspective* (1976) Vol. VIII 72; but see L.B. Sohn, 'International Arbitration in Historical Perspective: Past and Present', in A.H.A. Soons (ed.), *International Arbitration: Past and Prospects* (1990) 9, 10.

[16] Documents of the mediation: (1985) 24 *ILM* 1; E. Lauterpacht, 'Whatever Happened to the Beagle Channel Award?', in *Le Droit International au Service de la Paix, de la Justice et du Développement* (1991) 359.

1.2 Diplomatic settlement in early modern times

Despite evidence that at least the idea circulated already in 1726,[17] it is the 1794 Jay Treaty, between the United Kingdom and its former colony the United States, that is credited for the revival of institutional arbitration, and its foundation upon international law.[18] The Anglo-American agreement did not yet create a fully judicial form of arbitration. Though many cases settled under the Treaty were decided expressly on legal principles, political considerations were still part of the process.[19] The Jay Treaty did not instantly alter arbitral practice: throughout the 19th century there were still requests for unreasoned awards decided by foreign sovereigns.[20]

The Congress of Vienna in 1814-1815 marked the beginning of permanent multilateral diplomacy: the Great Powers of Europe agreed to convene regularly for the maintenance of peace and stability on the Continent. In 1822 Colombia and Peru also established an institution for peaceful settlement, which they called a 'super-arbitrator and conciliator'.[21] This may be the first significant reference to conciliation, though the 'conciliator' was not an expert in amicable settlement, but rather an international conference with state delegates acting upon government instructions.

In Europe, the idea of a family of nations bound by shared principles gained practical importance. In 1856, the Congress of Paris concluded the Crimean War, and at the same time formalised the ideal of comprehensive multilateral diplomacy by formally allowing the Ottoman Empire into the Congress frame-

---

[17] In a proposal by the Austrian Emperor to the Dutch Republic: C.G. Roelofsen, 'The Jay Treaty and All That; Some Remarks on the Role of Arbitration in European Modern History and its 'Revival' in 1794', in A.H.A. Soons (ed.), *International Arbitration: Past and Prospects* (1990) 201, 208.

[18] E.g., I. Brownlie, *Principles of Public International Law* (6th edn. 2003) 672; J.H. Ralston, *International Arbitration from Athens to Locarno* (1929) Vol. VII; A.M. Stuyt, *Survey of International Arbitrations 1794-1989* (1990). Further: J.L. Simpson and H. Fox, *International Arbitration* (1959); H.T. King and M.A. Le Forestier, 'Origins of Modern International Arbitration', (1996) 51 *Dispute Resolution Journal* 42.

[19] M.O. Hudson, *International Tribunals: Past and Future* (1944) 3.

[20] E.g., the *Portendic Claims* (*UK* v. *France*) unreasoned award by the King of Prussia 1843; J.B. Moore, *International Arbitrations* (1898) Vol. 5, 4937; the *San Juan de Furca* Case (1871-1872) decided by the German Emperor; J.B. Moore, *International Arbitrations* (1898) Vol. 1, 196-236, 229; H.T. King and M.A. Le Forestier, 'Origins of Modern International Arbitration', (1996) 51 *Dispute Resolution Journal* 42, 46; K. Strupp, 'Le droit du juge international de statuer selon l'équité', (1930) 33 *Recueil des Cours* Vol. III 357, 368.

[21] *Cot* 29. A comparable institution was envisaged during the Congress of Panama of 1826, which brought together most Latin American States: R.J. Alfaro, 'Signification internationale du Congrès de Panama', in H. Accioli and others, *Hommage d'une Génération de Juristes au Président Basdevant* (1960) 10, 18.

work. The European system explicitly took it upon itself to spread and defend the law of nations. At the same time, over forty States pledged that if a serious dispute would arise, they would, as far as the circumstances allowed, have recourse to the good offices of a friendly Power before going to war.[22] The fact that third party assistance was practised mostly by the Great Powers to impose their will did, however, lead the smaller States to suspect mediation as a means of interference.[23] At the Hague Peace Conference in 1899 some effort was required to get passed the bad reputation that the method had so acquired.

1.3 The 1899 Hague Peace Conference

Alarmed first of all by the arms race then taking place, the Russian Tsar in 1898 requested the Queen of the Netherlands to host the first global intergovernmental conference expressly called to maintain the peace.[24] The Hague Peace Conference of 1899, attended by government delegations from around the world, adopted two Conventions, one on humanitarian law, another on the peaceful settlement of disputes (the 1899 Hague Convention).[25]

The latter convention declared that, as far as circumstances would allow, parties in dispute would have recourse to mediation before they would resort to arms. Third parties would also have the right, and even the moral obligation, to offer mediation of their own volition, without this being considered an unfriendly act by any of the parties in conflict.[26] These provisions were criticised by Politis, who held that to formalise a pre-existing moral obligation would give rise to unwanted mediation, and raise suspicions with the parties in dispute.[27]

---

[22] A.G. Koroma, 'The Peaceful Settlement of International Disputes', (1996) 43 *NILR* 227, 228; T.P. Conwell-Evans, *The League Council in Action* (1929) 7.

[23] N. Politis, 'L'Avenir de la médiation', (1910) 17 *RGDIP* 136, 142. Until that time it was common to term both mediation and armed interference with an existing conflict as 'intervention', mediation being 'unarmed' intervention. Cf., E. de Vattel, *Le Droit des Gens* (1758) Vol. I ch III [37].

[24] M. Robinson, *Arbitration and the Hague Peace Conferences* (1936) 6; D.J. Bederman, 'The Hague Peace Conferences of 1899 and 1907', in M.W. Janis (ed.), *International Courts for the Twenty-First Century* (1992) 9.

[25] Convention With Respect to Laws and Customs of War on Land (29 July 1899) and the Convention for the Pacific Settlement of Disputes (29 July 1899); J.B. Scott (ed.), *The Hague Conventions and Declarations of 1899 and 1907* (1915); The Permanent Court of Arbitration *Basic Documents* (1998); J.B. Scott (ed.), *The Reports of the Hague Conferences of 1899 and 1907* (1917); A. Eyffinger, *The 1899 Hague Peace Conference* (1999).

[26] Hague Convention (1899) Arts. 2 and 3. W. Schücking, *Das Völkerrechtliche Institut der Vermittlung* (1923).

[27] N. Politis, 'L'Avenir de la Médiation', (1910) 17 *RGDIP* 136, 155-156.

The Convention recommended arbitration as 'the most effective, and at the same time the most equitable' means with regard to disputes of a legal nature which diplomacy has failed to settle.[28] To facilitate the recourse to this procedure, the Permanent Court of Arbitration (PCA) was established. The International Bureau, the secretariat of the PCA, maintains a list of names of up to four people selected by each Signatory Power, who can act as arbitrator in any case brought to the Court by common accord of the disputing parties.[29]

While rules for arbitration were given for essentially legal disputes, another procedure was developed for the clarification of the issues out of which a dispute may arise. Just a year before the First Hague Conference, in 1898, the conflicting reports of the facts surrounding the explosion of the American battleship *Maine* in the Havana harbour had ignited a war between Spain and the United States.[30] With many others, Russian Conference delegate De Martens believed that war could have been prevented if there had been a mechanism to establish the truth behind the incident. He proposed the establishment of international commissions of inquiry, independent bodies of experts charged with clarifying situations of controversy.[31] Their use would be obligatory in disputes not involving honour or vital interests.[32] Serious objections were however raised, especially by Germany and the Balkan States, who were concerned about the intrusive nature of inquiry commissions and the threat they could pose to State sovereignty. The articles on inquiry were eventually adopted, but included the provision that they would not be used when honour or vital interests were at stake, and that in any case their employment remained optional. Moral pressure would have to do the rest. Article 9 of the Convention reads:

> 'In differences of an international nature involving neither the honour nor vital interests, and arising from a difference of opinion on points of fact, the Signatory Powers recommend that the parties, who have not been able to come to an agreement by means of diplomacy, should, as far as circumstances allow, institute an International Commission of Inquiry, to facilitate a solution of these differences by elucidating the facts by means of an impartial and conscientious investigation.'

---

28 Hague Convention (1899) Art. 16.

29 P. Hamilton and others (eds.), *The Permanent Court of Arbitration: International Arbitration and Dispute Resolution* (1999); W.E. Butler, 'The Hague Permanent Court of Arbitration', in M.W. Janis (ed.), *International Courts for the Twenty-First Century* (1992) 43.

30 N. Bar-Yaacov, *The Handling of International Disputes by Means of Inquiry* (1974) 33.

31 The method was not completely unknown: as early as 1622 the Netherlands and Tunisia established a fact finding commission for the purpose of investigating violations of their peace treaty by private individuals. J.H.W. Verzijl, *International Law from a Historical Perspective* (1976) Vol. VIII 56.

32 Russian Draft Art. 14 in J. Brown Scott (ed.), *The Proceedings of the Hague Peace Conferences; The Conference of 1899* (1920) 797-800.

The commissions, to be formed upon special agreement between the Parties, would, unless otherwise agreed, consist of two nationals of each of the States in question. These four together would choose a fifth member to be the umpire.[33] The commission would hear both parties, and establish the facts of the case upon the information provided to it by the parties.[34] Article 14 of the Convention did not leave any misunderstandings regarding the nature of the procedure:

> 'The report of the international commission of inquiry is limited to a finding of facts, and has in no way the character of an award. It leaves the Powers in dispute entire freedom as to the effect to be given to this finding.'

Nonetheless, establishment of the facts is often interwoven with answering legal questions, as proved to be the case when the first inquiry commission was set-up in 1904. A serious conflict erupted when, during the Russo-Japanese war, the Russian Baltic fleet mistook British fishing vessels for the Japanese navy, killed two fishermen and sunk one ship.[35] French mediation prevented the so-called *Dogger Bank* incident to develop into a war, by suggesting the application of the inquiry provisions of the 1899 Hague Convention. The Convention was applied liberally: not only did this case arguably involve the 'honour' of one of the parties, the commission also went beyond establishing the facts by advising on responsibility for the incident. Nevertheless, the chosen method proved highly successful, through a mixture of factual investigation and tactful diplomacy. Russia was found to be responsible, but the Russian admiral was not personally held to blame.[36] Russia subsequently paid compensation, and so resolved amicably what at some point could have been a *casus belli.*

On the basis of this experience, the Second Hague Conference, convened in 1907, substantially elaborated the inquiry procedure in the 1907 Convention for the Pacific Settlement of Disputes.[37] The 1907 Hague Convention made no significant changes to the 1899 Hague Convention's provisions on mediation and good offices.[38] The development of the inquiry commissions prepared the way for the development of modern conciliation. The *Dogger Bank* Case al-

---

[33] Hague Convention (1899) Arts. 10, 11, 32.

[34] Hague Convention (1899) Art. 12.

[35] N. Bar-Yaacov, *The Handling of International Disputes by Means of Inquiry* (1974) ch 3; A. Mandelstam, 'La commission internationale d'enquête', (1905) 12 *RGDIP* 161, 351.

[36] For the report and the inquiry: J. Brown Scott (ed.), *The Hague Court Reports* (1916) 403.

[37] Hague Convention (1907) Arts. 9-36. Proposals by the Russian delegation to make the method compulsory were rejected.

[38] Cf., A. Eyffinger, 'A Highly Critical Moment: Role and Record of the 1907 Hague Peace Conference', (2007) 54 *NILR* 197.

ready established that stating the facts is easily intertwined with legal questions, and easily touches upon diplomatic considerations.[39] The case also proved that a carefully phrased non-binding report can sometimes do more than a binding legal award for the maintenance of self-respect and the continuation of peaceful relations.

1.4 **Inquiry since 1907**

The lessons of the Dogger Bank inquiry were taken one step further by the United States government, which in 1911 and 1912 negotiated a novel kind of treaty of general dispute settlement with United Kingdom and with France. These 'Taft' or 'Knox'-Treaties no longer mentioned the protection of honour and vital interests and allowed inquiry commissions to make recommendations.[40] Though these treaties never came into force, they provided inspiration for US Secretary of State Bryan, who in 1913 and 1914 concluded a great number of dispute settlement treaties with a wide range of countries, collectively known as the 'Bryan Treaties'.[41] Influenced by the experiences of the Spanish-American War and the *Dogger Bank* Case, Bryan saw inquiry essentially as a means to prevent war by cutting through the confusion and stalemate that, he believed, often preceded armed conflict. The Bryan Treaties provided for compulsory inquiry in the case of a dispute, and the postponement of resort to force until after the issuing of a report. To forestall political inaction in the face of crisis, the commissions could also spontaneously offer their services to the parties. The Bryan Treaties inspired many other inquiry agreements. In 1915, Argentina, Brazil and Chile concluded a three-way arrangement for inquiry commissions.[42] In 1919 the United Kingdom concluded inquiry agreements with Chile[43] and with Brazil.[44] In 1923, a collective of American States adopted the Gondra Treaty, which established two permanent inquiry commissions authorised to deal with disputes between any of the ratifying States.[45]

---

[39] It was therefore termed 'judicative conciliation', in A.H. Snow, *Judicative Conciliation* (1916).

[40] R. Donner, 'The Procedure of International Conciliation: Some Historical Aspects', (1999) 1 *Journal of the History of International Law* 103, 109.

[41] J. Brown Scott (ed.), *Treaties for the Advancement of Peace* (1920).

[42] Ibid., 147.

[43] Treaty of Investigation (Chile-United Kingdom) (28 March 1919, entered into force 23 October 1919, abrogated 4 April 1922): United Kingdom *Treaty Series* (1920) No. 3 (Cmd. 518); *Habicht* 5.

[44] Treaty of Investigation (Brazil-United Kingdom) (4 April 1919, entered into force 11 March 1921): United Kingdom *Treaty Series* (1921) No. 8 (Cmd. 1278); *Habicht* 7.

[45] Treaty to Avoid or Prevent Conflicts between the American States (Gondra Treaty) (3 May 1923) United States *Treaty Series* (1927) No. 752; *Habicht* 77.

In practice, inquiry commissions were only used a few times, mostly for maritime disputes similar to the *Dogger Bank* incident.[46] After 1922 their functions were taken over by conciliation commissions, which had by then evolved out of the concept of inquiry. One exceptional inquiry commission was that set-up in 1962 to deal with the *Red Crusader* Case between the United Kingdom and Denmark. In 1961 an incident occurred at sea, involving a Danish governmental ship and British fishermen. The Danes arrested the fishermen, but several Danish agents were subsequently abducted by the British, to which the Danish ship responded by firing on the fishing vessel. The inquiry commission investigated the incident and allocated legal responsibility in its report. The report led to successful settlement negotiations between the two States.[47] More recently a bilateral inquiry commission was created following an allegedly Chilean plot that killed Mr Letelier and Mrs Moffitt in the United States. Using a Bryan Treaty, the United States in 1988 brought a claim against Chile. Chile agreed to make an *ex gratia* payment to the amount necessary if responsibility had been accepted or established. The inquiry commission was charged with determining the sum. Contrary to the original treaty, the report was in advance accepted as binding.[48] In these last two cases, then, the inquiry commissions were used not, as originally intended, to provide objective information about a conflict situation that could lead to war, but rather as quasi-judicial means to settle sensitive issues that were considered unfit for arbitration.

1.5 The League of Nations and the propagation of conciliation

The outbreak of WWI in 1914 brought a temporary end to the hopes of achieving world peace through law and diplomacy. The Third Hague Peace Conference, planned for 1915, was cancelled. The world crisis fuelled the conviction that war should in the future be prevented by some collective organisation of States.[49] Governments as well as private individuals devised numerous plans

---

[46] In 1912 the *Tavignano* maritime incident between Italy and France was settled successfully: J. Brown Scott (ed.), *The Hague Court Reports* (1916) 413. The sinking of the *Tiger* in 1917 off the Spanish coast was settled between Spain and Germany: N. Bar-Yaacov, *The Handling of International Disputes by Means of Inquiry* (1974) 156-171. In this case the report was in advance accepted to be binding. Furthermore, the 1916 German sinking of the Dutch ship *Tubantia* was settled successfully in 1922: ibid. 171-179.

[47] (1967) 35 *ILR* 485; G. Timsit, 'Le fonctionnement de la procédure d'enquête dans l'affaire du "Red Crusader"', (1963) 9 *AFDI* 460; N. Bar-Yaacov, *The Handling of International Disputes by Means of Inquiry* (1974) 179-197.

[48] J.G. Merrills, *International Dispute Settlement* (4th edn. 2005) 56.

[49] F.P. Walters, *A History of the League of Nations* (1952), Vols. I, II; J.H. Lantané, *Development of the League of Nations Idea; Documents and Correspondence of Theodore Marburg* (1932) Vols. I, II; D.H. Miller, *The Drafting of the Covenant* (1928) ch 3 Vols, I, II.

for a comprehensive political institution, sometimes conceived in the form of a universal conciliation commission.[50] US President Wilson became the greatest protagonist of a future League of Nations.[51]

The Covenant establishing the League was adopted in 1919.[52] An Assembly, comprising all member States, would discuss international affairs.[53] A Council, comprising the Great Powers and a number of periodically elected other States, would have special responsibilities, especially in matters relating to international peace.[54] In practice, the use of the organisation was limited, because at all times some of the most important States were not Members.[55] The establishment of the League was accompanied by the creation of the Permanent Court of International Justice (PCIJ). Some of the projects for the establishment of a League contained references to conciliation, but the method did not obtain a place in the eventual arrangements. The Covenant of the League distinguished between on the one hand situations of war or the threat of war, which could be brought to the attention of the Council by any member State or by the Secretary-General,[56] and on the other hand 'any dispute likely to lead to a rupture, which is not submitted to arbitration or judicial settlement.'[57] The latter could only be submitted to the Council by any Member party to the dispute.

If a dispute came before the Council, the parties to the dispute were allowed to take part in the discussions.[58] The Council would appoint a Rapporteur, an individual on the Council who was to follow the case in detail and mediate between the parties in private meetings. The Rapporteur was responsible for guiding the discussion and drawing-up a report on the state of affairs.[59] In

---

[50] C. de Visscher, 'Les commissions de conciliation et la Societé des Nations', (1922) 19 *RGDIP* 410, 413.

[51] Presidential Address to Congress (8 January 1918). For his Fourteen Points: J.H. Lantané, *Development of the League of Nations Idea; Documents and Correspondence of Theodore Marburg* (1932) Vol. II.

[52] Covenant of the League of Nations (28 June 1919), 1 *LNTS* 7.

[53] League Covenant Art. 3(3).

[54] League Covenant Art. 4(4); A.H. Philipse, *Le Rôle du Conseil de la Société des Nations dans le Règlement Pacifique des Différends Internationaux* (1929); O. Hoijer, *La Solution Pacifique des Litiges Internationaux: Avant et Depuis la Société des Nations* (1925).

[55] The United States did not ratify the Covenant. Germany became member in 1926 but left in 1933. Japan, an original member, withdrew the same year. The Soviet Union joined in 1933, but abandoned it in 1938: M.O. Hudson, 'The Members of the League of Nations', (1935) 16 *BYIL* 130.

[56] League Covenant Art. 11.

[57] League Covenant Art. 15.

[58] T.P. Conwell-Evans, *The League Council in Action* (1929) 127 ff.

[59] Example of the 1924 *Mosul* Case (*Turkey* v. *UK*), T.P. Conwell-Evans, *The League Council in Action* (1929) 129 and the *Polish/Lithuanian* Case (1920) ibid. 131.

some cases the Council established inquiry commissions.[60] League inquiry commissions consisted of neutrals, and were authorised to suggest a solution to the dispute. A dispute would normally be discussed both publicly and privately. It was believed that pressure from a supposedly intrinsically pacifist public opinion would increase the chances of a peaceful settlement. Such diversified mediation was not without success.[61]

In the first few years, there was much faith in the League and its methods. For instance, in 1925 Greece responded to a border incident with Bulgaria by invading its neighbour.[62] Bulgaria did not to resist, but instead made an immediate appeal to the League. The League instantly and effectively ordered both States to cease hostilities and to withdraw behind their respective borders. An inquiry commission was then set-up, which declared that the Greek government was exclusively responsible for the hostilities, and expressed its opinion that Greece should make reparations. The commission's report, which also proposed measures to prevent further border incidents, was adopted by the Council and the matter was settled.

Initially, it seemed that the Covenant gave the League of Nations exclusive authority to deal with any dispute that threatened the peace[63] or was 'likely to lead to a rupture'.[64] While settlement by means of arbitration[65] was also expressly allowed outside of the League framework, amicable third party settlement was only referred to in relation to the Assembly and the Council.[66] As the Assembly was too large a body for settlement discussions, it was thought that all disputes should eventually be dealt with by the Council.[67] The dominance of the Great Powers in that body did not sit well with the smaller Powers. Already in 1920 Sweden and Norway proposed an amendment to the effect that before bringing a dispute before the League, member States should submit their differences to a bilateral conciliation commission modelled on the Bryan

[60] T.P. Conwell-Evans, *The League Council in Action* (1929) 135 ff.

[61] M.O. Hudson, *International Tribunals: Past and Future* (1944) 225. W. Schücking, *Das Völkerrechtliche Institut der Vermittlung* (1923) 228 ff.

[62] K. Ahooja-Patel, *The Greco-Bulgarian Dispute before the League of Nations, 1925-1927* (1974); T.P. Conwell-Evans, *The League Council in Action* (1929) 155-160.

[63] League Covenant Art. 11.

[64] League Covenant Art. 15(1)

[65] And, after amendments came into force on 26 September 1924, judicial settlement.

[66] Though regional understandings such as the Monroe Doctrine would retain their validity: League Covenant Art. 21.

[67] During the drafting of the Covenant amendments were introduced by several smaller Powers to include references to bilateral conciliation. These were however rejected by the Great Powers, who preferred referral to the Council. D.H. Miller, *The Drafting of the Covenant* (1928) Vol. I 305. During the drafting process the British Lord Cecil had assured the neutral Powers that the Covenant would not be incompatible with bilateral methods of settlement. O. Hoijer, *La Solution Pacifique des Litiges Internationaux* (1925) 407.

Treaties.[68] These proposals were rejected on the basis that they were too complicated, while there were also doubts about their compatibility with the League framework: States should not be encouraged to circumvent the established system. After further reflection, however, in 1922 a resolution favouring the development of bilateral conciliation was adopted.[69] The Assembly declared bilateral settlement agreements, including conciliation treaties, compatible with the Covenant, and even encouraged their conclusion by providing model provisions. Eventually, the legalism that had gripped the League gave way to new developments.

1.6 The beginning of modern conciliation

Forms of conciliation were already practised widely by the Swiss cantons[70] when in 1919, on the basis of a report written by Max Huber, the Swiss government launched a policy of concluding conciliation agreements.[71] Unlike US Secretary of State Bryan,[72] who saw his treaties as means to prevent war, Huber advocated his variation on inquiry, in which the commission could be empowered to make proposals based on its findings, primarily as a way to avoid the political costs of arbitration or judicial settlement. Conciliation would open new possibilities for diplomatic settlement by combining the values of political negotiations with those of independent and non-binding advice: 'La conciliation permet de céder tout en laissant entière la question de principe'.[73]

Tied in with this idea was the notion that some disputes were inherently non-justiciable: they were not fit for adjudication, because they were political, not legal disputes. The first conciliation treaty, signed between Germany and Switzerland, expressly stipulated as much.[74] This treaty was soon followed by

[68] On the Scandinavian proposals: C. de Visscher, 'Les commissions de conciliation et la Société des Nations', reprinted as Annex 2, (1922) 19 *RGDIP* 410, 431. Discussion, ibid. 415-423; W. Schücking, *Des Volkerrechtliche Institut der Vermittlung* 278-283; H. Wehberg, 'Die Vergleichskommissionen im modernen Völkerrecht', (1958) 19 *ZfAÖRV* 551, 556 ff.

[69] Assembly Res (22 September 1922), *League of Nations Official Journal* (1922) (special No. 9) 6; C. de Visscher, 'Les commissions de conciliation et la Société des Nations', Annex 1, (1922) 29 *RGDIP* 410, 429; C. Gorgé, 'L'évolution de la conciliation internationale', 54 *RDILC* (1927) 58, 82-90.

[70] F. Münch, 'Die Schweizerische Initiative zu zweiseitigen Abmachungen über die friedliche Beilegung von Streitigkeiten', (1966) 26 *ZfAÖRV* 705, 717-718.

[71] 'Rapport du Conseil fédéral à l' Assemblée fédérale concernant les traités internationaux d'arbitrage', (1919) 71 *Feuille Fédéral Suisse* Vol. V 808.

[72] J. Efremoff, 'L'Organisation de la conciliation comme moyen de prevenir des guerres', (1937) 59 *Recueil des Cours* Vol. I 99.

[73] 'Rapport du Conseil fédéral à l'Assemblée fédérale concernant les traités internationaux d'arbitrage', (1919) 71 *Feuille Fédéral Suisse* Vol. V 808, 820.

[74] Treaty of Conciliation, Arbitration and Compulsory Adjudication (Germany-Switzerland) (adopted 3 December 1921, entered into force 25 May 1922), Preamble; 12 *LNTS* 281. Some

treaties with many other States, also outside Europe. The 1922 League Resolution on conciliation gave important support to the initiatives by Switzerland and the Scandinavian States. The agreements established permanent commissions, and frequently provided for compulsory arbitration for legal disputes and compulsory conciliation for all other disputes. Meanwhile, other European States initiated their own conciliation policies. Soon they had created a web of dispute settlement commitments, eventually numbering some 200 treaties.[75]

Judging from the fact that treaties were frequently concluded between far-flung countries, the general desire to settle any future disputes was at least as important a motivation as was the rationale of preventing war. The ideal of conciliation was shared enthusiastically by governments and lawyers alike. The conciliation movement was successful in also including some States that were not favourable to arbitration. The Soviet Union concluded six conciliation treaties.[76] States learned from each other in the development of the language of conciliation treaties. The Treaty of Conciliation, Arbitration and Compulsory Adjudication between Switzerland and France of 1925 laid down what would become standard terms of reference.[77] In the Americas more than in Europe, conciliation was primarily seen as a means to prevent war, as borne out by the public discussions and the language of the treaties. The commitments created by the various Bryan treaties rapidly expanded with the conclusion of various multilateral dispute settlement treaties.[78] The most important of these was the Gondra Treaty, which integrated the various inquiry agreements into a comprehensive dispute settlement arrangement.[79] The 1929 Treaty of Washington modified the inquiry commissions to include conciliation functions.[80] The quick

writers choose a different definition of conciliation treaties and name the first conciliation treaty the Treaty of Investigation (Brazil-United Kingdom) (4 April 1919, entered into force 11 March 1921): United Kingdom *Treaty Series* (1921) No. 8 (Cmd. 1278): V.D. Degan, 'International Conciliation: Its Past and Future', in P. Fischer, H.F. Köck and A. Verdross, *Völkerrecht und Rechtsfilosofie* (1980) 261, 267 or that of Chile and Sweden (1920) (26 March 1920), 4 *LNTS* 273: *Cot* 80 (though Cot agrees that the 1921 treaty is of a new kind).

[75] P.J.I.M. de Waart, *Het Onderhandelingselement in de Vreedzame Regeling van Geschillen tussen Staten* (1971).

[76] Cf., M.O. Hudson, *International Tribunals: Past and Future* (1944) 226.

[77] Treaty of Conciliation, Arbitration and Compulsory Adjudication (France-Switzerland) (6 April 1925) Art. 6(1): M. Habicht, *Post-War Treaties for the Pacific Settlement of International Disputes* (1931) 226. This entailed a minor modification of similar terms first laid down in the Treaty of Conciliation (Sweden-Switzerland) (signed 2 June 1924, entered into force 14 February 1925), ibid. 84. The French-Swiss terms were included in the General Act of 1928.

[78] The first being the Convention for the Establishment of International Commissions of Inquiry (7 February 1923): United States *Treaty Series* (1925) No. 717.

[79] Treaty to Avoid or Prevent Conflicts between the American States (3 May 1923), United States *Treaty Series* (1927) 752.

[80] General Treaty of Inter-American Arbitration (5 January 1929, entered into force 28 October 1929), United States *Treaty Series* (1929) 780; C.C. Hyde, 'The Place of Commissions of

succession of American dispute settlement agreements eventually resulted in a complicated situation of overlapping commitments.[81]

Meanwhile, the League had further aspirations to guarantee international peace. In 1924 it prepared the Geneva Protocol,[82] which was intended to strengthen the League Covenant with a commitment to disarmament and by making the settlement of disputes by pacific means compulsory.[83] The Protocol favoured arbitration and judicial settlement over non-binding methods. Signatories to the Protocol agreed that, unless it were out of self defence or on direction of the League, they would in no case resort to war, either with one another, or with a State which in the event would accept all obligations arising out of the Protocol.[84] The Protocol never entered into force.

1.7 The summer of peaceful settlement

Remarkable progress was made in 1925, when Belgium, United Kingdom, Czechoslovakia, France, Italy and Poland jointly concluded dispute settlement treaties and various treaties of territorial guarantee with their former enemy Germany, collectively known as the Locarno Treaties.[85] These provided for compulsory arbitration or judicial settlement with optional conciliation of legal disputes, and compulsory conciliation by permanent commissions for all other disputes.[86] The treaties were never used. The German re-occupation of the Rhineland in 1936, contrary to the guarantees given in 1925, meant the *de facto* end of the Locarno Treaties. At the time of their conclusion though, the Treaties were heralded as a great advancement for the cause of peace, allowing for Germany's inclusion in the League of Nations, and inspiring a surge of conciliation and arbitration treaties,[87] as well as more far-reaching instruments. At the

---

Inquiry and Conciliation Treaties in the Peaceful Settlement of Disputes', (1929) 10 *BYIL* 96, 102-107; G.H. Hackworth, *Digest of International Law* Vol. VI (1943) 8.

[81] F. Galo Leoro, 'Peaceful Settlement of Disputes – an overview', (1994) Inter-American Juridical Committee Doc 34/94.

[82] Protocol for the Pacific Settlement of International Disputes (opened for signature 2 October 1924), *League of Nations Official Journal* (1924) (special No. 21) 20.

[83] Art. 3 provided for acceptance of the compulsory jurisdiction of the International Court. P. Noel-Baker, *The Geneva Protocol* (1925); H. Wehberg, 'Le Protocol de Genève', (1925) 7 *Recueil des Cours* Vol. II 1.

[84] Geneva Protocol Art. 2.

[85] The four dispute settlement treaties: Treaties of Conciliation, Arbitration and Compulsory Adjudication (Belgium-Germany) (Czechoslovakia-Germany) (France-Germany) and (Germany-Poland) (all 16 October 1925), 54 *LNTS* 289-363.

[86] C.C. Hyde, 'Commissions of Conciliation and the Locarno Treaties', (1926) 20 *AJIL* 103; C. Gorgé, 'L'évolution de la conciliation internationale', 54 *RDILC* (1927) 58, 96.

[87] *Cot* 82-83

League, the French Foreign Minister Aristide Briand famously spoke: 'Arrière les fusils, les mitrailleuses, les canons! Place à la conciliation, à l'arbitrage, à la paix!'[88]

The General Act on the Pacific Settlement of International Disputes (the 1928 General Act) was adopted by the Assembly of the League of Nations on 26 September 1928,[89] and was acceded to by twenty-three States, though many made reservations. Modelled on the dispute settlement provisions of the Locarno Treaties, the Act also provided for judicial or arbitral settlement of all legal disputes, optionally preceded by conciliation.[90] Parties could use either permanent or *ad hoc* commissions, which were also competent in all disputes not submitted to judicial settlement. The Act was updated by the UN General Assembly in 1949, without alteration to the conciliation provisions, and without attracting more ratifications.[91]

The international movement for peaceful settlement reached its highest point that summer of 1928. One month before the conclusion of the General Act, the Kellogg-Briand Peace Pact was signed, the first instrument to declare war illegal as an instrument of national policy.[92] Only wars of self-defence or on behalf of the world community would henceforth be allowed. Sixty-three States ultimately adhered to the treaty, which is arguably still in force. While declaring war in principle illegal was a monumental advance,[93] the weakness of the Pact is that it does not prescribe sanctions. Even if it would have done so, the willingness for concerted enforcement action was often not available at the time, as was demonstrated for instance following the Japanese invasion of Manchuria. Nevertheless in 1933 a large number of American States also concluded the Saavedra Lamas Treaty, which aimed to protect against war also those States that were not party to it, stipulated that territorial conquests would not be recognised, and that in the case of aggression the parties would 'make

---

[88] G. Unger, *Aristide Briand* (2005) 516.

[89] 93 *LNTS* 343. J.L. Brierly, 'The General Act of Geneva, 1928', (1930) *BYIL* 19; C. Tomuschat, 'The 1928 General Act for the Pacific Settlement of Disputes Revisited', in N. Ando and others (eds.), *Liber Amicorum Judge Shigeru Oda* (2002) 977.

[90] The General Act was invoked as granting jurisdiction in the *Nuclear Tests* Cases (*Australia* v. *France*) and (*New Zealand* v. *France*) (*Judgement*), (1974) *ICJ Rep* 253 in which the Court did not come to decide the point, and the *Aegean Sea Continental Shelf* Case (*Greece* v. *Turkey*), (1978) *ICJ Rep* 3 where the Court did not find jurisdiction. Whether the 1928 General Act was still in force was studiously avoided by the ICJ in the *Aerial Incident* Case (*Pakistan* v. *India*), (2000) *ICJ Rep* [26] (but see the negative answer by Judge Oda in his Separate Opinion). J.G. Merrills, 'The International Court of Justice and the General Act of 1928', (1980) 39 *Cambridge Law Journal* 137.

[91] UNGA Res (28 April 1949), (1950) 102 *UNTS* 912.

[92] General Treaty for the Renunciation of War as an Instrument of National Policy (27 August 1928), (1929) 94 *LNTS* 57.

[93] For recent informed and vocal support see G. Unger, *Aristide Briand* (2005) 532 ff.

every effort for the maintenance of peace'.[94] The Saavedra Lamas Treaty also made conciliation compulsory for all kinds of disputes.[95]

1.8 The Lauterpacht opposition

Despite the enthusiasm of many, one man dared to give strong opposition to conciliation. In his *The Function of Law in the International Community* of 1933, Hersch Lauterpacht agitated against the support given by many lawyers and politicians for the method. He held that the attention for conciliation undermined the potential for binding legal settlement through arbitration and the PCIJ:

> 'There is no occasion for self-congratulation because States have agreed to meet before a body of conciliators authorized to propose recommendations which Governments are not bound to accept. The practical result of conciliation and of other "alternative means" is not to substitute one mode of peaceful settlement for another of equal force and value. The effect is to substitute a series of *attempts at* settlement for a settlement proper.'[96]

Lauterpacht considered that conciliation may have become an 'obstacle to progress' by reducing the rule of law to one of various options of settlement,[97] and 'through the elimination of the recourse to rigid law' to spread 'the allaying oil of sweet reasonableness over the waves of the controversy'[98] while at the same time allowing States to appear to be committed to genuine peaceful settlement of disputes: 'Thus, under the cloak of a mere difference in procedure a check is being put on the reign of law between nations.'[99]

The major purpose of his influential book was to disprove the significance then attached to the notion of 'political' disputes, and to demonstrate that no dispute need be above the law. Lauterpacht's criticism of conciliation should be seen in this light: he perceived the propagation of conciliation as a means to perpetuate the pernicious notion of a separate category of inherently non-justiciable disputes. In his criticism, Lauterpacht concentrated on the propagation of conciliation as a means to prevent war; a means to deal with highly charged

94 Inter-American Anti-War Treaty of Non-Aggression and Conciliation (Saavedra Lamas Treaty) (10 October 1933), 163 *LNTS* 393 Art. 3.

95 Saavedra Lamas Treaty Art. 4.

96 H. Lauterpacht, *The Function of Law in the International Community* (1933) 267.

97 Ibid.

98 Ibid., 261.

99 Ibid., 436.

disputes, those traditionally involving the 'honour' or 'vital interests' of States, i.e., the 'non-justiciable' or 'political' conflicts.[100]

Lauterpacht pointed out that despite the fact that conciliation had not had much success in preventing war, it continued to be included in many international instruments with just that rationale. As the method did not serve its original purpose, Lauterpacht held, continuing its adoption was either inaccurate or dishonest. He did not deny that conciliation could be useful in some minor instances, but this admission was marginal: it would be 'to err on the side of optimism' to assume that conciliation could effectively deal with matters of, for instance, migration or territory.[101] The following sections review what the practice of conciliation has been. At the end of this first part of the chapter, Lauterpacht's criticism is revisited.

1.9 Conciliation commissions until 1940

Compared to the number of conciliation treaties that were concluded at the time, the number of conciliation commissions that actually met in the inter-war years is small.[102] Assessment is troubled by the possibility that cases have been kept confidential. It is known that a German-Soviet conciliation commission met several times in the late 1920s and early 1930s, but its proceedings are unknown.[103] Notably, in 1929 Bolivia and Paraguay employed an *ad hoc* conciliation commission to settle the dispute of the *Chaco* border incident, but did so without reference to the treaties they had earlier concluded for such cases.[104] The commission saw temporary success in advising on how to avoid resumption of hostilities. It eased tensions, brought the parties back to the *status quo ante* and led them to re-establish diplomatic links. In 1931 a German-Lithuanian commission, set-up under a pre-existing treaty,[105] dealt with a dispute involving the expulsion of Germans from Memel and the interpretation of a trade

---

[100] See chapter I 1.2 and 1.3.

[101] H. Lauterpacht, *The Function of Law in the International Community* (1933) 264.

[102] Cf., M.O. Hudson, *International Tribunals: Past and Future* (1944) 229; H. Wehberg, 'Die Vergleichskommissionen im modernen Völkerrecht', (1958) 19 *ZfAÖRV* 551, 567 ff.

[103] H. Wehberg, 'Die Vergleichskommissionen im modernen Völkerrecht', (1958) 19 *ZfAÖRV* 551, 567.

[104] G.H. Hackworth, *Digest of International Law* Vol. VI (1943) 41-51; *Proceedings of the Commission of Inquiry and Conciliation, Bolivia and Paraguay, March 13, 1929 –September 13, 1929* (1929); L. Woolsey, 'Bolivia – Paraguay Dispute', 23 (1929) *AJIL* 110 and (1930) 24 *AJIL* 122; H. Arbo, 'Le conflit entra la Bolivie et le Paraguay à propos du Chaco boréal', (1929) 36 *RGDIP* 528.

[105] Treaty of Conciliation, Arbitration and Compulsory Adjudication (Germany-Lithuania) (29 January 1928), M. Habicht, *Post-War Treaties for the Pacific Settlement of Intenational Disputes* (1931) 670.

agreement.[106] Acting in a legal manner, the conciliation was successful. Under an existing agreement with Portugal,[107] France unilaterally instituted proceedings regarding a bilateral trade dispute before a conciliation commission, but the parties reached a settlement before the first meeting of the commission.[108] Applying a treaty existing between them,[109] Belgium and Luxembourg successfully settled a dispute regarding the smuggling of alcohol and their treaty of economic union.[110] The commission, whose report was the basis of the settlement, was presided over by Max Huber. Another commission was seized by Denmark and Lithuania in 1937 regarding Lithuanian payment for railway construction.[111] The commission's law-based settlement proposal could not bring the parties to an agreement.[112] The parties did, however, reach a settlement later.[113] In the same year, the Dominican Republic and Haiti created a conciliation commission, deviating to some extent from the applicable 1929 Treaty of Washington. With the assistance of the commission they were able to solve a crisis that had erupted over frontier incidents.[114]

A special place is reserved for the *Wal-Wal* dispute between Italy and Abyssinia.[115] A frontier incident in Abyssinia involving troops from Italian Somaliland was quickly referred, by the Abyssinians, to a commission as provided for in a pre-existing bilateral treaty.[116] The terms of reference of the commission were not clear on whether it was to be a conciliation commission or an arbitration tribunal.[117] The Italians, under Mussolini, used this opportu-

---

[106] *Cot* 91; H. Wehberg, 'Die Vergleichskommissionen im modernen Völkerrecht', (1958) 19 *ZfAÖRV* 551, 568; D. Schindler, *Die Schiedsgerichtbarkeit seit 1914* (1938) 25.

[107] Treaty of Conciliation, Arbitration and Compulsory Adjudication (France-Portugal) (7 July 1928); *Habicht* 793.

[108] H. Wehberg, 'Die Vergleichskommissionen im modernen Völkerrecht', (1958) 19 *ZfAÖRV* 551, 570-572.

[109] Treaty of Conciliation, Arbitration and Compulsory Adjudication (Belgium-Luxembourg) (17 October 1927); *Habicht* 628.

[110] H. Wehberg, 'Die Vergleichskommissionen im modernen Völkerrecht', (1958) 19 *ZfAÖRV* 551, 568-570; D. Schindler, *Die Schiedsgerichtbarkeit seit 1914* (1938) 25.

[111] Under the Treaty of Conciliation, Arbitration and Compulsory Adjudication (Denmark-Lithuania) (11 December 1926), 67 *LNTS* 335.

[112] *Cot* 92; cf., P. Hamilton and others (eds.), *Permanent Court of Arbitration International Arbitration and Dispute Resolution* (1999) 287; 'Report du Conseil Administratif de la Cour permanente d'Arbitrage' 1938-7/8; idem, 1939-6/7; J.P.A. François, 'La Cour Permanente d'Arbitrage', (1955) 87 *Recueil des Cours* Vol. I 535 ff.

[113] *Cot* 92.

[114] *Cot* 90; (1929) 23 *AJIL* Off Doc 76; P.J.I.M. de Waart, *The Element of Negotiation in the Pacific Settlement of Disputes between States* (1973) 371.

[115] P.B. Potter, 'The Wal Wal Arbitration', (1936) 30 *AJIL* 27; Q. Wright, 'The Test of Aggression in the Italo-Ethiopian War', (1936) 30 *AJIL* 45; P.B. Potter, *The Wal Wal Arbitration* (1938).

[116] Treaty of Conciliation and Arbitration (Italy-Abyssinia) (2 August 1928); *Habicht* 805.

[117] Italy-Abyssinia Treaty Art. 5.

nity to successfully frustrate the commission's work, and to obscure the imminence of Italy's attack. Despite involvement of the League of Nations, Italy invaded Abyssinia.

1.10 Diplomatic settlement in international organisations since 1945

Even though in the 1930s the conclusion of dispute settlement agreements continued in significant numbers, the international movement for peaceful settlement gradually lost momentum. Multinational diplomacy was discredited by the failure of the League to deal with the Japanese invasion of Manchuria, the Italian invasion of Abyssinia, and the Spanish Civil War. The acceptance by Britain and France of Nazi claims on Czechoslovakia at Munich in 1938 ended the hope for international security based on law and diplomacy in the existing constellation. The outbreak of WWII in 1939 removed the constellation itself.

As in the previous World War, plans emerged for a new international organisation. The United Nations was established in 1945. The use of force in international relations was prohibited.[118] A powerful Security Council, with Great Power veto rights, was attributed primary responsibility for peace and security. A General Assembly representing all member States received comprehensive political competence, with secondary responsibilities in the field of peace and security. For judicial settlement, the PCIJ was reconstituted as the International Court of Justice. The United Nations invigorated the position of the Secretary-General of the Organisation. In law and in practice, the head of the Secretariat obtained significant responsibilities, and would gradually become closely involved in international mediation.[119]

The UN became an important forum for diplomacy and the development of international law, but was hindered almost from the start by the political divisions of the Cold War. In 1949 the General Assembly favoured the return to the relatively successful League practice of settling disputes with the help of an individual. This implied that the rapporteur would take the lead in Council

---

[118] UN Charter Art. 2(4). See chapter I 2.7.

[119] United Nations *Handbook on the Peaceful Settlement of Disputes between States* (1992) 130; K. Skjelsbaek and G. Fermann, 'The UN Secretary-General and the Mediation of International Disputes', in J. Bercovitch, *Resolving International Conflict* (1996); C.S.R. Murthy, 'The Role of the UN Secretary-General since the End of the Cold War', (1995) 35 *IJIL* 181; H. Caminos and R. Lavalle, 'New Departures in the Exercise of Inherent Powers by the UN and OAS Secretaries General: The Central American Situation', (1989) 83 *AJIL* 395; V. Pechota, 'The Quiet Approach: A Study of the Good Offices Exercised by the United Nations Secretary-General in the Cause of Peace', in K. Venkata Raman (ed.), *Dispute Settlement through the United Nations* (1977) 577.

meetings as well as in the direct negotiations. The Cold War situation did however not allow for such delegation of political control. It was only in the second half of the 1950s that, as an alternative, Secretary-General Hammerskjöld made his office into that of the permanent rapporteur, which now lends the post much of its public prestige.[120]

The organisation sometimes attempted to break through deadlocks by means of direct mediation under Security Council supervision. For instance, after the creation of Israel in 1947/1948, a UN mediator, Count Bernadotte, was appointed to work towards an Arab-Jewish agreement. Upon the assassination of the Count, the General Assembly established the Conciliation Commission for Palestine, which was to deal with various aspects of the Arab-Jewish dispute in that region.[121] The commission was to consist of several States appointed by the Great Powers.[122] Its terms of reference comprised mediation, advisory and executive functions, in particular organising repatriation and providing assistance to the refugees. The commission was to report to the General Assembly, which provided the commission with instructions. The commission, which continues to exist, is therefore not a conciliation commission in the normal sense of the word.[123] The complications inherent in the constitution of the commission were greatly increased by the intransigence of the parties. The commission's mediation functions have been superseded by various *ad hoc* initiatives.

There were other occasions when the United Nations created 'conciliation commissions' which in fact were intended as mediation bodies. These were equally were unsuccessful. In 1960, in response to the instant collapse of the newly independent former Belgian Congo, the General Assembly requested the Advisory Committee on the Congo to appoint the Conciliation Commission for the Congo, in consultation with the Secretary-General.[124] The com-

---

[120] B. Urquhart, *Hammarskjold* (1974). The possibility of appointing the Secretary-General as rapporteur for a specific question was recalled in the 'Declaration on the Prevention and Removal of Disputes and Situations which may Threaten International Peace and Security and on the Role of the United Nations in this Field', UNGA Res 43/51 (1988) Annex Art. 8.

[121] UNGA Res 194 (III) (11 December 1948); United Nations *Yearbook 1948-1949* (1950) 18, 197-199, 203-207; J.C. Hurewitz, 'The United Nations Conciliation Commission for Palestine: Establishment and Definition of Functions', (1953) 7 *International Organization* 482; 'Security Council' (1965), 19 *International Organization* 331-353, 335 ff; F.S. Hamzeh, *International Conciliation with Special Reference to the Work of the United Nations Conciliation Commission for Palestine* (1963); F.S. Hamzeh, *United Nations Commission for Palestine 1949-1967* (1968); D.P. Forsythe, *United Nations Peacemaking – The Conciliation Commission for Palestine* (1972).

[122] The parties to the dispute were not themselves consulted. The individual members of the Commission receive their instructions from their respective governments. F.S. Hamzeh, *United Nations Commission for Palestine 1949-1967* (1968) 31.

[123] See chapter I 3.1.

[124] UNGA Res 1474 (ES-IV), 20 September 1960; United Nations *Handbook on the Peaceful Settlement of Disputes between States* (1992) 48; U Thant, *View from the UN* (1978) 125-128; G. Abi-Saab, *The United Nations Operation in the Congo 1960–1964* (1978) 83.

mission, composed of representatives of fifteen African and Asian States, was unable to mediate due to the reluctance of the parties, and some States even withdrew from the commission because of disagreement with the UN. The commission could only report on ongoing events.[125] The conflict became entangled in the Cold War, escalated rapidly, and the parties were intransigent or could not be relied upon. There was little opportunity to test whether the set-up and mandate of the commission itself were at all suitable. In 1961 a second Conciliation Commission for Congo was created, this time composed of seven members appointed by the President of the General Assembly.[126] As the Congolese government ignored the commission, it was unable to perform its functions.[127]

1.11 Conciliation since 1945

The proliferation of international institutions and means of communication after WWII gave governments improved possibilities to settle disputes by negotiation. This did not, however, limit the use of conciliation, which resurfaced with some success. In 1946 France and Siam established an *ad hoc* conciliation commission composed of diplomats to make a recommendation regarding Siamese demands for frontier rectification. The essentially political suggestions made by the commission were at first rejected by Siam, but accepted later when the government changed.[128] In the *Vitianu* Case in 1949, Switzerland unilaterally applied for conciliation under an existing treaty with Romania, to deal with a dispute regarding alleged espionage by Mr. Vitianu. Romania refused to participate in the work of the commission.[129] In the *Gorm and Svava* Case of 1952 discussed earlier,[130] Belgium and Denmark conciliated a dispute of legal responsibility over two Danish ships lost during the German invasion in 1940.[131] The commission presented the parties with its conclusions and recom-

[125] UNGA Doc A/4711 (1960).

[126] UNGA Res 1600 (XV), 15 April 1961.

[127] United Nations *Handbook on the Peaceful Settlement of Disputes between States* (1992) 48; U Thant, *View from the UN* (1978) 5 ff, 129.

[128] S. Bastid, 'La commission de conciliation franco-siamoise', in C. Rousseau (ed.), *La Technique et les Principes du Droit Public: Etudes en l'Honneur de Georges Scelle* (1950) 1.

[129] R. Probst, 'Die Schweiz und die internationale Schiedsgerischtbarkeit', (1960) 17 *Schweizerisches Jahrbuch für internationales Recht* 99, 131-132; P. Guggenheim, 'Völkerrecht', (1950) *Schweizerisches Jahrbuch für internationales Recht* 123, 146.

[130] See chapter I 4.1.

[131] H. Rolin, 'Une conciliation belgo-danoise', (1953) 57 *RGDIP* 353; N.V. Boeg, 'Le différend dano-belge au sujet des navires danois 'Gorm' et 'Svava'', (1953) 23 *Acta Scandinavica Juris Gentium* 48; F.M. van Asbeck, 'La tâche et l'action d'une commission de conciliation', (1955) *NTIR* 3 and 208-219.

mendations, but did not give detailed legal reasoning. In the *Japanese 4% Loan* Case and the *Tokyo 5% Loan* Case, two disputes between French investors and Japanese governmental borrowers were also settled through a form of conciliation, by of the proposals of respectively the President of the World Bank and an expert acting on behalf of the President of the IMF.[132]

In 1955 Switzerland and France attempted conciliation to settle two disputes at once: one arising out of the costs of internment in Switzerland during the war of Polish divisions previously fighting for France, and one regarding alleged illegal activities of France in Switzerland. The commission, established under the existing treaty,[133] investigated both disputes and based its recommendations on legal considerations. The first matter was settled amicably. The second issue was abandoned for lack of evidence.[134] In 1956 Switzerland also conciliated a dispute over certain tax exemptions for Swiss nationals in Italy. The commission considered the case on a legal basis, but did not share its legal reasoning with the parties. It acted in this manner in an effort to avoid intransigence, believing that the losing party would not budge if it could reasonably disagree with the reasoning. The parties subsequently arrived at a mutually acceptable solution.[135]

In the same year, in the *Roula* Case Greece and Italy applied an existing treaty[136] and conciliated a dispute regarding compensation for destruction by Italy of a neutral Greek ship during WWII.[137] The commission applied principles of equity and the parties accepted the recommendations. In 1957, in the *F.OABV* Case, France and Morocco agreed to submit to an *ad hoc* conciliation commission their dispute over the French interception of an aeroplane carrying the Algerian rebel leader Ben Bella, immediately after his audience with the Moroccan King. External pressure and disagreement within the commission prevented the conciliators from doing their work.[138]

---

[132] The *Japanese 4% Loan* Case, (1955) 29 *ILR* 5 was settled in 1955, the *Tokyo 5% Loan* Case followed in 1960, (1966) 29 *ILR* 11; *Cot* 96.

[133] Treaty of Conciliation, Arbitration and Compulsory Adjudication (France-Switzerland) (6 April 1925); M. Habicht, *Post-War Treaties for the Pacific Settlement of International Disputes* (1931) 226.

[134] S. Bastid, 'La commission de conciliation franco-suisse', (1956) 2 *AFDI* 436; P. Guggenheim, 'Droit international public', (1954) 11 *Schweizerisches Jahrbuch für Internationales Recht* 173, 201.

[135] M. Breton-Jokl, 'La commission permanente de conciliation italo-suisse', (1957) 3 *AFDI* 210; (1958) 25 *ILR* Vol. I 313.

[136] Treaty of Conciliation, Arbitration and Compulsory Adjudication (Greece-Italy) (23 September 1928); *Habicht* 825.

[137] P. Hamilton and others (eds.), *The Permanent Court of Arbitration: International Arbitration and Dispute Resolution* (1999) 291-293; J.P.A. François, 'Le Palais de la Paix en 1956', (1957) 4 *NTIR* 69.

[138] C. Rousseau, 'Echec de la procedure d'enquête et de conciliation dans l'affaire du deroutement de l'avion transportant de Rabat a Tunis les chefs nationalistes algériens le 22 octobre 1956', (1958) 62 *RGDIP* 691; 'l'Affaire du F. OABV', (1958) 4 *AFDI* 282.

Meanwhile, new bilateral and multilateral peaceful settlement treaties were being concluded.[139] In 1948 the American States devised the Pact of Bogotá, a comprehensive dispute settlement treaty, replacing various older treaties, and laying the foundations of the Organisation of American States.[140] In 1957 the Council of Europe attempted to co-ordinate the European bilateral efforts with the European Convention on the Peaceful Settlement of Disputes, a broad instrument that has not had its desired impact.[141] In 1961, after several years of preparation and consultation with various experts, rapporteur Rolin submitted an extensive report on conciliation to the Institut de Droit International.[142] The practical experiences with conciliation in the 1950s had resulted in the widespread perception of the method as akin to non-binding arbitration. The appointment of jurists as conciliators, the cases submitted to them, and the expectations of the parties had all contributed to this development. The discussions of the Institute therefore revolved around a legal conception of conciliation, which is reflected in the model conciliation procedure the Institute adopted.[143]

In the 1960s Switzerland launched a new initiative to conclude bilateral treaties. The model treaty it produced was in many ways similar to the 1957 European Convention, but did away with the old-fashioned distinction between political and legal disputes, and ensured establishment of a commission also when one of the parties does not co-operate.[144] In the Swiss model, compulsory conciliation should precede settlement by binding procedures. A number of new treaties resulted, including one with the United Kingdom.[145] The momentum had gone, however. In the 1960s and 1970s very few disputes are known to have been submitted to conciliation.[146]

---

[139] United Nations *A Survey of Treaty Provisions for the Pacific Settlement of International Disputes 1949-1962*.

[140] American Treaty on Pacific Settlement (Pact of Bogotá) (20 April 1948), 449 *UNTS* 30: E. Turlington, 'The Pact of Bogotá', (1948) 42 *AJIL* 608; C.G. Fenwick, 'Revision of the Pact of Bogotá', (1954) 48 *AJIL* 123.

[141] (29 April 1957), 320 *UNTS* 243; H. Miehsler, 'The European Convention for the Peaceful Settlement of Disputes', in H. Kipp and others (eds.), *Um Recht und Freiheit* (1977).

[142] 48 *Annuaire de l'Institut de Droit International* (1959) Vol. I 5. See chapter III 3.

[143] 49 *Annuaire de l'Institut de Droit International* (1961) Vol. II 193, 374 (French) 385 (English). In 1968, the International Law Association (ILA) also discussed conciliation, on a report by Louis Sohn: ILA *Report of the Fifty-Third Conference* (1968) 15, 34.

[144] The model treaty is incorporated in a report on the conciliation policy of the Swiss government: Schweizerische Bundesrat *'Botschaft'*, (1966) 26 *ZfAÖRV* 723, 732; F. Münch, 'Die Schweizerische Initiative zu Zweiseitigen Abmachungen über die Friedliche Beilegung von Streitigkeiten', (1966) 26 *ZfAÖRV* 705.

[145] The treaty with the UK differs in some respects from the Swiss model: Schweizerische Bundesrat *'Botschaft'*, (1966) 26 *ZfAÖRV* 723, 740-742.

[146] While it may be disputed whether the unsuccessful effort by US Ambassador Webster in the dispute between the United Kingdom and Guatemala over Belize may be qualified as concili-

As discussed earlier,[147] Victor Umbricht succeeded in allocating the assets and liabilities of the East African Community that until 1977 united Kenya, Tanzania and Uganda.[148] Papal mediation from 1978 to 1985 arguably prevented a war between Chile and Argentina over a disputed arbitral award over delimitation in the Beagle Channel.[149] The dispute was concluded with the adoption of a new conciliation treaty.[150] In 1980, as discussed further below,[151] Iceland and Norway agreed to constitute a bilateral conciliation commission. Expert conciliators were able to settle the maritime delimitation between Iceland and the Norwegian island of Jan Mayen. Their skilful combination of legal and political considerations opened new perspectives for conciliation. In the *Taba* Case of 1986, an arbitral tribunal, dealing with delimitation of the border of Egypt and Israel in the Sinai, simultaneously and unsuccessfully attempted conciliation; the arbitration concluded the matter instead. On the whole, therefore, until the 1960s conciliation had continued its pre-WWII record of application. After 1960, however, conciliation commissions became rare, and were all created *ad hoc*. The creation of new conciliation provisions and mechanisms, however, continued apace.

1.12 Later multilateral treaties and conciliation

The apparent demise of comprehensive non-binding bilateral settlement agreements was counterbalanced by an increase of conciliation commitments in the many multilateral agreements concluded in that same period.[152] The socialist States and many newly independent States did not favour binding settlement of disputes, in part because of their concern over a supposed Western bias of the international legal system, in part as a consequence of their own cultural and economic preferences. The drafting of the dispute settlement mechanism of the

ation; he acted alone and was styled a 'mediator', but after investigating the dispute proposed a draft treaty to settle the dispute: K.R. Simmonds, 'The Belize Mediation', (1968) 17 *ICLQ* 997.

147 See chapter I 4.3.

148 V. Umbricht, *Multilateral Mediation: Practical Experiences and Lessons* (1989).

149 The original award (2 May 1977), (1978) 17 *ILM* 634. Documents of the mediation: (1985) 24 *ILM* 1; E. Lauterpacht, 'Whatever Happened to the Beagle Channel Award?', in *Le Droit International au Service de la Paix, de la Justice et du Développement* (1991) 359.

150 Treaty of Peace and Friendship (Argentina-Chile) (28 November 1984}, (1985) 24 *ILM* 11 Annex 1.

151 See chapter III 3.4.1.

152 E.g., Protocol of Buenos Aires (27 February 1967), 721 *UNTS* 324 among other things elaborated the powers of the Permanent Council to address disputes that came to its attention (see the current ch XII of the OAS Charter): F. Galo Leoro, 'Peaceful Settlement of Disputes – an overview', (1994) Inter-American Juridical Committee Doc 34/94 (on file with author).

1969 Vienna Convention on the Law of Treaties is a case in point.[153] Most Western States favoured the continuation of the trend towards compulsory binding settlement, while the majority of African, Asian and communist States was successful in substituting the draft arbitration provisions with a legally oriented but non-binding form of conciliation.[154]

In other cases, references to mediation and conciliation were seemingly included as a matter of course, without much attention to particular procedures that should be followed.[155] This was not the case with the conclusion of the 1982 Convention on the Law of the Sea, which provides a detailed and much debated compulsory conciliation procedure, inserted for those types of cases for which there was not a majority of States in favour of arbitration or judicial settlement.[156] As in most multilateral treaties, conciliation is also mentioned as an optional method before other methods of settlement are attempted. This Convention later had significant influence on the conclusion of subsequent multilateral agreements.[157]

At the United Nations, where many multilateral agreements originated, it became standard practice for each multilateral treaty to contain its own dispute settlement system.[158] Only some of these treaties actually set out a specific mechanism for conciliation, and thereby often copy provisions of preceding multilateral agreements in the same field. This practice results in a fragmented system of dispute settlement, as any dispute is to be referred to its own special

---

[153] I. Sinclair, *The Vienna Convention on the Law of Treaties* (2nd edn. 1984) 226-233; R.D. Kearney and R.E. Dalton, 'The Treaty on Treaties', (1970) 64 *AJIL* 495, 545 ff.

[154] See chapter III 3.2.

[155] E.g., Framework Convention on Tobacco Control (21 May 2003), (2003) 42 *ILM* 520 Art. 27; Agreement for the Establishment of the Indian Ocean Tuna Commission (25 November 1993), 1927 *UNTS* 330 Art. 23; Israel-Palestine Liberation Organisation Interim Agreement on the West Bank and the Gaza Strip (28 September 1995), (1997) 36 *ILM* 551 which refers in Art. 21 to a conciliation procedure to be agreed upon later. The Israel-Jordan Treaty of Peace (26 October 1994), (1995) 34 *ILM* 43 has an unspecified referral to mediation and conciliation. International Treaty on Plant Genetic Resources for Food and Agriculture (3 November 2001) Annex II part 2 (available on <ftp://ftp.fao.org/ag/cgrfa/it/ITPGRe.pdf>) (25 July 2006); Convention on the Prior Informed Consent Procedure for Certain Hazardous Chemicals and Pesticides in International Trade (11 September 1998), (1999) 38 *ILM* 1 Art. 20(4); Protocol to the Convention on Long-Range Transboundary Air Pollution on Further Reduction of Sulphur Emissions (14 June 1994) Art. 9(6), (1994) 33 *ILM* 1540. See further chapter IV 1. In this light it is notable that Energy Charter Treaty Art. 26(3)(a) allows for conciliation or arbitration in State/investor disputes, and that it refers to the rules of ICSID, which provides both, but that it nowhere stipulates that ICSID arbitration may follow ICSID conciliation and further only speaks of arbitral awards.

[156] See chapter IV 1.

[157] E.g., the Protocol to the Convention on the Prevention of Marine Pollution by Dumping of Wastes and Other Matter (7 November 1996), (1997) 36 *ILM* 1.

[158] T. Meron, 'Norm Making and Supervision in International Human Rights: Reflections on Institutional Order', (1982) 76 *AJIL* 754, 754.

conciliation commission.[159] This has so far not developed into a practical problem, as none of the conciliation provisions of multilateral treaties has ever led to actual conciliation proceedings. Should this nevertheless occur, problems can arise regarding the competence of a commission; a dispute may be related to a number of treaties, each with their own conciliation provision.[160] Issues of *res judicata* and *lis pendens* do also come up in new alternative dispute settlement mechanism created since the 1990s, the non-compliance procedure (NCP).[161] Included in multilateral agreements on the environment to promote compliance, NCPs combine elements of various settlement methods, and mobilise pressure to ensure that its results are implemented.

Alternatives to conciliation also emerged in other multilateral agreements. Sometimes treaty bodies were established to facilitate settlement between States, or even between States and individuals.[162] Renewed attention for conciliation came in another form. In 1995 the United Nations adopted the UN Model Rules of Conciliation,[163] and in 1996 the Permanent Court of Arbitration followed with similar rules.[164] Both are discussed in more detail below.[165]

1.13 Commercial State/non-State conciliation

Meanwhile, the development of international law benefited from the success of international commercial dispute settlement through arbitration and other settlement methods. The delays and costs of litigation in the national and international private sector spurred the development of variations on mediation and conciliation, collectively known as Alternative Dispute Resolution (ADR).[166] For dispute settlement in international commerce, parties frequently adopt the

---

159 R.R. Churchill and G. Ulfstein, 'Autonomous Institutional Arrangements in Multilateral Environmental Agreements: A little noticed phenomenon in International Law', (2000) 94 *AJIL* 623, 643 ff.

160 See chapter I 3.4, 3.5, chapter IV 6.5.

161 See chapter IV 6.

162 E.g., the early GATT working parties and the later GATT panels: see chapter IV 4, and the work of the European Commission on Human Rights under Art. 28(1)(b) of the European Convention on Human Rights: see chapter IV 3, and other examples mentioned there.

163 UNGA Res 50/50 (1995) Annex.

164 Permanent Court of Arbitration *Basic Documents* (1998) 153.

165 See chapter II 2.

166 While in private law in the United States it is common to consider arbitration among ADR methods, this is not so in many other countries. In public international law the terminology is rarely used, as, leaving aside arbitration, the methods referred to are suitably named 'diplomatic dispute settlement'. Considering this use, it is preferable to understand ADR in international law as also excluding arbitration. Contrast: F. Orrego Vicuña, *International Dispute Settlement in an Evolving Global Society* (2004) 99-100.

dispute settlement rules provided by either the International Chamber of Commerce (ICC) or the United Nations Commission on International Trade Law (UNCITRAL). The rules emanating from these bodies do not regulate an area of substantive law. They are procedural rules, which parties may choose to include in a contract in case a dispute arises, or which they may adopt once a dispute has arisen.

The International Chamber of Commerce (ICC) concerns itself with business disputes of an international character, but not involving States. The ICC offers an arbitration procedure, widely used by (larger) private parties. The ICC also used to offer a conciliation procedure, which was infrequently applied.[167] In 2001 this procedure was replaced by the ICC ADR Rules,[168] which are elementary and flexible. They provide for the appointment of an independent person, the neutral, either by the parties or by the ICC itself. The parties, in consultation with the neutral, may agree on the dispute settlement method to be used. In the absence of an agreement, the dispute shall be mediated.[169] Jurisdiction is granted by a clause in the parties' contract, by a special agreement or by acquiescence.

The United Nations Commission on International Trade Law developed the UNCITRAL Conciliation Rules in 1980.[170] In 2002 UNCITRAL also adopted a Model Law on International Commercial Conciliation, to be used as a model for States creating their own conciliation legislation.[171] Without stating it expressly, the UNCITRAL Conciliation Rules are meant for private international

---

167 ICC Rules of Conciliation and Arbitration (1 January 1988), (1989) 28 *ILM* 231. E.A. Schwartz, 'The Resolution of International Commercial Disputes under the Auspices of the ICC International Court of Arbitration', (1995) 18 *Hastings International and Comparative Law* 719; L.C. Reif, 'Conciliation as a Mechanism for the Resolution of International Economic and Business Disputes', (1990-1991) 14 *Fordham International Law Journal* 578, 612 ff; Report of the Secretary-General (1999) 'United Nations Decade of International Law', (2000) 39 *ILM* 966; for the history of ICC conciliation going back to 1921: S. Hamilton, 'ICC Conciliation: A Glimpse into History', ICC International Court of Arbitration Bulletin Special Supplement (2001) 23.

168 On <http://www.iccwbo.org/court/english/rules/rules.asp> (5 October 2007). 'The New ICC ADR Rules', (2001) 12 *World Arbitration and Mediation Report* 301.

169 ICC ADR Rules Art. 5.

170 UNGA Res 35/52 (1980); I.I. Dore, *Arbitration and Conciliation under the UNCITRAL Rules: A Textual Analysis* (1986); G. Hermann, 'Commentary on the UNCITRAL Conciliation Rules', (1981) 6 *Yearbook of Commercial Arbitration* 170; P. Sanders, *Quo Vadis Arbitration* (1999) 359-372, 378-393, 407-413.

171 On <http://www.uncitral.org/uncitral/en/uncitral_texts.html> (5 October 2007); UN Doc A/57/18 (2002); J.M. Jacquet, 'La loi-type de la CNUDCI du 24 Juin 2002 sur la conciliation commerciale internationale', (2004) *Revue de l'Arbitrage* 1; P. Sanders, *The Work of UNCITRAL on Arbitration and Conciliation* (2004) 199; L. Miguel Diaz and N.A. Oretskin, 'The US Uniform Mediation Act and the Draft UNCITRAL Model Law on International Commercial Conciliation', (2002) 670 *Practising Law Institute / Litigation and Administrative Practice Course Handbook Series* 791.

business disputes, similar to the ICC ADR Rules. Unlike the latter, however, the UNCITRAL Conciliation Rules are not linked to an institutional framework. This means among other things that the parties will themselves have to set-up a commission, and make *ad hoc* arrangements for administrative services. On the other hand, the UNCITRAL Conciliation Rules are more elaborate than the ICC ADR Rules, while not as comprehensive as the ICSID framework for conciliation. Like the ICC ADR Rules, they allow the parties to modify any provisions as they see fit.[172] Due to the confidential nature of UNCITRAL conciliation, there is no certainty regarding the practice of UNCITRAL conciliation. Inspired by the UNCITRAL Conciliation Rules, in 1996 the Permanent Court of Arbitration adopted the PCA Conciliation Rules, as well as, in 2002, the PCA Optional Rules for Conciliation of Disputes Relating to Natural Resources and/or the Environment (PCA Environmental Rules).[173]

1.13.1 *ICSID*

The increased internationalisation of trade, and the failure of attempts at a multilateral investment treaty,[174] resulted in thousands of bilateral investment treaties concluded between a great number of States; thousands of such treaties contain a reference to arbitration and conciliation of disputes through the International Centre for the Settlement of Investment Disputes (ICSID).[175] ICSID is an international body originating in the International Bank for Reconstruction and Development (IBRD or World Bank). In order to facilitate the resolution of investment disputes, and thereby to increase the flow of capital by providing for confidence and security.[176] ICSID provides procedural rules and administrative assistance for the resolution of conflicts between a State party

---

[172] UNCITRAL Conciliation Rules Art. 1 s 2. ICC ADR Rules Art. 1 allows such modification, but subject to the approval of the ICC itself.

[173] <http://www.pca-cpa.org/upload/files/ENV%20CONC.pdf> (5 October 2007); see chapter II 2.

[174] N.J. Schrijver, 'De treurige lotgevallen van de pogingen tot opstelling van een multilateraal investeringsverdrag', (2001) 49 *SEW-Tijdschrift voor Europees en Economisch Recht* 7.

[175] D. Bodansky, J.R. Cook and E. Brown Weiss, 'Invoking State Responsibility in the Twenty-First Century', (2002) 96 *AJIL* 798, 813; S.M.G. Koopmans, 'De onbekende en genereuze bescherming van Nederlandse investeringen in het buitenland', (2006) 81 *Nederlands Juristenblad* 74.

[176] Convention on the Settlement of Investment Disputes between States and the Nationals of Other States (18 March 1965) (ICSID Convention), (1965) 4 *ILM* 524. C.H. Schreuer, *The ICSID Convention: A Commentary* (2001); A. Broches, 'The Convention on the Settlement of Investments Between States and the Nationals of Other States', (1972) 136 *Recueil des Cours* 330; M. Hirsh, *The Arbitration Mechanism of the International Centre for the Settlement of Disputes* (1993).

and an investor from another State party,[177] ICSID may also be called upon to appoint a conciliator or arbitrator in instances where the parties cannot agree to a joint appointment of a conciliator or arbitrator, or where the parties have conferred appointing power to ICSID.[178] ICSID provides the most formal and detailed of international conciliation provisions: in addition to the regulations in the ICSID Convention, there are the more detailed ICSID Conciliation Rules and the Institutional Rules,[179] which describe in detail the procedure for conciliation as well as arbitration. The conciliation rules indeed resemble the arbitration rules in many respects; their lengthy nature is caused largely by the detail on procedural issues such as the appointment and replacement of conciliators, the conduct of the hearing and the formalities of closing the proceedings. They give the overall impression that ICSID conciliation can be a lengthy and complicated undertaking. It can be argued that this appearance may have contributed to the limited use made of the rules.[180]

Despite a rapidly growing number of cases submitted to ICSID arbitration, only two disputes are known to have been settled through conciliation,[181] of only of one of those, *Tesoro/Trinidad and Tobago*, some details have entered

---

[177] In addition, ICSID in 1978 established the Additional Facility, operating outside the framework of the Convention, having its own 'Conciliation (Additional Facility) Rules' (11 June 1979), (1982) 21 *ILM* 1443. The Centre is permitted to assist in the settlement of disputes in which either the State or the investor's State is not party to the Convention or when the dispute is not directly related to investment, provided it is not an 'ordinary commercial' one.

[178] ICSID Convention Arts. 1(2) and 6. U. Onwuamaegbu, 'The Role of ADR in Investor-State Dispute Settlement: The ICSID Experience', (2005) 22 *News from ICSID* (2) 12; M. Hirsch, *The Arbitration Mechanism of the International Centre for the Settlement of Investment Disputes* (1993).

[179] 'Rules of Procedure for Conciliation Proceedings' (ICSID Conciliation Rules) and Rules of Procedure for the Institution of Conciliation and Arbitration Proceedings (ICSID Institution Rules) on <http://www.worldbank.org/icsid/basicdoc/basic-en.htm> (5 October 2007).

[180] As also argued by Ms. Obaida, ICSID senior counsel responsible for the conduct of two ICSID conciliation cases, in a conversation with the author (26 July 2006), though ICSID conciliator Mr. Hanotiau holds that the detail of the rules do not affect the chances of success (interview with the author, 4 August 2006).

[181] One case *SEDITEX/Madagascar* (CONC/82/1) was halted before the constitution of a commission, but a case between the same parties was conciliated in 1994 CONC/94/01. N.G. Ziadé, 'ICSID Conciliation', (1996) (2) 13 *News from ICSID* 3. *Tesoro Petroleum Co/Trinidad and Tobago* (CONC/83/1) was settled: L. Nurick and S.J. Schnably 'The First ICSID Conciliation', (1986) 1 *ICSID Rev Foreign Investment Law Journal* 340; Remarks by A.R. Parra, 'ICSID and New Trends in International Dispute Settlement', (1993) 87 *ASIL Proc.* 2, 3; L.C. Reif, 'Conciliation as a Mechanism for the Resolution of International Economic and Business Disputes', (1990-1991) 14 *Fordham International Law Journal* 578, 605-607; A. Broches, 'The Experience of the International Centre for the Settlement of Investment Disputes', in S. Rubin and R. Nelson (eds.), *International Investment Disputes: Avoidance and Settlement* (1985) 75; ICSID Annual Report (1986) 8.

the public domain, these are discussed further below.[182] A fourth file was opened in 2003, which did not lead to actual conciliation.[183] In a fifth case, between an investor and Togo, the three member commission issued a report in April of 2006.[184] The report unfortunately remains confidential, but it is known that the conciliation resulted from a conciliation clause in the contract in dispute,[185] that the parties did not reach a settlement, and proceeded to arbitration. A new case was registered in August 2007.[186] Where relevant, references to the ICSID Conciliation Rules are included throughout this work.

1.14 The proliferation of conciliation options through the OSCE

The political changes after 1989 made possible the further development of dispute settlement in the Organisation for Security and Cooperation in Europe (OSCE). In 1991 the OSCE adopted the so-called Valetta Mechanism, which is optional for each member State.[187] Under it, a party can unilaterally request the establishment of a commission, but the party requires co-operation of the other party in the selection of the commission's members. The commission, confusingly entitled 'Mechanism', shall assist the parties in identifying a suitable procedure for the settlement of disputes.[188] The Mechanism may however, on the request of one of the parties, also give substantive advise on the dispute, and thus fulfil the role of a traditional conciliation commission. The provisions allow for major reservations, and are subsidiary to any other settlement mechanism in place between the parties in dispute. Recognising the limited value of the Valetta Mechanism, the member States set out to develop various other procedures. They could not agree to choose option one over the other, and therefore adopted all those proposed. One of these is the OSCE Conciliation Commission.[189] Where the Valetta Mechanism, at least initially, only aims to identify a suitable method of dispute settlement, the OSCE Conciliation

182 See chapter III 2.2.

183 In 2005 a settlement was reached before the commission was constituted in *TG World Petroleum Limited* v. *Republic of Niger* (CONC/03/1); Herbert Smith 'Arbitration Update' (brochure) (January 2004).

184 Togo Electricité/Togo (CONC/05/01). <http://www.worldbank.org/icsid/> (5 October 2007).

185 On the basis of conversations by the author with administrator Ms. Obadia (26 July 2006).

186 Shareholders of SESAM/Central African Republic (CONC/07/1).

187 Valetta Provisions for a CSCE Procedure for Peaceful Settlement of Disputes of 8 February 1991, (1991) 30 *ILM* 390 as modified in Annex 1 of the Decision on Peaceful Settlement (15 December 1992), (1993) 32 *ILM* 556. K. Oellers-Frahm, 'The Mandatory Component in the CSCE Dispute Settlement System', in M.W. Janis (ed.), *International Courts for the Twenty-First Century* (1992), 195.

188 Valetta Provisions Art. 8.

189 Decision on Peaceful Settlement of Disputes Annex 3.

Commission is a means of settlement itself. The OSCE Commission is constituted by the parties from the list of names drawn-up under the Valetta provisions. The OSCE Commission is however unlikely ever to be used, considering the other settlement means adopted at the same time, in particular the OSCE Court of Conciliation and Arbitration discussed below.

Another innovation introduced in 1992 is the provision for 'directed conciliation', which applies to all States members.[190] When applying these rules, the Ministerial Council or the Senior Council of the OSCE, by 'consensus minus two' instructs two parties in dispute to submit their controversy to a conciliation procedure, even if neither party has given its consent. This procedure builds on an analogy with the right of the UN Security Council to call upon the parties to settle their disputes by the means enumerated in Article 33(1) of the Charter.[191] The practical importance is however limited, as directed conciliation is subsidiary to any other settlement method the parties may have agreed to. Furthermore, either party may veto the application of the rules for directed conciliation if it considers that the dispute is related to territory or defence.[192] Lastly, no sanctions are available if the directive is not followed.

More impact can be made by the 1992 OSCE Convention on Conciliation and Arbitration within the OSCE (OSCE Convention).[193] It provides a comprehensive and compulsory mechanism for the settlement of any dispute. Any State in dispute may unilaterally initiate the establishment of a conciliation commission or arbitral tribunal. To this end the Convention established a Court of Conciliation and Arbitration (the OSCE Court).[194] It consists of a list of persons appointed by their state, who may be called upon on an *ad hoc* basis. The conciliation procedure itself prescribes that recommendations are made on the basis of the law and the parties' OSCE commitments. The importance of the OSCE Convention lies in that it provides compulsory jurisdiction for both conciliation and arbitration, and does not allow any reservations other than those expressly authorised.[195] Unlike in directed conciliation, the use of the method cannot be refused on the grounds of for instance national defence or

---

190 Decision on Peaceful Settlement of Disputes Annex 4.

191 Art. 33(2) UN Charter. M. Bothe, 'The Various Dispute Settlement Procedures: General International Law and OSCE Practice', in M. Bothe and others (eds.), *The OSCE in the Maintenance of Peace and Security* (1997) 367, 377.

192 Decision on Peaceful Settlement Annex 4 Art. 5 sub c.

193 Decision on Peaceful Settlement of Disputes Annex 2. H. Steinberger, 'The Conciliation Procedure Established by the Convention on Conciliation and Arbitration within the OSCE', in L. Caflisch (ed.), *The Peaceful Settlement of Disputes between States: Universal and European Perspectives* (1998) 67.

194 OSCE Convention Art. 1 and 10.

195 OSCE Convention Art. 34. For the allowable reservations: Art. 19(4) and 26(2) OSCE Convention.

territorial integrity. All things combined, the Convention could broaden substantially the range of compulsory dispute settlement.

Even though the OSCE Convention makes explicit that it is only subsidiary to other agreed forms of dispute settlement, this is only effective if these agreements expressly stipulate their exclusivity.[196] In addition, though existing mechanisms are to be respected, nothing is stated regarding *future* agreements concerning dispute settlement. To maintain the right to refer disputes to other procedures, the parties are to make a reservation to that effect, as is done in practice.[197] Some States that did not sign-up to the OSCE Court saw the Court as an attempt to limit compulsory adjudication. However, the respect for existing and – through the reservations – future dispute settlement agreements substantially limits the practical constraints, but thereby also limits the added value of the OSCE mechanism. In addition to the fact that some of the most important members are not party to the OSCE Convention, those who are party to it generally are also party to other settlement agreements.[198] In practice none of the OSCE conciliation procedures has so far been used.[199]

1.15 **The Belize/Guatemala differendum**

In the new century, a long-standing territorial dispute between Belize and Guatemala resulted in an important modern instance of conciliation.[200] The two

---

[196] OSCE Convention Art. 19(1)(b). L. Caflisch, 'The OSCE Court of Conciliation and Arbitration: Some Facts and Issues', in M. Bothe and others (eds.), *The OSCE in the Maintenance of Peace and Security* (1997) 381; L. Caflisch, 'La subsidiarité des méchanismes de la Convention de 1992', in L. Caflish (ed.), *The Peaceful Settlement of Disputes between States: Universal and European Perspectives*, 55.

[197] S. Jacobi, 'Subsidiarity and Other Obstacles to the Use of the OSCE Dispute Settlement Procedures', in M. Bothe and others (eds.), *The OSCE in the Maintenance of Peace and Security* (1997) 425, 439.

[198] Ibid., 440-444; K. Oellers-Frahm, 'The Mandatory Component in the CSCE Dispute Settlement System', in M.W. Janis (ed.), *International Courts for the Twenty-First Century* (1992) 195, 202.

[199] Cf., H.B. Reimann, 'Le règlement pacifique des différends à l'OSCE', in M.G. Kohen (ed.), *Promoting Justice, Human Rights and Conflict Resolution through International Law* (2007) 891.

[200] For the history of the dispute: L.R. Scheman and J.W. Ford, 'The Organisation of American States as Mediator', in S. Touval and I.W. Zartman (eds.), *International Mediation in Theory and Practice* (1985) 197, 219. See also the legal opinion on the dispute given on request of Belize by E. Lauterpacht, S.M. Schwebel, S. Rosenne and F. Orrego Vicuña, 'Legal Opinion on Guatemala's Territorial Claim to Belize' (November 2001) available on: <http://www.belize-guatemala.gov.bz/legal-opinion.pdf> (5 October 2007). The history, the commencement of the conciliation and the legal opinion are analysed in J.G. Merrills, 'The Belize-Guatemala Territorial Dispute and the Legal Opinion of January 2002', (2002) 2 *The Global Community* 77.

countries were in dispute since the independence of Belize in 1981. On the basis of interpretation of treaties of the 18th and 19th century, Guatemala maintains a claim to a large part of the territory of Belize.[201] The dispute also concerns contested migration in the border region. Already before Belize's independence the dispute had been subject to diplomatic dispute settlement, when at the request of the United Kingdom and Guatemala, the United States appointed Ambassador Webster to propose a settlement. He however proposed a draft treaty that in effect placed a future independent Belize under tutelage of Guatemala, an option that was unacceptable to the Belizeans and the United Kingdom.[202]

With the active involvement of the OAS, in 2000 the parties agreed each to appoint one independent non-national 'facilitator' to form a commission to deal with the 'differendum', and agreed to the commission's terms of reference. The facilitators were to 'assist the Governments of Belize and Guatemala to find formulae for a peaceful and definitive resolution of the territorial differendum between the two countries.' The facilitators subsequently recommended that:

> 'to this end, the Facilitators taking due account of all relevant factors (e.g. legal, historical, political etc.) will prepare and present proposals to the Parties for a comprehensive, definitive, honourable, and permanent resolution (...).'[203]

The facilitators consulted with the parties 'and all others whose cooperation might facilitate progress'.[204] A facilitator appointed by Honduras was to join their work to the extent the discussions considered maritime areas in the Gulf of Honduras.[205] In 2002 the facilitators presented a comprehensive set of proposals to deal with the international territorial border, maritime delimitation, settlements in the border regions and financial assistance to the parties in the form of a Trust Fund.[206] They also called for the creation of an ecological park, jointly operated with neighbouring Honduras. The proposals were to be put to referenda in both Belize and Guatemala.

---

201 M. Gorina-Ysern, 'OAS Mediates in Belize-Guatemala Border Dispute' (December 2000) ASIL Insights on <http://www.asil.org/insights/insigh59.htm> (5 October 2007).

202 K.R. Simmonds, 'The Belize Mediation', (1968) 17 *ICLQ* 997.

203 Cited in 'Belize-Guatemala Territorial Differendum: Proposals from the Facilitators' (30 August 2002) [II]; <www.belize.gov.bz/features/proposals/belize_guatemala_differendum.html> (20 April 2003).

204 Ibid.

205 J.G. Merrills, 'The Belize-Guatemala Territorial Dispute and the Legal Opinion of January 2002', (2002) 2 *The Global Community* 77, 93.

206 'Belize-Guatemala Territorial Differendum: Proposals from the Facilitators' (30 August 2002).

The proposals avoided any mention of historic entitlement or blame; there was no reference to the application of legal principles to the claims. The proposals regarding the delimitation of the territorial seas, also involving the rights of Honduras, demonstrate how the facilitators attempted to appear to be fully even-handed; they set out explicitly that each party should accept some of the positions of the other sides.[207] The use of an independent panel, investigating the dispute, and proposing a solution in a report to the parties, implies that this was an example of conciliation in all but name. The exercise was carefully conducted in such a way as to allow the parties to relinquish their position while maintaining their insistence on entitlement, just as Max Huber had propagated conciliation in 1919.

The proposals were well received by the OAS, and became the basis of discussions between the parties. However, Guatemala did not accept them, and the proposed referenda are not yet held. Nevertheless, on the basis of the proposals, through further OAS mediation, the parties in 2003 agreed to far-reaching 'confidence building measures', including rules against inflammatory public statement, a permanent OAS presence in the border region, and a special regime for settlers.[208] In 2005 the parties concluded a more elaborate Agreement on a Framework for Negotiations and Confidence Building Measures Between Belize and Guatemala,[209] which provides for continuing negotiations with the assistance of the OAS. It also provides that the OAS Secretary-General may recommend that elements of the differendum be submitted to international adjudication. The parties agreed to put such recommendations to their national authorities.

In conclusion, while the dispute is not yet resolved, it presently appears that the conciliation exercise has successfully put both sides on a path to peaceful settlement. The details in the latest Agreement suggest a narrowing of the contentious issues. The confidence building measures on OAS assistance, on dealing with settlers in contested border areas, and on protecting human rights, demonstrate the positive contribution made by various forms of non-binding third party settlement.

---

[207] Ibid., pt B [4].

[208] Agreement to Establish a Transition Process and Confidence Building Measures Between Belize and Guatemala (7 February 2003) on <www.oas.org/OASpage/press_release.asp?sCodigo=E-168/03> (18 January 2004).

[209] Agreement on a Framework for Negotiations and Confidence Building Measures Between Belize and Guatemala (7 September 2005) on <http://www.oas.org/documents/Belice_Guatemala/English_200dpi.pdf> (5 October 2007).

1.16 Lauterpacht revisited: a measure of success

Nowadays, Lauterpacht's dismissal of a category of inherently non-justiciable disputes is commonly shared. Any dispute that involves competing legal claims is a legal dispute, and no dispute is non-justiciable because of its political nature; no legal dispute is beyond the reach of the law. Any drive to initiate conciliation on such basis is therefore unfounded. In this respect, Lauterpacht's criticism has held good. His broad dismissal of conciliation must however be given more nuances, based essentially on the record of conciliation.

The number of conciliation cases does not match the number of treaties concluded for the purpose. Some seven commissions were convened in inter-State disputes between 1920 and 1940, seven cases were heard between 1940 and 1960.[210] In all of those cases, except for two, a partial or complete success was achieved following the initiation of conciliation.[211] In the *Taba* Case in the 1980s the conciliation failed, but an arbitral award successfully concluded the dispute. Several cases since then have seen complete success (*Jan Mayen*, *East African Community*) or at the least a positive effect (*Belize/Guatemala*).

The importance of the successes depends on the importance of the respective cases. Conciliation has not obviously served to prevent war, as Lauterpacht rightly predicted, then going against contemporary beliefs. Nevertheless, its use in for instance the Bolivia/Paraguay *Chaco* dispute in 1929[212] and in the *Belize/Guatemala* Case from 2000 to 2002 did serve to alleviate serious tensions. It is not unreasonable to assume that also the facts of the *East African Community* Case between Tanzania, Kenya and Uganda could have resulted in military confrontation.[213] Most conciliation successes, however, occurred in less tense situations, such as the various named disputes regarding financial compensation for war damage or lost investments. The *Jan Mayen* conciliation counts as a successful case of maritime delimitation. Lauterpacht was right in warning that conciliation does not ensure the rule of law, and may be used as cloak to hide the face of agreed norms. In the *Jan Mayen* Case, Iceland explicitly agreed to conciliation on the basis that that procedure allowed for the incorporation of non-legal considerations, in particular Iceland's economic interests, in any settlement of the dispute.

---

210 Acknowledging doubt about the Soviet-German commission. *Cot* 89-97; H. Wehberg, 'Die Vergleichskommissionen im modernen Völkerrecht', (1958) 19 *ZfAÖRV* 551.

211 The exceptions being the *Vitianu* Case (Switzerland/Romania) and the *F.OABV* Case (France/Morocco).

212 'Proceedings of the Commission of Inquiry and Conciliation, Bolivia and Paraguay, March 13, 1929–September 13, 1929' (1929); L. Woolsey, 'Bolivia – Paraguay Dispute', (1929) 23 *AJIL* 110 and (1930) 24 *AJIL* 122.

213 The war between Tanzania and Uganda during the proceedings had an essentially different origin.

Lauterpacht appears not to have appreciated sufficiently that there are many options in-between war and the application of the law through adjudication. Disputes, whether they threaten the peace or not, may well be settled by the various means of diplomatic dispute settlement, without a need for a binding interpretation of the applicable law. While all disputes can be addressed by the courts, parties frequently prefer to avoid litigation; conciliation has shown to be one among many possible alternatives.

A limited number of matters has been successfully settled through conciliation, and the method continues to inspire the further development of settlement methods. Moreover, where Lauterpacht considered that it was 'to err on the side of optimism' to assume that conciliation could effectively deal with matters of, for instance, migration or territory,[214] in the case of France and Siam, as in the case of Belize and Guatemala,[215] a conciliation commission has at least had beneficial results. Practice has shown, nevertheless, that the major strength of the procedure has not been in preventing war.

As set out above, by far most known cases in which the parties made use of conciliation were thus settled. These disputes were mainly smaller cases between friendly neighbours, involving claims for financial compensation. Lauterpacht's opposition can thus be said to have been partially right, but also to have overlooked that conciliation can perform useful functions in less significant disputes, as was also the rationale of the Swiss government when it proposed conciliation.[216] Building on this record, the United Nations and the Permanent Court of Arbitration both decided that it would be useful to develop new model rules of conciliation. These initiatives are the subject of the next part of this chapter.

PART TWO

THE DEVELOPMENT OF MODEL RULES

2. The Development of Recent Model Rules

In the 1990s both the United Nations and the Permanent Court of Arbitration adopted new sets of rules for the conduct of conciliation.[217] By doing so, the

---

214 H. Lauterpacht, *The Function of Law in the International Community* (1933) 264.

215 See chapter II 1.15.

216 'Rapport du Conseil fédéral à l'Assemblée fédérale concernant les traités internationaux d'arbitrage', (1919) 71 *Feuille Fédéral Suisse* Vol. V 808, 820.

217 UNGA Res 50/50 (1995) Annex; Permanent Court of Arbitration *Basic Documents* (1998) 153.

organisations re-affirmed the interest of the international community in conciliation, as in 1992 the OSCE had done with its various conciliation provisions. Their respective rules provide a model for States to fashion their own conciliation procedure, but also offer the assistance of the organisations. The rules also suggest new directions international conciliation may take, and at the same time give rise to a number of problems. Prominent among these are questions of the aim of conciliation, the relation between conciliation and the impartiality of the organisations involved, and the composition of the conciliation commission.

Model rules of conciliation had been developed since the early days of conciliation.[218] In 1961 the IDI adopted Regulations on the Procedure of International Conciliation (IDI Conciliation Rules).[219] Following the close involvement of the League of Nations with conciliation,[220] also the United Nations had developed a tradition of propagating the method.[221] On the basis of that tradition, in 1989 the General Assembly supported an Amicable Dispute Settlement Scheme,[222] which gave general guidelines for the establishment of commissions of good offices, mediation and conciliation. As pointed out by Lavalle,[223] the Scheme was flawed. In 1995 it was replaced by the adoption of the UN Model Rules of Conciliation for Disputes between States (UN Conciliation Rules).[224]

The UN Conciliation Rules attempt to revive the practice of bilateral conciliation by providing a detailed procedure. Parties are free to exclude or amend any of the provisions.[225] As with the IDI Conciliation Rules, it was intended

---

[218] E.g., the model conciliation treaty designed by Max Habicht in 1931: *Habicht* 1028-1040. In 1960 Switzerland prepared a Model Treaty of Conciliation, Judicial Settlement and Arbitration reprinted with introduction: K. Oellers-Frahm and A. Zimmerman (eds.), *Dispute Settlement in Public International Law: Texts and Materials* (2001) 302.

[219] See chapter III 3. For the preparatory report and written observations of other members: (1959) 47 *Annuaire de l'Institut de Droit International* Vol. II 5. The discussion and the rules: (1961) 49 *Annuaire de l'Institut de Droit International* Vol. II 193, 374 (English tr 385).

[220] C. de Visscher, 'Les commissions de conciliation et la Société des Nations', (1922) 29 *RGDIP* 410, 429. A Resolution of 25 September 1926 invited the Council to offer its good offices for the conclusion of arbitration and conciliation treaties.

[221] United Nations *Handbook on the Peaceful Settlement of Disputes between States* (1992), 45-48; C. Peck, *The United Nations as a Dispute Settlement System. Improving mechanisms for the prevention and solution of conflict* (1996).

[222] UNGA Decision 44/415 (4 December 1989).

[223] R. Lavalle, 'The Amicable Dispute Settlement Scheme Brought to the Attention of States by the United Nations General Assembly in 1989: A Critical Commentary', (1991) 42 *Austrian Journal of Public International Law* 163. Nevertheless, the General Assembly still referred to it, together with the subsequent UN Conciliation Rules, in UN GA Res 57/26 (2003).

[224] The UN Model Rules result from an initiative by Guatemala; letter to the Secretary-General (6 July 1990) UN Doc A/45/143 GAOR Annexes (45) 147.

[225] UN Conciliation Rules Art. 1.

that the UN Conciliation Rules would be adopted in bilateral treaties. Furthermore, the UN Conciliation Rules should provide assistance in cases that parties decide *ad hoc* for the conciliation of their dispute, or if under an existing agreement the dispute is to be referred to conciliation, but the agreement does not provide for procedural rules.[226] The latter situation is likely to occur, as conciliation is frequently included in bilateral and multilateral agreements, often without providing for any details of procedure.[227]

Guatemala, the sponsor of the draft UN Conciliation Rules, emphasised that the proposal built on past discussions and experience. Special mention was given of the IDI Conciliation Rules and of the UNCITRAL Conciliation Rules.[228] The final version of the UN Conciliation Rules, however, bears little resemblance to the IDI Conciliation Rules, and even less to the UNCITRAL Conciliation Rules.

The PCA had been involved with conciliation since 1937, and had hosted the Danish/Lithuanian Conciliation Commission,[229] the French/Swiss Commission,[230] and the Greek/Italian *Roula* Commission.[231] Further, in 1962 it had issued Rules of Arbitration and Conciliation for Settlement of International Disputes Between Two Parties of Which Only One is a State.[232] These rules, which gave a directing role to conciliation commissions, failed to attract interest. Since the revitalization of the PCA in the 1990s,[233] it has adopted various model rules for conflict resolution,[234] among which are the PCA Op-

---

226 UN Doc A/49/33 (1994) 36.

227 See chapter II 1.12.

228 Recommended by the General Assembly: UNGA Res 35/52 (1980).

229 'Permanent Court of Arbitration- Circular Note of the Secretary-General', (1960) 54 *AJIL* 937, 938; 'Report du Conseil Administratif de la Cour Permanente d'Arbitrage', 1938-7/8 idem, 1939-6/7; J.P.A. François, 'La Cour Permanente d'arbitrage', (1955) 87 *Recueil des Cours* Vol. I 535-538.

230 P. Hamilton and others (eds.), *The Permanent Court of Arbitration: International Arbitration and Dispute Resolution* (1999) 288-290. PCA Secretary-General J.P.A. François acted as secretary to that commission, while he presided the third and last commission employing the Court in the *Roula* Case.

231 P. Hamilton and others (eds.), *The Permanent Court of Arbitration: International Arbitration and Dispute Resolution* (1999) 291-293; J.P.A. François, 'Le Palais de la Paix en 1956', (1957) 4 *NTIR* 69, 71; *Cot* 95; 'Report du Conseil Administratif de la Cour permanente d'Arbitrage', (1955) 7 and (1956) 6.

232 (1963) 57 *AJIL* 500.

233 J.J. van Haersolte-van Hof, 'The Revitalization of the Permanent Court of Arbitration', (2007) 54 *NILR* 395; B.E. Shifman, 'The Revitalization of the Permanent Court of Arbitration', (1995) 23 *International Journal of Legal Information* 284. For further proposals: S.M.G. Koopmans, 'The PCA in the Field of Conciliation and Mediation: New Perspectives and Approaches', in Permanent Court of Arbitration (ed.), *International Alternative Dispute Resolution: Past, Present and Future* (2000) 67.

234 E.g., the Permanent Court of Arbitration issued Optional Rules for Arbitrating Disputes between two States (1992), Optional Rules for Arbitrating Disputes between Two Parties of which

tional Conciliation Rules (PCA Conciliation Rules). The PCA Conciliation Rules closely resemble the conciliation rules issued by UNCITRAL.[235] The changes the PCA made relate mainly to the availability of the Secretary-General for the appointment of conciliators, and the offer of administrative support from the International Bureau. In 2002, the PCA also adopted Optional Rules for Conciliation of Disputes Relating to Natural Resources and/or the Environment (PCA Environmental Rules).[236] The reason for the development of these rules lies in the fact that there is a growing number of multilateral environmental treaties including a reference to conciliation, without providing for any specific conciliation procedure.[237] The PCA Environmental Rules cater for the distinctive characteristics of environmental disputes in particular by referring to lists of expert conciliators, as well as lists of technical and scientific experts, to be maintained by the PCA. In addition, the PCA Environmental Rules in certain places refine the general PCA Conciliation Rules.

In the following sections a comparison is made between the UN Conciliation Rules and the PCA Conciliation Rules, with reference to the PCA Environmental Rules where these significantly differ. The PCA Conciliation Rules brief and flexible, while the UN Conciliation Rules are more extensive and formal. This reflects their respective intended audiences. In the PCA it was thought that the concept of conciliation is flexible enough to equally apply to inter-State disputes and disputes in which only one party is a State, a State enterprise or an international organisation. Its conciliation rules are also seen as a basis, given certain changes, for settling multi-party disputes.[238] The UN Conciliation Rules are intended for use by States only.[239] This disparity should

only One is a State (1993), Optional Rules for Arbitration involving International Organisations and States (1996), Optional Rules for Arbitration between International Organisations and Private Parties (1996): Permanent Court of Arbitration *Basic Documents* (1998); '97th Annual Report of the Permanent Court of Arbitration' (1997) Annex 10; D.P. Ratliff, 'The PCA Optional Rules for Arbitration of Disputes Relating to Natural Resources and/or the Environment', (2001) 14 *Leiden Journal of International Law* 887.

235 UNCITRAL Optional Conciliation Rules: (1981) 6 *Yearbook Commercial Arbitration* 165-169. The UN's Sixth Committee chose not to follow the suggestion made by UNCITRAL (UN Doc A/ 46/383 (1991)) to model its draft rules after the UNCITRAL Conciliation Rules. For the UNCITRAL Conciliation Rules: I.I. Dore, *Arbitration and Conciliation under the UNCITRAL Rules: A Textual Analysis* (1986); I.I. Dore, *The UNCITRAL Framework for Arbitration in Contemporary Perspective* (1993).

236 Permanent Court of Arbitration *Optional Rules for Conciliation of Disputes Relating to Natural Resources and/or the Environment* (2002).

237 P. Sands and R. MacKenzie, 'Guidelines for Negotiating and Drafting Dispute Settlement Clauses for International Environmental Agreements', International Bureau of the Permanent Court of Arbitration (ed.), *International Investments and the Protection of the Environment* (2001) 305. See further chapter II 1.12.

238 Introduction to the PCA Conciliation Rules: Permanent Court of Arbitration *Basic Documents* (1998) 157-158.

239 UN Conciliation Rules Art. 1.

not in all respects be decisive. Both sets of rules can be adapted to specific situations. Unlike the case of the PCA Conciliation Rules however, adapting the UN Conciliation Rules for a particular dispute without prior agreement with the United Nations may have consequences for the assistance provided by the Organisation. The services of the PCA on the other hand are made available to all States and State enterprises, as well as to international organisations wishing to make use of them.

2.1 The framework of the UN and PCA Conciliation Rules

Under the UN Conciliation Rules, prior to commencement of the proceedings the parties are to agree on a definition of the dispute as well as on procedural aspects such as the number and names of the conciliators.[240] To these ends, they may request the assistance and advice of the UN Secretary-General.[241] The terms of reference of the conciliation commission are broad. It is the task of the commission, acting independently and impartially, to assist the parties in reaching an amicable settlement.[242] The UN Conciliation Rules read:

> 'The commission shall refrain from presenting in its report any final conclusions with regard to facts or from ruling formally on issues of law, unless the parties have jointly asked it to do so.'[243]

The result of settlement is paramount: only if the commission does not succeed in reaching a settlement during meetings with the parties does the commission submit formal proposals. To this end, both the parties and the commission may make proposals at any time.[244] The UN Conciliation Rules also contain detailed rules on the conduct of the procedure. The commission, consisting of three or five persons, should try to make decisions unanimously, but may, if this proves impossible, also decide by majority. Abstentions are not allowed.[245] If it considers the submission of recommendations fruitless, it may decide only to draw-up a procès-verbal to that effect.[246]

The proceedings are meant to be insulated from further claims or proceedings, as all statements and documents are to remain confidential,[247] and as no

---

240 Ibid., Art. 2.

241 Ibid., Art. 19.

242 Ibid., Art. 7.

243 Ibid., Art. 20(2); cf., IDI Conciliation Rules Art. 7, last sentence.

244 UN Conciliation Rules Art. 16 and 17. ICSID Conciliation Rules Art. 22(2) reserves this right only for the commission.

245 UN Conciliation Rules Art. 18.

246 Ibid., Art. 20(4).

247 Ibid., Art. 25(1).

party may before any other court or tribunal invoke statements, views, offers or admissions made by the other party or the commission's report or recommendations, unless the parties otherwise agree.[248] No provision is made to prohibit conciliators from becoming arbitrators.[249]

The PCA Conciliation Rules are meant to be as flexible as possible. For instance, they prescribe the selection of only one conciliator, unless the parties choose otherwise.[250] The PCA and its Secretary-General may assist in the selection of conciliators, and may provide administrative assistance.[251] It is the role of the conciliator to assist the parties in reaching an amicable settlement. The PCA Conciliation Rules set out clearly that in the performance of his duties, the conciliator will be guided by principles of objectivity, fairness and justice, giving consideration to, among other things, the rights and obligations of the parties and the circumstances surrounding the dispute, including any previous practices between the parties.[252] This may be understood to mean that the principal basis for a recommendation for settlement is the law, but that other circumstances, and previous practices, may be a reason for deviation. The PCA Environmental Rules copy the above provision, but add: 'The conciliator will make proposals to preserve the respective rights of the parties, and to prevent and/or mitigate serious harm to the environment falling within the subject of the dispute.' The phrase 'preserving the respective rights', suggests that the conciliator is in principle to adopt a legal approach. The alternative reading, that the addition would only provide a basis for recommending interim measures for the duration of the conciliation, does not appear correct; 'preserving the respective rights' is not named as a discretionary option, to be considered upon application of one of the parties. To the contrary, the conciliator 'will' make such proposals. Nevertheless, the conciliator must in his proposals also incorporate the necessity of avoiding serious harm to the environment; this may be a non-legal consideration to be taken into account.

The PCA Environmental Rules offer a novelty in that they explicitly provide that the conciliator may propose an 'implementation committee' to assist the parties in implementing the settlement agreement.[253] Such committee may, *inter alia*, request the parties to provide reports on their implementation of the settlement, and may monitor their compliance. The provision, however optional, is reminiscent of non-compliance procedures included in modern mul-

[248] Ibid., Art. 28(1).

[249] An article to that effect: A/47/33 Art. 39 (1992) was deleted in the later versions. The rule does however appear in the PCA Conciliation Rules Art. 19.

[250] PCA Conciliation Rules Art. 3; PCA Environmental Rules Art. 3.

[251] PCA Conciliation Rules Arts. 4(3) and 8; PCA Environmental Rules Arts. 2, 4, 8.

[252] PCA Conciliation Rules Art. 7.

[253] PCA Environmental Rules Art. 12.

tilateral environmental treaties.[254] Similar to implementation committees in non-compliance procedures, these implementation committees may be granted the competence to propose measures to be taken against a party that does not meet its obligations. However, the implementation committee mentioned in the PCA Environmental Rules is but an option to be agreed upon by the parties at the moment a settlement is reached, and its competences are at that time to be determined by the parties. Therefore, the provision is of interests as a novel suggestion for inclusion in the conciliator's proposals, but must not be taken to signify any constraint on the conciliation procedure or on the parties.

Notably, the conciliator may meet with the parties in joint or separate sessions.[255] Unlike judicial proceedings, parties may provide the conciliator with information not to be disclosed to the other party.[256] This is different from the UN Conciliation Rules. There, meetings should be plenary; only at the final stage, when the dispute has been exhaustively presented by both sides and the commission is about to render its recommendations, can separate sessions be held.[257] Moreover, the UN Conciliation Rules require all documented information to be passed on to the other party.[258]

2.2 The aim of the proceedings

The terms of reference of both the UN- and the PCA Conciliation Rules indicate a more goal-oriented approach to conciliation than was adopted by the traditional settlement agreements, in which the work of the commission itself was of primary importance.[259] To differing degrees the rules make clear that the procedure is only an instrument, at any time to be trumped by an impending compromise. In traditional conciliation, the commission would have taken the lead, drawing-up formal recommendations and setting a time limit for a reply. The European Convention for the Peaceful Settlement of Disputes of 1957 serves as an example of this traditional approach:

---

254 See chapter IV 6.

255 PCA Conciliation Rules Art. 9(1).

256 PCA Conciliation Rules Art. 10.

257 UN Conciliation Rules Arts. 11(2) and 20(1).

258 UN Conciliation Rules Arts. 25(2) and (3).

259 This distinction is also noted with regard to the UNCITRAL Conciliation Rules by one of its drafters, Howard Holtzmann, who later drafted the PCA Conciliation Rules. H.M. Holtzmann, 'Dispute Resolution in Europe under the UNCITRAL Conciliation Rules', in D. Bardonnet (ed.), *Le Règlement Pacifique des Differends Internationaux en Europe: Perspectives d'Avenir* (1991) 293, 301. However, Habicht already noted such a shift in the French-Swiss treaty of 6 April 1925; *Habicht* 1026-1028. In that and similar instruments however, the task of the conciliators remains primarily that of investigation and working towards a report.

> 'The task of the Special Conciliation Commission shall be to elucidate the questions in dispute, to collect with that object all relevant documents and information by means of enquiry or otherwise, and to endeavour to bring the parties to an agreement. It may, after the case has been examined, inform the parties of the terms of settlement which seem suitable to it and lay down the period within which they are to make their decision.'[260]

In contrast, the UN Conciliation Rules, under the heading 'Fundamental Principles' provide:

> 'The commission, acting independently and impartially, shall endeavour to assist the parties in reaching an amicable settlement of the dispute. If no settlement is reached during the consideration of the dispute, the commission may draw up and submit appropriate recommendations to the parties for consideration.'[261]

The primary aim is a settlement during the course of the proceedings, leaving the initiative as far as possible to the disputing parties: the commission shall 'endeavour to assist'. In the PCA Conciliation Rules the overriding goal of reaching agreement dominates the terms of reference to such an extent that the procedure may also turn into mediation, abandoning the instruments of investigation and a report altogether. Article 7 reads:

> '(3) The conciliator may conduct the conciliation proceedings in such a manner as he considers appropriate, taking into account the circumstances of the case, the wishes the parties may express, including any request by a party that the conciliator hear oral statements, and any special need for a speedy settlement of the dispute.
> (4) The conciliator may, at any stage of the conciliation proceedings, make proposals for a settlement of the dispute. Such proposals need not be in writing and need not be accompanied by a statement of the reasons therefore.'

The conciliator has complete freedom, subject to the parties' wishes, to vary the conduct of the exercise as he sees fit. The flexibility inherent in the PCA formula is enhanced by the preference for a sole conciliator: a single individual may more easily vary the focus of his attention. The approach has consequences for the conduct of the deliberations, the position of the conciliators, and for the issuing of a report. The conciliators are required to try where possible to engage the parties in negotiations parallel to the conciliation proceedings. Moreover, the parties are encouraged to propose solutions themselves.[262] The

[260] European Convention for the Peaceful Settlement of Disputes Art. 15(1).
[261] UN Conciliation Rules Art. 7.
[262] PCA Conciliation Rules Art. 12; UN Conciliation Rules Art. 16.

conciliators can be required to provide additional assistance.[263] In this respect, one can think of arranging meetings between individuals relevant to the dispute or of organising an independent audit during or after the proceedings. Furthermore, a report or even a procès-verbal does not always have to be issued.[264]

2.3 The offer of organisational assistance

Both the UN and the PCA offer their assistance in the initiation and conduct of any undertaking to conciliate in accordance with their respective rules. The assistance of the UN Secretary-General may be requested if the parties cannot agree on the definition of the subject of the dispute, or on any other aspect of the modalities of the proceedings.[265] During the proceedings the commission may also request his advice or assistance at any time regarding the administrative or procedural aspects of the work.[266] Furthermore, a UN official may be appointed to act as secretary of the conciliation commission.[267] Finally, provision is made for the delivery of the documents of the conciliation procedure, once concluded, to the Secretary-General for safekeeping.[268] The PCA Conciliation Rules are slightly less elaborate, in that there is no clause involving the PCA Secretary-General in the delineation of the dispute. In practice, this should not bar his assistance. His services are explicitly offered with regard to the appointment of conciliators,[269] complementary to the organisational assistance of the International Bureau.[270] The contribution of the PCA Environmental Rules lies for a large part in the additional assistance the PCA may offer. The Secretary-General may be requested to submit to the parties a list of persons considered to have expertise in the subject-matter of the dispute, or, on the request of the conciliator, the Secretary-General may provide an indicative list of scientific or technical experts for the conduct of specialist investigations.[271]

---

263 PCA Conciliation Rules Art. 7(1).

264 A procès-verbal was required by the Rules of Arbitration and Conciliation (1962) s II Art. 15 prepared by the PCA and by the IDI Conciliation Rules Art. 9.

265 UN Conciliation Rules Art. 2. It thereby exceeds the role of a (residual) appointing authority, such as performed by the Director-General of the Food and Agricultural Organisation (FAO) in respect of the International Treaty on Plant Genetic Resources for Food and Agriculture, Annex II, part 2 Art. 3 and 4.

266 Ibid., Art. 19.

267 Ibid., Art. 10.

268 Ibid., Art. 23.

269 PCA Conciliation Rules Art. 4(3).

270 PCA Conciliation Rules Arts. 8 and 9.

271 PCA Environmental Rules Arts. 4(4) and 7(4) respectively.

The above gives rise to a number of questions. First, as both sets of rules provide that the parties may modify them by common agreement, the rules as finally agreed upon may differ substantially from the original models. The UN and the PCA offer their assistance when their rules are applied, but do not indicate when the alterations to the rules go so far that they can no longer be considered the UN or PCA Conciliation Rules. It may then be unclear whether the parties can still call on the help of the relevant organisation.[272] Therefore, unless the UN and the PCA are willing to facilitate conciliation generally, prior consultation will be necessary.

The close involvement of both organisations may also raise questions of neutrality. Because of his high political profile, this seems especially relevant to the Secretary-General of the United Nations. The UN Conciliation Rules are not the first to involve him in conciliation proceedings. The General Act of 1949 speaks in general terms about it,[273] while for instance the Law of the Sea Convention refers to him as an appointing and depository authority,[274] and the Vienna Convention on the Law of Treaties stipulates that the Secretary-General 'shall provide the Commission with such assistance and facilities as it may require'.[275] Where the role envisaged there seems to be of a passive nature, the present provisions may be seen as more substantial, and therefore more likely to draw the Organisation into political controversy.

The issue of neutrality was addressed by the Legal Counsel of the UN.[276] He held the view that as long as the request for assistance to the Secretary-General comes from the two parties jointly, his involvement may be assimilated to a request for the provision of good offices, and therefore falls within his function under the Charter and does not compromise the required neutrality of his position. It is submitted that this suggests too limited a view of what conciliation can entail. It is not excluded that the UN Conciliation Rules would be adopted in a treaty providing for compulsory conciliation. In that case, though there would be prior agreement, parties may disagree in the particular circumstances as to the appropriateness of the proceedings. The Secretary-General will then automatically be involved, and may have to choose sides in deciding whether or not to lend his assistance.

---

272 A similar complication can arise under the ICSID Convention, which offers the assistance of ICSID for conciliation conducted in accordance with the limited conciliation provisions set out in the Convention (Art. 32-35), but in Art. 33 allow parties to agree to rules other than the separate and highly elaborate ICSID Conciliation Rules (see chapter II 1.13.1).

273 1949 General Act Art. 9(2).

274 UNCLOS Conciliation Annex V Arts. 3 sub e and 7(1).

275 Vienna Convention on the Law of Treaties Annex Art. 7.

276 A/47/33 (1992) 64-65. In the same statement the Legal Counsel strongly opposed the possibility of involvement of the Secretary-General upon the request of one party only.

A more remote concern is that an undertaking may in itself compromise the appearance of neutrality. In the first place, because of the political character of conciliation, and the open terms of reference, there is a possibility that the outcome of the proceedings goes against international law or equitable principles. The linkage of the procedure with the UN may then affect the latter's purpose to

> 'bring about by peaceful means, and *in conformity with the principles of justice and international law*, adjustment or settlement of international disputes or situations which might lead to a breach of the peace.'[277]

Any such breach will of course be primarily the responsibility of the participating States, which are required by the UN Charter to settle their disputes 'by peaceful means in such a manner that international peace and security, *and justice*, are not endangered.'[278] Some concern is nonetheless warranted because of the importance to avoid even the appearance of partiality of the Secretariat: this is less a concern for the settlement efforts by the Security Council and the General Assembly.

A second point involving the appearance of impartiality is the position of third parties. Despite the required consensus between the States setting-up the commission, there may be third States who consider the undertaking prejudicial to their interests or position. Neither the PCA Conciliation Rules nor the UN Conciliation Rules provide for intervention by a third party or for the consideration of its interests.[279] Though the conciliation procedure cannot result in decisions that are binding upon third parties, other States may well have an interest in having their views presented, for instance when the conciliation concerns maritime delimitation. This is one of the reasons for which intervention is under certain conditions allowed in cases before the International Court of Justice.[280] In case of conciliation with UN involvement, the third party may, even if incorrectly, perceive the Organisation as condoning its exclusion.

It is understandable therefore that there was discussion on the appropriateness of the UN Secretary-General as the person to give assistance to disputing parties. By contrast, the Permanent Court of Arbitration does not have the political profile of the United Nations, and can therefore be less troubled by appearances. At the same time, the PCA has traditionally been favoured as a forum

---

[277] UN Charter Art. 1(1). Emphasis added.

[278] UN Charter Art. 2(3). Emphasis added.

[279] Both the 1949 General Act Art. 35(2) and the 1957 European Convention for the Peaceful Settlement of Disputes Art. 32(2) mention the possibility that the parties agree to invite a third State to intervene.

[280] ICJ Statute Arts. 62 and 63.

for conciliation.[281] Nevertheless, a proposal to conduct conciliation under the UN Conciliation Rules with the assistance of the Secretary-General of the Permanent Court of Arbitration was not accepted.[282]

2.4 The composition of the commission

The composition of a conciliation commission will be an important factor in its work and success. The approaches taken by the UN and the PCA are quite different in this respect, while both notably strive to limit the role of national members in any commission. In most cases, and in conformity with the arbitration and inquiry provisions of the Hague Conventions, conciliation commissions consist of five persons.[283] Normally, the parties may appoint a member of their own nationality, while they agree jointly to the remaining three.[284] Cot considers this composition 'an ideal working arrangement which enables the interests of all to be taken into account'.[285] Both the PCA- and the UN Conciliation Rules deviate from this practice. The UN Conciliation Rules leave the parties a choice between three or five conciliators.[286] In the case of a three-person commission, each party appoints one, who may not be of its nationality. Together the parties select the president of the commission. No nationals will therefore be appointed.[287] When preference is given to a five-person commission, each party may appoint one national. The remaining three are to be nationals of third States, agreed upon by the parties jointly.[288] In this case then the national members remain outnumbered. Though unanimity is the aim of the commission, if this cannot be achieved decisions shall be taken by major-

[281] IDI Conciliation Rules Art. 14 recommend the PCA. Wehberg considered 'gerade das Haager Milieu ausgezeichnet für die Arbeit der Vergleichskommissionen': H. Wehberg, 'Die Vergleichskommissionen im modernen Völkerrecht', (1958) 19 *ZfAÖRV* 551, 588.

[282] Informal working document (on file with author).

[283] Cf., F.M. van Asbeck, 'La tâche et l'action d'une commission de conciliation', (1956) *NTIR* 1, 4.

[284] E.g., General Act of 1949 Art. 4. The IDI Conciliation Rules do not deal with the issue of composition, though they exclusively speak of a 'commission', and thereby rule out the possibility of a sole conciliator: *Habicht* 1006. An interesting variation was made in the Treaty of Conciliation and Arbitration between Estonia, Finland, Latvia and Poland (17 January 1925), 37 *LNTS* 359 which established a commission comprising appointees of all four parties and one external member.

[285] *Cot* 109.

[286] The PCA Environmental Rules Arts. 3 and 4 leave a choice of one, three or five conciliators. In the case of three or five conciliators, two, respectively four, are party-appointed.

[287] In private international law this is a common situation, e.g., UNCITRAL Conciliation Rules Art. 3.

[288] UN Conciliation Rules Arts. 3, 4 and 5.

ity. Therefore, one or even both national conciliators can be outvoted.[289] The PCA Conciliation Rules prefer a sole conciliator, but give the parties the possibility to opt for two or three.[290]

Sole conciliators are not completely unknown in the settlement of disputes involving private parties.[291] The UNCITRAL Conciliation Rules provide for one conciliator, in order to minimise expenditure and to expedite proceedings: 'It is easier to act informally and confidentially with a sole conciliator'.[292] Nevertheless, they also explicitly allow the parties to agree to appoint a commission of two conciliators.[293] Until the *Belize/Guatemala* Case in 2000, there was no precedent for a commission of two conciliators.[294] In discussing the UNCITRAL Conciliation Rules, Dore remarks that an odd number of conciliators is not essential, since there is no requirement to impose a decision.[295] The third option mentioned in the PCA Conciliation Rules – a commission consisting of one national of each of the parties and a neutral president – is more common.[296]

The fully foreign three person commission provided for in the UN Conciliation Rules is a rarity, but the innovation was not based on much discussion.[297] Though the number of conciliators was much debated at the UN, the absence of a neutral element was not. The only precedent for a completely foreign composition of a three-member commission was the irregular case of Haiti and the Dominican Republic in 1938.[298] When the success of conciliation is dependent

---

[289] Ibid., Art. 18.

[290] PCA Conciliation Rules Art. 3: 'There shall be one conciliator unless the parties agree that there shall be two or three conciliators. Where there is more than one conciliator, they ought, as a general rule, to act jointly.'

[291] Only the Treaty of Conciliation, Arbitration and Compulsory Adjudication (Hungary-Switzerland) (signed 18 June 1924, entered into force 13 May 1925) provided for a sole conciliator: 34 *LNTS* 389. A sole conciliators was used in a few *ad hoc* cases: the *Japanese 4% Loan* Case (1966) and the *City of Tokyo 5% Loan* Case, *East African Community* Case: see chapter I 4.3.

[292] I.I. Dore, *Arbitration and Conciliation under the UNCITRAL Rules: A Textual Analysis* (1986) 26.

[293] UNCITRAL Conciliation Rules Art. 3.

[294] Commissions of four members were provided for in treaties concluded by the Soviet Union. *Cot* 109.

[295] I.I. Dore, *Arbitration and conciliation under the UNCITRAL Rules: A Textual Analysis* (1986) 26.

[296] E.g., the *Belgium/Luxembourg* Case (1934); D. Schindler, *Die Schiedsgerichtbarkeit seit* 1914 (1938) 25; and the *SS Roula* Case (*Greece* v. *Italy*) (1955-56).

[297] E.g., Informal document of the Working Group of the Special Committee on the Charter of the United Nations and on the Strengthening of the Role of the Organisation: UN code Chart WG.93 (4 March 1993) and the summary of the discussion in 1994 attached to a letter of the Secretary-General (5 December 1994) Doc ref LA/COD/30 (on file with author).

[298] A.M. Stuyt, *Survey of International Arbitrations 1794-1989* (1990) 576. The commission was not constituted as provided for in the General Treaty of Inter-American Arbitration Art. 4.

on the involvement of the disputing parties and on the trust they have in the conciliators, the elimination of the national element is an important departure from the known procedure.

Both the PCA and UN Conciliation Rules leave it to the parties to choose the final number of conciliators. Though flexibility is often praised, this option does require a separate decision and therefore negotiations. Unlike with the appointment of the neutral members on the commission, the rules do not prescribe recourse to a third party to settle the issue. The size of the commission is therefore among the first obstacles towards conciliation.[299] Here, however, both rules offer the assistance of their respective Secretaries-General.

2.5 Conclusion

The rules prepared by the United Nations and the Permanent Court of Arbitration indicate that the international community retains an interest in the settlement of international disputes through conciliation. They aim to be as flexible as possible, and explicitly provide that the parties may modify them as they see fit. This corresponds to the development in commercial dispute settlement allowing a method to be adapted to the needs of the parties. Unlike the PCA Conciliation Rules, however, the UN Conciliation Rules still specify that they are only to be used by States.

In addition to application *ad hoc*, the models are meant for incorporation in treaties dealing with a particular subject-matter. In the latter case the parties may make recourse to conciliation compulsory, and therefore require provisions on, *inter alia*, the competence of the commission to decide its competence, and on the appointment of conciliators for reluctant parties. The UN Conciliation Rules and the PCA Conciliation Rules do not take this into account. The PCA Environmental Rules, however, do include special provisions in case parties have agreed that conciliation is compulsory, and that therefore one party may make a unilateral application.[300]

While the discussed rules largely follow the commonly perceived interest in flexibility, they paradoxically also try to limit the national control over the proceedings by altering the traditional composition of commissions. It may be assumed, however, that many States prefer to be able to appoint a national of their own on the commission, as has been regular practice. Particularly because of the general reluctance of States to use conciliation in practice, this alteration seems to be ill-advised. Though it may be too early to draw any

---

[299] The suggestion was made by Austria to specify a standard size so that no additional agreement would be necessary UN Doc A/46/383 (1991) 4.

[300] PCA Environmental Rules Arts. 2(3), 4, 16.

conclusions, neither the UN Conciliation Rules nor their PCA counterparts have yet been used. The UN Conciliation Rules have so far not been included or referred to in the multilateral treaties that were adopted under the UN's auspices.

3. Conclusions: The Development of Inter-State Conciliation

Inter-State conciliation, while building on old roots of mediation and inquiry, arose essentially out of two strands of thought: to prevent war and to provide an alternative to adjudication. Driven by the enthusiasm surrounding the pacific ideal, conciliation developed into a globally recognised and institutionalised form swiftly upon its appearance. Initial hesitation by the League of Nations quickly changed into active support. Many bilateral and several multilateral treaties on dispute settlement came to include conciliation provisions. The method thereby developed into an independent system with its own characteristics.

The burgeoning of conciliation led to later disappointment. The idea that it could be a decisive tool in the prevention of war proved unjustified already in the 1930s, despite some occasional successes in easing tensions between belligerent parties. Moreover, the belief that there are kinds of disputes that are inherently non-justiciable was also lost. This abandoned doctrine was part of the motivation of many partisans of conciliation when they presented conciliation as an alternative to adjudication. In this light, Lauterpacht's criticism of the concept of non-justiciability led him also to attack conciliation as an essentially misguided concept.

It indeed appears correct that many general agreements on conciliation were superfluous. It has however not been demonstrated that these treaties were actually damaging, either to international law or to peaceful relations. At least the conclusion of conciliation treaties helped to spread the idea of diplomatic settlement around much of the world.

The actual bilateral conciliation cases, though small in number, still indicate that conciliation can be useful as potential alternative to adjudication, or to other means of dispute settlement. Almost all were successfully concluded. Practice shows that there is no use for a broad network of specific bilateral dispute settlement treaties such as was created between the two World Wars. In most cases of actual use, parties could probably also have agreed to set-up a commission if one had had not yet existed. Further, all modern instances of conciliation involved commissions created *ad hoc*.

Such *ad hoc* commissions will benefit from the guidance and institutional frameworks created by the UN and PCA. While the first provide a more detailed procedure intended for inter-State disputes, the latter may be used efficiently for all kinds of disputes, though to that end they give slightly less procedural guidance. Together, these sets of rules effectively pre-empt the need for further bilateral treaties. They do however leave open certain questions, such as regarding the involvement of the international organisations themselves. Other questions, such as on the place of law in conciliation, and on the relation of conciliation with law, shall be addressed in the next chapter.

Chapter III
CONCILIATION AND THE LAW

Conciliation is a diplomatic settlement method, producing non-binding recommendations. It is unlike the binding methods of arbitration and adjudication, which rely on application of the law. Nevertheless, in the conduct of conciliation proceedings the conciliators and the parties encounter law in various ways. Law may be the starting point of the argumentation by the parties, it may be the basis of consideration by the conciliators. Further, conciliation proceedings could potentially prejudge the dispute in case it moves on to adjudication or other settlement methods. The first part of this chapter addresses the role of law in international conciliation generally. It starts in section one with highlighting the roles the parties, conciliators and the dispute play in shaping the proceedings. It proceeds to set out two 'ideal types' of political and legal conciliation. Section three revisits the debate on conciliation by the Institut de Droit International in 1961, and reviews some conciliation alternatives that should have been included in that discussion. The second part of this chapter considers various ways in which conciliation may involve legal problems, such as prejudice and the independence of conciliators. It concludes by investigating the potential of precedent.

PART ONE
THE ROLE OF LAW IN CONCILIATION

1. Conciliation and Practice

The practical role of conciliation in any given dispute is dependent on the role of the parties, the conciliators and the dispute. The following highlights some essential variables at issue.

1.1 The role of the parties

It is the parties who decide on conciliation as a settlement method, it is they who initially decide how the procedure is construed, and it is they who have to

S.M.G. Koopmans, Diplomatic Dispute Settlement

accept or reject the outcome. Therefore, the parties in dispute have by far the most important roles in the use and success of conciliation, whatever the merits of the conciliators' work may be.

Having decided on conciliation as a potential settlement method, States are to agree terms of reference for the conciliators to work with. Such terms may be loosely formulated, such as 'to assist the parties in finding a solution' or they may describe in detail the basis of considerations to be made by the commission. An example of the latter option is found in the terms of reference of the commission set-up to address the *Jan Mayen* dispute, which called for consideration of, among other things, one party's strong economic interest, as well as geographical and geological features.[1] In this respect it is also important whether the terms of reference are found in a pre-existing treaty (as was the case for most cases in the 1920s, 1930s and 1950s), or were created for the particular dispute at hand (as in the *Taba* and *Jan Mayen* Cases), or even evolved with the handling of the dispute. More important than the terms of reference, however, will be whether the parties demand obedience to such terms of reference, and themselves abide by them. As discussed below,[2] the practice of conciliation in the middle of the 20th century frequently deviated substantially from the terms applicable to the commission.

Further choices to be made by the parties include the number of conciliators: in the original format a commission normally had five members,[3] but in more recent times parties have occasionally opted for a single expert, such as Victor Umbricht in the *East African Community* Case.[4] Parties also explicitly or implicitly choose a *type* of conciliator, be it a lawyer, a diplomat, a politician or a technical expert. Simultaneously, they may opt for full time or part time conciliators. This choice may be brought forward, and thereby complicated, if conciliators are selected in advance of the dispute, such as in the creation of permanent commissions to be seized whenever a dispute arises.

Eventually, the success or failure is fundamentally dependent on the position taken by the parties towards the settlement process. Do they enter the endeavour in good faith, are they willing to co-operate with the commission and with the other party? It is remembered that in the *Vitianu* Case Romania

---

[1] Agreement concerning Fishery and Continental Shelf Questions (Iceland-Norway) (28 May 1980) Art. 9(3), (1981) 20 *ILM* 797.

[2] See chapter III 2.

[3] F.M. van Asbeck, 'La tâche et l'action d'une commission de conciliation', (1956) *NTIR* 1, 4. Similarly, the Commission of Mediation, Conciliation and Arbitration of the OAU: Art. 23 Protocol of the Commission of Mediation, Conciliation and Arbitration.

[4] See chapter I 4.3. Similarly: the *Yugoslavia Succession* Case. A. Watts, 'State Succession: Some Recent Practical Legal Problems', in V. Götzand and others (eds.), *Liber Amicorum Günther Jaenicke – Zum 85. Geburtstag* (1998) 397. See chapter I 3.2.

refused to appoint conciliators, despite an obligation to do so.[5] In other cases, such as the *Gorm and Svava* Case, the friendly relations and co-operative attitude displayed by the parties were credited by the conciliators as the reason of success.

1.2 The role of the conciliators

Other relevant factors in the use and success of conciliation lie with the persons charged with making the contribution offered by the procedure: the conciliators. Their understanding of their role can determine which way the process develops. Victor Umbricht, for example, appears from his record of the *East African Community* Case as a modest but tenacious conciliator.[6] Despite occasional ruptures between the parties and accusations levied at the conciliator, he persevered, occasionally pressed his proposals, but managed to maintain the impression that the parties were always in control, and that his proposals were solely the expressions of what was put forward by the parties themselves. Conciliators can also take it upon themselves to conduct shuttle diplomacy, moving between parties to discuss possibilities, as was done by Judge Bellet in the *Taba* conciliation case.[7]

Another choice to be made by conciliators, particularly those appointed by the parties from their own nationals, is whether they conduct themselves as a neutral counsellor, or as an advocate of their State. While both stances may potentially make a positive contribution to the process, the positioning may affect the nature of the co-operation among conciliators and the effort itself. A conciliator considering himself a representative of one of the parties is likely to introduce the negotiations into the bosom of the commission. He may therefore inform the other members of what is acceptable to his side, while at the same time strengthening the confidence of his State in the work of the commission. A more neutral conciliator, on the other hand, is more likely to look for the middle ground, or for principles applicable to the dispute, on which basis it might be resolved. A neutral conciliator is also likely to have more personal persuasiveness for *both* parties, considering his disinterested contribution to the process.

In this respect, it is interesting to note that Cot is of the opinion that a vital characteristic of conciliation lies in the fact that the conciliation commission has no political power.[8] This appears to be incorrect. Though the incidence of

---

5 R. Probst, 'Die Schweiz und die internationale Schiedsgerischtbarkeit', (1960) 17 *Schweizerisches Jahrbuch für internationales Recht* 99, 131-132.

6 V.H. Umbricht, *Multilateral Mediation* (1989).

7 See chapter I 4.2.

8 See chapter I 3.1.

conciliation by persons with substantial political clout is indeed seemingly non-existent, there is no reason to call conciliation involving political heavyweights something other than conciliation. Moreover, the conduct of the commission as a respectable and balanced advisor of what would be reasonable to accept, can in itself generate political power suitable to pressure the parties into settlement. The *Jan Mayen* commission for instance, composed of the leading experts of each party plus a highly respected neutral chairman, appears to have formulated recommendations which, also because of the standing of the commission, were politically very difficult to reject.[9]

Lastly, a choice available to the commission is the provision of services following conclusion of the proceedings. It can for instance make itself available to resolve differences of interpretation regarding the recommendations, or regarding the ensuing settlement agreement. In this respect, permanent bodies will have an advantage over *ad hoc* institutions. The secretariat of OSCE Court of Conciliation, for instance, can serve as a permanent point of contact in assisting the parties in the elaboration of their settlement, and as liaison with the panel of conciliators in case their continued help is requested.

1.3 The role of the dispute

In addition to the parties and the conciliators, the use and success of the effort of conciliation is also dependent on the nature and development of the dispute itself, even if the parties and the conciliators would be the unchanged. A dispute that concerns the interpretation of a maritime incident involving the loss of life, while one of the parties is at war (*Dogger Bank*), will get different treatment than one involving the loss of only a ship, when the primary cause of the loss was a common enemy (*Gorm and Svava*). This is so even if both cases involve the ascertaining of historical facts and the allocation of legal responsibility. Also, certain disputes give rise to attention by other States or by international organisations, while others do not. If, as in the *Chaco* Case between Bolivia and Paraguay, there is a close interest by a major power such as the United States, parties may feel more pressed, but may also obtain additional rewards if the settlement is to the satisfaction of that outside power. Further, the public attention given to a particular case may influence the proceedings drastically, as demonstrated by the rupture following public pronouncements by one conciliator in the *F.OABV* Case.

There are many variables in the process of conciliation.[10] Parties, conciliators and the dispute itself can each vary in many ways, resulting in as many

---

[9] See chapter III 3.4.1.

[10] Mediation studies occasionally question when a dispute is 'ripe' for settlement: I.W. Zartman, *Ripe for Resolution: Conflict and Intervention in Africa* (1989); S. Touval and I.W.

different conciliation procedures. It is exactly because of this that there is good reason to identify a small number clear conceptions of conciliation, which carry in them essential distinguishing characteristics of the method. If clear conceptions can be distilled, the use of conciliation should be better understood.

2. Two Conceptions of Conciliation

Even though conciliation can take on many forms, two conceptions of conciliation can be distinguished: legal conciliation and political conciliation. These conceptions embody two identities of conciliation with distinct characteristics, while both identities fall within the common understanding and definitions of conciliation. They are two ideal types, in the sense of idealised abstractions.[11] Any proceedings in practice may comprise elements of both conceptions, though it should at least theoretically also be possible for proceedings to be just one or the other. The conceptions of political and legal conciliation address the way the conciliation is conducted. The ideal types regard, among other things, the terms of reference, the pursuit of conciliation by the parties and by the conciliators, the content of the commission's recommendations and the way in which parties respond to them. These conceptions suggest alternative methods to apply to conciliation, all within the understanding of the constitutive elements of conciliation.[12] It is proposed to distinguish between:

Political conciliation: The arguments used can include economic, historical, strategic and any other relevant considerations. Legal considerations may be among them, but where they are they do not carry any preponderant weight: the value attached to them depends on how important anyone thinks they are (they do not 'trump' other considerations);[13] and

---

Zartman (eds.), *International Mediation in Theory and Practice* (1985). Discussions have long focussed on the achievement of 'a mutually hurting stalemate.' J. Wilkenfeld and others (eds.), *Mediating International Crises* (2005) ch 6, and C.A. Crocker, F. Osler Hampson and P. Aall (eds.), *Herding Cats: Multiparty Mediation in a Complex World* (1999).

[11] The concept of ideal-types was developed by Max Weber: J.W. Harris, *Legal Philosophies* (2nd edn. 1997) 267.

[12] See chapter I 3.

[13] Theoretically a more 'purely political' form of conciliation is also conceivable, in which legal considerations are excluded completely. However, arguments of justice and entitlement are bound to be involved at least implicitly in any relevant discussion. As such arguments necessarily relate to law, also discussions on an exclusively political basis will involve legal thought.

> **Legal conciliation**: The conciliation involves a legal analysis of the case. Non-legal considerations are taken into account only in so far as the law recognises them as relevant.[14]

It is important to note that the types only relate to the conduct of conciliation. The types do not refer to the basis of any eventual settlement between the parties, for that is beyond the conciliation itself. Strictly law-based recommendations issued by the commission may still be followed by a purely political compromise between the parties.

This division of conciliation conceptions is relevant because of the confusion that has hindered an effective overview of the method. While the early drafters of conciliation provisions thought of conciliation in political terms, many practitioners chose a legalistic approach. Further, discussions of the method tend to be either inconclusive about the substantive aspects of the procedure,[15] or to adopt one of the forms exclusively.[16] While the current separation does not enable a clean categorisation of all cases, it may assist understanding the variable nature of conciliation. It should be clear, meanwhile, that the ideal types remain abstractions, and that any given procedure is in practice likely to combine elements of both. The distinction of ideal types indeed suggests that practice, as will be discussed further, is less clear. An 'ideal type' is not necessarily ideal for any given situation.

2.1 Political conciliation

Conciliation was developed as an alternative to the judicial process. The Swiss government, when in 1919 it pioneered a policy of concluding conciliation treaties, explicitly presented the method as a means to avoid litigation: in international politics, as in people's personal lives, 'recourse to a judge can undoubtedly produce a judgement, but is at the same time a source of resentment and can therefore give rise to new conflicts.'[17] Two aspects of litigation in

---

[14] A controversial topic with international courts and tribunals. It has long been a source of criticism of the ICJ, for instance in the *Nuclear Tests* Cases (*Australia and New Zealand* v. *France*), (1974) *ICJ Rep* 457. The opposite objection, that the Court does not take into account extra-legal, political arguments is also of long-standing, e.g., in the *South West Africa* Cases (*Second Phase*) (*Liberia and Ethiopia* v. *South Africa*) (*Judgement*), (1966) *ICJ Rep* 6, and in criticism of the Advisory Opinion *Legal Consequences of the Construction of a Wall in the Occupied Palestinian Territory* (*Advisory Opinion*), (2004) *ICJ Rep*.

[15] E.g., *Cot* especially 181-189.

[16] E.g., F.M. van Asbeck, 'La tâche et l'action d'une commission de conciliation', (1956) *NTIR* 1.

[17] 'Rapport du Conseil fédéral à l'Assemblée fédérale concernant les traités internationaux d'arbitrage', (1919) 71 *Feuille Fédéral Suisse* Vol. V 808, 819 (own tr).

particular are in play. First, there are the social, financial and political costs involved in bringing a difference to court. Second, it is the articulation of the dispute in terms of the law that can bring it to a higher level of controversy, and that invites the formulation of strong and opposite claims.[18] If recourse to a third party is necessary, avoiding the language of the law may, among other things, serve to limit the adversarial character of the proceedings. At the same time, it allows the dispute to be settled on other grounds than if the law were strictly applied.[19] The Swiss argued: 'La conciliation permet de céder tout en laissant entière la question de principe.'[20] Matters of the law were therefore to be avoided as much as possible, allowing for all parties to insist on the righteousness and legality of their position, while in practice conceding enough to reach a satisfactory compromise.[21] The liberty of the commission to ignore the law offers the parties the liberty to submit any kind of dispute to it:

> '[la procédure de conciliation] peut être introduite dans toutes les circonstances, même dans les conflits de haute politique, d' une part, parce que la proposition de conciliation n'est liée à aucune règle de droit, mais peut s'attacher exclusivement à des considérations tirées de l'équité et de l'opportunité, et, d'autre part, parce que les Parties conservent toute leur liberté d'action.'[22]

The commission would however be asked to take into consideration all aspects of the dispute. Legal claims are therefore not wholly excluded. Indeed, in addition to finding the facts, clarifying the legal situation for the commission's own deliberations, in order to assess what may be a fair compromise, is in this conception a legitimate occupation for conciliation commissions.[23] The law is here however only an instrument, an accessory to the overriding goal of finding a politically acceptable compromise.[24] The standard terms of reference of politi-

---

[18] On the use of the language of law as a political instrument: J.G. Collier and A.V. Lowe, *The Settlement of Disputes in International Law* (1999) 3-5.

[19] C. Gorgé, 'L'évolution de la conciliation internationale', 54 *RDILC* (1927) 58, 79-80.

[20] 'Rapport du Conseil fédéral à l'Assemblée fédérale concernant les traités internationaux d'arbitrage', (1919) 71 *Feuille Fédéral Suisse* Vol. V 808, 820.

[21] A particular example in the EAC case: V.H. Umbricht, *Multilateral Mediation: Practical Experiences and Lessons* (1989) 169.

[22] 'Message du Conseil fédéral à l'Assemblée fédérale concernant la ratification du traité d'arbitrage et de conciliation conclu, le 3 décembre 1921, entre la Confédération suisse et le Reich allemand', (1922) 73 *Feuille Fédéral Suisse* Vol. I 187, 193.

[23] E.g., 'Message du Conseil fédéral à l'Assemblée fédérale concernant l'approbation du traité de conciliation et d'arbitrage conclu, le 18 juin 1924, entre la Suisse et la Hongrie', (1924) 76 *Feuille Fédéral Suisse* Vol. III 638.

[24] The *France/Siam* Case was entirely composed of diplomats: S. Bastid, 'La commission de conciliation franco-siamoise', in C. Rousseau (ed.), *La Technique et les Principes du Droit Public: Etudes en l'Honneur de Georges Scelle* (1950) 1.

cal conciliation are contained in the General Act for the Pacific Settlement of International Disputes adopted by the League of Nations in 1928:

> 'The task of the Conciliation Commission shall be to elucidate the questions in dispute, to collect with that object all necessary information by means of enquiry or otherwise, and to endeavour to bring the parties to an agreement. It may, after the case has been examined, inform the parties of the terms of settlement which seem suitable to it, and lay down the period within which they are to make their decision.'[25]

The task of any commission is to find a solution to the dispute. By implication, this allows the conciliators to propose anything that has a chance of being accepted. What guidelines do the terms provide? First, the commission is to 'elucidate the questions in dispute'. This refers to the investigative function of the commission, the inheritance of the fact-finding commissions from which the thought of conciliation developed. It is the task of the commission to collect all useful information, by way of inquiry or otherwise.[26] Naturally, for a good understanding of the dispute, it is important that the commissioners obtain all relevant insights. The commission is therefore normally given explicit competence to request all information from the parties, and the parties always have an obligation to co-operate in good faith.[27] The clarification of the facts, positions and issues remains, however, at all times subjected to the final goal: that of reaching an agreement. Just as the commission should avoid antagonising the parties with controversial legal assessments, it should not delve into the basics of the dispute when this can endanger amicable settlement. This caution is especially relevant when after the initial investigation the commission turns to the discussions with the parties, and even more so when it issues its recommendations.[28]

After, and possibly even during the investigation stage, the commission is to bring the parties to an agreement. It is only following conclusion of the investigation of the dispute, and only if the commission deems it desirable, that

---

[25] 1928 General Act Art. 15(1).

[26] Nguyen Quoc Dinh, 'Les commissions de conciliation sont elles aussi des commissions d'enquête?', (1967) 71 *RGDIP* 565.

[27] Typically, the 1928 General Act Art. 13 provides: 'The parties undertake to facilitate the work of the Conciliation Commission, and particularly to supply it to the greatest possible extent with all relevant documents and information, as well as to use the means at their disposal to allow it to proceed in their territory, and in accordance with their law, to the summoning and hearing of witnesses or experts and to visit the localities in question.'

[28] E.g., the French-Swiss commission, when dealing with Swiss allegations of illegal French operations on Swiss soil, avoided a hearing which would have involved delicate issues. P. Reuter, 'Le droit au secret et les institutions internationales', (1956) 2 *AFDI* 46, 50.

the standard provisions allow the commission to outline its own proposals. In practice, however, it should be possible for the commission to issue informal proposals or recommendations at any time that this may facilitate a settlement.[29] It should nevertheless be ensured that a partial agreement will not complicate reaching a comprehensive settlement.

In political conciliation, any argument that may seem reasonable to both parties may do as the basis of the commission's recommendations. Economic and financial interests, strategic and diplomatic considerations, anything can be taken into account. Frequently the wide range of interests affected by any dispute will favour settlement. This wide range may then also provide the way out: a party can give up some particular interests in one field for compensation in another. This flexibility is not available in judicial settlement. It is mostly this flexibility that, in the perception of the Swiss pioneers of conciliation, allows both parties to compromise politically, without relinquishing their principles.

2.2 **Legal conciliation**

The terms of reference of the traditional bilateral dispute settlement treaties of early to mid-20th century do not refer to any norms to be applied, but rather focus on the desired outcome, a proposal acceptable to all. They therefore provide for political conciliation, as set out above. Nevertheless, the absence of a reference to international law did not stand in the way of it being used as a guide by those who practiced conciliation. This shows that in conciliation the terms of reference are not decisive, but that the approach taken in practice will depend essentially on the views on the dispute by conciliators and parties. In those conciliation undertakings of which we know the details, disputes were often treated in a legal manner.[30]

In the *French/Swiss* Case of 1956 the adjudicatory approach was especially noted.[31] The 1925 French-Swiss Treaty of Conciliation, Arbitration and Com-

---

[29] In the procedures for commercial conciliation this is a normal feature. For instance, the possibility of issuing proposals during the course of the undertaking is given explicitly in the UNCITRAL Conciliation Rules Art. 7(4) UNGA Res 35/52 (1980) and the Convention on the Settlement of Investment Disputes between States and the Nationals of Other States (18 March 1965) (ICSID Convention) (1965) Art. 34(1), 4 *ILM* 524.

[30] E.g., the *Germany/Lithuania* Case, the *France/Switzerland* Case, the *Switzerland/Italy* Case and the *Roula* Case, of which the work of the commissions is known to some extent: chapter II 1.9.

[31] S. Bastid, 'La commission de conciliation franco-suisse', (1956) 2 *AFDI* 436; F.M. van Asbeck, 'La tâche et l'action d'une commission de conciliation', (1956) *NTIR* 1; F.M. van Asbeck, 'La procédure suivi par la commission de conciliation franco-suisse', (1956) *NTIR* 209; A. Gros, 'Remarques sur la conciliation internationale', in *L'Evolution du Droit Public; Etudes Offertes à Achille Mestre* (1956) 279.

pulsory Adjudication on which the commission's jurisdiction was based,[32] included the same terms of reference for a conciliation commission as those of the 1928 General Act, cited above as an example of political conciliation. However, president Van Asbeck in his inaugural address recalled that if the conciliation effort would not succeed, the matter would be referred to the International Court of Justice. In that light, 'on pourrait regarder notre examen comme la répétition générale d'un procès devant la Cour.'[33] Therefore,

> '[i]l ne peut y avoir de doute qu'il nous incombe à nous d'élucider d'abord les positions *juridiques* réciproques des deux Parties (...) pour tâcher de donner un avis objectif aux Parties, un avis qui, le cas échéant, pourrait s'exprimer entre autres sur les chances de succès d'une action à intenter devant la Cour.'[34]

By considering the procedure as a non-binding preliminary round of adjudication, Van Asbeck held that conciliation was essentially an adversarial legal process. He rhetorically asked whether it was not only the law that could 'place us on solid ground, from where we can pursue the possibilities of settlement'.[35] Therefore, conciliation proceedings should closely resemble international litigation, with the exception coming at the end, as the judgement or award is non-binding.[36]

Another example in which in practice legal conciliation overtook a more political conception is provided by ICSID. The ICSID Convention gives the following purpose to conciliation commissions:

> 'It shall be the duty of the Commission to clarify the issues in dispute between the two parties and to endeavour to bring about agreement between them upon mutually acceptable terms. To that end, the Commission may at any stage of the proceedings and from time to time recommend terms of settlement to the parties. The parties shall cooperate in good faith with the Commission in order to enable the Commission to carry out its functions, and shall give their most serious consideration to its recommendations.'[37]

While it is assumed that investigation of the dispute will assist settlement, the terms of reference are political in nature. They do not refer to legal rules or

---

32 (6 April 1925); M. Habicht, *Post-War Treaties for the Pacific Settlement of International Disputes* (1931) 226.

33 F.M. van Asbeck, 'La tâche et l'action d'une commission de conciliation', (1956) *NTIR* 1, 6.

34 Idem, 7.

35 Idem, 7

36 F.M. van Asbeck, 'La procédure suivi par la commission de conciliation franco-suisse', (1956) *NTIR* 209.

37 ICSID Convention Art. 34(1).

other considerations: the only concern is to allow the parties to reach agreement. While the elaborate ICSID Conciliation Rules describe formal aspects similar to standard arbitration rules, for instance in the appointment and replacement of the conciliators and in the rules on submissions, they do not imply that the conciliation effort itself should resemble arbitration.[38] Further, persons on ICSID's list of potential conciliators should be 'persons of a high moral character with recognised competence in the fields of law, commerce, industry or finance, who may be relied upon to exercise independent judgement.'[39] Law is thus only one of the possible areas of expertise of a potential conciliator. When, on the other hand, recourse is had to arbitration within the ICSID framework, legal expertise is a necessary condition for appointment. Unlike the case of ICSID arbitration, when a State has accepted conciliation this does not relieve it of the possible use of diplomatic protection by the State of the investor.[40] Where it is considered inappropriate for the arbitral proceedings to coexist with the exercise of political pressure on behalf of the investor, its acceptance in the course of conciliation supports a political conception of ICSID conciliation.

Nevertheless, the deliberations in *Tesoro/Trinidad and Tobago*, the first case settled under the ICSID conciliation rules, were essentially of a legal character.[41] The conciliator, Lord Wilberforce, followed the line of the *Gorm and Svava* Case when he set out that his task was:

> 'to examine the contentions raised by the parties, to clarify the issues, and to endeavour to evaluate their respective merits and the likelihood of their being accepted, or rejected, in Arbitration or Court proceedings, in the hope that such evaluation may assist the parties in reaching an agreed settlement.'[42]

With such an understanding of the conciliator's mandate, irrespective of the terms of reference, the proceedings amounted to a form of legal conciliation. It is understood that the parties would also have had the possibility of resorting to arbitration, if conciliation should have failed. The parties succeeded in reaching an amicable settlement on the basis of the recommendations.

---

[38] E.g., ICSID Conciliation Rules Art. 5-12, 25-28.

[39] Idem, Art. 14(1).

[40] Idem, Art. 27.

[41] *Tesoro Petroleum Co/Trinidad and Tobago* ISCID Case No. CONC/83/1; L. Nurick and S.J. Schnably, 'The First ICSID Conciliation', (1986) 1 *ICSID Rev Foreign Investment Law Journal* 340, 347.

[42] From the recommendation issued by Lord Wilberforce (5 February 1985) quoted in L. Nurick and S.J. Schnably, 'The First ICSID Conciliation', (1986) 1 *ICSID Rev Foreign Investment Law Journal* 340, 348.

The choice to deal with disputes in legal terms can be understood in large part because most conciliators were jurists. Judging from the composition of the commissions that were activated in the 1930s and 1950s, the relevant governments had come to see conciliation as requiring judges and professors of law.[43] Only the commission in the dispute between France and Siam, where the matter of boundary rectifications was not considered a legal question, consisted exclusively of diplomats.[44] These instances suggest that many conciliators had a different conception of conciliation from those who pioneered the settlement method. These practical views would then override, if necessary, any conception of political conciliation laid down in the applicable terms of reference. By the 1950s, most known instances of conciliation amounted to a form of legal conciliation. In the course of time, therefore, a different form of conciliation had almost completely replaced the original conception of political conciliation. The remaining controversies concerned the degree to which the law should be the centre of the conciliation effort.

3. The Central Debate

In the decades following the initiation of conciliation, the legal conception appeared to have replaced the political. It is in this setting that two of conciliation's leading proponents pursued a debate at the heart of the evolution of the method. The protagonists, François and Rolin, had both had been involved in the 1952 *Gorm and Svava* Case, which had laid down a creative approach to the task of the commission.[45] The commission had first made an inventory of all reasonable legal interpretations of the facts of the dispute. By consensus, it then discarded the least acceptable of these, leaving those legal readings accepted by some, but not by other conciliators. It had thereby identified the area of doctrinal legal dispute. The commission then assessed the chances of success of the various competing legal views, then weighed the various claims. On this basis the amount of the claim was calculated, and this amount became the proposed settlement amount. The final result was thus reminiscent of an award by a tribunal, with the important difference that the commission did not issue any potentially controversial legal pronouncements.

---

[43] For example, both the France/Swiss commission and the Belgian/Danish commission were composed of three judges or law professors, plus two diplomats. The presidents were always lawyers.

[44] S. Bastid, 'La commission de conciliation franco-siamoise', in C. Rousseau (ed.), *La Technique et les Principes du Droit Public: Etudes en l'Honneur de Georges Scelle* (1950) 1.

[45] H. Rolin, 'Une conciliation belgo-danoise', (1953) 57 *RGDIP* 353.

This approach would later also be followed by two separate conciliations conducted by sole conciliators, in two cases concerning devaluation of Japanese loans.[46] While pointing out that it was not the task to give a judicial pronouncement, in both cases the conciliator proceeded to interpret the legal clauses of the contracts, and thereby established the relative merits of the claims. At the same time, the making of controversial legal assessments which could obstruct amicable settlement was avoided as much as possible. Instead the focus was on the relative value of the respective legal arguments, combined with an 'equitable' consideration of the legitimate expectations at the time the loan was formalised. After some legal argument, in both cases the conciliator came up with a proposed settlement inspired by the law, but not explicitly traceable to it.

A related option was adopted by the Italian/Swiss Commission in 1956.[47] The commission assessed the claims of the parties on their legal merits, but conveyed the observations unofficially, during the proceedings, so that they could form a basis for further negotiations with guidance from the conciliators. To keep the conciliation from being dominated by debates over the finer legal issues, the Commission's legal opinion was given without the reasoning that it was based upon. The absence of the legal grounds lessened the value of the opinion, thereby making it harder for the favoured party to renounce further conciliation and rely exclusively on its legal case. The Italian/Swiss Commission subsequently created a sub-commission consisting of the two national commissioners, assisted by economic and financial experts. This sub-commission was able to draft an agreement that, after some modifications, was adopted by the whole commission, and eventually by the parties themselves.

3.1 The debate

As practice shows, at the end of the 1950s different opinions existed on the extent to which legal determinations can contribute to amicable settlement. François made clear that he saw conciliation essentially as a form of advisory arbitration: it is the task of any commission to deal with a dispute on a legal basis, the difference with arbitration being that the final report is not binding on the parties. The commission was to inform the parties of their positions and chances if the case were to be judged. He adopted the view of the *Gorm and Svava* commission, which:

---

[46] *Japanese 4% Loan* Case, (1966) 29 *ILR* 5 and *Tokyo 5% Loan* Case, (1966) 29 *ILR* 11.

[47] M. Breton-Jokl, 'La commission permanente de conciliation italo-suisse', (1957) 3 *AFDI* 210; (1958) 25 *ILR* Vol. I 313; (1954) 11 *Annuaire Suisse de Droit International* 202.

> 'à juste titre a conçu son rôle non comme celui d'un juge, mais d'un conseil, avocat ou avoué, interrogé par un client sur les chances de succès d'un action judiciaire et l'opportunité d'une transaction, avec cette difference que la consultation lui est demandée par les *deux* parties.'[48]

The phrasing owes much to an earlier statement of the same by Rolin.[49] François, however, concluded that:

> 'l'élaboration de la proposition d'arrangement devient une opération *juridique*, une espèce d'instance prélable à examen par la Cour de Justice ou les arbitres, et non l'oeuvre de spéculation ou de sondage psychologique qu'on pourrait supposer; le résultat est de la plus grande importance pour les parties en cause.'[50]

He believed that the commissions should at least be free to determine whether conclusions regarding facts or the law would be helpful in achieving a settlement.[51] If at all possible, legal conclusions should be stated in the report. Essentially, he believed that the law would provide an argument for acceptance of the recommendations. Without it, the opinion of the commission would have little importance to the parties, and it would be hard for any government to make a settlement acceptable to its parliament.[52]

Rolin, on the other hand, had drawn different lessons from the same experience.[53] He believed that any judicial determination by the commission would make the favoured party intransigent. The commission should therefore take account of legal and factual matters and clarify the situation, but not judge it.[54] Specifically, it should refrain from any definitive opinion on legal or factual matters unless explicitly asked to do so.[55]

Some writers, notably André Gros and Julius Stone, argued that by assimilating conciliation to arbitration, the potential contribution of conciliation to

---

[48] J.P.A. François, 'La Cour Permanente d'Arbitrage', (1955) 87 *Recueil des Cours* Vol. I 456, 537. See H. Rolin, 'Une conciliation belgo-danoise', (1953) 57 *RGDIP* 353; N.V. Boeg, 'Le différend dano-belge au sujet des navires danois 'Gorm' et 'Svava'', (1953) 23 *Acta Scandinavica Juris Gentium* 48.

[49] H. Rolin, 'Une conciliation belgo-danoise', (1953) 57 *RGDIP* 353, 358.

[50] J.P.A. François, 'La Cour Permanente d'Arbitrage', (1955) 87 *Recueil des Cours* Vol. I 456, 537.

[51] (1961) 49 *Annuaire de l'Institut de Droit International* Vol. II 237.

[52] Ibid., 205, 252. P. Reuter seems to support François' legal conception of conciliation but emphasised the difficulties this entailed: 'Principes de droit public', (1961) 103 *Recueil des Cours* Vol. II 635.

[53] H. Rolin, 'Une conciliation belgo-danoise', (1953) 57 *RGDIP* 353 and H. Rolin, 'L'Heure de la conciliation', (1957) 3 *European Yearbook* 1, 12.

[54] (1961) 49 *Annuaire de l'Institut de Droit International* Vol. II 238, 241-242.

[55] H. Rolin, 'L' Heure de la conciliation', (1957) 3 *European Yearbook* 1, 12.

the settlement of disputes was neglected.[56] It should be the objective to find creative solutions, uninhibited by legal constraints, which allow for the settlement of any controversy without affecting the legal position of the parties in case the conciliation effort fails. The conciliator's role should be that of a friend in a social dispute rather than that of a legal counsel. Stone remarked:

> 'It follows also that clarification of the legal position by the conciliators should rarely rise above a very secondary role, except in the unusual case of an open flouting of clear legal rights without claim of justice, by a party who is subject to the compulsory jurisdiction of a tribunal of law in case the conciliation fails.'[57]

Having been the Agent in the *France/Switzerland* Cases, in which president Van Asbeck pursued a purely legal conception of conciliation, Gros pointed at the interpretation of conciliation as a kind of adjudication as the principal reason for its lack of application.[58]

The debate came before the Institute of International Law in 1961, when the experts were invited to decide on a model procedure of conciliation. Rolin was Rapporteur. Already in 1959 he had sent out a questionnaire regarding conciliation, which resulted in a range of views submitted by leading jurists.[59] The final text Rolin put before the Institute reflected his views:

> 'The President of the Commission may accompany his communication with a statement, either orally or in writing, of the principal reasons which, in the opinion of the Commission, appear likely to persuade the Parties to accept a settlement. He will refrain in this statement from setting forth definitive conclusions with reference to disputed facts or from formally deciding questions of law involved, unless the Commission has been requested to do so by the Parties.'[60]

François submitted an alternative: the commission would refrain from giving definitive conclusions regarding the facts or the legal matters arising in the matter, unless:

---

[56] 'Letter of Julius Stone', (1959) 48 *Annuaire de l'Institut de Droit International* Vol. I 88, 89-91. A. Gros, 'Remarques sur la conciliation internationale', in *L'Evolution du Droit Public; Etudes Offertes à Achille Mestre* (1956) 279.

[57] 'Letter of Julius Stone', (1959) 48 *Annuaire de l'Institut de Droit International* Vol. I 88, 90.

[58] A. Gros, 'Remarques sur la conciliation internationale' in *L'Evolution du Droit Public; Etudes Offertes à Achille Mestre* (1956) 279, 283. For an early statement of these views see the remarks made by J. Basdevant, (1927) 33 *Annuaire de l'Institut de Droit International* Vol. II, 867.

[59] (1959) 48 *Annuaire de l'Institut de Droit International* Vol. I 45 ff.

[60] Regulation on the Procedure of International Conciliation Art. 7 (English trans) (IDI Conciliation Rules'), (1961) 49 *Annuaire de l'Institut de Droit International* Vol. II 385.

> 'the commission deems that observations regarding the facts or the statement of its legal opinion would facilitate the purpose of its mission, provided that the terms of reference do not oppose this.'[61]

Rolin carried the day by a large majority, but many of the best known names sided with his opponent.[62] The IDI had thereby decided in favour of the less exclusively legal conception of conciliation as proposed by Rolin. The school of thought led by François, however, saw its views adopted in many multilateral treaties concluded in the years ahead.

The importance of the debate is not so much in the adoption or rejection of either the views of Rolin or François, but that it entrenched the view that conciliation was in essence a legal method of settlement.[63] The issue whether legal conclusions should be made explicit or not diverted attention from the legitimate question whether the commission should be occupied with the application of legal principles in the first place. Only a small minority voiced doubts about whether conciliation should be assimilated to legal settlement at all. Building on the tradition in which conciliation was first conceived, they argued that conciliation should be thought of as a political method of facilitation, not a variation of a legal method. They were insufficiently heard. There appeared only to be one conception of conciliation.

3.2 The legal conception and multilateral treaties

The legal conception of conciliation became formalised in many of the multilateral treaties drafted from that time onwards. Of special significance is the Vienna Convention on the Law of Treaties, which explicitly adopted the legal conception of conciliation.[64] This resulted from a last minute compromise between the countries favouring a comprehensive binding settlement procedure for disputes arising under the Convention, essentially the Western States, and those States opposing any third party intervention for ideological reasons (the communist States) and cultural reasons (certain African and Asian States).[65]

---

[61] Ibid., 264 (own tr).

[62] Rolins proposal was adopted by 44 votes to 13. François was however supported, *inter alia*, by Guggenheim, Rousseau, Wehberg, Verzijl and Charles de Visscher, (1961) 49 *Annuaire de l'Institut de Droit International* Vol. II 266.

[63] To this day, e.g., R. Donner, 'The Procedure of International Conciliation: Some Historical Aspects', (1999) 1 *Journal of the History of International Law* 103, 123.

[64] Cf., R. Donner, 'The Procedure of International Conciliation', (1999) 1 *Journal of the History of International Law* 104.

[65] I. Sinclair, *The Vienna Convention on the Law of Treaties* (2nd edn. 1984) 226-233; R.D. Kearney and R.E. Dalton, 'The Treaty on Treaties', (1970) 64 *AJIL* 495, 545; S. Rosenne, 'The Settlement of Treaty Disputes under the Vienna Convention of 1969', (1971) 31 *ZfAÖRV* 1.

After long negotiations, in an effort to break the stalemate, the final agreement contained in Article 66 of the Convention provides that disputes regarding the law of treaties concerning the interpretation or application of the *jus cogens* provisions may eventually be submitted to the ICJ, while for disputes concerning invalidity, termination and suspension of the operation of treaties, compulsory conciliation is provided. Such compulsory conciliation replaced the provision for arbitration as originally supported by the Western States. To dampen concern over the lack of legal safeguards for the application of the Convention, it was decided to increase the legal nature of conciliation by providing for legally oriented conciliators and by allowing explicit legal conclusions.[66] Not only should the list of conciliators prescribed by the Convention only contain the names of qualified jurists, more importantly the Convention explicitly refers to legal conclusions that the conciliators may reach:

> 'The report of the Commission, *including any conclusions stated therein regarding the facts or questions of law* shall not be binding on the parties and it shall have no other character than that of recommendations submitted for the consideration of the parties in order to facilitate an amicable settlement of the dispute.'[67]

The commission is given discretion to include legal or factual conclusions in its report if it considers this useful for the settlement of the conflict.

The provisions of the 1969 Convention were repeated in compulsory conciliation provisions of the 1978 Vienna Convention on Succession of States in Respect of Treaties[68] and became standard drafting policy.[69] Similarly, the 1980 UNCITRAL Conciliation Rules, designed for dispute settlement involving private parties, also approximate legal conciliation:

> 'The conciliator will be guided by principles of objectivity, fairness and justice, giving consideration to, among other things, the rights and obligations of the par-

---

[66] Vienna Convention on the Law of Treaties Art. 66.

[67] Idem, Annex Art. 2 (emphasis added).

[68] Annex Art. 6 (1978), 72 *AJIL* 971. Generally: R. Lavalle, 'Dispute Settlement under the Vienna Convention on Succession of States', (1979) 73 *AJIL* 407.

[69] E.g., Convention on the Representation of States in Their Relations With International Organisations of a Universal Character (1975), (1975) 69 *AJIL* 730; Convention on the Law of the Sea; Annex to the Vienna Convention on Succession in Respect of State Property, Archives and Debts (1983), (1983) 22 *ILM* 298 and the Vienna Convention on the Law of Treaties between States and International Organisations or Between International Organisations (1986) Annex, (1986) 25 *ILM* 543. A distinct approach was taken in the penultimate draft of the Articles on State Responsibility (provisionally adopted by the ILC in 1995): 'Report of the International Law Commission 48th Session' Art. 56 and UN Doc A/51/10 Annex I reprinted in (1998) 37 *ILM* 440. The ILC chose political conciliation, adopting the terms of reference of the General Act for the Peaceful Settlement of International Disputes (1949), while at the same time introducing the requirement that the conciliators are qualified jurists. These provisions were deleted in the final draft.

ties, the usages of the trade concerned and the circumstances surrounding the dispute, including any previous business practices between the parties.'[70]

Before that however, the adoption of the 1975 Convention on the Relations between States and International Organisations pushed the inclusion of legal considerations one step further:

> 'The report *shall* include the Commission's conclusions upon the facts and questions of law and the recommendations which it has submitted to the parties to the dispute in order to facilitate a settlement of the dispute.'[71]

This wording indicates that the commission is obliged to take up a legal role. On a strict reading, however, it is possible to understand the obligation placed on the commission only to involve the inclusion of legal conclusions *if it makes any.* If the clause is so understood, the commission could decide not to make any legal assessments, and therefore it would not have to include any in her report. The same interpretation is possible for the related clause in the 1982 Law of the Sea Convention:

> 'Its report shall record any agreements reached and, failing agreement, its conclusions on all questions of fact or law relevant to the matter in dispute and such recommendations as the commission may deem appropriate for an amicable settlement.'[72]

Freedom is granted as regards the recommendations ('may deem appropriate'). There appears to be no discretion not to include legal conclusions.

The legalistic views of conciliation adopted in the 1975, 1978 and 1982 Conventions are surpassed by an ambiguous provision in the 1992 Framework Convention on Climate Change and other conventions following its example. If its compulsory conciliation procedure is applied, the commission is asked to deliver a 'recommendatory award', which the parties are to consider in good faith.[73] The use of the term 'award' indicates that the framers were thinking of

---

[70] UNCITRAL Conciliation Rules rule 7(2).

[71] Convention on the Representation of States in their Relations with International Organisations of a Universal Character Art. 85(7) [emphasis added]. U. Villiani, 'A New Conciliation Procedure: The Vienna Convention on the Representation of Sates in Their Relations with International Organisations of a Universal Character', (1978-1979) 4 *Italian Yearbook of International Law* 31; J. Ritter, 'La Conférence et la Convention sur la Répresentation des Etats dans leurs Rélations avec les Organisations Internationales', (1975) 21 *AFDI* 471.

[72] LOSC Annex V Art. 7(1).

[73] Framework Convention on Climate Change Art. 14(5). Similar: Oslo Protocol to the 1979 Convention on Long-Range Transboundary Air Pollution of Further Reduction of Sulphur Emissions (14 June 1994), (1994) 33 *ILM* 1540 Art. 9(6).

arbitration. This seems to imply that the recommendation issued by a commission under the Convention would be a non-binding legal declaration rather than a proposed amicable settlement.[74]

By the 1990s the legal conception of conciliation was thereby dominant in multilateral treaties. This development stemmed from many factors, not in the least its treatment by conciliators themselves. Through their involvement in academic debate such as in the IDI, a notion of the method evolved which had little connection to the original view of conciliation as a political means of settlement. The legal conception was used and further strengthened when, in the drafting of multilateral treaties, there was held to be a need for an alternative to adjudication. Conciliation, already seen as a legal method, could fulfil that role, explicitly adorned with legal characteristics, such as jurist-conciliators and a prescription to the commission to express legal opinions.

3.3 The supremacy of the law?

If the parties use conciliation as a substitute for arbitration in matters they would otherwise have resolved judicially, the legal approach to conciliation may be a worthwhile alternative. This assumes, however, that the parties can accept at least partially negative conclusions, and share the intention to settle on the basis of the report. For when they accept losses in conciliation, the parties are not able to hide behind the binding authority of a judge. If, on the other hand, conciliation is initiated by parties who do not share a willingness to settle on the basis of as yet unknown recommendations, the legal approach can create complications. If it is the essence of the law to provide reliable guidelines for action, law will be an obstacle when all that is desired is latitude to reach a compromise of interests. The solid basis that law may provide for a proposal may also foster controversy if a party considers that the law as applied does not do it justice.

For a multilateral treaty regime legal conciliation has additional value in those cases where no possibility is created to submit the case to adjudication. Judicially inspired conciliation then offers the best chance at a principled settlement. Sometimes States are only willing to subscribe to written norms if the settlement mechanism does not produce binding decisions, as was the case for instance with several subjects covered by the 1982 Convention on the Law of the Sea. If then, when disputes arise, all settlements are free-standing *ad hoc* compromises, this can undermine the legal regime in which the other parties

[74] This appears a weaker form of 1925 Geneva Protocol Art. 4 (never entered into force), which provided that if the parties did not follow-up a unanimous conciliation report with arbitration, the conciliation report would be binding upon them.

also have an interest.[75] Most multilateral treaties do therefore in fact incorporate legalistic elements in the conciliation system.[76]

Nevertheless, the conciliation provisions in multilateral treaties have to our knowledge not been applied up to the present. The discrepancy between the popularity of the method in treaty provisions and the neglect of those provisions in practice may well add to the original criticism of legal conciliation voiced by Stone and Gros. For apparently only when the matter is not of major importance, and acceptance of the recommendations is assured in practice, as was the case with nearly all cases in the 1930s and 1950s, does legal conciliation offer significant advantages over arbitration.

The proper place for the legal assessments is also dependent on the character of the dispute. Sometimes parties can concur with a certain result because it seems to both of them to be just or at least practical. It is however rare that both parties agree with – rather than acquiesce in – judgements given by courts or tribunals. In many of these cases, parties accept the final decision, not necessarily because they concur with the findings, but because they had agreed that the decision would be final and binding.[77] If however, as is the case with conciliation, there is no such agreement, a seriously controversial verdict emanating from legal conciliation is not likely to be the basis of amicable compromise. This could be different if after the conciliation proceedings one of the parties can unilaterally initiate a binding legal procedure. In that case the conciliators may use their recommendations to provide an indication of what can be expected in adjudication. If the parties have not explicitly asked for a legal assessment, it should therefore be left to the conciliators in any particular case to see whether there is room for explicating a legal basis for their recommendations.

It is important to note that not all conciliation is legal conciliation, and that law-based conciliation does not necessarily have to be advisory (i.e., non-binding) arbitration. The discussants at the IDI overlooked the fact that commissions are not necessarily exclusively composed of lawyers. Furthermore, the IDI discussion focused on the final report in which the legal conclusions could be incorporated. The report is however not necessarily the focal point of the procedure. In the exercise of its functions the commission is likely to be involved in discussions with the parties before the delivery of the final recom-

---

[75] A highly critical assessment is made by R. Bindschedeler in *Judicial Settlement of International Disputes – An International Symposium* (1974) 163; H. von Mangoldt, 'Arbitration and Conciliation', ibid., 417, 487.

[76] See chapter IV 2.

[77] Incidentally, the difference between consensual submission and unilateral application is less than often assumed: C. Schulte, *Compliance with Decisions of the International Court of Justice* (2004) 405-413.

mendations. A commission may indeed be more successful if issuing the report can be avoided altogether. Conciliation, including legal conciliation, is therefore a more diverse method than it was credited for by either François or Rolin. On this understanding, the following sections investigate some alternative options developed in theory and practice.

3.4 **Some alternatives**

Whether or not the IDI discussion was the cause, a fact is that very few conciliations would follow. The 1960s only saw the two mentioned Japanese cases, which were both *ad hoc* procedures not between states, but between creditors and respectively Japan and the city of Tokyo.[78] In inter-State relations, only a fact-finding commission was set-up, in the *Red Crusader* Case of 1965.[79] It was not until 1981 that a new inter-State conciliation commission was created, and this deviated substantially from the traditional model. Its terms of reference represented a fresh look at the possibilities of conciliation.

3.4.1 *The* Jan Mayen *conciliation Case*

In the *Jan Mayen* Case, an *ad hoc* conciliation undertaking by Norway and Iceland, law and politics were combined in a novel way. The aim was to settle the outstanding maritime delimitation issues in the area around the Norwegian island of Jan Mayen, 292 nautical miles off the coast of Iceland.[80] The commission consisted of the Ambassadors Anderson of Iceland and Evensen of Norway, with the American Richardson as chairman. All three headed their respective delegations to the United Nations Conference on the Law of the Sea. The two nationally appointed conciliators had previously been involved in the bilateral negotiations that led to the conciliation agreement. The combination of political and legal expertise enabled the Commission to draw on both in

---

[78] See chapter II 1.11.

[79] See chapter II 1.4.

[80] Conciliation Commission on the Continental Shelf Area between Iceland and Jan Mayen: Report and Recommendations, (1981) 20 *ILM* 797. The resulting treaty: Agreement on the Continental Shelf between Iceland and Jan Mayen (Iceland-Norway) (22 October 1982), (1982) 21 *ILM* 1222. J. Evensen, 'La délimitation du plateau continental entre la Norvège et l'Islande dans le secteur de Jan Mayen', (1980) 26 *AFDI* 711; E.L. Richardson, 'Jan Mayen in Perspective', (1988) 82 *AJIL* 443; R.R. Churchill, 'Maritime Delimitation in the Jan Mayen Area', (1985) 9 *Marine Policy* 16; J.I. Charney, 'Progress in International Maritime Boundary Delimitation Law', (1994) 88 *AJIL* 227; F. Dalgaard-Knudsen, 'The Greenlandic Offshore Area', (1992) 5 *New York International Law Review* 63; D.W. Bowett, 'Contemporary Developments in Legal Techniques in the Settlement of Disputes', (1983) 180 *Recueil des Cours* Vol. II 169, 188 ff.

its search for a settlement, something required by the unclear state of the law as well as by the substantial political concerns the issue raised, especially for Iceland. The terms of reference reflect this:

> 'The Commission shall have as its mandate the submission of recommendations with regard to the dividing line for the shelf area between Iceland and Jan Mayen. In preparing such recommendations the Commission shall take into account Iceland's strong economic interest in these sea areas, the existing geographical and geological factors and other special circumstances.'[81]

The three conciliators were of the view that in the relevant area the law was 'far from completely crystallised'.[82] They decided therefore to focus on a fair division of the resources rather than on producing an artificial dividing line. To this end a detailed study was commissioned to establish a factual basis for any recommendations. First the draft Convention on the Law of the Sea was used to establish the island status of Jan Mayen and its legal entitlement to part of the continental shelf.[83] For the division of the area the conciliators turned to the geological report, which focused on the how the shelf is related to Jan Mayen, an issue of potential legal importance, and, secondly, on the prospects for finding valuable oil in the region, a politically sensitive issue. As the relevant shelf area geologically belonged neither to Jan Mayen nor to Iceland but turned out to be a submerged micro-continent of its own, no legal arguments could be raised on that basis.[84] The chances of lucrative oil exploitation were considered to be limited. The Commission thereupon reverted to its mandate, which was to take account of the special circumstances, in particular the needs of Iceland. The report continues:

> 'It follows from the mandate that the Conciliation Commission shall not act as a court of law. Its function is to make recommendations to the two governments which in the unanimous opinion of the Commission shall lead to acceptable and equitable solutions of the problems involved. Although not a court of law, the Commission has thoroughly examined state practice and court decisions in order to ascertain possible guidelines for the practicable and equitable solution of the questions concerned.'[85]

The commission then referred to the development of the Law of the Sea and the case law of the ICJ. Considering the broad scope of considerations open to

---

[81] Agreement on the Continental Shelf (Iceland-Norway) Art. 9(3).
[82] E.L. Richardson, 'Jan Mayen in Perspective', (1988) 82 *AJIL* 443, 445.
[83] Report and Recommendations, (1981) 20 *ILM* 797, 803.
[84] Ibid., 822-823.
[85] Ibid., 823.

the commission, and taking account of the favourable treatment already accorded to Iceland regarding its Exclusive Economic Zone (EEZ), the Commission proposed an option not offered by the developing law at the time, namely to create a zone of joint development, with special rules on exploration and investments.[86]

In many respects the recommendations, on the basis of economic and political considerations, favoured Iceland. About the proposed joint development zone Chairman Richardson wrote:

> 'This approach to dispute resolution is more naturally arrived at by the more flexible method of negotiation between the parties than through a formal adjudicative process. It can thus take into consideration a wide range of political and economic interests that would not necessarily be relevant in a claim as of right.'[87]

The parties eventually reached an agreement incorporating the commission's recommendations. It is clear that the final settlement would have been very different if the matter had been put to the International Court of Justice instead, as did indeed happen in the delimitation in the area between Jan Mayen and Greenland.[88]

The *Jan Mayen* conciliation thus represented a new mixture of political and legal conciliation. This form of dispute settlement finds an analogy in the beginnings of contemporary arbitration with the *Alabama Claims* Case, concerning the construction of Confederate warships in England during the American civil war. The resolution of the dispute was made possible by a special agreement in which the UK agreed to arbitrate on the basis of certain principles which were dear to the United States *as if they were law*.[89] In the *Jan Mayen*

---

[86] Ibid., 825 ff. The novelty of the recommendation did of course not imply it was contrary to existing law.

[87] E.L. Richardson, 'Jan Mayen in Perspective', (1988) 82 *AJIL* 443, 449.

[88] *Case Concerning Maritime Delimitation in the Area between Greenland and Jan Mayen* (*Denmark* v. *Norway*), (1993) *ICJ Rep* 38. The Court adopted the equidistance line and then modified it, guided by special circumstances. There was strong criticism from Judge Oda and Schwebel regarding the open-ended approach taken by the Court. Apparently for reasons of convenience the Court found a single boundary for both the continental shelf and the fisheries zone boundaries. It was however not in the position to prescribe a joint development zone. Denmark was not treated as favourably as was Iceland in the conciliation case: M.D. Evans, 'Less than an Ocean Apart: The St Pierre and Miquelon and Jan Mayen Islands and the Delimitation of Maritime Zones', (1994) 43 *ICLQ* 678, 692 ff; M.D. Evans, 'Case Concerning Maritime Delimitation in the Area between Greenland and Jan Mayen', (1994) 43 *ICLQ* 697; J.I. Charney, 'Maritime Delimitation in the Area between Greenland and Jan Mayen', (1994) 88 *AJIL* 105.

[89] The United Kingdom did not agree that the principles proposed by the United States formed part of international law, but accepted their application by the tribunal in this case. J.B. Moore, *History and Digest of International Arbitrations to which the United States has been a Party* (1898) Vol. I 543. Award: ibid., 653.

Case, by stating certain principles beforehand, the parties ensured that any recourse to legal considerations would be embedded in a politically agreed framework. Some ten years later, the example would be followed by the OSCE.

3.4.2 *OSCE conciliation*

The OSCE Convention on Conciliation and Arbitration,[90] concluded in 1992, provides for a compulsory conciliation mechanism, and simultaneously established a Court of Conciliation and Arbitration at Geneva.[91] The Court consists essentially of a list of persons appointed by their state, who may be called upon on an *ad hoc* basis. The OSCE Convention makes a clear distinction between the Members of the Court who may be called upon to arbitrate, and those who may conciliate. Arbitrators 'must possess the qualifications required in their respective countries for appointment to the highest judicial offices or must be jurisconsults of recognised competence in international law.'[92] The conciliators on the other hand 'must be persons holding or having held senior national or international positions and possessing recognised qualifications in international law, international relations, or the settlement of disputes.'[93] Consequently, the conciliator-members of the Court tend to be more politically oriented than the arbitrators, who are generally (former) judges.

This difference is reflected in the terms of reference: 'The function of arbitration is to decide, in accordance with international law, such disputes as are submitted to it.'[94] A conciliation commission on the other hand should 'assist the parties in finding a settlement in accordance with international law and their OSCE commitments.'[95] Though the reference to international law in the conciliation provisions does evoke several questions, it is clear that the conciliation procedure is intended to be a more political procedure than arbitration. Uncertainty exists over what 'OSCE commitments' the conciliators have to take into account, and how these may derogate from international law. OSCE Court Members Caflisch and Vajic reason that the reference to international law could be understood in a limited way, excluding the dispositive rules of

---

90 Convention on Conciliation and Arbitration within the OSCE contained in the Decision on Peaceful Settlement (15 December 1992) Annex 2, (1993) 32 *ILM* 557.

91 OSCE Convention Arts. 1, 10. The Court was established in May 1995, with former French Minister of Justice and former President of the Constitutional Council Robert Badinter as President and Former German Foreign Minister Hans-Dietrich Genscher as Vice-President.

92 OSCE Convention Art. 4(2).

93 Ibid., Art. 3(2).

94 Ibid., Art. 30.

95 Ibid., Art. 24.

international law.[96] This would however leave the conciliation commission only with the imperative to respect legal rules and obligations that cannot or may not be changed by bilateral agreement: *jus cogens* and obligations *erga omnes*.[97] That the obligations arising from such law have to be respected by any proposal emanating from the OSCE Court does however speak for itself, and would not have needed specification in the Convention.[98] It is therefore submitted here that the framers' intention was to include the whole of international law as the inspiration for a settlement.[99] The law will have to be regarded, but proposed settlements may depart from it where this better honours the OSCE commitments or other political considerations that favour amicable settlement and security and co-operation in Europe. Mentioning international law in the way the terms of reference here do seems a mistake, and it would be better to acknowledge this than interpret it out of existence, especially since it has led some to understand recourse to OSCE conciliation to mean requesting a legal opinion.[100]

Following this interpretation, OSCE conciliation is a blend of political and legal conciliation much like that adopted in the *Jan Mayen* Case. There is scope for approaches that are legally inspired, but in which the conciliators do not spell out the legal basis of their recommendations. This way the parties may

---

[96] N. Vajic, 'Diplomatic Settlement or Adjudication? Advantages and Drawbacks', in L. Caflisch (ed.), *The Peaceful Settlement of Disputes Between States: Universal and European Perspectives* (1998) 17, 22-23; L. Caflisch, 'The OSCE Court of Conciliation and Arbitration: Some Facts and Issues', in M. Bothe and others (eds.), *The OSCE in the Maintenance of Peace and Security* (1997) 381-397, 393-394.

[97] The Vienna Convention on the Law of Treaties Art. 53 identified *jus cogens* as 'norms accepted and recognised by the international community of States as a whole as a norm from which no derogation is permitted and which can be modified only by a subsequent norm of general international law having the same character' comprises such prohibitions as that of torture, slavery and the use of force. See *Case Concerning Armed Activities on the Territory of the Congo* (*Jurisdiction and Admissibility*) (*DR Congo* v. *Rwanda*), (2006) *ICJ Rep* [64], [125]. The concept of obligations *erga omnes* was recognised by the ICJ in the *Barcelona Traction* Case (*Belgium* v. *Spain*) (Second Phase), (1970) *ICJ Rep* 4, 32 and again in the *East Timor* Case (*Portugal* v. *Australia*), (1995) *ICJ Rep* 90, 102; J.A. Frowein, 'Die Verpflichtungen erga omnes im Völkerrecht und ihre Durchsetzung', in R. Bernhardt and others, *Völkerrecht als Rechtsordnung Internationale Gerichtsbarkeit Menschenrechte: Festschrift für Hermann Mosler* (1983) 241-262.

[98] A proposal contrary to *jus cogens* would be null and void when adopted.

[99] The summary given by Court President Robert Badinter is ambiguous: 'la Commission proposera aux parties un règlement équitable du litige, respecteux des principes du droit international.' 'La Cour de Conciliation et d'Arbitrage au sein de l'OSCE', (1999) 1 *International Law Forum* 99, 101.

[100] E.g., S. Jacobi, 'Subsidiarity and Other Obstacles to the Use for the OSCE Dispute Settlement Procedures', in M. Bothe and others (eds.), *The OSCE in the Maintenance of Peace and Security* (1997) 425, 451.

reach a settlement on the basis of their faith in the commission, rather than on the basis of their acceptance of a certain application of the law. Specifying the relevant considerations in advance, as is prescribed in the *Jan Mayen* and OSCE examples, can prove a viable alternative. It can facilitate the work of the conciliators, and at the same time identify the extent of the applicability of the law. The alternatives provided additional illustration that the ideal types of political and legal conciliation are indeed abstractions, and that there are possibilities to combine elements of both.

PART TWO

LEGAL CONSEQUENCES OF CONCILIATION

4. Impartiality Prejudice and Precedent

The process of conciliation also involves important procedural legal aspects. These have received remarkably little attention from writers and from conciliation commissions. The issues of secrecy and prejudice, as well as the possibility of precedent are discussed below. First, however, the basic question of the independence of the conciliator should be discussed.

4.1 The impartiality of the conciliator

It is notable that in inter-State conciliation, contrary to conciliation in international commercial relations involving private parties, there is no apparent concern about the independence or impartiality of the conciliators.[101] In conciliation involving private parties, such as covered by the ICC ADR Rules, the 'neutral', whether or not designated by the parties themselves, has to provide the ICC with a statement of independence, stating any facts or circumstances which might be of such nature as to call into questions his or her independence in the eyes of the parties.[102] A somewhat less demanding provision is included in the ICSID Conciliation Rules. They provide that the appointed conciliator shall sign a declaration stating among other things:

---

[101] Impartiality must be understood to refer to the absence of personal prejudice, whereas independence refers to the absence of material ties that could influence actions. In this view, impartiality concerns conviction, whereas independence concerns freedom to act. The distinction is infrequently made, and shall also not be pursued here.

[102] ICC ADR Rules Art. 3.

> 'To the best of my knowledge there is no reason why I should not serve on the Conciliation Commission constituted by the International Centre for Settlement of Investment Disputes with respect to a dispute between ... and ...'[103]

In public international affairs, considering the lack of provisions on this issue, impartiality is seemingly not a major concern. While many conciliation rules do provide for the appointment of persons who are not nationals of any of the States involved,[104] this does not amount to a guarantee of impartiality.

The absence of further provisions can have various reasons. First, unlike conciliation conducted under the supervision of a conciliation institution over which the concerned parties have relatively little control, such as ICSID or the ICC, States normally set-up their own conciliation commissions. States rarely rely on a third party to do this. Second, international conciliation takes place under close scrutiny of the States involved; they are expected to ensure that the conciliators meet the required standards, and may therefore not need the conciliator to state publicly that he is independent. Third, there may be occasions where any partiality or dependence on a powerful outside party is actually desired, in that his involvement could lead to recommendations supported by such outside party. There are nonetheless some good reasons to adopt measures to ensure independence of conciliators, at least of the non-national members of conciliation commissions.

Prospective conciliators are increasingly likely to have had some professional or personal link with any of the States in dispute. Further, if the parties adopt the legal conception of conciliation, the conciliators are presumed to act in a manner similar to judges. Even nationally appointed *ad hoc* judges to the ICJ are to act impartially.[105] Such obligation should then also apply to conciliators practicing legal conciliation. It fits with this understanding that the only significant comment on the impartiality of conciliators in inter-State conciliators came from Van Asbeck, a strong supporter of the legal conception.[106] When he presided (as a non-national chairman) over the French/Swiss commission, he emphasised that the national members were an integral part of the commission, and on that basis also supposed to be equally impartial. Their connection to the parties could only serve to ensure that the vision of their governments was sufficiently addressed, and that they could explain the recommendations of the commission to their home countries.

---

[103] ICSID Conciliation Rules rule 6.

[104] E.g., LOSC Annex V Art. 3(g); PCA Optional Conciliation Rules Art. 4(3); 1978 Vienna Convention on Succession of States in Respect of Treaties, (1978)17 *ILM* 1488 Annex Art. 2.

[105] Cf., Art. 31 and 20 ICJ Statute.

[106] F.M. van Asbeck, 'La tâche et l'action d'une commission de conciliation', (1956) *NTIR* 1, 4-5; F.M. van Asbeck, 'La procédure suivi par la commission de conciliation franco-suisse', (1956) *NTIR* 209, 219.

The impartiality of the conciliators is a greater concern in legal conciliation than in political conciliation, essentially because legal conciliators must be expected to apply the law objectively, whereas there is less scope to apply political considerations objectively. Traditionally, conciliation rules do not devote much attention to the topic. Unless States desire political conciliation, there may be reason for States to regard this issue more carefully, as they already do in international arbitration.

4.2 Prejudice and the *France/Siam* Case

The issue of prejudice has left notable traces in conciliation history. Without aiming to bind the parties, procedural rules frequently stipulate that the parties 'consider in good faith'[107] the recommendations issued by the commission, or should give them 'reasonable regard.'[108] These clauses demand a serious effort at settling the dispute on the basis of the recommendations, but do not oblige the parties to accept them. The fact that conciliation procedures are not binding does not, however, mean that they cannot have legal consequences. The more law-based a proceeding is, the more relevant the issue of prejudice becomes.

Paradoxically, the clearest example of prejudice in fact derives from a conciliation commission that did not consider legal claims at all, and moreover concerns an omission in conciliation rather than an adverse admission. In 1946 France and Siam agreed to set-up a conciliation commission to address the Siamese demands for frontier rectification. The commission duly issued a report that suggested some minor adjustments, which were however rejected by the Siamese government. When shortly thereafter a new ruler came to power, he accepted the recommendations.[109]

When Cambodia subsequently obtained independence from France, it disputed the presence of Thailand (formerly Siam) around the Temple of Preah Vihear, and in 1959 instituted proceedings before the ICJ.[110] The Court found in favour of Cambodia, basing itself on a detailed study of the history of the claims of the area, noting in particular Thailand's acquiescence in the allocation of the Temple to Cambodia in various official maps.[111] The conciliation case received special attention:

---

[107] E.g., Framework Convention on Climate Change Art. 14(6).

[108] E.g., Agreement on the Continental Shelf (Norway-Iceland) Art. 9.

[109] S. Bastid, 'La commission de conciliation franco-siamoise', in C. Rousseau (ed.), *La Technique et les Principes du Droit Public: Etudes en l'Honneur de Georges Scelle* (1950) 1.

[110] *Case Concerning the Temple of Preah Vihear* (*Cambodia-Thailand*) (*Merits*), (1962) *ICJ Rep* 6.

[111] Criticised in P.C.W. Chan, 'Acquiescence/Estoppel in International Boundaries: Temple of *Preah Vihear* Revisited', (2004) 3*CJIL* 421.

> 'here therefore was an outstanding opportunity for Thailand to claim a rectification of the frontier at Preah Vihear on the ground that the delimitation embodied a serious error which would have caused Thailand to reject it had she known of the error of 1908-1909. In fact, although Thailand made complaints about the frontier line in a considerable number of regions, she made none about Preah Vihear. She even (12 May 1947) filed with the Commission a map showing Preah Vihear as lying in Cambodia. Thailand contends that this involved no adverse implications as regards her claim to the Temple, because the Temple area was not in issue before the Commission, that it was other regions that were under discussion, and that it was in relation to these that the map was used. But it is precisely the fact that Thailand had raised these and other questions, but not that of Preah Vihear, which requires explanation.'[112]

In its pleadings, Thailand chose to focus on refuting the merits of Cambodia's claims, rather than challenging the use made by that State of the proceedings of the conciliation commission.[113]

It is thus possible that in later proceedings one of the parties wants to use the statements and admissions, or in the case of Thailand, even the omissions, made by the other party in the course of the conciliation. If the original undertaking fails and the dispute moves on to adjudication, one party may claim that the bargaining position of the other indicates that it was willing to admit responsibility, was about to settle for a certain sum, or that it had accepted a statement of facts. In addition, it is likely that a favoured party will want to use the recommendations of the conciliation commission in support of its own case.

The possibility to prejudge matters in the course of conciliation can be a serious threat to the effectiveness of the proceedings. For fear of repercussions the parties may be incapable of negotiating freely, unwilling to make any offers and to change the *status quo*. In adjudication such reluctance would not be a major problem, as the resolution of the matter is then in the hands of judges, who have the power to substitute their own assessments for those of the disputants. In conciliation, however, it is eventually up to the parties to find common ground.

If the commission works mainly on the basis of legal assessments, as in legal conciliation, the value of its work as a reference for subsequent proceedings may be significant. The complication this constitutes exists all the more when the parties do indeed come to an agreement on the basis of these recommendations. When a conflict arises out of this agreement, the perception could easily arise that the parties concurred in the commission's legal assessments

---

[112] *Case Concerning the Temple of Preah Vihear* (*Cambodia-Thailand*) (*Merits*), (1962) *ICJ Rep* 6, 28-29.

[113] *Case Concerning the Temple of Preah Vihear* (1962) ICJ Pleadings Vol. I 569 and Vol. II 314-5.

that underlay the recommendations the disputants later agreed upon. This is even if the agreement only extended to the dispositive parts of the recommendations, without necessarily sharing all reasoning on which they were based.

As it is the purpose of conciliation to get the disputants to come to agreement, and as this is more likely to happen if they do not have to concern themselves with any consequences of the undertaking itself, it should be attempted to prevent any possible prejudice of possible later proceedings. Several ways have been developed to do so.

4.3 Secrecy and records

For much of the history of conciliation, the essential safeguard against prejudice was the imperative of secrecy. The foremost reason for secrecy will however have been to allow the parties and the commission to act independently from political pressures of public opinion and other international actors.[114] The confidentiality of the conciliation proceedings seems to have carried with it the implicit assumption that the documents would not later be used in court. Little is known of the early cases of conciliation in part for this reason: records were as a rule not published.

With few written provisions, the requirement of secrecy remains embedded in the general principles of diplomacy. A standard clause is found in the 1957 European Convention for the Peaceful Settlement of Disputes:

> 'The work of the Special Conciliation Commission shall not be conducted in public unless the Commission with the consent of the parties so decides.'[115]

Reasons for deciding otherwise include educating the public about the need for a certain compromise, or a demand by the public to be informed.

One approach to preventing prejudice without maintaining secrecy was adopted in the 1952 *Gorm and Svava* Case. There, the commission president decided not to issue a written recommendation, but to read the text aloud to the parties, who were able to take notes. That way, it was thought, they could communicate the reasoning of the commission to their capitals, without possessing an authoritative document that could be perceived to affect the parties' rights.[116]

The *F.OABV* Case proved how politically important discretion is. In 1956 the French air force intercepted an aeroplane flying the Algerian rebel leader

---

[114] Cf., P. Reuter, 'Le Droit au Secret et les Institutions Internationales', (1956) 2 *AFDI* 46, 47.

[115] European Convention for the Peaceful Settlement of Disputes Art. 11.

[116] H. Rolin, 'Une conciliation belgo-danoise', (1953) 57 *RGDIP* 353, 358.

Ben Bella and four of his colleagues to Tunisia after their meeting with the King of Morocco in Rabat.[117] The dispute that subsequently arose between Morocco and France was submitted to an *ad hoc* conciliation commission. During the hearings in 1958 an article appeared in the French press alleging an informal legal statement made by the commission chairman Charles de Visscher, a statement denied by De Visscher himself. The agent for Morocco thereupon denounced these occurrences in a press conference. With the working situation deteriorated, and when then the majority of the members voted not to hear Mr Ben Bella as a witness, the Moroccan and Lebanese members of the commission left. The work of the commission therefore came to a premature end.

Three years later the Conciliation Rules prepared by the Institut de Droit International gave great emphasis to the secrecy of proceedings: five of its fifteen articles are devoted to it. The conciliation proceedings as well as the documents that result from them would not be made public unless the parties agreed. Diverging from the 1957 European Convention on Peaceful Settlement, the decision to publish was reserved to the parties only, and no longer involved the commission.[118]

Another issue is where to leave the records of the commission. In the absence of a provision the documents were sometimes left with the commission's president, a private person, imposing on him the responsibility to safeguard them. An obviously better solution is to deposit the documents with an international organisation.[119]

4.4 The no-prejudice clause

In 1955 the French-Swiss Commission gave both parties its report, also containing legal conclusions, in strict confidentiality. A heading was added to the text, saying that the document was not to prejudice the legal positions of the parties. They were also told not to use the document in any court proceed-

[117] C. Rousseau, 'Echec de la procedure d'enquête et de conciliation dans l'affaire du deroutement de l'avion transportant de Rabat a Tunis les chefs nationalistes algériens le 22 octobre 1956', (1958) 62 *RGDIP* 691; 'L'Affaire du F. OABV', (1958) 4 *AFDI* 282.

[118] IDI Conciliation Rules Arts. 10-14, in particular Art. 13; *Cot* 196-199 for a discussion on secrecy regarding witness statements under the IDI Conciliation Rules.

[119] This was earlier done by the French-Siamese Commission: S. Bastid, 'La commission de conciliation franco-siamoise', in C. Rousseau (ed.), *La Technique et les Principes du Droit Public: Etudes en l'Honneur de Georges Scelle* (1950) 1, 19 and the French-Swiss commission: F.M. van Asbeck, 'La procédure suivi par la commission de conciliation franco-suisse', (1956) *NTIR* 209, 216 and is prescribed in the IDI Conciliation Rules Art. 14 and in the UN Conciliation Rules Art. 23.

ings.[120] Bastid doubted that such a prohibition would hold in practice.[121] In this case the matter did not come to the test.

At the IDI meeting in 1961 Jenks and Fitzmaurice pointed out that in order to avoid prejudging subsequent legal cases, it was not adequate simply to regulate secrecy. In some instances it may be necessary to inform the public of the reasons that led to – or prevented an agreement. It would therefore be better to judge the need for secrecy on a case by case basis, allowing for publicity when necessary, without affecting the legal positions of the parties in dispute. The principle that no matter should be prejudged had to be distinguished.[122] As a result of their interventions, a special clause was inserted in the Preamble of the IDI Resolution:

> 'no admission or proposal formulated during the course of the conciliation procedure, either by one of the Parties or by the Commission, can be considered as prejudicing or affecting in any manner the rights or the contentions of either Party in the event of the failure of the procedure; and, similarly, the acceptance by one Party of a proposal of settlement in no way implies any admission by it of the considerations of law or of fact which may have inspired the proposal of settlement.'

Such a provision has become common.[123] A no-prejudice clause is also included in both the UNCITRAL and ICSID Conciliation Rules.[124] Following the example of the UNCITRAL Conciliation Rules, the PCA Conciliation Rules contain an explicit prohibition on:

---

[120] F.M. van Asbeck, 'La procédure suivi par la commission de conciliation franco-suisse', (1956) *NTIR* 209, 215.

[121] S. Bastid, 'La commission de conciliation franco-suisse', (1956) 2 *AFDI* 436, 439.

[122] (1961) 49 *Annuaire de l'Institut de Droit International* Vol. II 210 -215, 218-220. See also the comments submitted by Lord McNair, (1959) 48 *Annuaire de l'Institut de Droit International* Vol. I 85, 85-86.

[123] E.g., the Treaty of Conciliation, Judicial Settlement and Arbitration (United Kingdom-Switzerland) (1965) of which Art. 13(5) reads: 'No admission or proposal formulated during the course of the procedure of conciliation, either by one of the Contracting Parties or by the Commission, shall prejudice or affect in any manner the rights or the contentions of either Contracting Party in the event of the failure of the procedure of conciliation. Similarly, the acceptance by a Contracting Party of a finding, recommendation or draft settlement, formulated by the Commission, shall in no way imply any admission of the considerations of law or of fact upon which such finding, recommendation or draft settlement may have been based'.

[124] ICSID Convention Art. 35; UNCITRAL Conciliation Rules Art. 20. The 2002 *UNCITRAL Model Law on International Commercial Conciliation* provides explicitly in Art. 10(5) that this should not be held to imply that evidence that is otherwise admissible in arbitral or judicial proceedings, becomes inadmissible because it was used in conciliation.

> '[the introduction as evidence] in any arbitral or judicial proceedings, whether or not such proceedings relate to the dispute that is the subject of the conciliation proceedings: a) Views expressed or suggestions made by the other party in respect of a possible settlement of the dispute; b) Admissions made by the other party in the course of the conciliation proceedings; c) Proposals made by the conciliator; d) The fact that the other party had indicated its willingness to accept a proposal for settlement made by the conciliator.'[125]

This protection is extensive in that it also covers subsequent settlement proceedings that are not related to the dispute to be conciliated.[126] It should be noted, however, that the prohibition might be interpreted to say that there is no restriction placed upon the later use of those statements that are not themselves aimed at reaching a settlement, such as witness statements and the reports of experts. Such an interpretation would potentially restrict the willingness of States to involve such statements and report in conciliation. The clause is therefore better reinterpreted also to ban the future use of these submissions. In the UN Conciliation Rules a similar rule is included:

> 'Except as the parties may otherwise agree, neither party shall be entitled in any other proceedings, whether in a court of law or before any other body, entity or person, to invoke any views expressed or statements, admissions or proposals made by the other party in the conciliation proceedings, but not accepted, or the report of the commission, the recommendations submitted by the commission or any proposal made by the commission, unless agreed to by both parties.'[127]

Here, a problem arises out of the provision that statements, admissions and proposals cannot be invoked *if they are not accepted*. Presumably, they should be accepted by the party to which they are addressed. This then means that if they *are* accepted, the accepting party is entitled to invoke them at any subsequent occasion. This evidently runs counter to the principle of no prejudice, for a party only needs to accept an admission of the other in order to subsequently use it as an argument in court. The no-prejudice principle can be saved if the clause is interpreted in this way that only what is incorporated in a concluding agreement between the parties is understood as having been accepted in the sense of the article.

---

[125] Art. 20.

[126] Report of the Secretary-General 'Commentary on the Revised Draft of UNCITRAL Conciliation Rules' A/CN.9/180 in (1980) 9 United Nations *Commission on International Trade Law Yearbook* 100; I.I. Dore, *Arbitration and Conciliation under the UNCITRAL Rules: A Textual Analysis* (1986) 37.

[127] UN Conciliation Rules Art. 28(1).

4.5 The role of the conciliator in later proceedings

Another safeguard against prejudice, as found in the PCA Conciliation Rules, provides that unless the parties agree otherwise, the conciliator will not be involved in any later proceedings in the capacity of arbitrator or counsel, and that the parties undertake not to present the conciliator as a witness.[128] The UNCITRAL Conciliation Rules provide the same, without the possibility of the parties to agree otherwise.[129] The UN Conciliation Rules do not contain this rule.[130] Such a rule is a useful follow-up to the exclusion of evidence, as the conciliator will normally have additional information or insight that, if made available after the conciliation, can benefit a party in further court proceedings. Both the parties and the conciliator are held responsible. Nevertheless, only the parties are responsible for not introducing the conciliator as a witness.

The separation between conciliation and subsequent proceedings such as arbitration is not universally adopted outside public international law. In China, for instance, conciliation often runs concurrently with arbitration, and is also undertaken by the same tribunal deciding in arbitration.[131] Similarly, the arbitration laws of Hong Kong and Singapore also allow for an arbitrator simultaneously to act as a conciliator. Moreover, they provide:

> 'An arbitrator or umpire acting as conciliator – (a) may communicate with the parties to the reference collectively or separately.'[132]

Such a combination of conciliation and arbitration creates problems of due process.[133] It is a general principle of law that parties in litigation are entitled to know and respond to any statement by the other. Where in conciliation it can be permissible for the conciliator to discuss matters with the parties individu-

---

128 PCA Conciliation Rules Art. 19. Similarly, ICC ADR Rules Art. 7(3).

129 UNCITRAL Conciliation Rules Art. 19. The parties may however alter the Rules themselves as provided in Art. 1(2).

130 It appeared in an early draft but was soon deleted because of various criticism: UN Doc A/47/33 (1992) Art. 39 p. 61 and comments on p. 70. The PCA slightly modified the clause from the UNCITRAL Conciliation Rules Art. 19. It is also found in the ICSID Arbitration Rules Art. 1(4).

131 C. de Vera, 'Arbitrating Harmony: "Med-Arb" and the Confluence of Culture and Rule of Law in the Resolution of International Commercial Disputes in China', (2004) 18 *Columbia Journal of Asian Law* 149.

132 Singapore International Arbitration Act 17(3) (Amended 2001) and Hong Kong Arbitration Ordinance 2B(3) (1997). Further: P. Sanders, 'The Links between Arbitration and Conciliation', in K.P. Berger, et al. (eds.), *Festschrift für Otto Sandrock zum 70. Geburtstag* (2000) 823.

133 The fundamental principle of *audi et alteram partem*, as contained, e.g., in the European Convention on Human Rights, Art. 6.

ally, in arbitration each side should be allowed to contest the statements of the other.[134] If the parties agree to the conciliator becoming the arbitrator of the same dispute, they should arrange for the disclosure of the information known to one party and the arbitrator, but not to the other party. Provisions to that effect remain problematic, for they leave it to the conciliator/arbitrator to decide what information he considers material to communicate to the other party. A practical problem is that confidential exchanges are not normally recorded in writing. More importantly, a party may have provided the conciliator with sensitive information that *may not* be made known to the other party. Lastly, even if a conciliator/arbitrator manages to pass all these hurdles, parties may always doubt whether he has indeed done so, without a satisfactory way of having these doubts addressed. For these reasons, the promotion of conciliators to arbitrators in public international disputes should be prevented.

4.6 The exclusion of evidence

There is a difficulty with the prohibition of the use of the conciliator as a witness. If the dispute or some aspect of it comes before a national court, the applicable law may not respect any agreement to exclude evidence.[135] In that case, the conciliator, as witness, can be called nonetheless. If the court obliging the witness to give evidence is that of one of the States who were party to the conciliation, the forum State is in breach of its international obligation.

In situations before international courts or tribunals, when litigation is instituted between the same disputing parties, any use made by them of the conciliation material should be consensual. If not, the State submitting the material incurs legal responsibility,[136] but is then still up to the tribunal to assess the admissibility and value of the evidence.[137] Firm rules of evidence in public international law are developing but remain sparse.[138] While there is reason for an international tribunals not to ignore a no-prejudice clause, there is no certainty that it will respect it and declare inadmissible material brought in con-

---

[134] Cf., P. Sanders, *Quo Vadis Arbitration* (1999) 369.

[135] For the situation with the UNCITRAL Conciliation Rules: I.I. Dore, *Arbitration and conciliation under the UNCITRAL Rules: A textual Analysis* (1986) 36; generally: M. Breton-Jokl, 'La commission permanente de conciliation italo-suisse', (1957) 3 *AFDI* 210, 220.

[136] See chapter III 4.4.

[137] *Military and Paramilitary Activities in and Against Nicaragua* Case (*Nicaragua* v. *United States*) (*Merits*), (1986) *ICJ Rep* 40.

[138] C.F. Brower, 'Evidence before International Tribunals: The need for some standard rules', (1994) 28 *International Lawyer* 47; Generally: C.F. Amerasinghe, *Evidence in International Litigation* (2003); D.V. Sandifer, *Evidence Before International Tribunals* (rev. edn. 1975).

travention of it.[139] The ICJ has generally shown a flexible attitude as regards the substantive inadmissibility of evidence,[140] as have other courts.[141] Since the *Chorzow Factory* Case there is a presumption that evidence relating to settlement negotiations is inadmissible, and it is submitted that this should be understood to cover conciliation proceedings.[142] The above cited case of *Preah Vihear*, however, shows that the ICJ did not (yet) adopt this position. It has been argued more generally that there is no legal rule binding a tribunal to exclude certain evidence.[143] In the end, therefore, the primary rules regarding the submission or request of evidence resulting from conciliation remain the instruments of the relevant courts to which the evidence is to be submitted – and these are often silent on this point.

4.6.1 *An exception*

In contrast to the efforts to avoid future legal repercussions of conciliation proceedings, one multilateral conciliation procedure was designed to augment the legal value of its potential results. The 1975 Convention on the Representation of States in International Organisations stands out as providing a most judicial conciliation procedure. For one, it provides that if the organisation involved is so authorised, the commission may recommend that it requests an advisory opinion from the International Court of Justice.[144] Second, the provisions on the composition of the commission are rationalised to ensure that it will be set-up. If the two party-appointed members of the commission cannot agree on the selection of a chairman, or if one of the parties has not appointed a member of its own, the chief administrative officer of the organisation is entitled to appoint a qualified jurist as chairman.[145] It is upon this appointment that the commission will start to function, even if it is incomplete.[146]

---

[139] On a related point, Amerasinghe finds there is neither an established rule that illegally obtained evidence is excluded, nor one that it is not. He holds, however, that the starting point should be a presumption that no one should benefit from his own wrong. C.F. Amerasinghe, *Evidence in International Litigation* (2003) 179.

[140] S. Rosenne, *The Law and Practice of the International Court 1920-2005* (4th edn. 2006) Vol. III Procedure 1242 ff.; C.F. Amerasinghe, *Evidence in International Litigation* (2003) 164-167.

[141] E.g., the Inter-American Court of Human Rights: *Loayza-Tamayo* v. *Peru* (17 September 1997) Ser C No. 33 [42].

[142] *Chorzow Factory* Case (*Germany* v. *Poland*) (*Merits*), (1928) *PCIJ Ser A* No. 17, 51, also cited in *Frontier Dispute* (*Burkina Faso* v. *Mali*), (1986) *ICJ Rep* 554, 632. Further: *PepsiCo* v. *Iran* (1986) 13 Iran-US CTR 3, 28.

[143] C.F. Amerasinghe, *Evidence in International Litigation* (2003) 166.

[144] Vienna Convention on the Representation of States in their Relations with International Organisations of a Universal Character Art. 85(6).

[145] Idem, Art. 85(3).

[146] Idem, Art. 85(5).

There is of course little chance that a commission that is not supported by one of the parties in dispute can be successful in making an end to the conflict. The departure from the traditional model is justified by a clause intended to give some legal effect to the work of such an incomplete body. Article 85(7) of the Convention provides that in the absence of an agreement on the basis of the recommendations, 'any party to the dispute may declare unilaterally that it will abide by the recommendations in the report so far as it is concerned.' Naturally, the possibility of adopting the recommendations in the face of rejection by the other party exists in any case. The express inclusion in the Convention is however meant to confer legitimacy upon the party that does so, or at least to establish that behaviour in conformity with the recommendations is never illegitimate.[147]

Villani goes so far as to say that: 'If the existence of the aforesaid legal effect is accepted, it must be recognised that the report of the conciliation commission ultimately has an effect approaching that of an international judgement.'[148] This is an exaggeration: even if a convention provides for a unilateral declaration of acceptance of the report, the recommendations remain non-binding. If the commission was incomplete, the value of its findings will be all the more limited. Nonetheless, the provision does create a presumption in favour of the accepting party, and therefore provides a legal argument that could be used in subsequent proceedings. By including this article, the 1975 Convention departed from the idea that nothing in conciliation proceedings should prejudge the matter in any way, and instead opted for a further judicialisation of conciliation. It should be noted though that for unrelated reasons the Convention itself was no success, and that its form of judicial conciliation has not reappeared elsewhere.[149]

4.7 Questions of *res judicata* and *lis pendens*

It deserves frequent repetition that the outcome of conciliation proceedings is only a recommendation, and therefore not binding on the parties. A concilia-

---

[147] Cf., J, Ritter, head of the Swiss delegation, proposed the amendment in 'La conférence et la Convention sur la Representation des Etats dans leurs Relations avec les Organisations Internationales', (1975) 21 *AFDI* 471, 42; P. Pazartzis, *Les Engagements Internationaux en Matière de Règlement Pacifique des Différends entre Etats* (1992) 147 No. 92.

[148] U. Villani, 'A New Conciliation Procedure: The Vienna Convention on the Representation of Sates in Their Relations with International Organisations of a Universal Character', (1978-1979) 4 *Italian Yearbook of International Law* 31, 44.

[149] The 1975 Convention was adopted against the opposition of many of the States who host international organisations. It has not yet entered into force. The article on the conciliation procedure was however adopted with 63 in favour and 2 abstentions.

tion commission is by definition not able to render a judicial decision, and therefore cannot create *res judicata.* In this, conciliation is different from non-compliance procedures (NCPs), discussed in detail in the following chapter.[150] Unlike conciliation, NCPs function essentially as enforcement mechanism, though on the basis of amicable co-operation by the allegedly defaulting party. Therefore, in NCPs there may at least be a concern that the conciliation-like elements of the procedure prejudice later proceedings.[151]

On the other hand, like with NCPs, there is a remote possibility that conciliation may be affected by questions of *lis pendens.* This may occur for instance in cases of multilateral treaties providing for compulsory conciliation, where more than one State initiates conciliation proceedings, or in cases where conciliation proceedings take place between State A and State B, while arbitration proceedings on the same matter take place between State A and State C.[152] Multilateral treaties rarely provide detailed procedures for conciliation, let alone that they would address these eventualities.[153]

If all parties concerned consent, simultaneous conciliation proceedings may be joined into one, allowing for appropriate appointment powers for all concerned States.[154] This would be the easiest way to avoid complications. If this cannot be agreed to, however, there appears only to be the practical problem of stretching resources of the doubly affected State, but no legal reason not to have concurrent conciliation proceedings.

There may be differences in case of simultaneous occurrence of conciliation and arbitration, where conciliation is only an optional procedure suggested by the applicable multilateral treaty. If State A is about to agree to a settlement in conciliation with State B, its willingness to settle shall be affected by the convening of an arbitral tribunal on the same matter by State C, considering that such tribunal could make a determination binding on State A demanding concessions in addition to those agreed in conciliation with State B. While there is no legal obligation upon State C or on the arbitral tribunal, the latter may, by extending the principle of comity between judicial institutions to also

---

[150] See chapter IV 6.

[151] See chapter IV 6.

[152] Cf., M.A. Fitzmaurice and C. Redgwell, 'Environmental Non-compliance Procedures and International Law', (2000) 31 *NYIL* 35, 49.

[153] Unlike for instance the provisions of human rights bodies, which normally stipulate that a complaint cannot be submitted in simultaneous proceedings, or cannot be submitted twice to the same body: European Convention on Human Rights (24 November 1950), 213 *UNTS* 222 Art. 35(2)(b); American Convention on Human Rights (22 November 1969), 1114 *UNTS* 123 Art. 46(1)(c) and 47(d). On the general scarcity of rules in this area: Y. Shany, *The Competing Jurisdictions of International Courts and Tribunals* (2003) 212-213.

[154] Procedures for conciliation involving more than two parties occasionally occur, e.g., Convention on Biological Diversity Annex II Pt 2 Art. 2; LOSC Annex V Art. 3(g).

include conciliation bodies,[155] decide to stay its proceedings for a certain time, preferably until the conciliation effort with State B has been concluded,[156] unless the tribunal considers an interim award necessary to protect the rights of one of the parties. Applying the principle of comity does, however, presume that the matter before the two bodies is indeed the same or at least highly similar.[157] Following conclusion of the conciliation, or after the expiry of a certain grace period, the arbitral tribunal may then resume its work, provided that State C still wishes to press its claim. It is however also possible that in view of the pending arbitral proceedings, State A refuses to continue the conciliation proceedings, preferring to await the outcome of arbitration. The complications of *lis pendens* are related but more pressing for NCPs, and are therefore addressed at greater length in the sections discussing NCPs below.[158]

4.8 The creation of precedent

A distinction should be made between the issue of prejudice of conciliation on further proceedings on the one hand, and the precedential value of conciliation cases on the other. In the latter case, the question is whether one successful conciliation case can provide a form of case law for other conciliation or adjudication proceedings. A first prerequisite is that the commission's report is published, which is often not the case.[159] On points of procedure, at least, it is clear that the few cases of which details are known, have had significant impact on proceedings that followed. The precedent of *Gorm and Svava* was cited various times by Van Asbeck in his elaboration of the procedure to be followed by his commission.[160] The cases of the 1950s, including the *France/Siam* Case and the *F.OABV* Case, had a notable effect on the development of the IDI Conciliation Rules of 1961.

The precedential value of matters of substance depends on the characteristics of each particular case. The more the commission's report or the resulting settlement is inspired by the law, the more easily it be extrapolated to other

---

155 As applied in Arbitral Tribunal *Mox Plant* Case (*Ireland* v. *United Kingdom*) Order No. 3 [28] (24 June 2003), (2003) 42 *ILM* 1186, referring to the ECJ.

156 Cf., C. Söderlund, 'Lis Pendens, Res Judicata and the Issue of Parallel Proceedings', (2005) 22 *Journal of International Arbitration* 301, 312.

157 Y. Shany, *The Competing Jurisdictions of International Courts and Tribunals* (2003) 155.

158 See chapter IV 6.

159 In the investor-State practice of ICSID, where arbitral awards are normally published, none of the reports are published.

160 F.M. van Asbeck, 'La procédure suivi par la commission permanente de conciliation franco-suisse', (1956) 3 *NTIR* 209, 209 and 214.

cases. Furthermore, the stature of the recommendations may be dependent on the reputation of the conciliators. If they are well-known jurists, it is more likely that their recommendations will influence later proceedings. The writings of the experienced conciliators Huber, Rolin, François and Van Asbeck influenced the discussions at the IDI, but this was on matters of procedure rather than substance.[161] There is however no evidence of a standing body of precedent of substance carried over from one case to the next. Overall, the precedential value of cases is thought to be low, since even if the conciliators solely regarded the law, the non-binding nature of the undertaking can create a presumption of political, non-legal considerations having seeped into the commission's report.

Nevertheless, sometimes a case may break new ground by introducing new ways to look at legal issues. The well-publicised *Jan Mayen* conciliation case counts as such. It is said to have only limited value for other disputes because of the special considerations Iceland had negotiated for itself before the conciliation took place.[162] However, the special circumstances taken into account in this case may have had some effect on later maritime delimitation cases, especially the marginal consideration of the economic consequences of delimitation.[163] Churchill suggests that the commission's stated approach of finding 'acceptable and equitable solutions of the problems involved' influenced the language of the *Continental Shelf* Case (Libya/Tunisia),[164] in which the former Norwegian conciliator in the *Jan Mayen* Case, Evensen, sat as Judge *ad hoc*. The Court there states its aim to be 'to apply equitable principles ... and to balance up the various considerations in order to produce an equitable result.'[165]

The *Jan Mayen* conciliation left another mark on the case law of the Court. In 1986 El Salvador and Honduras by Special Agreement submitted to a Chamber their dispute about the land, island and maritime delimitation. In 1989 Nicaragua filed a Request to intervene in the maritime aspects of the dispute on the basis of Article 62 of the ICJ Statute. In support of its argument that it had an interest of a legal nature, Nicaragua mentioned, *inter alia*, the possibility that a

---

161 See chapter III 3.1.

162 R.R. Churchill, 'Maritime Delimitation in the Jan Mayen Area', (1985) 9 *Marine Policy* 16, 30-31.

163 *Gulf of Maine* Case (*US* v. *Canada*) (*Judgement*), (1984) *ICJ Rep* 246 and the *Jan Mayen* Case (*Denmark* v. *Norway*), (1993) *ICJ Rep* 38. About the roundabout approach of the ICJ: M.D. Evans, 'Less than an Ocean Apart: The St Pierre and Miquelon and Jan Mayen Islands and the Delimitation of Maritime Zones', (1994) 43 *ICLQ* 678, 692 ff; T.M. Franck, *Fairness in International Law and Institutions* (1995) 66-73. J.I. Charney and L.M. Alexander, *International Maritime Boundaries* (1993); M.D. Evans, *Relevant Circumstances and Maritime Delimitation* (1989).

164 (1982) *ICJ Rep* 3.

165 (1982) *ICJ Rep* 3, 60; R.R. Churchill, 'Maritime Delimitation in the Jan Mayen Area', (1985) 9 *Marine Policy* 16, 21.

joint development zone such as that created through the conciliation case involving Iceland and Norway would be instituted, something which would also affect Nicaragua.[166] The Chamber however ruled that this argument referred to too remote a contingency to justify an intervention.[167]

When Denmark brought the delimitation between Greenland and Jan Mayen to the Court, it explicitly attempted to find a precedent in the *Jan Mayen* conciliation case between Norway and Iceland.[168] The Court thought it 'understandable' that Denmark should seek similar treatment as Iceland. 'But in the context of relations governed by treaties, it is always for the parties concerned to decide, by agreement, in what conditions their mutual relations can best be balanced.'[169] Moreover, the law of delimitation does not prescribe that in the area around one island one consistent method should be applied. Therefore, the Court concluded that the fact that the conciliation case 'shares with the present dispute certain elements (identity of the island, participation of Norway) is of no more than formal weight.'[170]

The ICJ established two complementary reasons for not considering the conciliation case: one regarding the flexibility of the law of maritime delimitation, the other a general reference to the principle of no-prejudice. With this latter argument the Court seemingly classifies conciliation as a form of negotiation. Some nuance may be added. By a long and sustained practice of concluding bilateral treaties state practice and *opinio juris* may evolve, creating international law in their way. Conciliation reports, and the settlements that result from them, may contribute to the law in that way, and therefore remain of interest to the Court.[171] The deliberations of well-regarded commissions may still persuade the ICJ of new developments in state practice and legal thought. As for the *Jan Mayen* conciliation, it could not by itself establish a sustained pattern of changing state practice to affect the law. This situation was reinforced by the flexibility of application allowed by the law of maritime delimitation. It remains to be seen whether the Court will completely pass over

---

166 *Case Concerning the Land, Island and Maritime Frontier Dispute* (*El Salvador* v. *Honduras*) (*Application by Nicaragua for Permission to Intervene*), (1990) *ICJ Rep* 92, 108.

167 (1990) *ICJ Rep* 92, 125. The Chamber granted Nicaragua permission to intervene on another basis.

168 Similarly, the dissenting opinion of Danish Judge *ad hoc* Fischer, (1993) *ICJ Rep* 38, 311: 'I consider the Iceland/Jan Mayen delimitation which involves the very same island which is the subject of the present case to be highly relevant as a strong indication of what would be an equitable delimitation of the maritime area between Greenland and Jan Mayen.'

169 (1993) *ICJ Rep* 38, 77.

170 Idem.

171 R. Badinter, 'La Cour de Conciliation et d'Arbitrage au sein de l'OSCE', (1999) 1 *International Law Forum* 99.

the deliberations of conciliation commissions on disputes in which the law is less indeterminate.

5. Conclusions: Inter-State Conciliation and Law

The precedential value of conciliation cases is more noticeable in respect to the development of conciliation procedures themselves. With the often elementary procedural rules in the original conciliation agreement, a first major task for every conciliator is to adopt a working procedure. In this, the experience of previous commissions has proved to be of great importance. Especially the experiences of the *Gorm and Svava* conciliation, published by a member of the commission,[172] have influenced doctrinal development.[173] The discussions, culminating in the 1961 IDI debate, combined with the political desire to develop an alternative for adjudication in the dispute settlement under multilateral treaties, has influenced the use of conciliation drastically.

Over time, the original political conception of conciliation was effectively replaced with a legal conception. The latter could serve well in a limited number of cases, in particular in smaller cases between friendly neighbours, who from the outset were committed to accept the recommendations. In addition, legal conciliation served as a compromise solution for the drafting of dispute settlement provisions for many multilateral treaties, when States could not agree on either adjudication or non-legal, non-binding procedures. Nevertheless, by the gradual equating of conciliation with non-binding arbitration, conciliation lost part of its identity and thereby also lost much of its appeal in practice.

Despite the frequent inclusion of conciliation provisions in new treaties, the method has rarely been used since the 1960s. The most notable instances of conciliation since then were those, such as the *Jan Mayen* Case and the previously discussed *Belize/Guatemala* Case, in which conciliation had a much larger political element. It is therefore useful to construe an identity of conciliation that is broad enough to address any particular concerns of the parties in the specific dispute.

Legal and political conciliation, as ideal types, can be applied in practice, but their status as abstract models also indicates that in practice combinations of the two are possible. It has been shown that such combinations, devised *ad hoc*, can be successful in settling a range of disputes. Practice further suggests that if the parties have not explicitly asked for a legal assessment, it should be

---

[172] H. Rolin, 'Une conciliation belgo-danoise', (1953) 57 *RGDIP* 353, 358.

[173] E.g., the conciliator in the first ICSID conciliation *Tesoro Petroleum Co.* v. *Trinidad and Tobago* explicitly referred to the *Gorm and Svava* Case when choosing a law-based proceeding.

left to the conciliators to assess whether they should express a legal basis for their recommendations.

The discussion so far was on role of law in conciliation in general inter-State disputes, and on the legal effects of conciliation proceedings. It should now be assessed how conciliation can be used to address specific norms.

Chapter IV
CONCILIATION AND SPECIFIC NORMS

While conciliation procedures and mechanisms such as the UN Conciliation Rules and the OSCE Court lend themselves to settlement of inter-State disputes generally, various dispute settlement provisions are adopted for a specific area of law. Conciliation under such provisions can be termed 'area-specific conciliation'. The category of area-specific treaties relevant for conciliation is very broad, comprising all treaties providing norms for a certain subject-matter and also providing for conciliation.[1] Area specific treaties are particularly significant because their drafters were confronted with the tension between on the one hand the need to pragmatically solve any particular dispute, and on the other hand to maintain the integrity of the norms provided in the treaty.[2]

Due to the fact that the dispute settlement provisions in area-specific treaties are often very limited and only provide that 'a dispute may be submitted to mediation, conciliation or arbitration', there are many similarities in their dispute settlement provisions. These similarities do not, however, lead to a common system of dispute settlement. Frequently the instruments refer to various kinds of dispute settlement, without specifying institutional arrangements.[3] Also when institutional arrangements are provided, these are normally only designed for that agreement. By providing that in case of a dispute a conciliation commission or an arbitral tribunal may be established, the treaties in fact allow for a disparate practice of unrelated bodies and procedures.[4] There is no central conciliation commission for treaties on the environment or on arms control:

---

[1] It therefore only excludes treaties that solely address a procedure of dispute settlement such as the classic bilateral conciliation treaties) and those treaties not providing for conciliation.

[2] T. Gehring, 'International Environmental Regimes: Dynamic Sectoral Legal Systems', (1990) 1 *Yearbook of International Environmental Law* 35; N. Klein, *Dispute Settlement in the Convention on the Law of the Sea* (2005) 52.

[3] P. Sands and R. MacKenzie, *Guidelines for Negotiating and Drafting Dispute Settlement Clauses For International Environmental Agreements* (2000) 3, 6, 16 [brochure].

[4] R.R. Churchill and G. Ulfstein, 'Autonomous Institutional Arrangements in Multilateral Environmental Agreements: A Little Noticed Phenomenon in International Law', (2000) 94 *AJIL* 623, 643 ff.

there is no conciliation equivalent for the International Tribunal for the Law of the Sea (ITLOS),[5] though the proposal has been made several times.[6]

The first part of the Chapter will focus on the dispute settlement system created in the Law of the Sea Convention (LOSC), as well as on the dispute settlement systems of a wide range of multilateral environmental treaties. These instruments are selected because of the combination of broad scope, the active involvement of a great number of States in their implementation and because several such instruments also developed variations on conciliation. A review of these treaties shall offer insights into the means by which conciliation can be modelled to promote settlement on the basis of specific treaty norms.

The second part of this chapter discusses how this is done in other of settlement practices, in particular the one developed under the European Convention on Human Rights and the one that evolved from the General Agreement on Tariffs and Trade (GATT) to the World Trade Organisation (WTO). It is important to keep in mind that the resemblances with conciliation have to be balanced against the placement of these procedures within a judicial setting. The friendly settlement practices there occur in the face of a well-functioning system of implementation of legal obligations. The settlement practices there are thus part of an enforcement mechanism. Typically, when a particular dispute is not settled in the conciliation-like manner, it will be passed on to the judicial system, where a binding legal determination will follow. Nevertheless, while the third party settlement practices in these settings may not exemplify inter-State conciliation, there are various interesting point of overlap. This is also the case with another surveyed practice, that of the World Bank through its Inspection Panel. This concerns an instrument internal to the organisation itself, illustrating a different alternative to international conciliation.

Overlap may exist even more between conciliation and non-compliance procedures (NCPs), discussed in the last part of this chapter. NCPs form an attempt to regulate a certain area of substantive law, not only by providing concrete norms, but also by providing a central, institutionalised mechanism aimed at enforcing those norms. NCPs have developed a sizeable practice in a short number of years. Unlike the examples of the ECHR and GATT, however, there is so far no practice of adjudication backing-up any attempt at amicable settlement. In this light it should be assessed whether they may be seen as a new incarnation of conciliation, and how they deal with the tension between a de-

[5] It is noted that also ITLOS also does not have exclusive jurisdiction over disputes related to the law of the sea; its major contribution, however, is that it provides a focal point for area-specific dispute settlement.

[6] E.g., L. Caflisch, 'Cent ans de règlement pacifique des différends interétatiques', (2001) 288 *Receuil des Cours* 245, 460; see chapter I 3.3.3.

sire to respect the treaty norms on the one hand and a desire to refrain from adjudication on the other.

PART ONE

NORMS AND CONCILIATION

The first part of this chapter takes a closer look at what distinguishes area specific conciliation from general conciliation. In particular, it aims to identify how, while dealing with any individual dispute, a multilateral treaty regime can ensure that when two parties have recourse to its diplomatic settlement provisions, the norms and interests regulated in the treaty are made to play a part in the proceedings. First it looks at the obligatory and exclusive nature of a system. It then argues that there are four other important means of protecting the regime interests: expertise, neutral elements, norms and third parties.

1. Compulsion and Exclusivity

An important aspect of the effectiveness of an area-specific treaty is the commitment of the States Parties to applying its provisions. This commitment can be expressed by making the dispute settlement mechanism compulsory and exclusive. An important question is therefore whether the agreement contains compulsory conciliation: can a party unilaterally initiate proceedings, or does the use of the method require *ad hoc* mutual consent? Is the system exclusive, or can the parties decide to settle their dispute by means external to the mechanism? One of the most developed and influential,[7] though not yet used, area-specific conciliation mechanisms is contained in the United Nations Convention on the Law of the Sea (LOSC or the Convention).[8] It can be instructive, therefore, to review the example it sets.

---

[7] It is followed by, among others, the UNESCO Convention on the Protection of the Underwater Cultural Heritage (6 November 2001), (2002) 41 *ILM* 40; Protocol to the Convention on the Prevention of Marine Pollution by Dumping of Wastes and Other Matter (7 November 1996), (1997) 36 *ILM* 1; Agreement for the Implementation of the Provisions of the United Nations Convention of the Law of the Sea (10 December 1982) relating to the Conservation and Management of Straddling Fish Stocks and Highly Migratory Fish Stocks (4 August 1995), (1996) 34 *ILM* 1542. For an illustration of the inspiration sought in related conventions in drafting dispute settlement procedures, see COP 5th sess. of the Convention to Combat Desertification (20 August 2001) Doc. ICCD/COP(5)/8.

[8] (10 December 1982, entered into force 16 November 1994), (1982) 21 *ILM* 1261. M.H. Nordquist, S. Rosenne and L.B. Sohn (eds.), *United Nations Convention on the Law of the Sea 1989: A Commentary* (1989) Vol. V; R.R. Churchill and A.V. Lowe, *The Law of the Sea* (3rd edn. 1999); R. Lavalle, 'Conciliation under the United Nations Convention on the Law of the Sea: a

The Convention provides illustration of the difficulties involved in obliging States to the dispute settlement provisions of an area-specific treaty. The Convention, which entered into force in 1994, deals with a great variety of matters ranging from coastal State jurisdiction to the exploitation of the deep sea bed. It sets up a permanent International Tribunal for the Law of the Sea, but also allows for ways of bypassing this court.[9] It contains a comprehensive dispute settlement system, including provisions for compulsory adjudication and arbitration. Compulsory adjudication is agreed upon for disputes regarding the basic maritime rights and freedoms.[10] On the other hand, as part of a multi-layered compromise between pro- and anti- compulsory settlement negotiating parties,[11] the Convention allows States to exclude important cases from compulsory binding jurisdiction, including matters concerning military activities, delimitation and disputes in which the Security Council is involved.[12] The reason for this exclusion may be sought in 'vital national interests' or the protection of essential characteristics of sovereignty.[13] Specified other disputes can also be excluded, for which States have to accept compulsory conciliation instead.[14] For yet other disputes, conciliation is only recommend-

critical overview', (1997) *Austrian Review of International and European Law* 2:25-48; W. Riphagen, 'Dispute Settlement in the 1982 United Nations Convention on the Law of the Sea', in C.L. Rozakis and C.A. Stephanou (eds.), *The New Law of the Sea* (1983) 281; G. Jaenicke, 'Dispute Settlement Under the Convention on the Law of the Sea', (1983) 43 *ZfAÖRV* 813.

[9] N. Klein, *Dispute Settlement in the UN Convention on the Law of the Sea* (2005); G. Eiriksson, *The International Tribunal for the Law of the Sea* (2000); M.M.T.A. Brus, *Third Party Dispute Settlement in an Interdependent World* (1995) 23. On the fragmentation of dispute settlement: S. Oda, 'Dispute Settlement Prospects in the Law of the Sea', (1995) 44 *ICLQ* 863; J.I. Charney, 'The Implications of Expanding International Dispute Settlement Systems: The 1982 Convention on the Law of the Sea', (1996) 90 *AJIL* 69; A.E. Boyle, 'Dispute Settlement and the Law of the Sea Convention: Problems of Fragmentation and Jurisdiction', (1997) 46 *ICLQ* 37.

[10] States may choose to grant jurisdiction to the International Tribunal for the Law of the Sea, the International Court of Justice, or an arbitral tribunal. In case the parties' choices do not match, the dispute is submitted to arbitration: LOSC Art. 287.

[11] T. Treves, '"Compulsory" Conciliation in the U.N. Law of the Sea Convention', in C. Philipp (ed.), *Liber Amicorum Günther Jaenicke – Zum 85. Geburtstag* (1999) 611, 617-619.

[12] LOSC Art. 298(1). The condition of the non-involvement of the Security Council does grant an important opportunity to the permanent members of that organ to attempt to block any proceedings broadly related to international peace and security initiated against them.

[13] Cf., R.R. Churchill and A.V. Lowe, *The Law of the Sea* (3rd edn. 1999) 455.

[14] Compulsory conciliation is provided for in Arts. 297(2)(b), (3)(b), 298(1)(a). Note that Art. 298(a)(ii) provides that disputes excepted from binding legal settlement and conciliated under Art. 298(a)(i) shall, if no agreement is reached following conciliation, nevertheless be submitted to a binding legal settlement procedure 'by mutual consent'. This paradoxically still requires each party's consent to a procedure it up to that point had rejected. Further: M.M. Marsit, 'La conciliation dans la Convention des Nations Unies sur le Droit de la Mer', in *Colloque international, Monaco 27-29 Mars 2003* (2004) 343; A.O. Adede, *The System for Settlement of Disputes under the United Nations Convention on the Law of the Sea* (1987) 241-242; M.H. Nordquist, S.

ed.[15] For cases falling under the compulsory conciliation clauses, a mandatory procedure is laid down. In other cases, the provided procedure may be substituted or amended as the case arises.

It is notable that the essential reasoning behind the compulsory conciliation provisions regarding the conservation and management of living resources in the Exclusive Economic Zone was to avoid binding legal review of sovereign acts of coastal states.[16] To increase the insulation of coastal states against legal claims, LOSC Article 297 prescribes conciliation only when a coastal State has 'manifestly failed to comply' with specified obligations,[17] or has 'arbitrarily refused' a certain request.[18] Clearly, the intention of these clauses is to restrict conciliation on the basis of these claims to the extent possible, and then to instil in the conciliation commission an assumption favourable to the coastal state. Similarly, with regard to the coastal States' policies regarding foreign marine research, the conciliation commission is explicitly prohibited from 'cal[ling] in question the exercise by the coastal State of its discretion' to make certain determinations.[19] Thereby, the Convention goes very far in limiting the effective scope of conciliation to address grievances on the basis of its own norms.

The primary rule in the LOSC settlement mechanism is that parties are free at any time to settle any dispute that may arise regarding the Convention by whatever means they choose.[20] The system is therefore not exclusive but residual.[21] If the parties choose their own procedures, the mechanism of the Convention is only applicable when the other attempts at settlement were unsuccessful and further proceedings are not excluded by agreement between the parties.[22] Disputes under the Convention can for instance be brought before *ad hoc* arbitral tribunals, or be resolved by a regional agency. The Conven-

---

Rosenne, L.B. Sohn (eds.), *United Nations Convention on the Law of the Sea 1982: A Commentary* (1989) Vol. V 101 ff and 313 on the emergence of compulsory conciliation.

[15] This is implied by singling out conciliation as a commendable method of settlement. Cf., J.G. Merrills, *International Dispute Settlement* (4th edn. 2005) 190. It is a specification of the reminder already given in Art. 280 'Nothing in this Part impairs the right of any States parties to agree at any time to settle a dispute between them concerning the interpretation or application of this Convention by any peaceful means of their own choice.'

[16] LOSC Art. 297. N. Klein, *Dispute Settlement in the UN Convention on the Law of the Sea* (2005) 186.

[17] LOSC Art. 297(3)(b)(i).

[18] LOSC Art. 297(3)(b)(ii).

[19] LOSC Art. 297(2)(b).

[20] LOSC Art. 280.

[21] Y. Shany, *The Competing Jurisdictions of International Courts and Tribunals* (2003) 201.

[22] LOSC Art. 281. In those cases where the Convention prescribes compulsory conciliation, it is conceivable that the procedure will actually be used twice: once as the result of a *compromis* or standing arrangement between the parties, and, upon failure of the first attempt, once resulting from the obligation laid down in the Convention.

tion does, nevertheless, accord preference to procedures that end with a binding decision: if the parties have agreed to a binding method in another instrument, that agreement shall take precedence over other methods. This is, again, unless the parties agree otherwise.[23]

While this liberal subsidiarity regime may be thought to have excluded the conflicts of competence mentioned in relation to the OSCE system,[24] it has proven not to be failsafe. In the *Southern Bluefin Tuna* dispute an arbitral tribunal found that the dispute at hand arose both under LOSC and under the Southern Bluefin Tuna Convention (CCSBT).[25] Article 281 LOSC, on which the claimants argued that the jurisdiction of the Tribunal was based, provides that parties to a dispute may employ by common agreement any dispute settlement outside of LOSC, and that, if these efforts are unsuccessful, the LOSC dispute settlement procedures apply only where such agreement does not exclude any further procedure. The tribunal held that because the CCSBT did not provide for compulsory dispute settlement, for subject-matters under that Convention the parties had opted out of the compulsory settlement provisions of LOSC. Therefore, the relevant LOSC provisions could not be invoked, and a tribunal established on the basis of LOSC lacked jurisdiction.[26] Considering vocal criticism as well as support for the *Southern Bluefin Tuna* Tribunal's decision,[27] the wider effect of the award is still in dispute. In any case, States will have to be more careful in agreeing to dispute settlement clauses. A possible view of the award is that if one party initiates proceedings on the basis of an agreement providing for compulsory settlement, but the same dispute also arises under an

---

23 LOSC Art. 282.

24 See chapter II 1.14.

25 Award of the Arbitral Tribunal established under Annex VII LOSC, *Southern Bluefin Tuna* Case (*Australia and New Zealand* v. *Japan*) (*Jurisdiction and Admissibility*), (2000) 39 *ILM* 1359 [52]; Convention for the Conservation of the Southern Bluefin Tuna (10 May 1993), 1819 *UNTS* 360.

26 *Southern Bluefin Tuna* Case (*Jurisdiction and Admissibility*) [65].

27 E.g., T. Treves, 'Dispute-Settlement in the Law of the Sea: Disorder or System?, in M.G. Kohen (ed.), *Promoting Justice, Human Rights and Conflict Resolution through International Law* (2007) 927, 933 ff; N. Klein, *Dispute Settlement in the UN Convention on the Law of the Sea* (2005) 35-42; B.H. Oxman, 'Complementary Agreements and Compulsory Jurisdiction', (2001) 95 *AJIL* 277; D.A. Colson and P. Hoyle, 'Satisfying the Procedural Prerequisites to the Compulsory Settlement Mechanisms of the 1982 Law of the Sea Convention: Did the *Southern Bluefin Tuna* Tribunal Get it Right?,' (2003) 34 *Ocean Development & International Law* 59; B. Kwiatowska, 'The Southern Bluefin Tuna Arbitral Tribunal did get it right: a commentary and reply to the article by D.A. Colson and P. Hoyle', (2003) 34 *Ocean Development & International Law* 369; D.R. Rothwell and T. Stephens, 'Dispute Resolution and the Law of the Sea: Reconciling the Interaction between the LOS Convention and Other Environmental Instruments', in A.G. Oude Elferink and D.R. Rothwell (eds.), *Oceans Management in the 21st Century: Institutional Frameworks and Responses* (2004) 209, 221.

agreement with dispute settlement provisions that do not provide for compulsory settlement, application of the compulsory settlement provisions of the first agreement is excluded. This means that States wishing to further compulsory dispute settlement should ensure that any new agreement includes a 'saving clause' stipulating that nothing in that agreement is intended to affect any compulsory jurisdiction conferred under another agreement, and, if the agreement so provides, that the parties agree to submit any dispute arising under that agreement to compulsory dispute settlement, also if another agreement provides otherwise.

A related problem surfaced in the *Mox Plant* dispute between Ireland and the United Kingdom. The dispute revolves around Irish concerns for the environmental consequences of nuclear processing at a UK facility on the shore of the Irish Sea. Ireland appealed to a tribunal under LOSC Annex VII, claiming various breaches by the United Kingdom of LOSC, but also referring to the OSPAR Convention and EU law to support its case.[28] The Tribunal considered whether the references to the OSPAR Convention necessitated deference to the OSPAR dispute settlement system, on the basis that LOSC Article 281 and 282. The Tribunal was however not persuaded that the OSPAR Convention 'substantially covers the field of the present dispute so as to trigger application of articles 281 and 282 of [LOSC].'[29] The Tribunal, while still in the preliminary phase of deciding on jurisdiction, added the worthwhile gloss to the decision in the *Southern Bluefin Tuna* Case that in order to block application of the LOSC dispute settlement system, the competing legal instrument must 'substantially cover the field' of the claims in dispute. This rather loose language appears to imply that it must be closely scrutinised whether all of the claims in dispute are based on the competing legal instrument (such as the CCSBT or the OSPAR Convention), but that there is scope for the Tribunal to hold that, even though not all claims are or can be based on such instrument, the totality of claims 'substantially' can be related to that instrument, and therefore there is no residual jurisdiction for a tribunal established on the basis of LOSC.[30] The Tribunal was however not given the opportunity to later elaborate on that finding, as it did find that it had to suspend its work on another basis. The Tribunal was concerned that the dispute could in whole or in part be subject to the com-

---

[28] A. Cassar, 'Introductory Note to OSPAR/UNCLOS: Mox Plant Award and Order', (2003) 42 *ILM* 1116; Arbitral Tribunal *Mox Plant* Case (*Ireland* v. *United Kingdom*) Order No. 3 (24 June 2003), (2003) 42 *ILM* 1186.

[29] Arbitral Tribunal *Mox Plant* Case (*Ireland* v. *United Kingdom*) Order No. 3 [18].

[30] Cf., D.R. Rothwell and T. Stephens, 'Dispute Resolution and the Law of the Sea: Reconciling the Interaction between the LOS Convention and Other Environmental Instruments', in A.G. Oude Elferink and D.R. Rothwell (eds.), *Oceans Management in the 21st Century: Institutional Frameworks and Responses* (2004) 209, 225.

petence of the European Court of Justice, and that Ireland and the United Kingdom might possibly not have standing to issue proceedings.[31] LOSC Article 282, together with 'considerations of mutual respect and comity which should prevail between judicial institutions both of which may be called upon',[32] thereby provided a window for the Tribunal to allow for these issues to be settled elsewhere, and to postpone resumption until such time.

Subsequently, the ECJ, upon application by the European Commission, found that the Irish claims submitted to the Annex VII Tribunal were allegations regarding UK obedience of norms that had become part of EU law.[33] By appealing to an external arbitral tribunal Ireland usurped the competence of the Commission and the ECJ to ensure respect of EU law.[34] This was so irrespective of the fact that ITLOS, when earlier deciding on a request for provisional measures,[35] as well as the Annex VII Arbitral Tribunal when considering its jurisdiction, had held that they had *prima facie* jurisdiction to address the claims. In this case, then, LOSC Articles 281 and 282 were useful in cautioning the Tribunal and explicitly allowing for regard for jurisdiction of other, non-LOSC courts and tribunals. This assisted the Tribunal in deciding to put its work on hold. Nevertheless, considering the proactive protection by the European Commission and the ECJ of their respective competencies, is likely that there would also have been such a Judgement by the Court even if the Tribunal had decided to continue its deliberations.

These cases bring to light the challenges of a system of residual jurisdiction. Any concession to the exclusive nature of a conciliation system evidently opens possibilities to avoid its use, regardless of the merits of any tailor-made specifics of the provided conciliation system. At the same time, an open system allows for the realities of increasingly competing jurisdictions.

1.1 The case of other treaties

The choices made in the Law of the Sea Convention, in favour of compulsory conciliation but against an exclusive system, are also made in other area specific mechanisms[36] such as the Framework Convention on Climate

---

[31] Idem [20].

[32] Idem [28].

[33] ECJ Judgement C-459/03 (*Commission* v. *Ireland*) (*Mox Plant*) (30 May 2006) [184].

[34] The ECJ did not rule on the permissibility of Ireland's bringing other claims to an OSPAR Arbitral Tribunal: *Dispute Concerning Access to Information under Article 9 of the OSPAR Convention* (*Ireland* v. *United Kingdom*) (Final Award) (2 July 2003), (2003) 42 *ILM* 1118.

[35] *Mox Plant* Case (*Ireland* v. *UK*) (ITLOS Order 3 December 2001), (2002) 41 *ILM* 405.

[36] Nevertheless (unlike the final version of the Articles on Responsibility of States for internationally wrongful acts (adopted in 2001) UN Doc A/56/10 supp 10, which do not contain inde-

Change,[37] the Convention to Combat Desertification,[38] the Convention on the Prior Informed Consent Procedure for Certain Hazardous Chemicals and Pesticides in International Trade,[39] and the Convention on Biological Diversity (CBD).[40]

Compulsory conciliation has historically been the result of a diplomatic compromise between States favouring binding settlement and those opposing it. Accounts of the negotiations leading to the 1969 Vienna Convention on the Law of Treaties[41] and the 1982 Convention on the Law of the Sea[42] are clear in this respect. Conciliation was as far as States reluctant of adjudication were willing to go, and as much as others wishing reference to a Court could settle for. While compulsory conciliation guarantees that any dispute will have a forum, it also guarantees that no settlement will be reached without the *ad hoc* consent of the parties. Compulsory conciliation, as such, does however not ensure that the treaty norms will also be the basis of any conciliation proceedings, let alone that these norms will be reflected by any bilateral settlement that may come out of them. Compulsory conciliation, after all, only obliges parties to pursue the method, but not to adopt its outcome.

The example of the Law of the Sea Convention illustrates that even when the drafters of an agreement agree that there should be compulsory conciliation, it may still be difficult to effectuate the parties' obligation to settlement

---

pendent dispute settlement provisions) the Draft Articles on State Responsibility which had been provisionally adopted by the ILC in 1995 included an exclusive system of conciliation, (1998) 37 *ILM* 440 Art. 56 and Annex I. For the commentary on the articles concerning dispute settlement: 'Report of the International Law Commission 47th session' UN Doc A/50/10 supp 10. On the reasons for leaving the dispute settlement provisions out of the final version: J. Crawford, J. Peel and S. Olleson, 'The ILC's Articles on Responsibility of States for Internationally Wrongful Acts: Completion of the Second Reading', (2001) 12 *EJIL* 963, 965.

[37] United Nations Framework Convention on Climate Change Art. 14.

[38] (17 June 1994), (1994) 33 *ILM* 1328 Art. 29; M.A. Bekhechi, 'Une nouvelle étappe dans le developpement du droit international de l' environnement: la Convention sur la Desertification', (1997) 101 *RGDIP* 5.

[39] (11 September 1998), (1999) 38 *ILM* 1. Another example is the Convention on Non-navigational Uses of International Watercourses (1997). This, however, speaks in Art. 33 of compulsory fact-finding, in fact an incarnation of conciliation.

[40] 31 *ILM* 818 (1992) Art. 27. Also the Vienna Convention on the Law of Treaties is not fully exclusive, as Art. 66 allows the parties to set-up their own conciliation mechanism before the expiry of a twelve-month period, after which the special conciliation provisions of the Convention become mandatory.

[41] I. Sinclair, *The Vienna Convention on the Law of Treaties* (2nd edn. 1984) 226-233; R.D. Kearney and R.E. Dalton, 'The Treaty on Treaties', (1970) 64 *AJIL* 495, 545 ff.

[42] M.H. Nordquist, S. Rosenne and L.B. Sohn (eds.), *United Nations Convention on the Law of the Sea 1982: A Commentary* (1989) Vol. V; A.O. Adede *The System for Settlement of Disputes under the United Nations Convention on the Law of the Sea* (1987); N. Klein, *Dispute Settlement in the Law of the Sea Convention* (2005) 256.

under the treaty regime. Any effort to add elements of legal conciliation to a conciliation procedure may be undermined if parties are free to adopt another settlement method whenever a dispute arises. Therefore, the exclusivity of the regime is of great significance to the effectiveness of conciliation to address specific norms. Nevertheless, whether the settlement mechanism adopted in a treaty is exclusive or not, several other or additional options exist to promote the role of specific norms in the conduct of conciliation.

2. Norm Protection

In the application of conciliation provisions of area-specific agreements generally, promoting respect for the norms can be addressed in various ways. In the event, the role of such norms is not only an abstract interest of the treaty regime, but can be of specific interest also to third parties. They may have a stake in the outcome of the dispute itself, or they may later be confronted with the outcome as an example of State practice, or even of a form of precedent, that will affect their legal and political position. Perhaps even more important is the interest that a disputing party itself may have in the basis on which it will be invited by the conciliators to adopt or negotiate a settlement. To serve these interests and to balance countervailing political pressures, four essential features are used. First, treaties may provide for conciliators with expertise. Second, treaties may accord special place to neutrals. Third, they may expressly prescribe the basis of considerations. Fourth, they may create room for other external factors.

2.1 Expertise

When a distinct procedure is created by an area-specific agreement, its usefulness depends to a large extent on the way in which it concerns itself with the object and purpose of the underlying agreement. For non-binding settlement to work satisfactorily, the close involvement of the disputants in the deliberations is evidently essential. Nevertheless, it may be assumed that neutrals and experts in the field are best placed to protect the multilaterally regulated common interests in those fields. Clearly, experts can also be partial and will not always share a conception of the common good, but it can be assumed that generally they are more inclined to keep in mind the integrity of the regime in their field of expertise than others who are involved in the process on an exclusively diplomatic basis, and therefore presumed to be more oriented towards political settlement.

The requirement that conciliators are experts of the subject-matter under discussion is most easily included in legally oriented instruments as the Vienna Convention on the Law of Treaties. This requires that that the conciliators are qualified jurists.[43] Most other instruments, however, do not set such criteria. While the provisions in LOSC regarding adjudication allow for the selection of scientific or technical experts to sit with the judges,[44] there is no requirement of expertise when it comes to conciliation. It is only written that persons nominated by State Parties should enjoy 'the highest reputation for fairness, competence and integrity'.[45]

A notable provision is found in the LOSC Implementation Agreement regarding Straddling Fish Stocks (1995).[46] While the Agreement declares that the LOSC provisions on dispute settlement apply *mutatis mutandis*,[47] a separate article allows for the establishment of an *ad hoc* expert panel established by the disputants.[48] No further details are given for what appears to be a rudimentary form of conciliation by experts. A comparable, though different innovation is found in the provision of compulsory fact finding in the Convention on the Law of the Non-navigational Uses of International Watercourses. Here, a commission of experts is to investigate the dispute and issue a report on:

> 'its findings and the reasons therefore and such recommendations as it deems appropriate for an equitable solution of the dispute, which the Parties concerned shall consider in good faith.'[49]

This may be seen as fact-finding with an explicit objective to reach settlement.[50] It is however better understood as conciliation, only with the explicit requirement of area-specific expertise on the part of the conciliators. The mixture of the explicit aim of investigating the dispute, with the additional competence of suggesting a solution, is reminiscent of the work of the 1905 inquiry

---

[43] Vienna Convention on the Law of Treaties (1969) Art. 1 Annex. Note however that when a commission is set-up the parties may also appoint conciliators who are not on the list, and for whom no qualifications are explicitly required.

[44] LOSC Art. 289.

[45] LOSC Annex V Art. 2.

[46] Agreement for the Implementation of the Provisions of the United Nations Convention of the Law of the Sea (10 December 1982) relating to the Conservation and Management of Straddling Fish Stocks and Highly Migratory Fish Stocks (4 August 1995), (1996) 34 *ILM* 1542.

[47] Idem Art. 30.

[48] Idem Art. 29.

[49] Convention on the Law of the Non-navigational uses of International Watercourses Art. 33(8).

[50] Cf., R. Lapidoth, 'Dispute Settlement under the 1997 Convention on the Law of the Non-navigational Uses of International Watercourses', in M.N. Schmitt (ed.), *International Law Across the Spectrum of Conflict* (2000) 231, 241.

commission for the *Dogger Bank* incident, often presented as in fact the first conciliation commission.[51] On the whole, however, it appears that area-specific conciliation as it is currently provided for does not explicitly seek to protect the interests of the regime by the standard involvement of experts.

2.2 Neutral elements

Another way in which the treaty regime could be kept in view when settling bilateral disputes is by involving a neutrally appointed element in the conciliation commission. This is indeed commonly provided, though to varying degrees. In the Convention on the Law of the Sea, and in those conventions following its model, provision is made for a commission consisting of five persons.[52] Each party nominates two conciliators, one is nominated by the parties or the other nominees jointly. The neutral or third party element is therefore very limited. Slightly different, the Framework Convention on Climate Change provides for a three person commission, with only one non-national.[53]

A different possibility is displayed in the treaties following the example of the Vienna Convention on the Law of Treaties.[54] These allow the parties to each select one conciliator freely, and one non-national from a pre-existing list. The four nominees together select a fifth person as chairman.[55] This way, partisan influence within the commission is supposed to be diminished, to the benefit of community interests. There is however no good possibility of assessing whether including non-national conciliators indeed has this effect. In the few accounts given from within conciliation commissions, the members stress the collegiality and integrity of all members.[56] The instance of the *F.OABV* Case, in which the national conciliator and the non-national conciliator appointed by one party walked out of the proceedings over what appeared to be partisan grievances, was exceptional.[57] A question mark looms over the un-

---

[51] See chapter II 1.3.

[52] LOSC Annex V Art. 3. See also chapter IV 2.

[53] United Nations Framework Convention on Climate Change Art. 14(5).

[54] Vienna Convention on the Law of Treaties Art. 2 Annex; E.g., Convention on Succession of States in Respect of State Property, Archives and Debts (8 April 1983, not yet in force), (1983) 22 *ILM* 306, Annex.

[55] This differs from the practice in such public/private law models as the UNCITRAL Conciliation Rules (Art. 3), where there shall be one conciliator unless the parties agree on two or three, and the ICSID Convention (Art. 29), leaving the number of conciliators up to the parties, with three conciliators as the default option.

[56] E.g., E.L. Richardson, 'Jan Mayen in Perspective', (1988) 82 *AJIL* 443; F.M. van Asbeck, 'La tâche et l'action d'une commission de conciliation', (1956) *NTIR* 1

[57] C. Rousseau, 'Echec de la procedure d'enquête et de conciliation dans l'affaire du deroutement de l'avion transportant de Rabat a Tunis les chefs nationalistes algériens le 22 octobre 1956', (1958) 62 *RGDIP* 691.

characteristic *Taba* conciliation case, in which the three conciliators, of which two were nominated by the disputing states, instantly agreed that the conciliation work could best be done by the neutral chairman alone. It is unlikely that this self-disqualification has anything to do with doubts about the ability to properly apply the norms to the dispute.[58] It does nevertheless provide further support to the position that a neutral element is important to gain the confidence of both parties.

2.3 **Norms**

The most direct way in which the object and purpose of the treaty regime can kept in view in area specific conciliation is by explicitly making the legal norms the basis of consideration in the work of any commission. As discussed in chapter III, the legal conciliation tradition was explicitly adopted in the Vienna Convention on the Law of Treaties.[59] It refers to the competence of the commission to express conclusions on questions of law. This was taken further by in the LOSC provisions. The Law of the Sea Convention requires that the commission's report shall record, failing agreement, 'its conclusions on all questions of fact or law relevant to the matter in dispute'.[60] This provision can be seen to require that the commission considers the dispute in detail, and that its recommendations are based significantly on a legal analysis of the facts of the case. The law-based method was also included in for instance the Framework Convention on Climate Change and the Oslo Protocol on Sulphur Emissions, where they require that a conciliation commission renders a 'recommendatory award'.[61] This suggests that the process is really that of advisory arbitration, in which an adjudicatory process is followed, with the exception of its binding nature.

Since the 1990s, however, new conciliation provisions have not always required the inclusion of legal determinations. Frequently, the parties drafting the relevant agreements sufficed with minimal clauses such as that in the Convention on Biological Diversity: '[The commission] shall render a proposal for resolution of the dispute (...)'.[62] Romano argues that in this period, dispute

[58] As also the fierce criticism of the conciliator-turned-arbitrator in her dissent demonstrates: R. Lapidoth, 'Some Reflections on the Taba Award', (1992) 35 *GYIL* 224.

[59] See chapter III 3.2.

[60] LOSC Annex V Art. 7(1). The relevant text of the 1975 Vienna Convention on the Representation of States in Relations with International Organisations Art. 85(7): 'The report shall include the Commission's conclusions upon the facts and questions of law'.

[61] United Nations Framework Convention on Climate Change Art. 14(5); Oslo Protocol to the 1979 Convention on Long-Range Transboundary Air Pollution of Further Reduction of Sulphur Emissions Art. 9(6).

[62] Convention on Biological Diversity Annex II Part 2 Art. 5; also: OSPAR Convention Art. 32.

settlement clauses were less afterthoughts in the drafting of treaties, but instead increasingly came to be seen as essential elements thereof.[63] An important reason for not providing detailed terms of reference setting out the legal character of the conciliation would then be that institutionalised treaty regimes, through meetings of the parties or, as the case may be, the Secretariat of the relevant international organisation, may issue guiding norms that are not meant as binding. By not providing for legal conciliation, conciliation could serve to also accommodate these norms.[64] This limitation is however for two reasons not strictly necessary. First, any other norms or standards could be taken into account in any subsequent negotiation of the parties on the basis of the legal proposals by the conciliation commission. Second, to be more precise the terms of reference of such commissions could also refer to the additional norms and standards to be taken into account. That way it would be avoided, if such was indeed desired, that the conciliation turns into political conciliation, in which in principle any consideration could be at the basis of the commission's recommendations.

On the far end of the spectrum of legal conciliation are the terms of reference for friendly settlement of the former European Commission of Human Rights. As is discussed shortly, it performed conciliation-like functions regarding settlement between parties complaining of human rights violations by a State. The Commission had the power to reject settlements between the parties if, in the opinion of the Commission, these were not concluded 'on the basis of respect for human rights'.[65] According legal considerations such a predominant role makes the nature of such proceedings as a supervisory system. As Merrills pointed out:

> 'The fact that here, and in other human rights treaties, conciliation is more than a means of securing a settlement which the parties can accept, but has an additional – and crucial – substantive component, is clearly something which distinguishes friendly settlement under these arrangements from conciliation as generally understood.'[66]

It is important to note that the way in which the norms are addressed throughout any conciliation procedure will depend also on the position taken in the process by the parties themselves. If they plead their cases as lawyers, a legal process is likely to ensue. If they only wish to bargain, or to take a political

[63] C.P.R. Romano, *The Peaceful Settlement of Environmental Disputes* (2000) 42.

[64] T. Gehring, 'International Environmental Regimes: Dynamic Sectoral Legal Systems', (1990) 1 *Yearbook of International Environmental Law* 35, 51.

[65] Then Art. 28(1) European Convention on Human Rights.

[66] J.G. Merrills, *International Dispute Settlement* (4th edn. 2005) 78-79.

stance, the most law-oriented conciliation commission will find it hard to perform its functions as envisaged. This will be so all the more as, unlike the European Commission of Human Rights, conciliation commissions do not have the power to reject a settlement freely concluded between the parties.

2.4 Third parties

Other measures may be included in the regime to promote conformity of the settlement with norms. One such is the standard publication of the commission's report. This would allow third parties to review the recommendations, and to comment on them. It could have a restraining effect on potential settlements in flagrant disregard of applicable norms.[67] Due to the consensual nature of conciliation, however, a requirement of publication is not a common feature of its provisions. It is suggested that if drafting parties agree on compulsory conciliation on the basis that it is an alternative to adjudication, they should include the requirement of publication of the report. An explicit requirement to publish the commission's report could be a worthwhile contribution to demonstrating and promoting respect for the treaty norms through diplomatic settlement.[68]

Another possibility to protect the object and purpose of a multilateral agreement in any settlement mechanism is to give standing to third parties in the conciliation proceedings. To do so does, however, also create difficulties as regards the consensual nature of the method: adoption of any proposals resulting from conciliation will still depend on a positive decision by the parties. For instance, it could legally be made possible for others than the directly affected party to start conciliation proceedings against a party that violates another's rights. A distant analogy can be found in the existence of public prosecutors, who guard the legal order also when the victim does not act, or when there is no individually identifiable victim. Another way of involving third parties would be to grant a right of intervention in ongoing proceedings between two other parties. This is however problematic, first because of the consensual nature of diplomatic dispute settlement: the intervention considered here would take place without the consent of the disputants. Second, if intervention by a third party would not require the consent of the disputants, the latter may abandon this form of dispute settlement altogether, to avoid unwanted outside interference. Because of these difficulties, few examples of provisions for such third party involvement can be found. A different solution, however, is discussed in the second part of this chapter: the non-compliance procedure.

---

[67] This is a requirement in the revised friendly settlement practice of the European Convention on Human Rights (Art. 39).

[68] The modern *Jan Mayen* and the *Belize/Guatemala* Cases, where the reports were published, remain exceptional. See chapter II 1.15 and III 3.4.1 respectively.

Some examples of the inclusion of other parties do nevertheless exist. The Convention on the Law of the Sea provides three such options in conciliation: joint application, separate application and the submission of views. When States determine by agreement that they share the same interests, they shall join as one party in the proceedings. The two conciliators each party is entitled to, one national and one non-national, shall then be appointed jointly.[69] The party-appointed non-national may be substituted for an appointee of the joining state. A complication occurs if there are more than two parties on one side of the dispute. Then at least one of them shall not have its national on the commission. The Convention on Biological Diversity keeps things simpler: when several parties share the same interests, they shall appoint their members of the commission jointly by agreement.[70] Another possibility is that of a procedure involving three or even more separately operating parties.[71] In that case use may be made of the possibility to modify provisions of the regulations of the proceedings.

Alternatively, following the example of the Vienna Convention on the Law of Treaties,[72] LOSC offers the possibility that the commission, only with the consent of the parties, invites any State Party to submit its views to the commission.[73] Such submission of views is not to be equated with the possibility of intervention:[74] it only serves to better inform the commission of a situation, but does not grant any rights to the State submitting views. In no way does the State submitting views become a party to the proceedings.[75] The commission can value the views as it wishes, and nothing alters the rights of the parties to conclude a settlement as they see fit.

Lastly, a more remote example of protection of the regime interests by a third party is provided by the 1954 Hague Convention for the Protection of Cultural Property in the Event of Armed Conflict.[76] It introduces the possibil-

---

[69] LOSC Annex V Art. 3(g).

[70] Convention on Biological Diversity Annex II Pt 2 Art. 2.

[71] This possibility is opened by LOSC Art. 3(g) Annex V. The second sentence reads 'Where two or more parties have separate interests or there is a disagreement as to whether they are of the same interests, they shall appoint conciliators separately'. Art. 3(h) then provides that the provisions on the constitution of the commission are applied 'as far as possible'.

[72] Vienna Convention on the Law of Treaties Annex Art. 3.

[73] LOSC Art. 4 Annex V. For the submission of views on the basis of this article, consent is required. Though the article only speaks of States, it must also be possible for a non-state entity to submit its views, provided always that the parties consent.

[74] E.g., ICJ Statute Art. 62.

[75] This is notably different in the practice of the former GATT panels, as in that of the current WTO panels, as discussed shortly.

[76] Hague Convention for the Protection of Cultural Property in the Event of Armed Conflict (14 May 1954), 249 *UNTS* 240.

ity that a third party initiates a dispute settlement procedure between two parties. Protection of the interests of the international community is obviously difficult in times of war. Therefore, the 1954 Hague Convention expressly mentions the right of third parties, including the Director-General of UNESCO, to 'offer' mediation or conciliation. While this may appear not to affect the parties' rights, the offer can in fact amount to an initiative by the third party of settlement discussions between them, because the Convention notably provides: 'parties to the conflict shall be bound to give effect to the proposals for meeting made to them.' The provisions were repeated in the Second Protocol to the Hague Convention, adopted in 1999.[77]

The above review has shown that drafters of area-specific treaties have various means at their disposal to promote the respect for the norms of the treaties in any recourse to conciliation. The creation of an exclusive system, with compulsory conciliation, is a first step. If the system is not exclusive and compulsory, any tailor-made procedure is only applied if the disputing parties make a positive decision to select it. Additional measures to protect the treaty norms can be the inclusion of experts, and the enlargement of the neutral element in the commission. Further, the terms of reference may stipulate that the norms are to be the basis of deliberations. Lastly, broad standing may be given to other parties, who may then present the interests of outsiders in the proceedings.

These means are adopted in available mechanisms to varying degrees. None of these measures in themselves, or even in combination, ensures that settlement will occur on the basis of the treaty norms. The actual behaviour of the conciliators and that of the parties will likely trump the procedural bars. They are nevertheless available for those who wish to use them.

PART TWO

COMPLIANCE AND CONCILIATION

In view of the lack of practical experience with the conciliation provisions in multilateral area-specific agreements, it should be all the more worthwhile to study experiences obtained in various other systems in which a desire for amicable settlement in preference to adjudication is combined with an interest by drafters, parties and outsiders in maintaining the relevant norms. To that end, the second part of this chapter starts with a review of the practice and provi-

[77] Second Protocol to the Hague Convention (1954) for the Protection of Cultural Property in the Event of Armed Conflict (26 March 1999), (1999) 38 *ILM* 769, Art. 36(2).

sions developed in the system of the European Convention on Human Rights (ECHR). It then turns to the settlement practices in international trade law as developed in GATT and WTO, and continues by discussing the review practice of the World Bank. It concludes with a discussion of the functioning of non-compliance procedures (NCPs).

It is important to note that both in case of the ECHR and of the WTO, and to a lesser extent in GATT, any friendly settlement practice should be seen against the background of a functioning judicial system, having jurisdiction to issue a binding legal finding on each case that is not amicably settled, and that is established to protect a certain body of norms. Therefore, the conciliatory functions of the system take place within a setting of enforcement of rules. They are therefore distinct from the conciliation of general political inter-State disputes, such conflicts over a border or over debt payments. For NCPs, the situation is less clear, as in many cases there are doubts about the standing of the applicable norms, and there is an ambivalent relationship with other dispute settlement methods. Therefore, the discussion on NCPs will focus also on the legal nature of the relevant rules.

3. Friendly Settlement and The European Commission of Human Rights

While there are various other multilateral mechanisms for the protection of human rights,[78] none has such an impact, such an elaborate institutional machinery or produced such detailed case law as the 1950 Convention for the Protection of Human Rights and Fundamental Freedoms (European Convention on Human Rights).[79] Diplomatic third party dispute settlement is an essential feature of the Convention.[80] Until the body was abolished with the entry into force of Protocol No. 11 in 1999,[81] one of the main instruments in its

---

[78] E.g., the International Covenant on Civil and Political Rights (19 December 1966), 99 *UNTS* 171, which also provides for an optional conciliation commission in Arts. 41 and 42; the International Covenant on Civil and Political Rights (3 December 1966), 993 *UNTS* 3; the Convention for the Elimination of All Forms of Discrimination Against Women (18 December 1979), 1249 *UNTS* 13; the Convention Against Torture and Other Cruel, Inhuman or Degrading Treatment or Punishment (10 December 1984) GA Res 39/46, UN Doc A/Res/39/46 (1984).

[79] Convention for the Protection of Human Rights and Fundamental Freedoms (4 November 1950), 213 *UNTS* 221.

[80] D. Shelton, 'The Boundaries of Human Rights Jurisdiction in Europe', (2003) 13 *Duke Journal of Comparative and International Law* 95; A. Kiss, 'Conciliation', in R. St. James Macdonald and others (eds.), *The European System for the Protection of Human Rights* (1993) 703, 703.

[81] Protocol No. 11 (11 May 1994, entered into force 1 November 1999) *ETS* 155.

development was the European Commission of Human Rights.[82] While the Commission did not practice conciliation, its settlement work is of interest in the search for third party settlement mechanisms dealing with particular norms. This is so primarily because of the way in which a conciliation-like method was employed in relation to very sensitive rules, but also because the system itself underwent a significant change, which may inform developments in actual inter-State conciliation.

The Convention, modified over time by successive Protocols,[83] sets out fundamental human rights such as the right to life, the prohibition of torture, the right to a fair trial and the right to privacy.[84] It created a Court of Human Rights, that would hear allegations of breaches by a member State as regards any person within the jurisdiction of that State. Complaints could be brought by other member States, and, if the member State accepted the right of individual petition, also by individuals provided these had first exhausted domestic remedies. Gradually all member States – which by 1998 included nearly all States in Central and Eastern Europe – accepted this right, and also accepted the compulsory jurisdiction of the Court.

Complaints were first to be assessed by the Commission of Human Rights, a semi-judicial body comprised of legal experts.[85] The Commission could declare cases 'manifestly non-admissible', or could attempt friendly settlement of the case, and report and refer the case to the Court. If the case was not referred to the Court, the Commission's decision to that effect would be scrutinised by the Committee of Ministers, a political body. The Committee also supervised the implementation of the Court's decisions. This political element in the Convention's system did not, however, result in political restrictions on the work of the Commission or the Court.[86]

3.1 Settlement responsibility

The task of the Commission was first to decide whether an application was admissible.[87] Applications would be referred to a member of the Commission

[82] The commission was installed in 1954, and in 1955 was allowed to consider individual applications. K. Rogge, 'The European Commission of Human Rights', in M. de Salvia and M.E. Villiger (eds.), *The Birth of European Human Rights Law* (1998) 5.

[83] The fourteenth protocol was opened for signature on 13 May 2004.

[84] Respectively Art. 1, 2, 6 and 8 ECHR.

[85] Throughout its existence only one non-lawyer ever became a member. K. Rogge, 'The European Commission of Human Rights', in M. de Salvia and M.E. Villiger (eds.), *The Birth of European Human Rights Law* (1998) 5, 9.

[86] I. Cabral Barretto 'Le règlement amiable devant la Cour européenne des droits de l'homme', (2002) *Bulletin des Droits de l'Homme* (10) 27, 38; J.G. Merrills, *Human Rights in Europe* (4th edn. 2001) 292-296.

[87] The settlement work of the Commission should not be confused with the settlement activity of the Court before 1999: V. Berger, 'Le règlement amiable devant la Cour européenne des

who would act as Rapporteur for that case.[88] The admissibility test required the Commission to determine, among other things, that there was an alleged violation of one of the rights enumerated in the Convention, that the applicant was himself a victim of the alleged breach and that he had exhausted domestic remedies. A large share of applications was thus rejected. The investigation by the Rapporteur was aimed at establishing the facts of the case, often by studying the documents, but occasionally also by a hearing in Strasbourg. In exceptional cases the Rapporteur would visit the State in which the alleged breach had occurred.

During this investigation, the Commission was bound to 'place itself at the disposal of the parties concerned with a view to securing a friendly settlement of the matter on the basis of Human Rights as defined in this Convention.'[89] This friendly settlement function was of major interest in the design of the Convention system: it was explicitly provided in the Convention that the Court could only deal with a matter after the Commission had acknowledged the failure of its friendly settlement efforts.[90] In many cases the involvement of the Commission in this regard was limited to a written invitation to the State and to the applicant to suggest terms for settlement. The Commission would in all cases have to verify that the settlement was reached on the basis of respect for human rights.[91]

In 1991 the member States agreed to a more proactive settlement role for the Commission.[92] The practice developed that the Secretariat would proactively contact the applicant to inquire after his desired terms of settlement. These desires would then be communicated to the respondent State. Frequently, the Secretariat would act as intermediary, without any actual meeting between the parties. Further, the Rapporteur could suggest what he thought would be the

---

droits de l'homme', in F. Matscher and H. Petzold (eds.), *Protecting Human Rights: The European Dimension* (1988) 55; C.A. Nørgaard and H.C. Krüger, 'Article 28 § 1-b et § 2', in L.-E. Pettiti, E. Decaux and P.-H. Imbert (eds.), *La Convention Européenne des Droits de l' Homme; Commentaire Article par Article* (1999) 661, 662-663. Before the abolition of the Commission, the Court's activities in this field were even more limited than they are today, and consisted essentially of acknowledging settlements reached by the parties themselves.

[88] Rule 47 of the Rules of Procedure of the European Commission of Human Rights (as in force on 28 June 1993), available on <http://www.hrcr.org/docs/Eur_Commission/commrules2.html> (5 October 2007).

[89] Then Art. 28(1)(b) ECHR.

[90] Then Art. 47 ECHR.

[91] Then Art. 28(1)(b) ECHR. H.C. Krüger and C.A. Nørgaard, 'Reflections Concerning Friendly Settlement under the European Convention on Human Rights', in F. Matscher and H. Petzold (eds.), *Protecting Human Rights: The European Dimension* (1988) 329.

[92] C.A. Nørgaard and H.C. Krüger, 'Article 28 § 1-b et § 2', in L.-E. Pettiti, E. Decaux and P.-H. Imbert (eds.), *La Convention Européenne des Droits de l'Homme; Commentaire Article par Article* (1999) 661, 664 n 1.

likely conclusions of the Commission and the Court. In addition, it was possible for the Commission to issue a 'provisional opinion' on whether there was indeed a violation.[93] Such an opinion, originally only oral, but later also in writing,[94] could not be relied upon outside of the friendly settlement procedure, and could not bind the Commission. Nevertheless, it must be assumed that a provisional opinion issued by the Commission itself, as also suggestions expressed by the member of the Commission with primary responsibility for the case, would usually be a good prediction of the eventual conclusion of the Commission.

In some cases where it appeared that settlement was possible, but not on the basis of the proposals by the parties themselves, the Rapporteur could make a settlement proposal.[95] Such proposal could be a 'take it or leave it', purely financial settlement, though suggestions of change of administrative or legislative practices were occasionally made, and such suggestions could be subject to substantive discussions.[96] Occasionally, as in conciliation, a meeting would be convened.[97] In exceptional cases, such as when sensitive political issues were at issue, the Rapporteur would preside, otherwise it would be a member of the Secretariat.[98] Such meetings would be especially likely if they could resolve major issues, such as those that affected a larger number of applicants at the same time. On one such occasion a meeting chaired by the Rapporteur with government agents and several applicants and their representatives resulted in the simultaneous settlement of 23 cases.[99]

---

[93] Rule 55 Rules of Procedure of the European Commission on Human Rights. I. Cabral Barretto, 'Le règlement amiable devant la Cour européenne des droits de l'homme', (2002) *Bulletin des Droits de l'Homme* (10) 27, 30.

[94] C.A. Nørgaard and H.C. Krüger, 'Article 28 § 1-b et § 2', in L.-E. Pettiti, E. Decaux and P.-H. Imbert (eds.), *La Convention Européenne des Droits de l'Homme; Commentaire Article par Article* (1999) 661, 664 n 2.

[95] H.C. Krüger and C.A. Nørgaard, 'Reflections Concerning Friendly Settlement under the European Convention on Human Rights', in F. Matscher and H. Petzold (eds.), *Protecting Human Rights: The European Dimension* (1988) 329, 331.

[96] As confirmed in interviews with various Commission officials by the author in 2005/2006. Cf., C.A. Nørgaard and H.C. Krüger, 'Article 28 § 1-b et § 2', in L.-E. Pettiti, E. Decaux and P.-H. Imbert (eds.), *La Convention Européenne des Droits de l'Homme; Commentaire Article par Article* (1999) 661, 665.

[97] I. Cabral Barretto, 'Le règlement amiable devant la Cour européenne des droits de l'homme', (2002) *Bulletin des Droits de l'Homme* (10) 27, 31.

[98] In *Ramazan Cagirga* v. *Turkey*, Report of the Commission 7 July 1995 (No. 21895/93), three members of the Commission were involved in the negotiations.

[99] *J.S. and others* v. *the Netherlands*, Report of the Commission 23 January 1996 (No. 14561/89 ao). Also a 1991 meeting in Portugal which settled 14 cases simultaneously: A. Wampach, 'Pratiques de la Commission: ses relations avec les réquerants', in M. de Salvia and M.E. Villiger (eds.), *The Birth of European Human Rights Law* (1998) 339, 343-344.

It is remarkable, in this respect, that much of the settlement work was delegated. As noted, it was the Secretariat rather than the Rapporteur that would contact the parties. Further, unless the case was seen as being of major significance, it was the Secretariat rather than the Rapporteur, let alone a broader representation from the Commission itself, that would conduct the settlement efforts. While this division of labour inevitably reflected the heavy workload of the Commission, it also suggests that the settlement efforts were often not at the forefront of the system's functioning.

Usually, the party that appeared to be on the losing hand would favour a settlement. In this respect it has been remarked by insiders that also when the finding of a violation was predicted, and the State was willing to settle on favourable terms, occasionally the applicant's counsel would favour pursuing the case, for the apparent purpose of lodging a win in Strasbourg. A settlement would also be more likely if the State could limit itself to a monetary payment, rather than a change in the law or administrative procedure. Nevertheless, there have been several friendly settlements that consisted of such fundamental revisions.[100]

Any documents related to the settlement would remain confidential. In the event the settlement efforts were not successful, they were entirely without prejudice, and the parties were not allowed to mention their substance in any further proceedings.[101]

3.2 Settlement practice

No friendly settlements were concluded until 1965,[102] and only 31 until 1985, but then there were 345 from then until 1998.[103] In the later years, about one in seven cases declared admissible was settled amicably.[104] Apart from settle-

---

100 H.C. Krüger and C.A. Nørgaard, 'Reflections Concerning Friendly Settlement under the European Convention on Human Rights', in F. Matscher and H. Petzold (eds.), *Protecting Human Rights: The European Dimension* (1988) 329, 331.

101 D.J. Harris, M. O'Boyle, C. Warbrick, *Law of the European Convention on Human Rights* (1995) 602.

102 C.A. Nørgaard and H.C. Krüger 'Article 28 § 1-b et § 2', in L.-E. Pettiti, E. Decaux and P.-H. Imbert (eds.), *La Convention Européenne des Droits de l'Homme; Commentaire Article par Article* (1999) 661, 662.

103 S. Dollé, 'Friendly Settlement 14 Years On in the European Commission of Human Rights', in M. de Salvia and M.E. Villiger (eds.), *The Birth of Human Rights Law* (1998) 243, 243. For examples of settlements: P. Leach, *Taking a Case to the European Court of Human Rights* (2nd edn.) (2005) 71-77; A.H. Robertson and J.G. Merrills, *Human Rights in Europe* (3rd edn. 1993) 282-284.

104 N. Braza and M. O'Boyle, 'The Legacy of the Commission to the New Court under Protocol No. 11', in M. de Salvia and M.E. Villiger (eds.), *The Birth of European Human Rights Law* (1998) 377, 386.

ment through the Commission's efforts, cases could be struck out if the parties concluded a settlement independently.[105] Then, also, the Commission would have to assess whether it was nevertheless required to pursue the case so as to ensure respect for human rights.

Most settlements consisted of financial compensation for the applicant,[106] without an acknowledgement of a violation by the respondent government. According to Judge Cabral Barreto, the absence of such admission was essential to settling States.[107] The settlement would usually also include compensation of legal fees. As the Court maintained a policy of awarding only limited amounts, if at all, States must have been able to entice applicants to accept a more generous offer. Such attraction would have to be balanced against a desire by many applicants to have their complaint heard in Court and obtain a judgement. In cases concerning criminal matters, States would occasionally offer procedural interventions, such as reopening the procedure, pardoning the applicant, or ceasing prosecution. Regarding civil cases involving the State as a party, the State could offer to change its position in the proceedings, or not to execute a certain judgement. In immigration cases, States would sometimes offer residence permits. It was unusual though not unknown[108] that the settlement contained a formal apology to the alleged victim of a breach. If the complaint arose from a fundamental lapse in the government administration, States could also agree to introduce new legislation or alter administrative practice.

3.3 Settlement and compliance

It is notable that the Rapporteur directly responsible for the settlement effort would normally be the Commission member with the nationality of the respondent State. He would be selected in most instances because he was familiar with the language of the application and the government culture or the relevant State.[109] As the person concerned was appointed to the Commission on the

[105] Then (since 1990) Art. 30(1) and (3) ECHR. This competence now lies with the Court: Art. 37(1) ECHR.

[106] C.A. Nørgaard and H.C. Krüger, 'Article 28 § 1-b et § 2', in L.-E. Pettiti, E. Decaux and P.-H. Imbert (eds.), *La Convention Européenne des Droits de l'Homme; Commentaire Article par Article* (1999) 661, 669-673.

[107] I. Cabral Barretto, 'Le règlement amiable devant la Cour européenne des droits de l'homme', (2002) *Bulletin des Droits de l'Homme* (10) 27, 31.

[108] Cf., S. Dollé, 'Friendly Settlement 14 Years On in the European Commission of Human Rights', in M. de Salvia and M.E. Villiger (eds.), *The Birth of Human Rights Law* (1998) 243, 244 and C.A. Nørgaard and H.C. Krüger, 'Article 28 § 1-b et § 2', in L.-E. Pettiti, E. Decaux and P.-H. Imbert (eds.), *La Convention Européenne des Droits de l'Homme; Commentaire Article par Article* (1999) 661, 671 n 3.

[109] Prof H.G. Schermers, member of the Commission for 15 years, in an interview with the author on 4 December 2005.

nomination of his State, there could be doubts about his impartiality. Apparently, however, there have been little or no concerns in practice. This may have been partly due to the fact that he was assisted by members of the secretariat, whose involvement could imply a marginal check.

The options for settlement were restricted by two requirements. First, the essence of any settlement would be set out in a published report.[110] Second, and more important, the full Commission had the responsibility to assess whether the settlement was based on respect for human rights. If the Commission would find fault, it would reject the settlement and continue its deliberations. No such instances have been recorded, and it may be thought, therefore, that the requirement of approval by the Commission ensured that States could not simply buy off individual applicants, without rectifying any underlying failures in that State's handling of similar situations. It is however not unreasonable to question whether this system always functioned so well as intended, and as it is credited for my most commentators.[111] It is remarkable that on no occasion a friendly settlement reached by the parties was not accepted.[112] Insiders note that there were rarely if ever any discussions within the Commission on settlements supervised by a Rapporteur. While it may well be that in certain instances during the drafting stage the Commission saw to the modification of an otherwise unacceptable settlement, such a blank record does raise the legitimate question whether there was sufficient scrutiny of the settlements on respect for the norms set out in the Convention.

In this respect, most criticism is levied against the only inter-State case settled by means of the friendly settlement procedure in the Commission's time, an application brought in 1982 by Denmark, France, the Netherlands, Norway and Sweden regarding alleged serious violations of the Convention by Turkey's then military government. In 1985 a settlement was reached, in the formulation of which members of the Commission played an important part.[113] Delegates of the Commission investigated the allegations and conducted various meetings with the parties, both jointly and separately. The Commission also confidentially informed the parties of its preliminary views on the allegations.[114] The eventual settlement was based on proposals by the parties and sanctioned

---

[110] Then Art. 28(2) ECHR.

[111] E.g., N. Braza and M. O'Boyle, 'The Legacy of the Commission to the New Court under Protocol No. 11', in M. de Salvia and M.E. Villiger (eds.), *The Birth of European Human Rights Law* (1998) 377, 386.

[112] I. Cabral Barretto, 'Le règlement amiable devant la Cour européenne des droits de l'homme', (2002) *Bulletin des Droits de l'Homme* (10) 27, 34, 37.

[113] Cases No. 9940-9944/82; Report of the European Commission of Human Rights (7 December 1985), DR 44, 31.

[114] Idem [33].

by the Commission. It essentially contained promises by Turkey that breaches such as those complained of would not occur in the future, while the Commission accepted the responsibility to report on Turkey's compliance with its commitments.[115]

Several critics have written that by supporting this settlement in the face of clear breaches of fundamental human rights norms, by not demanding more from the Turkish government or having the Court rule on Turkey's violations, the Commission let undue political pressures prevail over respect for the human rights standards.[116] Critics have up to now however not accounted for the remarkable fact that shortly after the despised settlement, Turkey accepted the right of individuals to bring cases against it.[117] The acceptance of the right, which led to a flood of cases against Turkey and which has served to substantiate much further scrutiny, at first view appears surprising. Though there is no official confirmation, several discussions by the author with various persons with inside knowledge indicate that Turkey's acceptance of the right of individual application was in fact a tacit condition of the settlement struck with the member States who brought the complaint.[118] Following the inter-State complaint, and following the transfer of power in Turkey to a civilian government, Turkey was eager to develop its international standing and credibility. Further integration into the ECHR system was perceived as a significant sign of democratisation and Westernisation, and accepting the right of individual petition, and later also the full jurisdiction of the Court, would be both a major concession to the complaining States as well as a step towards regaining respectability.

On this understanding, the result of the friendly settlement procedure in this case was of much greater value that a mere conviction of Turkey regarding the particular complaints brought in 1983 would have been. Indeed, the settlement may have been one of the greatest achievements of the ECHR system. One may still be right to point out that the settlement did not adequately address the human rights violations dating from the moment of the application, but others may point out that the settlement function created a better result for the human rights situation than a conviction of Turkey by the Court could have provided.

---

[115] Idem [39].

[116] E.g., J.G. Merrills and A.H. Robertson, *Human Rights in Europe* (4th edn. 2001) 281.

[117] On 28 January 1987, little over a year after the adoption of the Commission's report on 7 December 1985.

[118] Due to the continuing sensitivity of this information, as well as the intangible nature of an unwritten understanding, the author here relies on many anonymous internal sources deemed highly credibly by him. In the absence of publicly available evidence, the author presents this insight as a highly credible assumption.

Nevertheless, questions about the friendly settlement practice remain. According to the Convention, any settlement should always be 'on the basis of respect for Human Rights as defined in the Convention and the protocols thereto'.[119] As stated, it was unusual that the settlement would contain a formal apology to the alleged victim of a breach. In fact, by far most friendly settlements included wording in which the State explicitly did not recognise that there was a breach of human rights standards. It is noted that some States were eager to offer a financial settlement, rather than introduce the required reforms.[120] This practice conflicts with the notion that if there was a breach, a State should remedy the mistake, not only for the applicant, but for all persons who at present or in the future could otherwise in the same way see their human rights violated. It would seem logical that the first step in making amends is to acknowledge that a violation has occurred, an acknowledgement that was (and remains) absent from most settlements.[121] It is questionable whether a State violating human rights can, with a financial payment alone, show sufficient respect for the norms as defined in the Convention. In this respect, Merrills and Robertson have noted:

> 'The aim of the Convention is not, as some people imagine, to create a procedure for putting governments in the dock and registering convictions against them if they infringe its provisions. The aim is rather to protect the individual's rights and encourage the Contracting States to respect them, first by specifying the rights concerned and then, where necessary, by providing arrangements for supervision and control.'[122]

This should not, however, lead to settlements that do not sufficiently respect human rights. The question here, therefore, is not whether friendly settlement is in itself an inappropriate option to avoid censure of a State by the Court, but whether in practice the friendly settlement option has managed to live up to the requirements set for it by the Convention itself.

There have been several cases in which, despite allegations of grave human rights abuses, a purely financial settlement was condoned by the Commission,

---

[119] Art. 38(1)(b) ECHR. This will be restated in a new Article 39 if and when the 14th protocol comes into effect.

[120] S. Dollé, 'Friendly Settlement 14 Years On in the European Commission of Human Rights', in M. de Salvia and M.E. Villiger (eds.), *The Birth of Human Rights Law* (1998) 243, 244, concerning complaints of unreasonable lengths of proceedings.

[121] In the Inter-American system States do occasionally apologize (and even agree to erect a monument to victims), and are occasionally also ordered by the Court to apologize: J.M. Pasqualucci, *The Practice and Procedure of the Inter-American Court of Human Rights* (2003) 254, 280-281.

[122] J.G. Merrills and A.H. Robertson, *Human Rights in Europe* (4th edn.) (2001) 282.

without acknowledgement of a breach, or a commitment to prevent such cases in the future.[123] A notable case is *Farrell* v. *the United Kingdom*[124] in which British security forces mistakenly killed a man in Northern Ireland, raising broader questions about the use of force by the soldiers there. The British government concluded a friendly settlement with the family concerned, consisting of a payment of £37,500, without acknowledging a breach or announcing new measures, only stating it was an 'unfortunate mistake'. The settlement was however followed by a number of similar cases, suggesting that there may indeed have been a structural problem underlying the incident. The Commission's lenient approach is also seen in *Can* v. *Austria*[125] and in *Skoogström* v. *Sweden*.[126] In both cases the Court agreed to strike a case off its list following a friendly settlement, on the basis that any lingering doubts about the legislative programme announced therein must be put aside because there was clear case law on the relevant issue, and that this provided sufficient clarity to the respondent government regarding its obligations.[127] It may be thought, however, that if the party violating the norm under discussion does not acknowledge the violation, it is insufficient confirmation of the norm that the Court solely relies on established case law.

Amicable settlement practices are especially controversial when applied to questions of human rights violations. Even more than in settlement discussions between States, discussions involving an individual and a government are normally on an unequal footing, allowing greater influence of power and resources in the negotiation.[128] Further, in State/individual relations, such as the maintenance of human rights, the development of a compromise, even if satisfactory to both parties, is likely to influence the situation for many other actors. Some, including the Inter-American Commission of Human Rights and the associated Court,[129] are of the opinion that grave human rights violations always require

---

[123] P. Sardaro, 'Jus Non Dicere for Allegations of Serious Violations of Human Rights; Questionable Trends in the Recent Case Law of the Strasbourg Court', (2003) *EHRLR* 601, 620; P. Frumer, *La Renonciation aux Droits et Libertés: La Convention Européenne des Droits de l'Homme à l'Epreuve de la Volonté Individuelle* (2001) 73-78.

[124] ECtHR (*Friendly Settlement*) 1984 Case No. 9013/80. D.J. Harris, M. O'Boyle, C. Warbrick, *Law of the European Convention on Human Rights* (1995) 601.

[125] ECtHR (*Friendly Settlement*) 30 September 1985 Case No. 9300/81.

[126] ECtHR (*Friendly Settlement*) 2 October 1984 Case No. 8582/79.

[127] In both cases the decisions of the Court were internally controversial: J.G. Merrills, *The Development of International Law by the European Court of Human Rights* (1993) 61.

[128] For a discussion of mediation and human rights in a domestic setting: A. Rycroft, 'The Mediation of Human Rights Disputes', (2002) *South African Journal on Human Rights* 287.

[129] The Court held that the Inter-American friendly settlement procedure should only be attempted by the Commission if the circumstances make that option suitable or necessary, and that when a State denies that a forced disappearance took place, there is no need for the Commis-

censure, regardless of any opportunity to settle.[130] In view of the requirement of respect for the norms as set out in the European Convention on Human Rights,[131] settlement should acceptable when commitments to alter the faulty situation are made, or when it is clear that the violation at issue was indeed an unfortunate mistake or grave exception unlikely to recur. Further, if the settlement forms part of a group of cases, it may be pragmatic to give more leeway to settlement of the bulk of these cases, as long as under the heading of the leading case among them, the State agrees to remedy the structural flaw that caused the violations. If there are doubts, however, the intention to uphold the norms of the Convention necessitates that a settlement should explicitly confirm the applicability of the norm to that case.[132] If it does not, the doubts created by the settlement necessarily undermine respect for the Convention and its institutions.

In the light of the above, it is all the more worrying that the new Court may be too eager to remove cases from its docket. Various cases can be mentioned in which the Court accepted a settlement and struck out applications on the basis of questionable offers to the applicants by the respondent Government.[133] The Court has even struck out cases in which the applicants rejected the settlement offered,[134] though some such actions have been criticised by other mem-

---

sion to attempt settlement: IACtHR *Velasquez Rodriguez* v. *Honduras* (*Preliminary Objections*) (26 June 1987) Ser C No. 1 [42]-[46]; IACnHR *María Teresa Guardado* v. *El Salvador* (Case No. 10.915) *Annual Report of the Inter-American Commission on Human Rights* (1993) Report 8/1994 [4]; H. Tigroudja and I.K. Panoussis, *La Cour interaméricaine des droits de l'homme* (2003) 132-134; F. Ang and E. Bergmand, 'Friendly Settlement and Striking Out of Applications', in P. Lemmens and W. Vandenhole (eds.), *Protocol No. 14 and the Reform of the European Court of Human Rights* (2005) 89, 96.

130 Even though the Inter-American Court may be criticised for allowing doubtful friendly settlements, e.g., the *Maqueda* Case (IACtHR Resolution 17 January 1995) Ser C No. 18 [27], where a settlement was accepted on the basis that it ensured the victim's freedom, regardless of other relevant allegations of violations. H. Tigroudja and I.K. Panoussis, *La Cour Interaméricaine des Droits de l'Homme* (2003) 139.

131 Art. 38(1)(b) ECHR.

132 For examples of how things went wrong in another system, see C.A. Odinkalu, 'The Individual Complaints Procedure of the African Commission on Human Rights: A Preliminary Assessment', (1998) 8 *Transnational Law and Contemporary Problems* 359, 374.

133 Striking out is regulated in Art. 37(1) ECHR. C.L. Rozakis, 'Únilateral Declarations as a Means of Settling Human Rights Disputes: A New Tool for the Resolution of Disputes in the ECHR's Procedure', in M.G. Kohen (ed.), *Promoting Justice, Human Rights and Conflict Resolution through International Law* (2007) 1003; F. Ang and E. Bergmand, 'Friendly Settlement and Striking Out of Applications', in P. Lemmens and W. Vandenhole (eds.), *Protocol No. 14 and the Reform of the European Court of Human Rights* (2005) 89, 96-101; P. Sardaro, 'Jus Non Dicere for Allegations of Serious Violations of Human Rights; Questionable Trends in the Recent Case Law of the Strasbourg Court', (2003) *EHRLR* 601, 620.

134 E.g., *Akman* v. *Turkey* ECtHR (*Judgement*) 26 October 2001, Case No. 37543/97; *Haran* v. *Turkey* ECtHR (*Judgement*) 26 March 2002, Case No. 25754/94.

bers of the Court.[135] In *Tahsin Acar* v. *Turkey* a decision to strike out a case has been overturned by the Grand Chamber of the Court.[136] It should also be noted, on the other side of the balance, that recently the Court for the first time rejected a settlement submitted by both parties, and continued deliberating the case, considering that respect for human rights required it to do so.[137]

Considering also that the Court rightly criticises governments for excessive delays their judicial proceedings, it evident that the new Court is under pressure, with an ever expanding case load.[138] While the friendly settlement option available in the European Convention may produce welcome results, experience shows that the availability of such an option also creates the risk that it negatively affects the implementation of the Convention's norms. If the Court is to function in accordance with the requirement of the Convention, it needs to be more cautious in accepting settlements in situations where a grave human rights violation has likely occurred.

3.4 Attempting settlement post-Commission

Since the abolition of the Commission in 1999, attempting friendly settlement between applicant and State and ensuring a settlement's respect for human rights became the responsibility of the new Court.[139] It was not an intention of the

---

[135] P. Leach, *Taking a Case to the European Court of Human Rights* (2nd edn.) (2005) 79-81. Cf., C.L. Rozakis, 'Unilateral Declarations as a Means of Settling Human Rights Disputes: A New Tool for the Resolution of Disputes in the ECHR's Procedure', in M.G. Kohen (ed.), *Promoting Justice, Human Rights and Conflict Resolution through International Law* (2007) 1003, 1011 ff. There are some similarities to the earlier discussions in the Court in *Skoogström* v. *Sweden*, ECtHR (Judgement) 2 October 1984: V. Berger, 'Le règlement amiable devant la Cour européenne des droits de l'homme', in F. Matscher and H. Petzold (eds.), *Protecting Human Rights: The European Dimension* (1988) 55, 57.

[136] *Tahsin Acar* v. *Turkey* ECtHR (*Preliminary Issue*) 6 May 2004, Case No. 26307/95 [7], [36].

[137] *Ukrainian Media Group* v. *Ukraine* ECtHR (*Judgement*) 12 October 2005 Case No. 72713/01.

[138] Lord Woolf and others, 'Review of the Working Methods of the European Court of Human Rights', (2005) 7 (paper) <http://www.echr.coe.int/ECHR/Resources/Home/LORDWOOLFREVIEWONWORKINGMETHODS.pdf> (5 October 2007); Registry of the European Court of Human Rights *Survey of Activities 2006* (2007) 2.

[139] Art. 38 ECHR and Rule 56(1) Rules of the Court. In Protocol No. 14 Amending the Control System of the Convention, CETS No. 194, opened for signature Strasbourg 13 May 2004, not yet entered into force, the relevant provision will become Art. 39, and will read that the Court has this faculty 'at any stage of the proceedings'. This change codifies existing practice, as the settlement function will not undergo fundamental change: F. Ang and E. Bergmand, 'Friendly Settlement and Striking Out of Applications', in P. Lemmens and W. Vandenhole (eds.), *Protocol No. 14 and the Reform of the European Court of Human Rights* (2005) 89. Generally: P. Lemmens and W. Vandenhole (eds.), *Protocol No. 14 and the Reform of the European Court of Human Rights* (2005).

11th Protocol to change the status of the friendly settlement activity,[140] as its drafters considered the friendly settlement practice an important success.[141] The transfer of the responsibility for attempting settlement to the Court has nevertheless had a negative effect on the substantive importance of this element of the Convention system. As could be expected, due to its judicial status, the Court does not wish to be involved in any negotiation process. Not only would that potentially draw the Court into political bargaining, to the extent that in pursuit of a settlement the Court would be informed of informal admissions by a party, or a willingness to concede certain points, the settlement process could also cloud the responsibility of the Court to reach an impartial decision on the basis of the principle of a fair trial which it is held to protect.[142] Further, unlike the Commission, the Court will not provide suggestions to the parties as to its possible ruling on the case. Its role in friendly settlement is thus severely limited: according to Leach 'little more than a post box'.[143]

To the extent the Court is involved in settlement efforts, this is now part of the tasks of the Registry. The Registry, however, maintains a role of importance, by using the wide discretion accorded to it by the Court. In a standard letter to the government and the applicant, setting out a summary of the facts of the case, the Registrar includes the phrase that the Court is available to assist the parties in attempting settlement.[144] In addition, the Registrar may also make reference to the outcome of previous, similar cases. Contrary to what is sometimes stated, at least some persons in the Registry take an active role in promot-

---

140 Council of Europe *Protocole No. 11 à la Convention de Sauveguarde des Droits de l'Homme et des Libertés Fondamentales et Rapport Explicatif* [brochure] (1994) [94] announces that a Judge, assisted by the Registry, can guide or encourage settlement. The changeover was primarily motivated by the growing workload and the expanding number of member States: A. Drzemczewski, 'A Major Overhaul of the European Human Rights Convention Control Mechanism: Protocol No. 11', in Academy of European Law (ed.), (1995) 6 *Collected Courses of the Academy of European Law* bk 2 121, 134.

141 N. Braza and M. O'Boyle, 'The Legacy of the Commission to the New Court under Protocol No. 11', in M. de Salvia and M.E. Villiger (eds.), *The Birth of European Human Rights Law* (1998) 377, 387

142 In the Inter-American system, the responsibility of friendly settlement is left to its Commission 'precisely because it is not a judicial body' IACtHR *Viviana Gallardo* (*Decision*) (13 November 1981) Ser. A No. G101/81 [24]. Further: J.M. Pasqualucci, *The Practice and Procedure of the Inter-American Court of Human Rights* (2003) 147 ff.

143 P. Leach, *Taking a Case to the European Court of Human Rights* (2nd edn. 2005) 72.

144 In the first few years following the 1999 revision, this would be the letter informing the parties of admissibility, but due to a change of working practice to reduce the Court's workload, the decision on admissibility and on the merits are now joined. (Interview with Ms A. van Steijn, Registry lawyer, 16 January 2006) In this, the practice appears to be similar to that of the Inter-American system, even though in that case it remains the Commission that issues the request. J.M. Pasqualucci, *The Practice and Procedure of the Inter-American Court of Human Rights* (2003) 148.

ing friendly settlement.[145] The responsible Registry official may make telephone calls to the parties, or in exceptional cases meet with them, to discuss terms of settlement. The Registrar cannot, however, authoritatively suggest – as the Commission used to do in the form of a provisional opinion, or the Rapporteur by informal suggestions – what in his view would be the likely outcome of a Court hearing. He may give indications of his preliminary personal assessment, but these are unlikely to carry the same predictive weight as the previous alternatives.

The new system thus creates fewer opportunities than before for pushing the parties towards settlement. With the delegation of the settlement function to the Registrar, there is less opportunity to weigh in on the parties, considering that, unlike the Commission's Rapporteur, the Registrar does not have a formal role in the shaping of the Court's findings. His influence, and moreover the time he has available for settlement, is necessarily more limited, despite the active interest taken in settlement by many Registry officials. It is therefore useful that a 'Group of Wise Persons' recently supported the increased efforts by the Registry, and also suggested that friendly settlement is also attempted at national or Council of Europe level.[146] In a reaction, the Court itself appears to be more reluctant to step up the friendly settlement efforts.[147]

A rare recent inter-State case, between Denmark and Turkey,[148] demonstrates that the friendly settlement process can still be useful. Here the parties themselves concluded a robust settlement. Following Danish complaints of Turkish human rights violations concerning a Danish citizen, Turkey acknowledged 'occasional and individual cases of torture and ill-treatment', paid a substantial sum in settlement, and committed to certain human right projects. The case was resolved essentially bilaterally, with occasional drafting advice by the Registry.

Unlike the situation in the Commission's time, in the revised system any settlement concluded between the parties is published.[149] In contrast to the reticence of the new Court to engage in friendly settlement activity, the Council of Ministers underlined the importance it attaches to attempting friendly

---

[145] As confirmed in off the record interviews with various Court officials by the author in January 2006.

[146] Report of the Group of Wise Persons to the Committee of Ministers, 10 November 2006, Council of Europe Doc SAGES (2006) 06 EN Def. [107-108].

[147] Opinion of the Court on the Wise Persons' Report, adopted 2 April 2007 <http://www.echr.coe.int/NR/rdonlyres/26457EAB-2840-4D71-9ED7-85F0F8AE0026/0/OpinionoftheCourtontheWisePersonsReport.pdf> (19 October 2007).

[148] *Denmark* v. *Turkey* ECtHR (*Friendly Settlement*) 5 April 2000, Case No. 34382/97.

[149] ECHR Art. 39. For examples of settlements: P. Leach, *Taking a Case to the European Court of Human Rights* (2nd edn. 2005) 74.

settlement, on the basis of alleviating the workload of the Court and providing a rapid and satisfactory solution for the parties.[150] It is noted that the sister institution of the Inter-American Court of Human Rights in the 1990s gradually placed more emphasis on its Commission's powers to attempt amicable settlement,[151] without suggesting that in practice this role has indeed increased.[152] Remarkably, despite the decline in attention in the ECHR system for friendly settlement, more friendly settlements have already been reached in the period since the abolition of the Commission than during the entire lifetime of the Commission.[153] This development is, however, due to the simultaneous settlement of classes of cases with respondent Governments, and to the settlement of very simple cases, in which the existence of a violation was clear.[154]

3.5 Conclusions

As discussed above, it was precisely in those instances where the Commission may be thought not to have concentrated on the law, where it may be criticised for not respecting its settlement responsibilities under the Convention. Here lies the essential problem for diplomatic settlement under area-specific treaties, a problem heightened both by the particularly sensitive nature of human rights norms, and by the power differences between States and individuals. It is argued that States have a significant advantage in negotiations with individuals, as they have more power and can benefit from their experience with such settlements. More fundamentally, there is tension between human rights and diplomatic solutions, because essential legal norms do not allow for compromise.[155] Such problems should be less distinct in conciliation in other fields, and in settlement between more equal parties.

---

150 Council of Europe/Committee of Ministers Res (2002) 59 (18 December 2002).

151 The evolution in statements from *Velasquez Rodriguez* v. *Honduras* (*Preliminary Objections*) (26 June 1987) [44] to *Caballera-Delgado and Santana* v. *Colombia* (*Preliminary Objections*) (21 January 1994) [27] and *Genie-Lacayo* v. *Nicaragua* (*Preliminary Objections*) (27 January 1995) [39].

152 Cf., J.M. Pasqualucci, *The Practice and Procedure of the Inter-American Court of Human Rights* (2003) 148; Art. 41 of the Rules of Procedure of the IACnHR <http://www.cidh.oas.org/Basicos/basic16.htm> (21 July 2006).

153 F. Ang and E. Bergmand, 'Friendly Settlement and Striking Out of Applications', in P. Lemmens and W. Vandenhole (eds.), *Protocol No. 14 and the Reform of the European Court of Human Rights* (2005) 89, 92.

154 I. Cabral Barretto, 'Le règlement amiable devant la Cour européenne des droits de l'homme', (2002) *Bulletin des Droits de l'Homme* (10) 27, 43.

155 F. Ang and E. Bergmand, 'Friendly Settlement and Striking Out of Applications', in P. Lemmens and W. Vandenhole (eds.), *Protocol No. 14 and the Reform of the European Court of Human Rights* (2005) 89, 95; P. Frumer, *La Renonciation aux Droits et Libertés: La Convention Européenne des Droits de l'Homme à l'Epreuve de la Volonté Individuelle* (2001) 75.

The extent to which the ECHR settlement practice can be seen as conciliation is discussed in relation with the GATT/WTO and World Bank Inspection Panel further below.[156] It is significant for the discussion of conciliation and norms generally, that while in the ECHR system the practical scope for diplomatic settlement activity has decreased since the system's revision, the use that is made of the remaining possibilities has been criticised, with some ground, for having allowed unwarranted deviation from the norms the system is intended to guard. Considering the sensitive nature of human rights norms in particular, it is clear that the role of conciliation-like methods can be significant, but its practice must be under constant scrutiny to avoid that an amicable settlement between the parties is detrimental to the system or to the rights of (one of) the parties.

The apparent abandonment of active settlement practice, and the delegation of such remaining settlement tasks to the Registrar, who has less time and less opportunity than the former Commission, exemplifies a trend toward judicialisation of dispute settlement.[157] Arguably, the existing law-based variation of conciliation practiced by the Commission was replaced by near exclusive adjudication. In this particular instance, however, it appears that the legalisation process was not undertaken deliberately by the member States, but lay in an unpremeditated refusal by the new Court to get involved in settlement activity. At the same time, despite occasional calls for the reinstitution of a more active settlement practice,[158] there are also calls for the reduction of the limited settlement activity that has survived.[159]

4. Settlement from GATT to WTO

The World Trade Organisation (WTO), created in 1994,[160] developed out of the 1947 General Agreement on Tariffs and Trade (GATT).[161] GATT may be

---

[156] In the conclusion to the present chapter.

[157] Cf., C. Baudenbacher, 'Judicialization: Can the European Model Be Exported to Other Parts of the World?', (2004) 39 *Texas International Law Journal* 381, 391.

[158] E.g., Report of the Group of Wise Persons to the Committee of Ministers, 10 November 2006, Doc SAGES(2006) 06 EN Def. [107-108]; I. Cabral Barretto, 'Le règlement amiable devant la Cour européenne des droits de l'homme', (2002) *Bulletin Des Droits de l'Homme* (10) 27, 45.

[159] F. Ang and E. Bergmand, 'Friendly Settlement and Striking Out of Applications', in P. Lemmens and W. Vandenhole (eds.), *Protocol No. 14 and the Reform of the European Court of Human Rights* (2005) 89, 95; P. Frumer, *La Renonciation aux Droits et Libertés: La Convention Européenne des Droits de l'Homme à l'Epreuve de la Volonté Individuelle* (2001) 75.

[160] The Marrakesh Agreement Establishing the World Trade Organisation (15 April 1994), (1994) 33 *ILM* 1144. E.-U. Petersmann (ed.), *International Trade Law and the GATT/WTO Dispute Settlement System* (1997); J. Cameron and K Campbell (eds.), *Dispute Resolution in the World Trade Organization* (1998).

[161] General Agreement on Tariffs and Trade (30 October 1947), 55 *UNTS* 194.

called ‘the accidental organisation’. Intended as an agreement to bridge the period until the establishment of the planned International Trade Organisation (ITO), it became the permanent platform for international trade when the creation of the ITO was frustrated. GATT’s unintended elevation meant that dispute settlement under various international trade agreements had to evolve gradually. This was reinforced by the fact that striving for consensus was the guiding principle in nearly all decision-making.

The tools provided in the agreement itself were not adequate to deal with the many disputes that would arise under the manifold agreements that were to be attached to it. What followed, therefore, was a creative though often tortuous construction of interpretations and additional dispute settlement instruments.[162] The following discussion therefore aims to combine the varying practice, while focussing also on the structural changes arising out of the transformation from GATT to WTO. The review further aims to allow assessment of how the methods as used relate to conciliation as understood here, and how these methods and the overall system could deal with applying the agreed norms.

4.1 Consultations and good offices

GATT Articles 22 and 23 created a basis for consultations. These could be initiated ‘with respect to any matter affecting the operation of this Agreement’.[163] Further, consultations should take place between parties if any of them considered that any benefit under the agreement was ‘nullified or impaired’, or if an objective of the agreement was impeded, by actions or omissions of another Contracting Party. The term ‘consultation’ must be understood to cover both consultation and negotiation, considering that in view of the applicable GATT norms, discussions between the parties are likely also to concern the granting of concessions or benefits.

Such consultation became one of the main features of the GATT system, both in numbers and in scope.[164] Little is known of the content of most consultations, as they were confidential and as settlements were generally not disclosed. However, for some subject-matters there was at least an obligation to disclose the fact that consultations were initiated, allowing for third parties to request to join in these discussions.[165] It was only with the advent of the WTO

---

[162] E.-U. Petersmann (ed.), *International Trade Law and the GATT/WTO Dispute Settlement System* (1997) 70 ff.

[163] GATT 1947 Art. 22. O. Long, *Law and its Limitations in the GATT Multilateral Trade System* (1985) 74-75.

[164] J.U. Kusumowidagdo, *Consultation Clauses as a Means of Providing for Treaty Obedience* (1981) 231.

[165] GATT 1947 Art. 22.

that a comprehensive obligation was created to notify bilateral settlements to the organisation.[166] If consultation would not have the desired result, the parties could request an appropriate body or individual to 'use their good offices with a view to the conciliation of the outstanding differences between the parties'.[167] The GATT Director-General would be the most likely intermediary. The method was not used frequently.[168] In most cases, the Director-General advised the parties to continue consultations, or to commence a panel procedure.[169] In the notable *Copper Dispute*, however, the Director-General appointed a representative to address a complaint by the European Community regarding high copper prices in Japan, something that was held to distort markets, while not necessarily being an infringement of GATT obligations.[170] In a note to the parties, the representative held that there was no violation, but that the parties should pursue negotiations concerning the tariffs applicable to relevant trade.[171] The parties accepted the advice.

4.2 Panel procedures and settlement

If no satisfactory solution could be obtained, the dispute would be put to the Contracting Parties, the denomination for the Contracting Parties acting collectively. Though that body could legally take certain decisions by majority voting, in practice it always strove for consensus, requiring that at least no State formally objected to a proposed decision. Rather than having all Contracting Parties collectively deal with a dispute in substance, a practice quickly developed in which a 'working party' would be set-up. This body, also deciding by consensus, would consist of five to twenty States, including the disputing parties. It could investigate the dispute, and at the same time attempt to negotiate a settlement.

---

[166] Y. Iwasawa, 'Settlement of Disputes concerning the WTO Agreement: Various Means other than Panel Procedures', in M.K. Young and Y. Iwasawa, *Trilateral Perspectives on International Legal Issues* (1996) 377, 380-381.

[167] 1979 Understanding Regarding Notification, Consultation, Dispute Settlement and Surveillance (1979 Understanding) [8] (28 November 1979) GATT Doc L/4907 (1979).

[168] Y. Iwasawa, 'Settlement of Disputes concerning the WTO Agreement: Various Means other than Panel Procedures', in M.K. Young and Y. Iwasawa, *Trilateral Perspectives on International Legal Issues* (1996) 377, 384.

[169] E.-U. Petersmann, *The GATT/WTO Dispute Settlement System: International Law, International Organizations and Dispute Settlement* (1997) 78; E. Canal-Forgues, *L'Institution de la Conciliation dans le Cadre du GATT* (1990) 41.

[170] Report of the Council 28 October 1988, GATT Doc L/6419.

[171] L/6456 (31 January 1989). A. Porges, *Guide to GATT Law and Practice: Analytical Index* (6th edn. 1995) Vol. 2 767.

From 1953 onwards, the instrument of working parties was gradually replaced with *ad hoc* 'panels' created by the Contracting Parties.[172] Even though the creation of a panel was also subject to consensus, there were only few instances in which a respondent party effectively blocked its creation. Over time, the Contracting Parties came to respect the right of any party to submit its dispute to a panel.[173] Panels comprised three or five experts. These were generally diplomats with a legal background, citizens of countries other than those in dispute. They did not take any instructions from any government.[174] The disputing parties would not be represented on the panel itself: instead, they were invited to present their case to it. The panel then drafted a report, assessing whether the conduct of the respondent party was in conformity with its GATT obligations.

The proceedings before the panel were of a judicial nature, with written submissions and oral pleadings, but were confidential. Panels focused on application of the GATT rules. In order to allow parties to correct the findings of the panel, and in order for them to make any policy adjustment following a negative panel report, the report was communicated to the parties in stages. First, the parties received the descriptive part of the draft report, setting out the facts of the case and the arguments presented by the parties themselves. To this they could make corrections. Subsequently, the parties would be the first to receive the final panel report, which then included legal findings. Subsequently, the report would be submitted to the Contracting Parties.

Communicating draft reports was an expression of the responsibility of panels to assist parties in reaching a friendly settlement.[175] Panels did not, however, actively assist parties in the negotiations. Actual settlement was the responsibility of the parties themselves. It was increasingly perceived that the panel undertook a quasi-judicial function.[176] The panel report, therefore, should not be seen as a proposal for a settlement. The essential ground on which a panel could be criticised was a perceived erroneous interpretation or application of the law. Should there be no settlement, the panel report could be referred to the collective body, which would be able to make a 'ruling' by adopting the report, possibly with modifications. The ruling could only be adopted by consensus,

---

[172] E. Canal-Forgues, *L'Institution de la Conciliation dans le Cadre du GATT* (1990) 160 ff.

[173] E.-U. Petersmann, *The GATT/WTO Dispute Settlement System: International Law, International Organizations and Dispute Settlement* (1997) 87 ff.

[174] See J.H.H. Weiler, 'The Rule of Lawyers and the Ethos of Diplomats; Reflections on the Internal and External Legitimacy of WTO Dispute Settlement', (2001) 35 *Journal of World Trade* 191, 194.

[175] 1979 Understanding [18].

[176] J.H. Jackson, 'The Legal Meaning of a GATT Dispute Settlement Report: Some Reflections', in N. Blokker and S. Muller (eds.), *Towards More Effective Supervision by International Organisations* 149, 152.

which required that also any party criticised in the panel report could formally object, and thereby prevent the adoption of a ruling. If the report was not adopted, it would have no legal status. A ruling, on the other hand, counted as an authoritative statement of GATT rights and obligations in that situation. There has always been a discussion on the importance of adopted reports for later practice,[177] as both parties and panels consistently referred to previous panel reports to support their contentions in new cases.[178] The panel report was not binding in itself, and all parties to a dispute had the opportunity to block its adoption by the Contracting Parties. Nevertheless, up to the 1980s, there were remarkably few problems with the adoption of panel reports.

The dispute settlement system was often commended for its efficiency and success, but it is submitted that for this it relied on the fact that normally no allowance was made for reparations or compensation.[179] The system was essentially prospective, and at most allowed for retaliation in reaction to ongoing breaches after a violation had already been confirmed.[180] While this implies a significant restriction on the available remedies, it will at the same time have meant that the threshold for success of a settlement was lower. After all, the complaining party knew that if it would push on for a binding ruling, it would still not get compensated for damages incurred. On the other hand, the respondent party knew that it could still settle the matter amicably without financial loss or too much damage to its reputation, whereas a panel report could condemn it, leading to unnecessary political fallout. The main objective of the GATT system was to protect the balance of concessions and advantages created in the GATT system.[181] It was not to decide on State responsibility, but to terminate violations as quickly as possible.

4.3 Settlement practice

In this light, it may not be surprising that in the GATT period more than 60% of disputes ended before the final report of the panel was issued.[182] It is remark-

---

[177] A. Chua, 'Precedent and Principles of WTO Panel Jurisprudence', 16 *Berkeley Journal of International Law* (1998) 171; J.H. Jackson, 'The Legal Meaning of a GATT Dispute Settlement Report: Some Reflections', in N. Blokker and S. Muller (eds.), *Towards More Effective Supervision by International Organisations* 149.

[178] D. Palmeter and P.C. Mavroidis, 'The WTO Legal System: Sources of Law', (1998) 92 *AJIL* 398, 400.

[179] E.-U. Petersmann, *The GATT/WTO Dispute Settlement System: International Law, International Organizations and Dispute Settlement* (1997) 78.

[180] As set out in the Annex to the 1979 Understanding Regarding Notification, Consultation, Dispute Settlement and Surveillance (the 1979 Understanding).

[181] O. Long, *Law and its Limitations in the GATT Multilateral Trade System* (1985) 71, 75.

[182] M.L. Busch and E. Reinhardt, 'Bargaining in the Shadow of the Law: Early Settlement in GATT/WTO Disputes' (2001), 24 *Fordham International Law Journal* 158, 161.

able, however, that on average 55% of cases closed before a panel was established. Only an additional 5 to 6% of cases was settled or withdrawn before the issuing of the panel report. Therefore, during the panel process itself few settlements were reached. Those that were concluded in such period, demonstrate a disproportionally high incidence of full or partial concessions by the defendant.[183]

The panel system became increasingly popular. More than 250 disputes have been submitted to procedures under GATT Article 23.[184] Until the late 1980s, almost all of the approximately 130 panel reports were adopted and of those, most were implemented.[185] Only in very few cases were reports revised by means of an 'understanding' negotiated in the GATT Council.[186] Only four reports were not adopted, and those involved major disputes. Nevertheless, even in those cases the parties did eventually reach a settlement.[187]

4.4 Settlement and compliance

In a book-length study, Canal-Forgues suggested that the GATT dispute settlement process was a form of conciliation, or at least analogous to it.[188] His concept of conciliation is the broader notion of mediation common in private international law.[189] More importantly, he considers that the rules of the GATT should not be seen as fully legal rules, but rather as general principles which serve as a point of departure or a guide.[190] On that assumption, it would appear that adjudication of GATT disputes is conceptually difficult, as there are no 'hard rules' to interpret and apply. Any process of third party determination of

---

183 This conclusion is suggested as a correction of the inferences of Busch and Reinhardt themselves (ibid., 163), who state that concessions by defendants appear significantly more likely to occur *after* a panel has been established, but *before* it has ruled, whereas according to their figures, only cases are more than times more often settled before the creation of a panel than during its proceedings.

184 E.-U. Petersmann (ed.), *International Trade Law and the GATT/WTO Dispute Settlement System* (1997) 74.

185 E.-U. Petersmann, *The GATT/WTO Dispute Settlement System: International Law, International Organizations and Dispute Settlement* (1997) 88; P. Pescatore, W.J. Davey and A.F. Lowenfeld, *Handbook of GATT/WTO Dispute Settlement* (1991) 77.

186 Until the breakdown associated with the trade negotiations of the Uruguay Round, which led to the establishment of the WTO, e.g., the *DISC* Case (1977), BISD 28 S/114; *Spring Assemblies* Case (1983), BISD 30 S/107, C/M/168.

187 *Soybeans* Case (1990) (GATT Doc L/5142); *Citrus Preferences* Case (1985) (GATT Doc L5776); *Canned Fruit* Case (1985) (GATT Doc L/5778) and the *Gold Coins* Case (1985) (GATT Doc L/5863).

188 E. Canal-Forgues, *L'Institution de la Conciliation dans le Cadre du GATT* (1990).

189 See chapter I 3.

190 E. Canal-Forgues, *L'Institution de la Conciliation dans le Cadre du GATT* (1990) 33.

GATT obligations then becomes an exercise in diplomatic dispute settlement. There are, however, insufficient indications that when the Contracting Parties, after extensive negotiation, agreed to grant specific concessions and create enumerated obligations, these were not understood as legal.[191]

The naming of the treaties and the discussions on alleged violations of the norms, both by the parties and by the panels, indicate that the GATT obligations were in fact perceived as more than points of departure, indeed seen as legal rules.[192] In this light, the GATT panels performed a useful and successful role in obtaining compliance with GATT legal norms. They did so without substantial use of any conciliation functions, as is underscored by the fact that the only very few disputes were settled during the panel process, and that the panels themselves did not aim for such settlement. Due to the effective mechanism of norm implementation by panels and Contracting Parties, however, also bilateral settlements were necessarily influenced by references to the applicable norms.

In the GATT system, panels increasingly came to be seen as performing a strict legal review, with occasional strong criticism if they were alleged to have made legal mistakes. The process, involving neutral experts, also allowed for the involvement of third parties, most notably through the submission of the dispute to the Contracting Parties in order to adopt the report. This way, protection of the treaty regime was built in to the system. The system evolved from one initially of negotiation and voluntary submission to a more judicial process, eventually paving the way for the near-binding judicialised method of the WTO.[193]

4.5 WTO: conciliation and judicialisation

The WTO dispute settlement system builds on the experience of the previous GATT period.[194] In the GATT system, States in dispute had various opportunities to prevent a binding decision regarding their case. They could block the

---

[191] J.H.H. Weiler 'The Rule of Lawyers and the Ethos of Diplomats; Reflections on the Internal and External Legitimacy of WTO Dispute Settlement', (2001) 35 *Journal of World Trade* 191, 194.

[192] E.g., R. Hudec, *Enforcing International Trade Law: The Evolution of the Modern GATT Legal System* (1993) chapter 7-10.

[193] J.H. Jackson, 'The Legal Meaning of a GATT Dispute Settlement Report: Some Reflections', in N. Blokker and S. Muller (eds.), *Towards More Effective Supervision by International Organisations* 149, 150 ff.

[194] DSU Art. 3(1). Further, the reformed GATT 1994 (General Agreement on Tariffs and Trade 1994 (15 April 1994), WTO Agreement Annex 1A, 1867 *UNTS* 187, (1994) 33 *ILM* 1153) still forms part of the WTO system.

formation of an investigating panel from being formed, or block the adoption of its report. Until the 1980s there were remarkably few instances of blockage, but this changed with the start of the negotiations of the Uruguay Round, when a number of problems crystallized. There was a growing tendency towards forum-shopping, made possible by the multiplicity of the GATT settlement systems. Delays were experienced in various stages of the procedure. The European Community and the United States began using the adoption of panel reports as a bargaining tool. Lastly, the United States increasingly adopted unilateral sanctions, arguing that the GATT system did not provide adequate protection. Market parties asked for more legal certainty in international trade. Several States demanded binding legal settlement.[195] There was however also a significant group of States that preferred to keep a diplomatic element in the process.

Eventually, the compromise embedded in the current WTO settlement system retains large parts of the GATT process. It provides a more judicialised and institutionalised settlement procedure, while also retaining some elements of diplomatic settlement. The main organ of the WTO is the Ministerial Council, which convenes at least once every two years.[196] The WTO Council, in which all members are represented, conducts the affairs of the organisation at all other times. It is this organ that under the name of the Dispute Settlement Body (DSB) administers the dispute settlement mechanism,[197] as set out in the Understanding on Rules and Procedures Governing the Settlement of Disputes (DSU).[198] The DSB is the ultimate guardian of all disputes concerning WTO law, making the WTO system exclusive of other dispute settlement systems,[199] though not of other rules of public international law.[200]

As under GATT, States with complaints concerning another's practices under the covered agreements should first enter into bilateral consultations.[201]

---

195 C. Baudenbacher, 'Judicialization: Can the European Model Be Exported to Other Parts of the World?', (2004) 39 *Texas International Law Journal* 381, 394; N. Saiki, 'WTO Rules and Procedures for the Settlement of Disputes – Their Formation: A Practitioner's View', in M.K. Young and Y. Iwasawa (eds.), *Trilateral Perspectives on International Legal Issues* (1996) 403, 410; P. Pescatore, W.J. Davey and A.F. Lowenfeld, *Handbook of GATT/WTO Dispute Settlement* (1991) 75.

196 WTO Agreement Art. 4(1).

197 WTO Agreement Art. 4(3).

198 Understanding on Rules and Procedures Governing the Settlement of Disputes, WTO Agreement Annex 2, 1869 *UNTS* 401, (1994) 33 *ILM* 1226.

199 DSU Art. 23. The WTO system itself does however make occasional exceptions for disputes under related trade agreements: E.-U. Petersmann, *The GATT/WTO Dispute Settlement System: International Law, International Organizations and Dispute Settlement* (1997) 180.

200 J. Pauwelyn, *Conflict of Norms in Public International Law: How WTO Law Relates to other Rules of International Law* (2003); D. Palmeter and P.C. Mavroidis, 'The WTO Legal System: Sources of Law' (1998), 92 *AJIL* 398.

201 DSU Art. 4(2).

These consultations should be notified to the DSB, though their initial aim is to reach a mutually satisfactory solution without its involvement.[202] It is reported, however, that bilateral consultations are not always reported to the organisation until after a settlement has been reached.[203] If no settlement is reached, the complaining State may request the DSB to establish a panel.[204] The DSB establishes *ad hoc* panels, adopts their recommendations and guards over the implementation of the outcome of the procedures, much as was the situation under GATT. Similarly, it decides by consensus.[205] A major innovation in the transition from GATT to WTO is however that in the DSB's administration of the panels, the rule of consensus is reversed: proposals are accepted, unless a contrary consensus exists.[206] For panel reports this means that except in the unlikely case that not even the winning party supports the recommendations made by the panel, the latter's proposals are always adopted.

The membership of the panels is similar to that under GATT, though it is now specified that nominations to a panel are made by the DSB, which should not be opposed, except for compelling reasons.[207] Unless the parties[208] or the DSB[209] decide otherwise, the terms of reference for the panel are to examine the matter in the light of the relevant provisions and to make such findings as will assist the DSB in making the recommendations or in giving the rulings provided for in that/those agreement(s).[210] These terms are elucidated by Article 11 DSU:

> 'The function of panels is to assist the DSB in discharging its responsibilities under this Understanding and the covered agreements. Accordingly, a panel should make an objective assessment of the matter before it, including an objective assessment of the facts of the case and the applicability of and conformity with the relevant covered agreements. Panels should consult regularly with the parties to the disputes and give them adequate opportunity to develop a mutually satisfactory solution.'

---

[202] DSU Art. 4(4) and (5). Third States may however be included in the consultations if the party whose practises are the subject of the consultations agrees that the third State has a substantial trade interest under agreements enumerated in the DSU (Art. 4(11) and footnote 4).

[203] M.L. Busch and E. Reinhardt, 'Bargaining in the Shadow of the Law: Early Settlement in GATT/WTO Disputes', (2001) 24 *Fordham International Law Journal* 158, 171.

[204] DSU Art. 4(7).

[205] DSU Art. 2(4) and footnote 1.

[206] M.E. Footer, 'The Role of Consensus in GATT/WTO Decision Making', *17 Northwestern Journal of International Law and Business* (1996/1997) 653; A.F. Lowenfeld, 'Remedies along with Rights: Institutional Reform in the New GATT', (1994) 88 *AJIL* 477, 483.

[207] DSU Art. 8(6)

[208] DSU Art. 6(2) and 7(1).

[209] DSU Art. 7(3).

[210] DSU Art. 7(1).

With the last sentence, the panel is given a passive role in the search for a settlement: any effort to negotiate a compromise remains the responsibility of the parties, while the panel will only 'give them adequate opportunity'. Nonetheless, whereas the panel's proceedings can lead to a binding decision, the preferable solution is reaching an agreement between the disputing parties before the conclusion of the panel proceedings. As in the GATT period, the panel issues its report in stages, allowing for the parties to comment on it, and possibly to use it in their negotiations. The panel bases itself exclusively on the law.[211]

The DSB will adopt the panel report unless either 1) consensus is reached that it should not be, or 2) if one of the parties brings the case before the newly created Appellate Body,[212] 'the most drastic innovation in GATT dispute settlement'.[213] Appeal is limited to issues of law covered in the panel report, and to legal interpretations developed by the panel.[214] The composition of the Appellate Body also has a more legal character: there is an emphasis on legal qualifications, and no government-related persons may be members.[215]

More than the GATT system, the WTO Agreement offers various ways for other parties pursuing the same issue to become involved, either as a party in the proceedings, or as an interested outsider. About one third of cases at the WTO involve multiple complainants. On the basis of the explicit requirement that the interests of third parties are taken into account, interventions have taken place in more than 80% of cases.[216] The Appellate Body has also decided to admit *amicus curiae* briefs from NGOs.[217] Further, to secure a certain degree of supervision over the content of a compromise, the amicable settlement of an issue formally raised under the consultation and dispute settlement procedures has to be notified to the DSB. Any member can then raise a point relating thereto.[218]

The clear judicialisation of dispute settlement in the WTO has not completely removed elements of conciliation. Article 5(3) DSU provides the possi-

---

211 J. Pauwelyn, *Conflict of Norms in Public International Law: How WTO Law Relates to other Rules of International Law* (2003) 459.

212 DSU Art. 16(4).

213 A.F. Lowenfeld, 'Remedies along with Rights: Institutional Reform in the New GATT', (1994) 88 *AJIL* 477, 483.

214 DSU Art. 17(6).

215 DSU Art. 17(3).

216 DSU Art. 9 resp Art. 10. E.-U. Petersmann, 'Alternative Dispute Resolution: What Lessons for the WTO?', in R. Briner and others, *Law of International Business and Dispute Settlement in the 21st Century* (2001) 615, 620.

217 *Shrimp-Turtle* Case, Appellate Body 12 October 1998, WTO Doc. WT/DS58/AB/R [99-110].

218 DSU Art. 3(6).

bility of requesting conciliation, mediation or good offices at any time by any party to the dispute. If the other party agrees, any of these methods can be applied at any time. Also, the Director-General of the WTO may himself *ex officio* offer such services.[219] Unlike the common understanding in public international law, the use of the terms good offices, conciliation and mediation here are not meant to refer to three separate dispute settlement methods. In the WTO[220] as previously in GATT[221] they are conflated into a general informal method of dispute settlement resembling mediation.

The percentage of amicable settlements in the WTO system is not much different from that under GATT before the breakdown in the 1980s, discussed above, though the number of cases has increased.[222] The system is generally considered to be a relative success,[223] even though there remain problems with compliance,[224] and there are various suggestions for improvement.[225] While the practice of dispute settlement generally did not radically change, the formal structure did. Some political elements dating from GATT times were also included in the WTO DSU. Unless the parties[226] or the DSB[227] decide otherwise, the panel has to examine the matter 'in the light of the relevant provisions' of the agreement 'and to make such findings as will assist the DSB in making the recommendations or in giving the rulings provided for.'[228] The phrase 'in the light of the relevant provisions' indicates that the settlement should be in *accordance* with the parties' rights and obligations, though other considerations

---

219 DSU Art. 5(6).

220 N. Komuro, 'The WTO Dispute Settlement Mechanism – Coverage and Procedures of the WTO Understanding', (1995) 29 *Journal of World Trade* (4) 5, 47.

221 E. Canal-Forgues and R. Ostrihansky, 'New Developments in the GATT Dispute Settlement Procedures', (1990) 24 *Journal of World Trade* (2) 67, 70-71.

222 W.J. Davey, 'The WTO Dispute Settlement System: The First Ten Years', (2005) 8 *Journal of International Economic Law* 17, 48; M.L. Busch and E. Reinhardt, 'Bargaining in the Shadow of the Law: Early Settlement in GATT/WTO Disputes', (2001) 24 *Fordham International Law Journal* 158.

223 E.g., V. Hughes, 'Accomplishments of the WTO Dispute Settlement Mechanism', in Y. Taniguchi, A. Yanovich and J. Bohanes (eds.), *The WTO in the Twenty-First Century* (2007) 185; the WTO-commissioned 'Sutherland Report': WTO Consultative Board *The Future of the WTO: Addressing Institutional Challenges in the New Millennium* (2005) 50 <http://www.wto.org/english/thewto_e/10anniv_e/future_wto_e.htm> (5 October 2007).

224 G.N. Horlick, 'Problems with the Compliance Structure of the WTO Dispute Resolution Process', in D.L.M. Kennedy and J.D. Southwick (eds.), *The Political Economy of International Trade Law* (2002) 636; Sutherland Report 53.

225 E.g., the various contributions Part II of: Y. Taniguchi, A. Yanovich and J. Bohanes (eds.), *The WTO in the Twenty-First Century* (2007).

226 DSU Art. 6(2) and 7(1).

227 DSU Art. 7(3).

228 DSU Art. 7(1).

can be taken into account.[229] Nevertheless, legal and binding settlement practice became the standard.[230] The panel's reports have become more legalised.[231] Panellists look more towards the possible review by the inherently more legally oriented Appellate Body, than to the scrutiny of the essentially political DSB. The latter gives little opportunity for overturning a panel's findings. The judicial nature of the WTO Dispute Settlement System has even led to concerns by some that supremacy of the judicial mechanism may undermine the political institutions and requirements of the WTO and its membership.[232]

4.6 Conclusions

Compared with dispute settlement mechanisms of many other area-specific treaties, the GATT/WTO system is exceptional. Throughout its long evolution, many disputes have in fact been addressed by it.[233] While it has not clearly laid down a conciliation procedure, it has developed various practices that include elements of it. A swift evolution took place in GATT, from negotiation and State-guided mediation to legal conciliation with elements of adjudication. The procedure was also remarkable because of the involvement of all Contracting Parties with any given dispute. Panellists based themselves on the law. Reports were seen as sources of law. The process was essentially conserved in the WTO, though the system became even more adjudicatory, especially through the creation of legal review in the Appellate Body, and through the near automatic adoption of the reports. In this, the GATT/WTO development is reminiscent of the European Convention on Human Rights, where an already strict variation on legal conciliation by the Commission was also replaced by more predominant judicial settlement.

The GATT/WTO developments were essentially driven by the desires of the parties to ensure respect for the agreed norms, and to that end to create an

---

229 DSU Art. 3(4) and (5).

230 A.F. Lowenfeld, 'Remedies along with Rights: Institutional Reform in the New GATT', (1994) 88 *AJIL* 477, 479; Y. Iwasawa, 'Settlement of Disputes concerning the WTO Agreement: Various Means other than Panel Procedures', M.K. Young and Y. Iwasawa (eds.), *Trilateral Perspectives on International Legal Issues* (1996) 377, 378.

231 Cf., J.H. Jackson, *The World Trade Organisation: Constitution and Jurisprudence* (1998) 98; see also E.-U. Petersmann, 'WTO Dispute Settlement Practice 1995-2005: Lessons from the Past and Future Challenges', in Y. Taniguchi, A. Yanovich and J. Bohanes, *The WTO* in the Twenty-first Century (2007) 38, 67 ff.

232 L. Bartels, 'The Separation of Powers in the WTO: How to Avoid Judicial Activism', (2004) 53 *ICLQ* 861.

233 E.-U. Petersmann (ed.), *International Trade Law and the GATT/WTO Dispute Settlement System* (1997) 74.

efficient system of legal assessment.[234] It appears, however, that in contemporary discussions on the perceived deficiencies of the WTO dispute settlement model, critics do not sufficiently account for the fact that the system evolved from a model of diplomatic dispute settlement, and that various States explicitly desired the retention of elements of diplomatic settlement also in the judicialised institutions of the panel, the Appellate Body and the DSB. One cannot criticise the WTO system for not working in a sufficiently adjudicatory manner, if the design of the system is not updated to be more adjudicatory.

It is remarkable, however, that in a joint statement by three former GATT/WTO Directors-General in 2001, States were urged not to use the WTO settlement system too eagerly, and to try first to settle the dispute through consultations or bilateral negotiations.[235] Since then a decline in cases is noted.[236] It is here suggested that excess pressure on the system could be relieved if more attention was given to the employment of diplomatic third party dispute settlement methods. Such a suggestion was not included in the long-term review recommendations by the Sutherland Report of 2005.[237] The Sutherland Report made modest proposals, largely to increase transparency and awareness, while only in passing addressing the amicable settlement options, but not proposing systemic amendments on that point.[238] It appears from the Sutherland Report and the reactions thereto, however, that the organisation is not willing to take that step, at least not yet. As long as that is the case, the WTO will possess a *sui generis* dispute settlement system, of which the political elements limit its functioning as outright adjudication. For the moment, nonetheless, the WTO has developed a workable quasi-judicial method to maintain the norms in the international trade regime. The DSU remains under revision.[239]

---

[234] N. Saiki, 'WTO Rules and Procedures for the Settlement of Disputes – Their Formation: A Practitioner's View', in M.K. Young and Y. Iwasawa (eds.), *Trilateral Perspectives on International Legal Issues* (1996) 403; P. Pescatore, W.J. Davey and A.F. Lowenfeld, *Handbook of GATT/WTO Dispute Settlement* (1991) 75; A.F. Lowenfeld, 'Remedies along with Rights: Institutional Reform in the New GATT', (1994) 88 *AJIL* 477.

[235] Joint Statement on the Multilateral Trading System, 1 February 2001, available on: <http://www.wto.org/english/news_e/news01_e/jointstatdavos_jan01_e.htm> (5 October 2007).

[236] K. Leitner and S. Lester, 'WTO Dispute Settlement 1995-2004: A Statistical Analysis', (2005) 8 *Journal of International Economic Law* 231.

[237] Consultative Board *The Future of the WTO: Addressing Institutional Challenges in the New Millennium* (2005) <http://www.wto.org/english/thewto_e/10anniv_e/future_wto_e.htm> (5 October 2007). Further: M.L. Movsesian, 'The Sutherland Report and Dispute Settlement', (2005) 2 *IOLR* 201 and other articles in that volume.

[238] Though W.J. Davey, 'The Sutherland Report on Dispute Settlement: A Comment', (2005) 8 *Journal of International Economic Law* 321, 325 points out the possibility that the suggestion that certain panel reports are subjected to an 'in-depth analysis by a reasonably impartial special expert group of the DSB' (Sutherland Report, 56 [251]) could create a new political check on judicial dispute settlement. Such check would however be prospective.

[239] In the Doha Declaration, Ministers abandoned the earlier deadline, and stated that revision of the system would not be part of a package deal. WT/MIN(1)/DEC 1, 20 November 2001

5. The World Bank Inspection Panel

Another alternative settlement method was developed in the World Bank. While it is evidently more remote from conciliation than the practices of NCPs, the ECHR and GATT, it is touched upon here because it suggests novel solutions to shared complications. The World Bank, the common name for the International Bank for Reconstruction and Development (IBRD) and the International Development Association (IDA),[240] is a multilateral development agency, providing billions of US dollars in loans to developing countries. It finances major projects in such countries, and thereby directly affects the lives of local populations. Until the early 1990s, there was no formal mechanism for the affected populations to address any complaints to the World Bank. Following sustained criticism regarding the effects of some of the investment projects, in 1993 the World Bank decided to set-up an Inspection Panel.[241] Other international financial institutions later followed this example by setting-up loosely similar compliance review bodies.[242]

5.1 The Inspection Panel's role

The Inspection Panel was to be an independent forum, through which people directly affected by the Bank's projects could request the Bank 'to act in accordance with its own policies and procedures',[243] such as on the appraisal and implementation of projects, and on the transparency and accountability of the Bank's operatives.[244] The members of the Panel are appointed by the World

---

<http://www.wto.org/english/thewto_e/minist_e/min01_e/mindecl_e.htm#dispute> (5 October 2007).

240 The larger World Bank Group also comprises the International Finance Corporation (IFC), the Multilateral Investment Guarantee Agency (MIGA) and the International Centre for Settlement of Investment Disputes (ICSID).

241 G. Alfredsson and R. Ring (eds.), *The Inspection Panel of the World Bank* (2001). I.F.I. Shihata, *The World Bank Inspection Panel in Practice* (2nd edn. 2000).

242 For example, in 2003 the European Bank for Reconstruction and Development (EBRD) set-up the Independent Recourse Mechanism, of which it approved the rules of procedure in 2004: <http://www.ebrd.com/about/integrity/irm/about/procedur.pdf> (5 October 2007); EBRD *Independent Recourse Mechanism: Guide to Making a Complaint about an EBRD-financed Project* (2004). In 2003 the Asian Development Bank (ADB) set-up the ADB Accountability Mechanism including a Compliance Review Panel, to replace the earlier 'Inspection Function': <http://compliance.adb.org/> (5 October 2007); in 1994 the Inter-American Development Bank (IADB) set-up an Independent Investigation Mechanism: <http://www.iadb.org/cont/poli/mecanism.pdf> (5 October 2007).

243 The Operating Procedures of the Inspection Panel, (1995) 34 *ILM* 503, 510.

244 I.F.I. Shihata, 'The World Bank Inspection Panel – Its Historical, Legal and Operational Aspects', in G. Alfredsson and R. Ring (eds.), *The Inspection Panel of the World Bank* (2001) 7, 16-17.

Bank itself, but they are not eligible to work for the Bank ever again. This should support the members' independence. There is no requirement that they are experts in the World Bank's policies and procedures.

The norms applied by the Panel to the workings of the Bank are the internal norms of the Bank itself, and not directly norms governing the relations between the bank and the directly affected people.[245] Nevertheless, a number of these internal norms embody norms of general international law applicable between the Bank and the borrowing State, and may also internalise international law applicable between the Bank and the affected persons. The World Bank also sets out to apply international law in its policies and operations.[246] It nevertheless goes too far to suggest, as some appear to do,[247] that the Inspection Panel is a quasi-judicial body charged with applying the World Bank's policies and procedures as rules of international law. The Operating Procedures limit the scope of the investigation by referring only to the policies and procedures of the World Bank itself.[248] Moreover, many public international rules governing a situation are not directly applicable to relations between the Bank and individuals. Nevertheless, in making its assessment, the Panel can also draw on general international law to substantiate its findings, and certain policies demand, *inter alia*, that a project is undertaken in conformity with domestic and international law.

The function of the Inspection Panel is reflected in part in the requirements set for its reports, which should include:

> '(a) a summary discussion of the relevant facts and of steps taken to conduct the investigation; (b) a conclusion showing the Panel's findings on whether the Bank has complied with relevant Bank policies and procedures; (c) a list of supporting documents which will be available on request from the Office of The Inspection Panel; and (d) statements of the majority and minority views in the absence of a consensus by the Panel.'[249]

This means that the Panel is engaged in a fact-finding mission, though it also contrasts these facts with the rules and policies the World Bank sets for itself, and on that basis comes to a (non-binding) assessment of the Bank's compli-

[245] A. Orakhelashvili, 'The World Bank Inspection Panel in Context', (2005) 1 *IOLR* 57, 58.

[246] A. Gowlland Gualtieri, 'The Environmental Accountability of the World Bank to Non-State Actors: Insights from the Inspection Panel', (2001) 72 *BYIL* 213, 221, 245.

[247] A. Orakhelashvili, 'The World Bank Inspection Panel in Context', (2005) 1 *IOLR* 57 *passim*; C. Chinkin, 'Normative Development in the International Legal System', in D. Shelton (ed.), *Commitment and Compliance: The Role of Non-Binding Norms in the International Legal System* (2000) 21, 33.

[248] Operating Procedures Art. 1, 52.

[249] Operating Procedures Art. 52.

ance. The judicial element in the procedure is marked by the provision allowing for dissenting opinions. The Inspection Panel is not authorised to make recommendations, as is a defining element of conciliation commissions.[250] Its primary function is not facilitating settlement, but is inspection, supervising the actions of the World Bank, with the intended additional effect of future deviation from rules and policies. It should already be clear from its name that the Inspection Panel is not a judicial body or a special kind of conciliation commission: it is an instrument of enforcement, semi-detached but emanating from and still linked to the World Bank itself.

Complaints regarding the World Bank's internal compliance may come from locally organised groups. Only in exceptional occasions can non-local NGO's represent the aggrieved.[251] Third parties may however submit *amicus curiae* briefs if they can demonstrate an interest in the proceedings.[252] The Panel reviews whether a complaint falls within the scope of its mandate, and may recommend to the Board of Executive Directors that it consents to an investigation. If an investigation is so authorised by the Board, the Panel may approach all World Bank staff, hear the aggrieved and obtain any external information. There is no express provision allowing the involvement of those making the complaints in the actual proceedings, though the Panel does in fact allow for their submissions. This again indicates that the panel is unlike a judicial or conciliation body. The Panel subsequently issues a report, on the basis of which the Management of the Bank should report and make recommendations to the Board, which will then decide on any action. At the end of the process, the reports and the recommendations are made public.

5.2 The Inspection Panel's practice

Most of the cases in which an investigation was conducted concerned large infrastructure projects related to irrigation, natural energy resources and electric power.[253] Most complaints alleged non-compliance by the Bank with its

---

[250] See chapter I 3.1.

[251] When there is no adequate or appropriate representation in the country concerned: Art. 4(c) and 11 Operating Procedures. E.g., the International Campaign for Tibet in the *Western Poverty Reduction Project* (China), Request RQ99/3, WBIP Report 28 April 2000. Further: I.F.I. Shihata, *The World Bank Inspection Panel in Practice* (2nd edn. 2000) 64-66, 73.

[252] Operating Procedures Preamble and Art. 50.

[253] E.g., *Reform Project for the Water and Telecommunications Sectors* (Paraguay) and *SEGBA V Power Distribution Project* (Argentina) Request 02/26, WBIP Report 23 August 2002, WBIP Annual Report 2004/2005, 41; *Bujugali Hydropower Project and others* (Uganda) WBIP Report 23 May 2002, WBIP Annual Report 2001/2002, 18; *Petroleum Development and Pipeline Project* (Chad) Request 01/22, WBIP Report 12 September 2001, WBIP Annual Report 2001/2002, 27.

environmental and social policies, such as the Environmental Assessment Policy, the Indigenous Peoples Policy and the Involuntary Resettlement Policy.[254]

The investigation by the Panel concerns the activities of the Bank, not those of the borrowing State.[255] The Inspection Panel may review whether the Bank attached the requisite conditions to the investment, whether the borrowing country was properly informed of the requirements, and whether the project was properly supervised by the Bank operatives. The Panel cannot, however, directly address any failures by the borrowing countries themselves: such criticism should be construed as criticism of the Bank operatives who would have failed to demand the compliance by the borrowing countries with its obligations.

Despite the limitations to the bases on which the Inspection Panel may review the work of the World Bank, its work and impact has generally been regarded favourably.[256] According to both activists and academics, from the moment of creation of the Inspection Panel, the Bank has shown increasing accountability and quality control. Nevertheless, as is evident from several instances of the Inspection Panel's investigations, there is at least occasionally substantial room for improvement in the performance of the Bank.[257] As a result of complaints lodged with the Inspection Panel some projects were cancelled,[258] but this has not necessarily stopped the borrowing countries from pursuing the projects with their own means.[259]

---

[254] L. Boisson de Chazournes, 'Compliance with Operational Standards: The Contribution of the Word Bank Inspection Panel', in G. Alfredsson and R. Ring (eds.), *The Inspection Panel of the World Bank* (2001) 67, 73 ff; I.F.I. Shihata, 'The World Bank Inspection Panel – Its Historical, Legal and Operational Aspects', in ibid., 7, 22 ff; B. Kingsbury, 'Operational Policies of International Institutions as Part of the Law-Making Process: The World Bank and Indigenous Peoples', in G. Goodwin-Gill and S. Talmon (eds.), *The Reality of International Law; Essays in Honour of Ian Brownlie* (1999) 323.

[255] World Bank, 'Conclusions of the Second Review of the World Bank Inspection Panel (20 April 1999), (2000) 39 *ILM* 249 [12].

[256] E.g., I.F.I. Shihata, *The World Bank Inspection Panel in Practice* (2nd edn. 2000) 260; S. Slemmer-Schulte, 'Introductory Note to the Conclusions of the Second Review of the World Bank Inspection Panel', (2000) 39 *ILM* 243, 246, but critically: E. Nurmukhametova, 'Problems in Connection with the Efficiency of the World Bank Inspection Panel', (2006) 10 *Max Planck Yearbook of United Nations Law* 397.

[257] E.g., *Coal Sector Environmental and Social Mitigation Project* (India) Request 01/23, WBIP Report 25 November 2002, WBIP Annual Report 2004/2005, 47; *Reform Project for the Water and Telecommunications Sectors* (Paraguay) and *SEGBA V Power Distribution Project* (Argentina) Request 02/26, WBIP Report 23 August 2002, WBIP Annual Report 2004/2005, 41.

[258] E.g., *Arun III Hydroelectric Project* (Nepal), Request 94/1, WBIP Report 25 October 1994; *Western Poverty Reduction Project* (China), Request RQ99/3, WBIP Report 28 April 2000.

[259] D. Hunter, 'Using the World Bank Inspection Panel to Defend the Interests of Project-Affected People', (2003) 4 *Chicago Journal of International Law* 201.

The Inspection Panel is primarily an instrument for the internal review of the Bank's functioning: it does not prescribe or prohibit, nor does it mediate or conciliate between the aggrieved and the Bank. The Inspection Panel does not pronounce on liability, and does not have the function of awarding or recommending financial or other satisfaction to those affected by the Bank's actions.[260] Still, the Inspection Panel is a notable example of increased accountability of international organisations. In addition, by means of this institutional scrutiny of the Bank's work, the Bank has also obtained an additional tool in its relations with borrowing countries. Bank officials can, by pointing at their own responsibilities and at the Inspection Panel oversight function, better explain to the borrowing countries why scrutiny of project implementation is important.

Indirectly, then, the existence of an Inspection Panel focussing only on the Bank itself can also improve the compliance with applicable norms by others. It challenges the implicit assumption in dispute settlement that a third party is required to guard over application of norms, and that in order to have a third party, there should first be a second party with which the first party can officially be in dispute.

Sometimes, as with the World Bank, the power difference between the first party and the potential second party, here the complaining groups of affected individuals, is so large that the larger party may avoid any third party dispute mechanism to address grievances.[261] International tribunals are considered out of the question, as these would disproportionally restrict the powerful party's freedom of action. Even non-binding settlement such as conciliation and mediation is considered inappropriate, for the same reason, but also because this would give too much of a comparable standing to incomparable entities, i.e., individuals *vis-à-vis* the World Bank.

The creation of the Inspection Panel is in this view a noteworthy alternative.[262] From the concept of consultation, it takes the notion that any exercise of sovereign power affecting outside parties can be improved by informing oneself of external considerations. Like area-specific conciliation, it focuses on conformity in accordance with applicable norms. As in conciliation, the outcome of an Inspection Panel review does not have a binding character on the Bank, in that the Bank is not obliged to abide by any findings of the Panel.

---

260 Applicants sometimes appear to have a different understanding, as for instance in the *Lesotho Highlands Water Project,* upon application of Swissbourgh Diamond Mines (Pty) Ltd and others (Request 99/15, WBIP Annual Report 1998-1999 20-23; WBIP Report 23 July 1999.

261 On the circumstances surrounding the development of the Inspection Panel: I.F.I. Shihata, *The World Bank Inspection Panel in Practice* (2nd edn. 2000) ch 1.

262 From the outside perspective of accountability in international law; from the perspective of the then management of the World Bank, the Inspection Panel was created at least as much for reasons of improving the Bank's efficiency. I.F.I. Shihata, *The World Bank Inspection Panel in Practice* (2nd edn. 2000) 2.

Unlike conciliation, however, the Panel's findings are not even necessarily submitted to the outside party. The complaining groups are not called to negotiate with the World Bank on the recommendations of the Panel. In fact, it is solely up to the Bank to decide what to do with the findings. Like NCPs, however, the Inspection Panel system allows for censure through a mobilisation of shame. It does not offer potential sanctions, as the Inspection Panel holds no power over the Bank. The Inspection Panel system shows how some elements of conciliation and of other dispute settlement systems can be used in asymmetrical relations to give a voice to small parties, and to promote compliance with specific norms also by large, powerful actors who refuse to agree to binding legal settlement.

6. Non-compliance Procedures

The period after WWII saw an exponential growth of international agreements codifying or creating international norms and arrangements, without, however, an equivalent rise in the use of dispute settlement mechanisms. Against this background, numerous agreements including non-binding norms developed.[263] In addition, States were frequently willing to create ambitious rules, without agreeing on adjudication as a means of enforcement.[264] An alternative form of dispute settlement, the NCP, developed as a result. This development coincided with a debate about the standing of the norms at issue. Norms classified as 'soft law' were thought to be of a different character, requiring a new kind of dispute settlement mechanism. Therefore, it is important to first address the notion of soft law.

6.1 Law, non-law and soft law

The status of non-binding norms and of norms in agreements lacking an enforcement mechanism producing binding results are frequently seen as soft law,[265] which is not fully binding but can nevertheless produce certain legal

[263] D. Shelton, 'Law, Non-law and the Problem of "Soft Law"', in D. Shelton (ed.), *Commitment and Compliance: The Role of Non-Binding Norms in the International Legal System* (2000) 1; J. Charney, 'Compliance with International Soft Law', ibid., 114, 116; E. Brown Weiss (ed.), *International Compliance with Nonbinding Accords* (1997).

[264] X. Wang and G. Wiser, 'The Implementation and Compliance Regimes under the Climate Change Convention and its Kyoto Protocol', (2002) 11 *Review of European Community and International Environmental Law* 181, 196; cf., D. Bodansky, J.R. Cook and E. Brown Weiss, 'Invoking State Responsibility in the Twenty-First Century', (2002) 96 *AJIL* 798.

[265] 'those international norms, principles and procedures that, by being outside the system of formal sources of the ICJ Statute Art. 38(1) or by lacking the requisite normative content to create

effects.[266] These norms would therefore be in an intermediate position between legal rules and non-binding statements. On that assumption, it is argued that these norms are not fit for binding legal dispute settlement such as through adjudication. After all, they are not the legal tools with which a judge can exercise his judicial function. Moreover, it is argued that States deliberately fashioned these rules as non-legal or semi-legal in order to avoid being held legally accountable for any breach. This would also explain the emergence, in particular in the field of the environment, of non-compliance procedures. These procedures are often presented as an alternative, to co-exist in the same agreement with the traditional dispute settlement methods of mediation, conciliation and adjudication. In practice, however, in these agreements NCPs are the only option for compliance review and dispute settlement that is actually applied.

The concept of soft law is however problematic. In the way it is often presented it conflates agreements containing imprecise norms, and those containing nominally non-binding norms, with agreements that lack a strong enforcement mechanism.[267] This creates a semblance of law for norms that were not designed as such.[268] However, it accords better with diplomatic practice and with the apparent intentions of drafters and judges to distinguish between norms that are intended to be legally binding, and others that are only aspirations, which create political or moral, but not legal obligations ('pledges' as Raustiala calls them).[269] In this light, indeterminate or imprecise norms are not necessarily non-binding; they may convey substantial discretion to the addressee, or there may be legitimate debate about their precise content. Distinguishing conceptually between binding and non-binding norms explains why in treaty negotiations parties often attach great importance to the legal or non-legal nature of the incorporated norms.[270] It must be added that non-binding, aspirational norms may still contribute to the development of legal norms, as

---

enforceable rights and obligations, are nevertheless capable of producing certain legal effects'. F. Francioni, 'International "Soft Law" a Contemporary Assessment', in V. Lowe and M. Fitzmaurice (eds.), *Fifty Years of the International Court of Justice* (1996) 167, 168.

266 K. Raustiala, 'Form and Substance in International Agreements', (2005) 99 *AJIL* 581, 586-587.

267 E.g., A.T. Guzman, 'The Design of International Agreements', (2005) 16 *EJIL* 579, 580 n 5; K. Zemanek, 'Is the Term "Soft Law" Convenient?', in G. Hafner and others (eds.), *Liber Amicorum Professor Ignaz Seidl-Hohenveldern* (1998) 843.

268 E.g., A. Orakhelashvili, 'The World Bank Inspection Panel in Context', (2005) 1 *IOLR* 57, 70-73.

269 A.T. Guzman, 'The Design of International Agreements', (2005) 16 *EJIL* 579, 580 n 5. Cf., K. Raustiala, 'Form and Substance in International Agreements', (2005) 99 *AJIL* 581, 587.

270 Cf., K.W. Abbott and others, 'The Concept of Legalization', (2000) 54 *International Organization* 401, 409; J. McCall Smith, 'The Politics of Dispute Settlement Design: Explaining Legalism in Regional Trade Pacts', (2000) 54 *International Organization* 137.

they can contribute to a change in practice and provide a basis for nascent *opinio juris*. Statements of moral obligations do not, however, in themselves create legal obligations.

Another distinction should be made between non-binding norms and the non-existence in an agreement of a binding dispute settlement mechanism. Whether a dispute settlement system is provided for or not, if rules are intended as legally binding, they remain susceptible to be applied in some international adjudicatory setting, for instance if the two States at variance over the concerned rules have both accepted the Optional Clause of the ICJ Statute.[271] Further, by agreeing to fashion certain norms as legal norms, the drafters agreed that these norms should have a 'compliance pull'[272] that is stronger than that of aspirational norms. Formally, then, if the rules are intended to be legally binding norms, there is no difference whether they are protected by a dispute settlement mechanism or not; its absence does not make such norms 'soft'.

It must be conceded to soft lawyers that if a purportedly legally binding norm is structurally violated without any response, the value of the norm is diminished.[273] The ultimate consequence is however that the norm becomes an aspiration, and loses its legal status. It is a different matter, however, if the States to which legally binding norms and/or aspirational norms apply, prefer to use other means for promoting compliance with these rules, or if they collectively prefer no compliance mechanism at all. It is then likely that the costs to them of using the available settlement mechanisms do not outweigh the benefits to be obtained by addressing a transgressor's violations.[274]

Already at the drafting stage, cautious States may recognise shared concerns, and accept norms as legally binding, but prefer not to face scrutiny in the form of compulsory enforcement and sanctions. In such situations, they are likely to prefer other methods of dispute settlement, or none at all. A more secure strategy to avoid forceful scrutiny would be to adopt the norms as aspirational rather than as legally binding. Faced with such different desires for the content and workings of a new set of norms, non-compliance procedures

---

[271] Art. 36(2) ICJ Statute.

[272] Cf., T.M. Franck, *Fairness in International Law and Institutions* (1995) 89.

[273] Cf., A.M. Weisburd, 'The Effect of Treaties and Other Formal International Acts on the Customary Law of Human Rights', (1995/1996) 25 *Georgia Journal of International and Comparative Law* 99, 100, 106.

[274] A.T. Guzman, 'The Design of International Agreements', (2005) 16 *EJIL* 579, 596; though Guzman appears to underestimate that not all international agreements consist of 'give and take' situations, but sometimes demand compliance of as many States as possible to further the drafter's goals, such as global environmental protection. The nature of the rules is significant; see E.-U. Petersmann, *The GATT/WTO Dispute Settlement System: International Law, International Organization and Dispute Settlement* (1997) 63.

appear to be one alternative meeting all parties somewhere along the way.[275] It is notable that the creation and application of various environmental regimes, including non-binding norms and including reliance on some form of non-compliance procedure, is considered to have been effective.[276] It is therefore worthwhile to assess how these regimes attempt to deal with disputes and alleged violations regarding their subject-matter, and the parallel operation of NCPs and area-specific conciliation. The concluding sections of this chapter will review whether NCPs may count as a new form of conciliation, or as an alternative to it.

6.2 The Montreal Protocol NCP

There are many multilateral environmental agreements that contain institutional arrangements tasked to guard agreed environmental norms.[277] Important examples include the 1973 Convention on International Trade in Endangered Species of Wild Fauna and Flora (CITES),[278] the 1989 Convention on the Control of Transboundary Movements of Hazardous Wastes and Their Disposal (Basel Convention)[279] and the 1992 United Nations Framework Convention on Climate Change (Climate Change Convention).[280] The main instrument of discussion and supervision of the norms created by these agreements is, for each agreement separately, a Meeting – or Conference of the Parties (MOP or COP).[281] This body meets at regular intervals to discuss the regime of the agreement and to decide on further measures.[282] The use of formal dispute settlement methods is uncommon. Implementation is pursued largely through

---

[275] On the objectives of NCPs see C. Redgwell, 'Non-Compliance Procedures and the Climate Change Convention', in B. Chambers (ed.), *Inter-Linkages: The Kyoto Protocol and the International Trade and Investment Regimes* (2001) 43, 44.

[276] E.L. Miles and others, *Environmental Regime Effectiveness: Confronting Theory With Evidence* (2002); O. Young (ed.), *The Effectiveness of International Environmental Regimes* (1999) contains various relevant case studies.

[277] U. Beyerlin, P.-T. Stoll and R. Wolfrum (eds.), *Ensuring Compliance with Multilateral Environmental Agreements: Academic Analysis and Views from Practice* (2006); A. Kiss and D. Shelton, *International Environmental Law* (3rd edn. 2004) 301 ff; R.R. Churchill and G. Ulfstein, 'Autonomous Institutional Arrangements in Multilateral Environmental Agreements: A Little Noticed Phenomenon in International Law', (2000) 94 *AJIL* 623.

[278] (3 March 1973) 993 *UNTS* 243.

[279] (22 March 1989) 28 *ILM* 657.

[280] (9 May 1992) 31 *ILM* 849.

[281] Also in non-environmental agreements, e.g., Framework Convention on Tobacco Control (21 May 2003), (2003) 42 *ILM* 520, Arts. 23 and 24.

[282] M. Fitzmaurice, 'Consent to Be Bound – Anything New under the Sun?', (2005) 74 *Nordic Journal of International Law* 483.

reporting and discussion.[283] At the same time, these bodies can further develop the treaty regime, by the adoption of new rules and aspirations.

Several agreements go beyond a MOP or COP, and also include special procedures for non-compliance, forming part of a specialised mechanism for consideration and conciliation: a non-compliance procedure. The first, and so far the most advanced among these is the NCP adopted under the 1987 Montreal Protocol[284] to the 1985 Vienna Convention for the Protection of the Ozone Layer[285] (the Montreal NCP).[286] Other non-compliance procedures, modelled on the Montreal example, are provided for or are currently being developed in a large number of environmental treaties,[287] in addition to the widely known Kyoto Protocol to the 1992 Framework Convention on Climate Change.[288]

---

283 E.g., X .Wang and G. Wiser, 'The Implementation and Compliance Regimes under the Climate Change Convention and its Kyoto Protocol', (2002) 11 *Review of European Community and International Environmental Law* 181.

284 (19 September 1987) 1522 *UNTS* 293.

285 (22 March 1985) 1513 *UNTS* 324.

286 The Montreal NCP, pursuant to the Montreal Protocol Art. 8 is contained in a decision by the Fourth Meeting of the Parties UNEP/Ozl.Pro.4/15 on <http://unfccc.int/2860.php> (5 October 2007).

287 The 1994 Oslo Sulphur Protocol on Further Reduction of Sulphur Emissions (14 June 1994), (1994) 33 *ILM* 1542; the 1979 Convention on Long-Range Transboundary Air Pollution (13 November 1979), 1302 *UNTS* 217; the 1992 Convention for the Protection of the Marine Environment of the North-East Atlantic (OSPAR Convention) (22 September 1992), (1993) 32 *ILM* 1069; the 1998 Aarhus Convention on Access to Information, Public Participation in Decision-Making and Access to Justice in Environmental Matters (25 June 1998), (1999) 38 *ILM* 517 and Decision I/7 Report of the First Meeting of the Parties UN Doc ECE/MP.PP2/Add8 (2 April 2004); the 2000 Cartagena Protocol on Biosafety (29 January 2000), (2000) 39 *ILM* 1027 to the Convention on Biological Diversity (5 June 1992), (1992) 31 *ILM* 818. The Convention entered into force in 2003: the non-compliance procedure was adopted by the MOP of 23-27 February 2004: MOP BS-I/7 on <www.biodiv.org/convention> (5 October 2007); the Rotterdam Convention on the Prior Informed Consent Procedure for Certain Hazardous Chemicals and Pesticides in International Trade (1998) (11 September 1998, as amended 24 September 2004), (1999) 38 *ILM* 1; amended version: <http://www.pic.int/en/ConventionText/ONU-GB.pdf> (5 October 2007); Stockholm Convention on Persistent Organic Pollutants (22 May 2001), (2001) 40 *ILM* 532.

288 Kyoto Protocol to the Framework Convention on Climate Change (11 December 1998), (1999) 37 *ILM* 22, elaborated in the Marrakesh Accords (10 November 2001) FCCC/CP/2001/13/Add.3, K.R. Gray, 'Eleventh Meeting of the Conference of the Parties to the *United Nations Framework Convention on Climate Change*/First Meeting of the Parties to the *Kyoto Protocol*' (2006) 10 ASIL Insight 8 (electronic, 3 April 2006); C. Brown, 'The Settlement of Disputes Arising in Flexibility Mechanism Transactions under the Kyoto Protocol', (2005) 21 *Arbitration International* 361; X. Wang and G. Wiser, 'The Implementation and Compliance Regimes under the Climate Change Convention and its Kyoto Protocol', (2002) 11 *RECIEL* 181, 189. On the negotiating history of the Marrakesh Accords: D.A. Wirth, 'The Sixth Session (pt two) and Seventh Session of the Conference of the Parties to the Framework Convention on Climate Change', (2002) 96 *AJIL* 648. For a comparison with the Montreal Protocol mechanism: L. Thomas, 'A Comparative Analysis of International Regimes on Ozone and Climate Change with Implications for Regime Design', (2003) 41 *Columbia Journal of Transnational Law* 795.

The procedures these instruments set-up require closer attention to see how they function and how they include features of conciliation. The focus here is on the leading example of the Montreal Protocol.

The purpose of the Montreal Protocol is the elaboration and implementation of the provisions of the Vienna Convention for the Protection of the Ozone Layer.[289] All parties to the Montreal Protocol are obliged annually to report on their imports and exports of controlled substances. The Montreal NCP stipulates that it is without prejudice to the operation of the dispute settlement system of the Vienna Convention,[290] which provides for optional adjudication and compulsory conciliation.[291] While the latter dispute settlement procedure is only rudimentary, the non-compliance procedure is substantially developed. The crux of the procedure is the Implementation Committee, which is supported by a Secretariat.[292] Any party to the Montreal Protocol, as well as the Secretariat, may report a presumed case of non-compliance to the Implementation Committee. A party may also report its own non-compliance. The Implementation Committee considers the information submitted to it.[293] If there is found to be non-compliance, the Committee aims to reach an amicable solution with the concerned State.[294] The Committee eventually reports to the MOP, which retains the final word regarding any settlement.[295] The Implementation Committee has no power to bind, and can only recommend.

The Committee is composed of government representatives. The ten members of the Committee represent States, the only condition for their selection being an equitable geographical distribution.[296] The expertise of the represen-

---

289 UNEP *Handbook for the International Treaties for the Protection of the Ozone Layer* (6th edn. 2003) 35; M. Ehrmann, 'Procedures of Compliance Control in International Environmental Treaties', (2002) 13 *Colorado Journal of International Environmental Law and Policy* 377, 390 ff.

290 Preamble Montreal NCP.

291 Vienna Convention for the Protection of the Ozone Layer Art. 11.

292 Under the Marrakesh Accords the Kyoto Protocol has obtained a more complex structure involving a Compliance Committee which 'shall function through a plenary, a bureau and two branches, namely, the facilitative branch and the enforcement branch'. Marrakesh Accords Art. II(1). The facilitative branch can be likened to the Montreal Protocol's Implementation Committee whereas the enforcement branch may revoke privileges and reduce emission allocations.

293 P. Sands and R. MacKenzie, 'Guidelines for Negotiating and Drafting Dispute Settlement Clauses for International Environmental Agreements', in International Bureau of the Permanent Court of Arbitration (ed.), *International Investments and the Protection of the Environment* (2001) 305, 321-322.

294 Montreal NCP Art. 8.

295 This is different under the Marrakesh Accords under the Kyoto Protocol, where the Enforcement branch of the Compliance Committee can make decisions, from which the concerned party may appeal on limited grounds to the Conference of the Parties, which may override the original decision by qualified majority. Marrakesh Accords Art. XI.

296 Montreal NCP Art. 5.

tatives in the committee is a matter at the discretion of each elected State party. In practice, States tend to appoint diplomats with subject-matter expertise.[297] The political composition of the Committee does not imply that upholding the norms is not an essential concern. While the first goal of the committee is to reach an amicable solution, this should be 'on the basis of respect for the provisions of the protocol',[298] just as is the requirement of friendly settlements under the European Convention on Human Rights.[299] The Committee evidently has a responsibility to ensure that any amicable solution should not entrench or condone a violation of the relevant rules. Any amicable solution, though possibly entailing interim measures for a transitional period, should result in bringing the deviant party in compliance.

The Implementation Committee's deliberations do not involve the party allegedly non-complying:

> 'no party, whether or not represented in the Implementation Committee, involved in a matter under consideration by the Implementation Committee, shall take part in the elaboration and adoption of recommendations on that matter to be included in the report of the Committee.'[300]

If a case of presumed or alleged non-compliance is initiated by a State other than the possibly defaulting party itself, the application is submitted to the Secretariat. The Secretariat then asks the concerned State for information, following which the Secretariat submits the request and the information to the Implementation Committee. The initiating State and the concerned State are therefore not pitted against each other before the Implementation Committee. The Committee studies the information provided. If the party appears not to be in compliance, the Committee requests the party to clarify the situation, and to provide a plan of action to bring it into compliance. Only if the Committee considers the case complicated, or sees a need to discuss the plan of action, the Party is invited to attend a meeting of the Committee.[301] The State concerned is allowed to participate in the discussion of the Implementation Committee, as is necessary in order to find an amicable solution, but it is not involved in elaborating the recommendations to the MOP. The MOP may, after receiving a report from the Implementation Committee:

---

[297] Interview with Mr. Lang, Deputy-Chief Officer of the Multilateral Fund for the Implementation of the Montreal Protocol (6 August 2004). On the former President of the Implementation Committee: Press Release Multilateral Fund for the Implementation of the Montreal Protocol (12 February 2004).

[298] Montreal NCP Art. 8.

[299] ECHR Art. 38(1)(b).

[300] Montreal NCP Art. 11.

[301] Report of the 14th Meeting of the Parties [138] (5 December 2002) UNEP/Ozl.Pro.14/9.

> 'taking into consideration the circumstances of the matter, decide upon and call for steps to bring about full compliance with the protocol, including measures to assist the Parties' compliance with the Protocol, and to further the Protocol's objectives.'[302]

Frequently, the MOP offers non-complying States temporary dispensation from the rules if they accept financial or administrative assistance packages with provisions for future compliance tied into them.[303] To this end, the regime is linked to the operation of the Montreal Protocol's Multilateral Fund (MLF); this allows for the creation of financial incentives.[304] Taking away the means of assistance is an important negative sanction. Another deterrent is the potential shaming of the defaulting party. There is evidence that at least some States are indeed concerned about their reputation in this way.[305] The report of the Implementation Committee is available to any person upon request.[306] The MOP may also suspend the Member's rights and privileges granted under the Protocol. The latter includes the possibility that the export of controlled substances to a defaulting party is suspended: something that could have a serious negative impact on the relevant economy. It is clear, therefore, that irrespective of the means it uses to achieve its ends, the objective of the NCP is to enforce the applicable rules and to bring parties into compliance. While interim solutions may be considered, the aim is always to ensure obedience with the applicable norms.

---

302 Montreal NCP Art. 9.

303 The example of Latvia in M.M. Goote, 'Noncompliance Procedures', (1999) 10 *Yearbook of International Environmental Law* 155; the example of Russia in O. Yoshida, 'Soft Enforcement of Treaties: The Montreal Protocol's Noncompliance Procedure and the Functions of Internal International Institutions', (1999) 10 *Colorado Journal of International Environmental Law and Policy* 95, 133-139.

304 In 2002 the Executive Committee of the Multilateral Fund had approved 510 new projects and activities, valued at over USD 261 million: 'Report of the 14th Meeting of the Parties' (5 December 2002) [237] UNEP/Ozl.Pro.14/9; Interview with Mr. Lang, Deputy-Chief Officer of the Multilateral Fund for the Implementation of the Montreal Protocol (6 August 2004).

305 A clear example was the intervention by the Maldives protesting against a draft warning against the Maldives despite having introduced a comprehensive plan of action: 'Report of the 14th Meeting of the Parties' (5 December 2002) [141] UNEP/Ozl.Pro.14/9; generally: E. Brown Weiss, 'Conclusions: Understanding Compliance with Soft Law', in D. Shelton (ed.), *Commitment and Compliance: The Role of Non-Binding Norms in the International Legal System* (2000) 535, 541-542; Cf., C.R. Kelly, 'Enmeshment as a Theory of Compliance', (2005) 37 *NYUJILP* 303. The same is held in the field of human rights, e.g., J.M. Pasqualucci, *The Practice and Procedure of the Inter-American Court of Human Rights* (2003) 345.

306 Montreal NCP Art. 16.

6.3 Settlement practice

For a long time, like seemingly all multilateral environmental regimes,[307] the Montreal Protocol NCP suffered from a poor record of reporting by many parties, in particular by poorer countries.[308] This is particularly important in a system in which information gathering depends to a large extent on the self-reporting of the parties, as is the case in all discussed instruments. Non-reporting may result from actual lapses in implementation, but naturally also from administrative failures. In any case, it makes it difficult to assess compliance, and thereby also the success of the regime. It is notable, however, that in recent years reporting reached satisfactory high levels,[309] though problems in certain areas remain.[310]

While the system relies on the willingness of each party to provide information that may be used against it, it also allows each and every party, as well as the central executive body,[311] to bring a case for alleged non-compliance to the Implementation Committee. This generous distribution of legal standing is a substantial innovation brought by NCPs. On the other hand, as pointed out by

---

[307] See also the contributions in O. Schram Stokke, J. Hovi and G. Ulfstein (eds.), *Implementing the Climate Regime* (2005) esp ch 3, 4,

[308] Kiss and Shelton are more positive: A. Kiss and D. Shelton, *International Environmental Law* (3rd edn. 2004) 305-306. But for example the President of the Implementation Committee under the Montreal Protocol Decision XIV/14 [129] (2002) reported that 50% of the Parties had reported within the specified period. Further, thirteen out of 180 parties had not reported any data at all: 'Report of the 14th Meeting of the Parties' (5 December 2002) NEP/Ozl.Pro.14/9; M.M. Goote, 'Noncompliance Procedures', 10 *Yearbook of International Environmental Law* (1999) 155-179; S. Thomas-Nuruddin, 'Protection of the Ozone Layer: The Vienna Convention and the Montreal Protocol', in P. Szaz (ed.), *Administrative and Expert Monitoring of International Treaties* (1999) 113; A. Chayes and A. Handler Chayes, *The New Sovereignty* (1995) ch 7.

[309] In 2004, 175 out of 184 Parties had reported their data over the previous year. With the exception of new Parties, all Parties had reported their baseline data: Report of the Sixteenth Meeting of the Parties to the Montreal Protocol on Substances that Deplete the Ozone Layer, UNEP Doc UNEP/Ozl.Pro.16/17 (16 December 2004) [145]-[147]. In 2005 the record improved further, though reporting on research, development and awareness dropped: Report of the Seventh Meeting of the Conference of the Parties to the Vienna Convention for the Protection of the Ozone Layer and the Seventeenth Meeting of the Parties to the Montreal Protocol on Substances that Deplete the Ozone Layer': UNEP Doc UNEP/OzL.Conv.7.7-UNEP/OzL/Pro.17/11 (25 January 2006) [176] and [181]. In October 2006 a higher number, 177, had complied with their reporting obligations, though with further increased membership, the relative reporting compliance level dropped to a limited extent: UNEP Doc UNEP/OzL.Pro.19/9/Add.1 (18 October 2006).

[310] K. Madhava Sharma, 'Compliance with the Multilateral Environmental Agreements to Protect the Ozone Layer', in U. Beyerlin, P.-T. Stoll and R. Wolfrum (eds.), *Ensuring Compliance with Multilateral Environmental Agreements: Academic Analysis and Views from Practice* (2006) 25, 32, 34.

[311] In this case the UNEP Ozone Secretariat. Montreal Protocol Annex IV Arts. 1, 2, 3, 7.

Francioni,[312] this recognition of the legitimate interests of the many simultaneously reduces the strength of the individual claim in legal dispute settlement.

The non-compliance procedure of the Montreal Protocol has seen several relative successes. The first major case, in 1995, concerned the non-compliance of Russia.[313] With public scrutiny, and by offering funds and assistance, in 2002 it could be reported that Russia was in compliance. Many other projects have been initiated involving a large number of essentially poor countries. Nevertheless, the overall implementation records of certain countries are a point of concern. Dozens of countries were found to be in non-compliance. Despite that, in most cases the Implementation Committee recommended, and the MOP decided, that the non-complying parties should continue to be treated as parties in good standing.[314] So far, strong responses have not been the Committee's strength; in most cases the Parties are reprimanded. The case of Azerbaijan, which demonstrated a recurrent inability to comply, was exceptional in that the MOP decided to cease export to it of controlled substances.[315] Though it is generally held that the procedure works well,[316] this is so especially in cases that are not too difficult.[317] The Committee has had to deal with an increasing number of matters of non-compliance in recent years.[318] Overall, however, the Montreal Protocol is lauded as a great success, achieving a worldwide reduction of 99% of relevant emissions in less than twenty years.[319]

---

312 F. Francioni, 'International "Soft Law" a Contemporary Assessment', in A.V. Lowe and M. Fitzmaurice (eds.), *Fifty Years of the International Court of Justice* (1996) 167, 177.

313 M. Ehrmann, 'Procedures of Compliance Control in International Environmental Treaties', (2002) 13 *Colorado Journal of International Environmental Law and Policy* 377, 406-409; 'Report of the 14th Meeting of the Parties' [133] (5 December 2002) UNEP/Ozl.Pro.14/9.

314 E.g., Decisions XVII/27 (Bangladesh); XVII/28 (Bosnia-Herzegovina); XVII/29 (Chile); XVII/30 (China); XVII/31 (Ecuador), etc.: Report of the Seventh Meeting of the Conference of the Parties to the Vienna Convention for the Protection of the Ozone Layer and the Seventeenth Meeting of the Parties to the Montreal Protocol on Substances that Deplete the Ozone Layer 57 ff.

315 Decision XVII/26, Report of the Seventh Meeting of the Conference of the Parties to the Vienna Convention for the Protection of the Ozone Layer and the Seventeenth Meeting of the Parties to the Montreal Protocol on Substances that Deplete the Ozone Layer 57.

316 K. Madhava Sharma, 'Compliance with the Multilateral Environmental Agreements to Protect the Ozone Layer', in U. Beyerlin, P.-T. Stoll and R. Wolfrum (eds.), *Ensuring Compliance with Multilateral Environmental Agreements: Academic Analysis and Views from Practice* (2006) 25, 37; E.L. Miles and others, *Environmental Regime Effectiveness: Confronting Theory With Evidence* (2002) 435; M.A. Fitzmaurice and C. Redgwell, 'Environmental Non-compliance Procedures and International Law', (2000) 31 *NYIL* 35, 62.

317 D.G. Victor, 'The Operation and Effectiveness of the Montreal Non-Compliance Procedure', in D.G. Victor, K. Raustiala and B. Skolnikoff (eds.), *The Implementation and Effectiveness of International Environmental Commitments: Theory and Practice* (1998) 137, 161 ff.

318 Submission by Australia: 'Review of the Implementation of the Non-Compliance Procedure for the Resolution of Non-Compliance Matters' UNEP/OzL.Pro.17/CRP.1 (21 November 2005) [4], [7].

319 Report of the Seventh Meeting of the Conference of the Parties to the Vienna Convention for the Protection of the Ozone Layer and the Seventeenth Meeting of the Parties to the Montreal

6.4 Compliance and responsibility

It must be acknowledged that NCPs are created in the environmental field precisely as a preferred alternative to traditional third party dispute settlement methods, such as conciliation and adjudication. One reason for this may be that the laws of State responsibility seriously complicate legal claims based on another's treaty obligations or *erga omnes* obligations, especially in the area of environmental law.[320] Who is to complain when all can complain, and how should competing complaints procedurally relate to each other? Should compensation be awarded to all, should the risk and cost of litigation be shared by all? The Articles of State Responsibility offer solutions for complications as regards multilateral treaty relationships,[321] for instance by distinguishing between injured States, who are directly affected and may thus claim compensation, and all other interested States, who may ask for a declaratory remedy or a cessation.[322] It is, however, not yet clear whether States, when drafting treaty obligations, or when conciliating on the basis of existing norms, are generally willing to adopt – and comply with – these distinctions. More important perhaps is a second argument used in support of the adoption of NCPs. It is frequently held that the traditional methods simply do not work: they are hardly ever applied, are antagonistic, and – at least the law-based binding methods – offer little scope for win-win solutions. Even when accepting that there is no such thing as soft law, breaches of environmental law are often difficult to determine, a victim is difficult to identify, and retaliation with a similar breach is not allowed.

By contrast, NCPs seem to function reasonably well. Parties apparently accept from the start that some States may not comply with the rules, and that this is an issue of common concern. Indeed, when a party's acts do not conform to a pre-established norm, the NCP offers a way to direct the party's attention to the norm, to communicate disapproval of non-conforming behaviour, and to investigate, propose and agree a course of action towards compliant behaviour.

Protocol on Substances that Deplete the Ozone Layer' UNEP/OzL.Conv.7/7 (25 January 2006) [177]; 'Report of the Twenty-sixth Meeting of the Open-ended Working Group of the Parties to the Montreal Protocol' UN Doc. UNEP/Ozl.Pro.WG/1/26/7 (12 July 2006) [3].

320 Cf., M.A. Fitzmaurice and C. Redgwell, 'Environmental Non-compliance Procedures and International Law', (2000) 31 *NYIL* 35, 37; J. Werksman, 'Compliance and the Kyoto Protocol: Building a Backbone into a "Flexible" Regime', (1998) 9 *Yearbook of International Environmental Law* 48, 58-61; M. Koskenniemi, 'Breach of Treaty or Non-compliance? Reflections on the Enforcement of the Montreal Protocol', (1993) 3 *Yearbook of International Environmental Law* 123, 125-127.

321 Draft Articles on Responsibility of States for Internationally Wrongful Acts UN Doc GOAR Supp 10 (A/56/10) in particular Art. 42 and 48.

322 They may request reparation if they act in the interest of the injured party: see Articles on State Responsibility Commentaries 323.

This occurs without the necessity of punishment or of supporting the *a contrario* interpretation that non-conformity is non-problematic. However, even if NCPs offer a channel for censure through debate and development rather than censure through outright punishment, the creation of an NCP could be said to affect the standing of the rules it protects.

Does an NCP diminish the value of the treaty norms? No, say those who may be called binding law relativists. Craik states that whether or not a procedure is binding is a social rather than a legal matter: 'The binding nature of the process has less to do with the availability of coercive legal remedies in the event of rejection than with the perception of the parties and the public that the process was fair and the result was reasonable.'[323] Boyle also believes that dispute settlement of any kind is essentially about the peer pressure needed to enforce settlements. The international institutions created for environmental law help mobilise the attention of the international community, by involving all in the compliance of others. Thereby, the expression of essential community pressure is actually better developed in this realm than in many others: 'Thus it is wrong to conceive of State responsibility, or the judicial settlement of disputes, as providing a stronger basis for the "enforcement" of international environmental law.'[324]

The relativists, however, assume that the non-binding procedures will in fact also suffice in preventing or remedying possible deviant behaviour. Though initial experiences with NCPs are positive, it cannot yet be concluded that they sufficiently prevent deviant behaviour. Moreover, through the operation of the NCP, for instance by allowing parties to delay their implementation of a relevant norm, it becomes very difficult to measure what in fact constitutes defiance of an obligation. Chayes and Chayes, sidestepping such controversy, held that enforcement should not be the basis of assessment in the first place: 'If we are correct that the principal source of non-compliance is not wilful disobedience but the lack of capability or clarity or priority, then coercive enforcement is as misguided as it is costly.'[325] If this is indeed the case, at least in the case of environmental agreements, then the aim as well as the means of NCPs can be different from those of traditional settlement methods. They then are educational tools for a transition period. As in school tests, it is acceptable to get it

---

323 A.N. Craik, 'Recalcitrant Reality and Chosen Ideals: The Public Function of Dispute Settlement in International Environmental Law', (1998) 210 *Georgetown International Environmental Law Review* 551, 557.

324 A. Boyle, 'Saving the World: Implementation and Enforcement of International Environmental Law Through International Institutions', (1991) 3 Environmental Law 229, 231.

325 A. Chayes and A. Handler Chayes, *The New Sovereignty* (1995) 22. Supported for instance by X. Wang and G. Wiser, 'The Implementation and Compliance Regimes under the Climate Change Convention and its Kyoto Protocol', (2002) 11 *RECIEL* 181, 182.

wrong sometimes, though faults do not change the required correct answers. NCPs should then, however, ultimately be replaced by a judicial procedure.

Several scholars note that good compliance records are generally associated with treaty commitments that do not deviate much or at all from the *status quo*.[326] Stronger commitments to change or convergence require stronger judicial oversight.[327] It is then assumed that well-functioning compliance mechanisms do not demand much effort from participating States. If these findings are substantiated, the apparent benefits of NCPs should be considered with caution. It will then be impossible to demonstrate their superior efficacy beyond doubt, as comparisons between different area-specific treaties demand assessment of how much a particular regime requires States to deviate from the *status quo ante*.

Nevertheless, from the perspective of implementing the object and purpose of treaty, at least in the environmental field, NCPs appear better at dealing with deviations than conciliation procedures. It was concluded that there are various ways in which in area-specific treaties the regime interests can be taken into account in a bilateral conciliation procedure.[328] However, even if conciliation is incorporated in the agreement on an exclusive and compulsory basis, the involvement of neutrals and experts is secured, the conciliators are bound to make their recommendations on the basis of the substantive norms and third parties are allowed to join the proceedings, the conciliation effort may still result in a bilateral compromise struck by two parties without reference to the norms. NCPs at least offer the involvement of a wider grouping of States in any settlement itself, and offer means of chastising deviating parties. NCPs have binding elements: they can lead to taking away certain rights conferred by the treaty. They can ultimately even lead to a decision by the other Contracting Parties to force a State out of the operation of the treaty.[329] NCPs do not, however, imply that non-compliance is necessarily met with an unequivocal legal rebuke. NCPs do increase the likelihood that the outcome of a dispute settlement effort is based on respect for the norms. In doing so, they greatly reduce the consensual diplomatic element of the mechanism as compared to conciliation. In this, they are comparable to the work of the European Commission of Human Rights. The more important assessment is however that, contrary to conciliation, NCPs are regularly used.

---

[326] G.W. Downs, D.M. Rocke and P.N. Barsoom, 'Is the Good News About Compliance Good News About Cooperation?', (1996) 50 *International Organization* 379.

[327] J. McCall Smith, 'The Politics of Dispute Settlement Design: Explaining Legalism in Regional Trade Pacts', (2000) 54 *International Organization* 137, 172.

[328] See chapter IV 1 and 2.

[329] Though such decision is generally unlikely, as in that scenario the removed party can no longer be held accountable for a violation of the treaty.

6.5 Prejudice

As they are placed alongside other dispute settlement methods, and as they may result in settlements and sanctions concerning disputes that directly affect other parties equally subject to and involved in the regime's operation, NCPs raise significant questions of litispendence and *res judicata*. This is so for instance when a State party is not satisfied with the claim brought in a non-compliance procedure against a third party's behaviour.[330] Particularly as one instance of a violation of a norm is opposable by all, there may be competing claims. All parties may submit their views to the Secretariat or the Implementation Committee, but they are free to pursue other means instead. Can a complaint against State A by State B be dealt with in the non-compliance procedure, while the same complaint against State A's behaviour, but by State C, is pursued through the traditional dispute settlement procedures? The preamble of the Montreal NCP offers more questions than answers with a seemingly simple statement: the NCP shall apply 'without prejudice to the operation of the settlement procedures laid down in Art. 11 of the Vienna Convention', i.e., the traditional settlement methods. The Montreal Protocol is, after all, a legally binding instrument with a potentially strong enforcement mechanism, providing for optional adjudication and compulsory conciliation.

As to *res judicata*, Koskenniemi is rightly categorical in his reading of the Montreal NCP,[331] that even if a solution has been reached within the Implementation Committee, the same matter can be taken up anew by any other party. Neither the settlement nor any finding by the Implementation Committee can become *res judicata*.[332] The Implementation Committee, like a conciliation commission, cannot take a binding decision. Only once the MOP has accepted the Implementation Committee's report does it become a binding decision of an authoritative body. However, the party bringing the complaint to the Implementation Committee must, as an emanation of the principle of good faith, be estopped from raising the claim in another forum until the issue is taken up in the MOP. Even though the MOP is not a judicial body, its decision, whether or not confirming the recommendations by the Implementation Com-

---

330 A. Reinisch, 'The Use and Limits of Res Judicata and Lis Pendens as Procedural Tools to Avoid Conflicting Dispute Settlement Outcomes', (2004) 3 *The Law and Practice of International Courts and Tribunals* 37; Y. Shany, *The Competing Jurisdictions of International Courts and Tribunals* (2003); T. Meron, 'Norm Making and Supervision in International Human Rights: Reflections on Institutional Order', (1982) 76 *AJIL* 754.

331 M. Koskenniemi, 'Breach of Treaty or Non-Compliance? Reflections on the Enforcement of the Montreal Protocol', (1993) 3 *Yearbook of International Environmental Law* 123, 150.

332 The precondition for *res judicata* is that the determination was legal and binding. Y. Shany, *The Competing Jurisdictions of International Courts and Tribunals* (2003) 245-255.

mittee, creates a new legal situation following a contentious procedure. In this the result may be likened to a plea bargain struck with the public prosecutor. Such settlements should therefore, unlike the present unsatisfactory situation, be protected against subsequent complaints on the same issue, by including in the NCP an explicit provision to that effect.

A further problem arises when the NCP and for instance arbitration proceedings are concurrently instituted by different parties over the same instance of alleged non-compliance.[333] If, upon application by party B, the non-complying State A has just agreed to an assistance package in the NCP, relinquishing some of its institutional rights, it would not be fair if, while awaiting confirmation by the MOP, an arbitral tribunal applied to by party C would demand provisional measures and full compliance under threat of reparations. If the NCP provisions state that they are without prejudice to the traditional dispute settlement procedures, would this have to mean that while the NCP is in process, it does not have any legal effect at all for third parties? Such an interpretation could defeat the purpose of the NCP, as any party disagreeing with the (expected) outcome of the NCP could then institute rival proceedings. Assuming this is not the intention of the regime, it must be held that as all parties agreed to the establishment of the NCP procedure, its practical application in a particular case must have some legal relevance for all parties. Therefore, it is submitted that an arbitral tribunal seized by a third party during the operation of a NCP should stay the proceedings until the NCP has resulted in a conclusive determination.[334] As discussed previously,[335] it may thereby also invoke the principle of comity existing as between judicial institutions, extending it to include NCP bodies.[336] It may decide to stay its proceedings for a certain time, unless the tribunal considers an interim recommendation or award necessary to protect the rights of one of the parties. In this, the commission or tribunal should consider whether the applicant's rights can also be protected by the institutional framework of the NCP. Upon conclusion of the NCP proceed-

---

[333] Cf., P. Sands, 'Non-compliance and Dispute Settlement', in U. Beyerlin, P.-T. Stoll and R. Wolfrum (eds.), *Ensuring Compliance with Multilateral Environmental Agreements: Academic Analysis and Views from Practice* (2006) 353; M.A. Fitzmaurice and C. Redgwell, 'Environmental Non-compliance Procedures and International Law', (2000) 31 *NYIL* 35, 49. On the wider issue of the simultaneous applicability of multilateral environmental agreement dispute settlement methods and those of the WTO: A. Gonzalez-Calatayud and G. Marceau, 'The Relationship between the Dispute-Settlement Mechanisms of MEAs and those of the WTO', (2002) 11 *RECIEL* 275.

[334] Cf., C. Söderlund, 'Lis Pendens, Res Judicata and the Issue of Parallel Proceedings', (2005) 22 *Journal of International Arbitration* 301, 312.

[335] See chapter III 4.7.

[336] E.g., Arbitral Tribunal *Mox Plant* Case (*Ireland* v. *United Kingdom*) Order No. 3 [28][(24 June 2003), (2003) 42 *ILM* 1186, referring to the ECJ.

ings the arbitral tribunal would then be at liberty to resume its work, provided that the requesting party, State C, confirms it still wishes to proceed. Preferably, the outcome reached in the NCP would have included the consent of that State, which on that basis should have committed to call for termination of the arbitration proceedings. Alternatively, respondent State A, as well as all others involved in the NCP, would know before the final determination in the NCP was reached that the dispute could be continued in arbitration proceedings. This knowledge could serve to inform the NCP outcome. While this proposed solution still leaves a degree of legal uncertainty for the respondent State, it appears the most suitable way to deal with the declared principle that the NCP shall not prejudice traditional settlement methods.

Conversely, when a case is already *sub judice*, it would seem inappropriate to allow for the initiation or continuation of proceedings within the Implementation Committee and the MOP to the point that such proceedings could be understood to have determined that there was in fact non-compliance of the relevant party.[337] This should not, however, bar any negotiations within or outside of the NCP that could lead to an amicable solution while the case is before a judicial body: the Implementation Committee or MOP should only refrain from reaching a conclusion on the record in dispute, so as not to influence the concurrent legal proceedings with a public finding.

To escape from the various factors pushing for a standstill of conflicting proceedings, it would be preferable to make clear in the settlement provisions that the NCP shall be employed first, before other procedures are tried: a *lis alibi pendens*-provision.[338] In the particular case of NCPs, the provision should include that the NCP takes temporal precedence over other methods, but that following the conclusion of the NCP other methods may be initiated. This does not yet solve the problem that the outcome of the NCP may be contested in later adjudicatory proceedings. That could only be done by excluding recourse to adjudication completely. Despite the frequently professed unsuitability of adjudication for the subject-matters for which NCPs are created, adjudication is never ruled out, undoubtedly in part in order to maintain the threat of legal and binding third party determinations, to curtail the political manoeuvring with the norms that remains a possibility within NCPs.

By creating non-compliance procedures in addition to traditional settlement methods, the drafters created the possibility of many complications, as addressed

---

[337] Cf., M. Koskenniemi, 'Breach of Treaty or Non-Compliance? Reflections on the Enforcement of the Montreal Protocol', (1993) 3 *Yearbook of International Environmental Law* 123, 159.

[338] Y. Shany, *Competing Jurisdictions of International Courts and Tribunals* (2003) 212. 218.

above. In practice, however, up to now no situations of concurrent proceedings are known, and new NCPs continue to be developed. So far, complaints are routed through the non-compliance procedures only. Thereby, these regimes ensure much more than conciliation can do – and more effectively, so far – that a settlement is reached that is at least to a significant extent influenced by the treaty norms. By adopting a NCP, parties do however relinquish much of the consensual aspects provided for by a choice for conciliation. The next section will, among other things, review whether NCPs may also be counted as forms of conciliation.

7. Conclusions: Inter-State Conciliation and Specific Norms

This chapter has discussed challenges of non-binding third party dispute settlement in a range of treaties setting out norms for a specific field. In particular, it investigated how area-specific agreements use conciliation as part of a dispute settlement system, and how they can attempt to ensure respect for norms. It was found that there are many ways in which conciliation provisions are included in such agreements, and that often there is only a very limited outline of a conciliation procedure. In several treaties, however, conciliation provisions are more elaborate. This is most notable in the 1982 Law of the Sea Convention, which has also had a substantial impact on later multilateral agreements. The drafting of that Convention also demonstrated that the adoption of a compulsory conciliation mechanism can be a compromise between those who favour binding dispute settlement and those who favour diplomatic methods.

As part of such compromise, considering that conciliation does not lead to binding settlement nor necessarily to judicial application of the rules, other elements can be built in, to further the respect for the treaty norms in any attempt at settlement through conciliation. The effect of such elements is significantly influenced by the importance attached to conciliation in the system itself: it is clearly greater if the relevant provisions exclude recourse to other mechanisms outside of the system, and if conciliation is not optional but compulsory, so that on the initiative of only one party the procedure is set in motion. Substantive elements to favour respect of the treaty's norms can be the inclusion of neutral third parties, who are ideally experts in the relevant norms, charged with assessing the dispute on the basis of these norms. Several such elements are indeed provided for in a wide range of treaties. Further, the mechanism can accord a place to outside parties with an interest in the dispute or just in upholding the norms. How all this is in fact implemented nevertheless depends to a large extent on the conciliators, as well as on the parties involved in the dispute. The parties remain in control of any concluding settlement.

Despite the leeway granted by conciliation, history suggests that the method will rarely if ever be used for multilateral treaty disputes. While States appear generally reluctant to initiate the use of international dispute settlement methods, this is even more so in the case of conciliation. Settlement practices with some resemblances to conciliation do take place in the ECHR and the WTO, but there it is normally in the face a binding judicial determination, and therefore as a method of last resort before judgement strikes. Alternatively, as in the case of the World Bank, a much weakened alternative to conciliation can be adopted by those public international parties who can successfully withstand any pressure to consent to any form of binding settlement, but still desire to be accountable.

Also when, in the case of particular multilateral treaties, State Parties are clear from the start that they wish as much as possible to avoid binding dispute settlement, conciliation is still not an alternative preferred in practice. This is so despite the fact that several such treaties include more elaborate conciliation provisions. Apparently, regardless of any negotiation of conciliation clauses during the drafting stage, in the practice of multilateral relations the method is only considered useful if it serves as a way to avoid a binding legal determination. As adjudication remains rare in any multilateral treaty relationship, conciliation is likely to remain even rarer. Nevertheless, some elements of conciliation have been employed to develop an alternative for conciliation, the NCP. In this light it may be of interest whether NCPs, but also the settlement practices of the ECHR, WTO and the other institutions discussed, may qualify as equivalent to conciliation procedures, as is sometimes suggested.[339]

7.1 Conciliation or variation

Eight constitutive elements of international conciliation have been enumerated:[340] (1) a method of settlement of international disputes, (2) which is not binding, (3) involving a commission, (4) appointed by the parties, (5) which is independent, (6) investigates the dispute, (7) and proposes a solution to the parties (8) to be presented in a report. The European Commission of Human Rights, with a few exceptions,[341] did not practice inter-State, but individual/

339 E.g., C.P.R. Romano, *The Peaceful Settlement of International Environmental Disputes* (2000) 89; A. Kiss, 'Conciliation', in R. St. James Macdonald and others (eds.), *The European System for the Protection of Human Rights* (1993) 703, 706.

340 See chapter I 3.1.

341 The Commission saw only 13 inter-State cases throughout its existence. Of these, only the abovementioned case against Turkey was settled with involvement of the Commission. See chapter IV 3.

State settlement. Its practice approximates the concept of conciliation in that, as an impartial institution, the Commission investigated the dispute and occasionally nudged the parties in the direction of settlement by assisting negotiations, frequently by giving an indication of its opinion on the merits of the complaint. GATT panels, on the other hand, investigated the dispute but would not push the parties towards compromise. Panels would only provide drafts of descriptive parts of the report, which, though they may have contained some clues as to the eventual findings, were not submitted primarily to encourage parties to compromise. Further, the panel process was increasingly perceived as judicial, both by the parties, the panellists and the treaty body that could decide to make the panel reports binding on the disputants. The World Bank Inspection Panel is farthest removed from the established understanding of conciliation, as it is not involved in settlement at all. It is set-up by one party, and no other party has formal standing before it: complainants can only bring a complaint, and there is no suggestion of negotiations with them.

However, also the European Commission of Human Rights did not practice conciliation in the established sense: it was not appointed by the parties, but – in part – only by one of them. It did not have as its principal aim to achieve a settlement. It could reject a settlement, and its central responsibility, declaring cases admissible or not, did have binding consequences on the parties. Further, active settlement work in the form of issuing provisional opinions and undertaking assisted negotiation was undertaken only in some cases.[342] More importantly, however, the Commission's practice differed from conciliation because it concerned itself primarily with ensuring compliance with a particular set of norms. As set out in its terms of reference and as confirmed in practice, the Commission was foremost an instrument in a supervision mechanism, and not a body aimed at reaching settlement. In this respect, the Commission shares characteristics with GATT panels and even with the Inspection Panel.

The closest to the established understanding of conciliation were the GATT working parties created in the 1940s and 1950s. On the basis of an assessment of the relevant GATT obligations, by means of a pragmatic process, they would produce proposals for the parties. On the other hand, the members of the working parties were States, and thus not independent experts appointed by the parties. The disputants themselves were also part of the membership. By concentrating on negotiating an acceptable settlement, rather than independently investigating the dispute, these working parties should rather be considered examples of inter-State mediation.

Does the non-confrontational character of the Montreal non-compliance procedure make it equivalent to conciliation? The Implementation Committee

[342] And then often involved only members of the Secretariat, not Commission members themselves.

is a standing body, elected periodically by all parties to the relevant agreement. Disputing parties have no ability to change the composition when a case arises. The committee is not independent either: its members are States, and the committee is responsible to the MOP. Nevertheless, conciliation elements are present in the way that there is an investigation of a possible dispute between a State and the MOP, the latter acting as the representative of all State Parties, including any State that brought the alleged non-compliance to the attention. The Committee aims to find an amicable solution. It draws-up a report, with recommendations, which is submitted to the COP/MOP. However, while amicable settlement is attempted with one party, the recommendations are addressed exclusively to the other. It is this other, the COP/MOP, that takes binding decisions. In conciliation, on the other hand, the recommendation is intended to be the basis for settlement negotiations between the parties.

More fundamentally, however, it is the underlying aim of a non-compliance procedure, as well as of the ECHR, GATT and World Bank mechanisms that set them apart from traditional conciliation. They are only marginally means to resolve questions of competing claims. They are in essence instruments to enforce compliance with specific norms, and thereby also tools to prevent disobedience of these norms. The absence of a party element, the 'mobilisation of shame' and, in the Montreal NCP, the possibility of ensuing sanctions make that these are not conciliation procedures in the normal sense, but rather flexible enforcement mechanisms.

7.2 **Norm protection**

Especially as regards multilateral agreements, the question is whether NCPs are appropriate and useful as the primary instrument for the maintenance of any specific legal regime. So far, many specialists of environmental matters are positive on NCPs, and more and more treaties include them. However, in NCPs tensions between application of norms and a rejection of adjudication exist more in the open. Certain questions of *res judicata* and *lis pendens* remain as yet unresolved problems for the proper administration of dispute settlement. States thus far deal with these tensions by avoiding them. It would be better to set out explicitly what the relationship is. It should then be provided that a party should exhaust one procedure, namely the NCP, before it may initiate others. Similarly, it should be provided that when different parties pursue the same claim against the same counter party in different fora, there shall at least be a rule that arbitral tribunals seized during the application of the NCP should stay proceedings until the NCP has led to a conclusion.

Another difficulty with NCPs is that such mechanisms imply that the State Parties to a regime accept and perhaps expect that non-compliance will not be exceptional. This would be an explanation why NCPs originate and exist in environmental treaties, and not in conventions on human rights. In the latter treaties, States express a strong commitment to uphold the agreed norms, the legal standing of which is not disputed. The unwillingness to pre-assume non-compliance is however not restricted to treaties involving such strong-felt or moral norms as human rights. It also applies, for instance, to maritime rights and the law of treaties. In such cases, non-compliance mechanisms are less appropriate than a compulsory conciliation mechanism containing the earlier enumerated elements promoting a greater role of norms in settlement activity. While such procedures of legal conciliation equally do not guarantee respect for the norms in a settlement, they nevertheless are more explicitly geared towards their implementation, and allow for an explicitly principled approach by the parties.

In asymmetrical relations, on the other hand, neither a non-compliance mechanism nor a classic conciliation mechanism may be feasible. In this respect the World Bank Inspection Panel represents a relevant alternative. While in individual cases a more powerful actor is frequently able to ignore the grievances of the smaller actor, the recurrence of such individual cases, coupled with the public perception concerns of the more powerful party, demand a dispute settlement procedure that takes into account the power differences. A dispute between parties of greatly varying standing can be addressed by investigating the case through a semi-independent institution created by the more powerful party itself. The example of the World Bank demonstrates that the review body may even restrict its assessment to the standards set by the powerful party itself, provided that these standards are reasonably objective and leave room for critical review of their creator's actions. The review institution can prod its founder into action due to the trust conferred upon it, as supporters as well as critics of the World Bank agree the Inspection Panel has done.[343] The impetus to act is further supported by the potential for embarrassment, if the founder should be seen to sideline its own review body.

In their own way, each of the institutions discussed here established a new option for dealing with the conflict between the need to apply certain adopted rules, and the desire to stay away from adjudication. One solution, as in the ECHR system, was to allow for friendly settlement on the basis of an indication of the applicability of the norms, while maintaining supervision over the settlement to respect the norms. This choice was preferable over the option of

[343] D. Hunter, 'Using the World Bank Inspection Panel to Defend the Interests of Project-Affected People', (2003) 4 *Chicago Journal of International Law* 201; I.F.I. Shihata, *The World Bank Inspection Panel in Practice* (2nd edn. 2000) 260; S. Slemmer-Schulte, 'Introductory Note to the Conclusions of the Second Review of the World Bank Inspection Panel', (2000) 39 *ILM* 243, 246.

having a quasi-adjudicatory process, as in GATT, but with the possibility of not adopting its findings. Eventually the power of parties to block adoption of the report can lead to a breakdown of the system, as indeed happened in GATT in the 1980s. Alternatively, a party may unilaterally adopt a review body to make findings on relations with others, even on the basis only of rules drawn up by itself. Such self-compliance review is a long way from classic diplomatic dispute settlement methods, but nevertheless a relevant option to prevent and possibly resolve disputes with others.

In both GATT and ECHR, a process of judicialisation eventually led to the reduction of substantive settlement work. This was so in part because the desire to stay away from adjudication diminished. Considering the benefits of binding determinations, or because of the other advantages of being part of the jurisdiction created by membership of both WTO and the Council of Europe, parties accepted binding determination of the agreed norms by means of adjudication. A further judicialisation may also eventually take place for other multilateral agreements, thereby vacating the need for NCP provisions.[344] Such judicialisation is also a constant call by NGOs and academics when it comes to the World Bank, but that organisation has at present little to gain by subjecting itself to a court. If it would do so, however, other reasons for settlement practices may emerge, as occurred in both the ECHR system and in the WTO: their adjudication systems became overburdened. It is clear that there will always be situations in which States will want to avoid adjudication, even though they cannot resolve their treaty dispute only by bilateral negotiation. It is then good to know that conciliation and related methods provide a range of possibilities to address the dispute while keeping an eye on the norms involved.

---

[344] M.A. Fitzmaurice and C. Redgwell, 'Environmental Non-compliance Procedures and International Law', (2000) 31 *NYIL* 35, 65.

Chapter V
THE USE OF INTER-STATE CONCILIATION

1. THE USE OF DIPLOMATIC DISPUTE SETTLEMENT

For the settlement of inter-State disputes a great number of settlement methods is available.[1] Recourse to non-binding methods such as conciliation is known as diplomatic dispute settlement, as, more than in the case of binding methods, success is dependent on a diplomatic agreement during and after their use. Diplomatic methods do not intend to replace normal diplomatic activity. In adjudication, on the other hand, the political agreement to settle in accordance with the third party procedure is give *before* the initiation of the proceedings: when a court or tribunal reaches a decision, there is a legal duty to abide by it.[2]

Another relevant distinction is that between legal and non-legal settlement methods. Legal methods rely on a strict application of the law to the particular dispute, whereas non-legal methods do not. Unless the parties rely on their joint and separate application of the law without recourse to outside parties, legal methods are dependent on the involvement of a third party, normally a body of independent legal experts, such as found in a court or in an arbitral tribunal. Settlement of disputes by adjudication results in an outcome binding on the parties. It is possible that a non-binding, diplomatic dispute settlement method is at the same time a legal method. This is the case when parties opt for advisory (non-binding) arbitration, or when they request a conciliation commission to handle a dispute on a strictly legal basis.

All settlement methods can be used in succession.[3] Various methods can be used simultaneously, such as when good offices are employed while a dispute

---

[1] See chapter I 2.

[2] Though this does not necessarily mean that parties will necessarily comply: e.g., the negotiations regarding judgement in the *Land and Maritime Boundary between Cameroon and Nigeria* Case (Cameroon and Nigeria; Equatorial Guinea intervening), (2002) *ICJ Rep* 303 discussed further below. Generally: C. Schulte, *Compliance with Decisions of the International Court of Justice* (2004).

[3] E.g., the negotiation of the 'Joint Notification to the Registrar of the International Court of Justice of the Dispute between Malaysia and Singapore Concerning Sovereignty over Pedra Branca/ Pulau Batu Puteh, Middle Rock and South Ledge' of 23 July 2003 and the underlying interna-

is before the International Court of Justice. Settlement methods may even blend into each other, such as when inquiry is used to clarify an issue submitted to mediation, or evolve out of each other, such as the mission termed 'of good offices' regarding the Cyprus problem, which turned into mediation with elements of arbitration.[4] Further, frequently a method is not called by its proper name, as in the 'facilitation' of the 'differendum' between Belize and Guatemala.[5] Lastly, there are various new forms of third party settlement, such as non-compliance procedures, which are still to be accorded a place in the canon of dispute settlement methods.

This fluid practice reinforces the need for a clear understanding of the core methods of dispute settlement. This may help those involved in the practice, whether through drafting a clause, selecting a method or actually attempting to settle a dispute. They can then place their work in a broader perspective, and become better aware of its limitations and possibilities. Of all the commonly mentioned methods, however, conciliation is probably the least understood. Despite a stormy appearance on the world scene in the early 20th century, one century later it still has an ambiguous status, is little practiced and rarely studied. Nevertheless, it retains a potentially important place in many dispute settlement mechanisms. It is therefore useful to revisit the identity of inter-State conciliation.

2. Finding the Identity of Conciliation

The identity of conciliation has always been elusive. Conciliation was practiced before it was invented,[6] and then emerged as a concept nearly simultaneously in both Europe and the Americas, based on overlapping but dissimilar ideas of preventing war and providing a new alternative to adjudication.[7] Considering also that, in private law, mediation and conciliation are often considered interchangeable,[8] it is important to review the debate on the definitional

---

tional agreements, jointly submitting a case to the ICJ <http://www.icj-cij.org/icjwww/idocket/imasi/imasiframe.htm> (26 July 2006).

[4] 'Report of the Secretary-General on his Mission of Good Offices', UN Doc S/2004/437. See chapter I 2.3.

[5] 'Belize-Guatemala Territorial Differendum: Proposals from the Facilitators' (30 August 2002). See chapter II 1.15.

[6] In the 1905 *Dogger Bank* Case, which was officially an inquiry procedure, but in fact proposed a solution to the dispute: see chapter II 1.3.

[7] See chapter II 1; chapter III 2.

[8] E.g., the UNCITRAL Model Law on International Commercial Arbitration (2001) Art. 1(3) UN Doc A/57/18; M. Rubino-Sammartano, *International Arbitration Law and Practice* (2001) 10-11; P. Sanders, *Quo Vadis Arbitration* (1999) 353; H.M. Holtzmann, 'Dispute Resolution in Eu-

elements of the method. It was found that the definitions that are now frequently repeated in literature are either to restrictive or too broad.

The method of conciliation distinguishes itself from mediation essentially in that conciliators investigate the dispute and subsequently propose a solution.[9] Conciliation is considered to be a more formal procedure than mediation: the conciliators assume an independent role, and do substantial work away from the parties.[10] By contrast, mediation is more informal, with relatively more time spent in discussions with the parties. Conciliators work towards settlement by means of preparing a report containing proposals for settlement,[11] while mediators only prepare a report if they consider this useful for their work towards a settlement.[12] It is understood that this criterion is open to debate, and that reasoned opinions may differ.[13]

In chapter I, the elements of a definition of conciliation were identified as: (1) a method of settlement of international disputes, (2) which is not binding, (3) involving a commission, (4) appointed by the parties, (5) which is independent, (6) investigates the dispute, (7) and proposes a solution (8) to be presented in a report.[14] Having these elements in mind, it is better possible to review the emergence, practice, problems and possibilities of the method in general inter-State relations. At the same time, considering the varied and fluent nomenclature of diplomatic settlement, related methods should not be let out of sight, just as conciliation-like practices in non-inter-State disputes can be relevant for a proper understanding of inter-State conciliation. It is nonetheless rather a factor inherent in inter-State conciliation itself that has for a long time limited a better view of the method, namely the confusion over the role it was to play among the range of settlement methods.

---

rope under the UNCITRAL Conciliation Rules', in D. Bardonnet (ed.), *Le Règlement Pacifique des Differends Internationaux en Europe: Perspectives d'Avenir* (1991) 293, 299.

[9] See chapter I 3.2.

[10] C.C. Hyde, 'The Place of Commissions of Inquiry and Conciliation Treaties in the Peaceful Settlement of Disputes', (1929) 10 *BYIL* 96, 101-102.

[11] E.g., 'Belize-Guatemala Territorial Differendum: Proposals from the Facilitators', (30 August 2002); 'Report and Recommendations of the Conciliation Commission on the Continental Shelf Area between Iceland and Jan Mayen', (1981) 20 *ILM* 797.

[12] E.g., as in the case of the 'Special Negotiator for Succession Issues' who wrote provided drafts of a settlement on the basis of international law for further negotiation by the parties, and who considered himself a mediator: A. Watts, 'Introductory Note to Agreement on Succession Issues between the Five Successor States of the Former State of Yugoslavia', (2002) 41 *ILM* 1.

[13] E.g., on whether the work of the sole conciliator in the *East African Community* Case was not in fact mediation, as he himself considered it: V. Umbricht, *Multilateral Mediation: Practical Experiences and Lessons* (1989).

[14] See chapter I 3.1.

2.1 Two ideas of conciliation

At the root of inter-State conciliation were initially two ideas, fuelled by the practical and doctrinal setting at the time of its introduction. The first driving thought was that an impartial commission of wise men, taking the time to investigate a *casus belli* while politicians and populations cooled off from their initial excitement, could effectively prevent the eruption of war.[15] The 1898 *Maine* incident in Havana,[16] which ignited the Spanish-American War, had great impact on the perceptions of international lawyers and diplomats. A few years later, the *Dogger Bank* Case demonstrated how a calm and independent investigation of a Russian/British naval incident could successfully resolve an sensitive issue. All this gave impetus to the work of the Second Hague Conference of 1907, and to the Bryan-treaties concluded by the US with American States.[17] After WWI, such pacific works were hailed by the international peace movement as well as by governments, mainly those of the smaller European and American powers: agreeing to conciliation became a welcome expression of commitment to the global ideal. This combined with the existing uncertainty about the status of 'political disputes', often held to be separate category of cases involving 'honour' and 'vital interests'.[18] These were frequently held to be non-justiciable. Conciliation thus appeared to be viable option to deal with them.[19]

The second idea underlying the development of conciliation was that it could add to the possibilities of dispute settlement, in particular by providing an alternative to adjudication. It was mainly this idea that in 1919 led the Swiss Government, encouraged by Max Huber, to adopt a policy of concluding conciliation treaties. It saw conciliation as a means not just to prevent war, but as a means for the settlement of any international dispute. Conciliation could help to avoid the political costs of arbitration or judicial settlement.[20] Added to these ideas was the fact that international adjudication, including arbitration, was then still in its early stages. The age-old tradition of referring disputes to foreign sovereigns for a binding decision had only just been replaced by the cre-

---

15 See chapter II 1.6.

16 N. Bar-Yaacov, *The Handling of International Disputes by Means of Inquiry* (1974) 33. See chapter II 1.3.

17 J. Brown Scott, *Treaties for the Advancement of Peace* (1920). See chapter II 1.4.

18 E.g., Treaty of Arbitration (Ecuador-Venezuela) (24 May 1921), *Habicht* 17; Treaty of Conciliation and Arbitration (Finland-Germany) (14 March 1925, entered into force 27 February 1926), 43 *LNTS* 367.

19 E.g., J. Efremoff, 'L'Organisation de la conciliation comme moyen de prevenir des guerres', (1937) 59 *Recueil des Cours* Vol. III 99.

20 'Rapport du Conseil fédéral à l' Assemblée fédérale concernant les traités internationaux d'arbitrage', (1919) 71 *Feuille Fédéral Suisse* Vol. V 808, 820.

ation of the Permanent Court of International Justice.[21] Further, while not essential to the reasoning of the Swiss government, it was a common belief that there were gaps in international law, which would not allow a court like the PCIJ to address just any international dispute.[22] The idea that some disputes were non-justiciable was not restricted to only to cases of 'high politics', but extended to other fields as well. On this basis the first conciliation treaty, concluded in 1921 by Switzerland and Germany, could explicitly consider that certain disputes were non-justiciable, and that these were to be submitted to conciliation.[23]

2.2 Legal and political conciliation

In addition to the diversity of ideas behind the initial development of conciliation, there have also been conflicting views on the way in which the procedure should be conducted, in particular on whether the work of the commission – and the way in which the parties approach it should be legally inspired or not. Remarkably, however, this conflict has up to now never been fully articulated. It is here proposed that there are in fact two 'ideal types' of conciliation, in the sense of idealised abstractions. Actual practice may approximate these types, but may also be a combination of both extremes.

The first type is that of political conciliation, in which the commission can base its settlement proposals on whatever appears to it to be most suitable. The arguments on which the commission bases its recommendations may include economic, historical, strategic and any other relevant considerations. Legal considerations may be, but are not necessarily among them. Where they are they do not carry preponderant weight.[24] In this conception, conciliation is a direct extension of normal diplomatic discussions, now aided by an independent body investigating the dispute.

By contrast, in legal conciliation, the commission makes recommendations on the basis of a legal analysis of the case. Non-legal considerations are taken into account only in so far as the law recognises them as relevant.[25] In the purest form of legal conciliation, the commission acts as an arbitral tribunal,

---

[21] It would survive up to the Beagle Channel Arbitration, in which as late as 1977 an arbitral award decided the delimitation dispute between Chile and Argentina, indirectly arising of out of a 1881 treaty between the two states referring to arbitration by the British Sovereign: H.T. King and M.A. Le Forestier, 'Papal arbitration', (1997) 52 *Dispute Resolution Journal* 74, 78.

[22] J. Fischer Williams, 'Justiciable and Other Disputes', (1932) 26 *AJIL* 31.

[23] Treaty of Conciliation, Arbitration and Compulsory Adjudication (Germany-Switzerland) (3 December 1921), 12 *LNTS* 281.

[24] See chapter III 2.

[25] Ibid.

pronouncing on the legal merits of the dispute, only lacking the power to bind the parties to its conclusions.

Both conceptions have been propagated and both have indeed been practised. The difference in approach was however rarely reflected in the terms of reference of the commissions, suggesting that it was the incidental perception of the task of the commission, as held by the commission members and possibly by the parties themselves, that determined the conduct and outcome of the proceedings. To the extent that the parties at the time of the proceedings actually favoured the adopted conception of conciliation, whether legal or political, such flexibility of the identity of conciliation may be applauded. To the extent that adopting this conception in a particular case was a result of unfamiliarity with the procedure or with the options available, an opportunity to choose was missed, resulting from an identity problem in need of resolution.

It is important to note that attempts at clarifying the nature of conciliation are not attempts to restrain its practice, or to discard as wrong or irrelevant instances that do not match the conceptions as set out. Rather, a clear identity of conciliation allows for the better discussion and assessment of the various possibilities on offer, and facilitates the selection of conciliation or of an alternative for adoption in settlement provisions. To this end, the conceptions should also be matched with practice.

3. The Practice of Conciliation

In inter-State disputes, conciliation was not used as frequently, or for as important cases, as originally envisaged. The 1905 *Dogger Bank* inquiry involving Russia and the United Kingdom appears to have been among the most important: it resolved what may have been a *casus belli* between two Great Powers.[26] It also established that inquiry into the facts is easily intertwined with legal questions, and also easily touches upon diplomatic considerations. The case further demonstrated that a carefully phrased non-binding report can sometimes do more than a binding legal award for the maintenance of self-respect and the continuation of peaceful relations. It provided inspiration for the development of the formal concept of conciliation itself.

The discussion of the subsequent practice of conciliation must take into account that secrecy and confidentiality make that relevant details of proceedings are often not known,[27] and may also have meant that even their occur-

[26] J.B. Scott (ed.), *The Hague Court Reports* (1916) 403 ff. See chapter II 1.3.

[27] E.g., the work of the German/Soviet conciliation commission, which met between 1929 and 1932, but the work of which is unreported: H. Wehberg, 'Die Vergleichskommissionen im modernen Völkerrecht', (1958) 19 *ZfAÖRV* 551, 567.

rence remains unknown. Nevertheless, some seven international commissions are known to have convened between 1920 and 1940, and seven more met between 1940 and 1960.[28] All of the cases dealt with, except for two, were settled successfully in whole or in part.[29] Since then, we may add several more inter-State cases, with a mixed record. First is the *Jan Mayen* Case of 1981, involving Iceland and Norway.[30] Here the parties drew-up exceptional terms of reference. The commission was to take account not only of nascent maritime law, but also explicitly of the economic needs of one of the parties. The commission's report became the basis for a settlement between the parties.[31] Second was the *East African Community* Case of 1977-1986, a case of political conciliation, in which a sole conciliator, invoking both principles, practice and the *status quo*, managed after many years to propose a successful settlement package for a dispute involving three States.[32] The *Taba* conciliation of 1986-1989, concurrent with arbitration of the same dispute, and involving a number of arbitrators simultaneously appointed as conciliators, was unsuccessful in settling the border demarcation dispute between Egypt and Israel. The case was however concluded by means of the arbitral award.[33] Lastly, in the *Belize/Guatemala* Case of 2000-2002, a commission of two non-nationals practiced political conciliation regarding a long-standing dispute concerning territorial claims and movements of settlers. The commission's report was not accepted by one of the parties,[34] but became the basis for further mediation by the OAS, and has resulted in easing tensions and the adoption of confidence building measures.[35]

Casting a wider net, one may also mention other inter-State cases. In 1983-1985 the European Commission of Human Rights was actively involved in

---

[28] Some writers use different definitions, and therefore name different numbers, cf., A.M. Stuyt, *Survey of International Arbitrations 1794-1989* (1990) 567-584; *Cot* 89-97; H. Wehberg, 'Die Vergleichskommissionen im modernen Völkerrecht', (1958) 19 *ZfAÖRV* 551; see chapter II 1.9; II 1.11.

[29] The fully unsuccessful cases were The *Vitianu* Case (Switzerland/Romania) and the *F.OABV* Case (France/Morocco). In both cases the commission never came to issue any recommendations, either because a national conciliator was not appointed, or because he (and a colleague) withdrew from the proceedings. See chapter II 1.

[30] See chapter III 3.4.1.

[31] For the commission's report: (1982) 62 *ILR* 108. For the resulting treaty: (1982) 21 *ILM* 1222

[32] V. Umbricht, *Multilateral Mediation: Practical Experiences and Lessons* (1989). See chapter I 4.3.

[33] (1987) 26 *ILM* 1. See chapter I 4.2.

[34] 'Belize-Guatemala Territorial Differendum: Proposals from the Facilitators' (30 August 2002).

[35] Agreement on a Framework for Negotiations and Confidence Building Measures Between Belize and Guatemala (7 September 2005) <http://www.oas.org/documents/Belice_Guatemala/English_200dpi.pdf> (5 October 2007). See chapter II 1.15.

reaching a friendly settlement between Turkey on the one hand, and Denmark, France, the Netherlands, Norway and Sweden on the other, concerning the alleged human rights violations committed by the Turkish military regime.[36] The resulting settlement was much criticised for relying on promises of improvement by the Turkish government and further discussions by it with the Commission, but it now seems that there was a secret unwritten addition to the settlement, in which Turkey committed to accepting the right of individual complaint to the European Court. If this is indeed the case, the settlement was a great success. In a more recent case between Turkey and Denmark, concerning an allegation of an individual breach of human rights, the Registry of the Court was involved in streamlining a draft settlement already worked out between the parties.[37]

A different line of practice developed regarding international trade disputes in GATT. The working panels used in the late 1940s and early 1950s, while really practising inter-State mediation, provided a useful forum for the settlement through assisted negotiations of various allegations of non-compliance with GATT norms. In view of the more independent and judicial character that States wished to give the process, they developed the GATT panels, which until the 1980s were highly successful. The panels practiced what may be thought to be a strict form of legal conciliation, issuing a legal opinion on the alleged GATT violations. Nevertheless, the panels formed part of a system of enforcement, relying on political pressure on disputants to co-operate in the adoption of the report. When in the 1980s certain States started to treat the process as indeed non-binding and on that basis refused the adoption of reports, the system itself was considered to have failed.

Various other cases are known of conciliation between States and private parties, such as the *Japanese 4% Loan* Case and the *Tokyo 5% Loan* Case, which were respectively settled on the basis of legally inspired proposals by the President of the World Bank and by an expert acting on behalf of the President of the IMF.[38] Further, the otherwise underused ICSID conciliation procedure has seen in *Tesoro/Trinidad and Tobago* a successfully settled case according to strict legal conciliation,[39] while another case was settled in all se-

---

[36] Report of the European Commission of Human Rights, 7 December 1985, DR 44, 31. See chapter IV 4.4.

[37] *Denmark* v. *Turkey* ECtHR Judgement (*Friendly Settlement*) 5 April 2000, No. 34382/97. See chapter IV 4.4.

[38] The *Japanese 4% Loan* Case, (1955) 29 *ILR* 5 was settled in 1955, the *Tokyo 5% Loan* Case followed in 1960, (1966) 29 *ILR* 11.

[39] *Tesoro Petroleum Co.* v. *Trinidad and Tobago* ISCID Case No. CONC/83/1; L. Nurick and S.J. Schnably, 'The First ICSID Conciliation', (1986) 1 *ICSID Rev Foreign Investment Law Jo*urnal 340, 347.

crecy.[40] This also reinforces the assumption that many successes and failures are not known because they remain covered by confidentiality obligations, or because parties simply do not wish them to be known. Nevertheless, the large majority of known cases was a partial or complete success. The importance of the success varies from case to case, and is best reviewed in the context of the ideas that drove the development of the method.

3.1 The founding ideas in practice

Some of the inter-State commissions helped to ease significant tensions between the countries, as in the *Chaco* Case,[41] in the *Dominican Republic/Haiti* Case[42] and in the *Belize/Guatemala* Case.[43] Most cases, on the other hand, concerned relatively technical issues between States enjoying friendly relations. These cases were often claims between neighbouring States for financial compensation regarding a manageable incident, such as the *Gorm and Svava* Case regarding the loss of ships,[44] the *France/Switzerland* Case regarding the payment of internment,[45] and the *Denmark/Lithuania* Case regarding payment for railway construction.[46]

For a settlement method in part built on the idea that it could prevent war, this should have created disappointment. As it turned out, in the fiery preparations for war, conciliation and other methods of settlement were often disregarded. In the Americas, multilateral treaties for peaceful settlement followed each other rapidly, but – despite some limited successes mentioned above – could not provide a sizeable enough check on aggression. Elsewhere, ignominy came when in 1936 Mussolini pretended to negotiate with Abyssinia over the implementation of a commitment to conciliation and arbitration, but in fact used this to hide his imminent invasion. The discredited pacifist idealism of the early 20th century and the period between the World Wars thereby also damaged conciliation. We have come a long way from the aspirations of the 1920s and 1930s.[47]

---

40 *SEDITEX* v. *Madagascar* (CONC/94/01). Further cases were either concluded before commencement of the commission's work or did not result in settlement. See chapter II 1.13.1.

41 L. Woolsey, 'Bolivia – Paraguay Dispute', (1929) 23 *AJIL* 110 and (1930) 24 *AJIL* 122.

42 (1929) 23 *AJIL* Off Doc 76.

43 'Belize-Guatemala Territorial Differendum: Proposals from the Facilitators' (30 August 2002). See chapter II 1.15.

44 H. Rolin, 'Une conciliation belgo-danoise', (1953) 57 *RGDIP* 353.

45 S. Bastid, 'La commission de conciliation franco-suisse', (1956) 2 *AFDI* 436.

46 P. Hamilton and others (eds.), *Permanent Court of Arbitration International Arbitration and Dispute Resolution* (1999) 287.

47 E.g., C. Gorgé, 'L'évolution de la conciliation internationale', 54 *RDILC* (1927) 58; J. Efremoff, 'L'Organisation de la conciliation comme moyen de prevenir des guerres', (1937) 59 *Recueil des Cours* Vol. I 99.

The other founding idea, that conciliation could be useful to avoid the political and other burdens of adjudication, does find support in case history. The smaller matters, in which States submitted rather technical disputes to commissions, could equally have been submitted to arbitration or an international court. Instead, the dispute was settled consensually. To the extent, however, that conciliation was supported as an alternative to adjudication because of intrinsic deficiencies in the judicial process, this motivation lost its appeal. Supported by the arguments of Hersch Lauterpacht,[48] the idea that no disputes are *inherently* non-justiciable became *communis opinio* in the decades following conciliation's founding. Disputes were less frequently excluded from a court's jurisdiction on grounds of non-justiciability.[49] Eventually there was no category of disputes left for which conciliation was the ultimate answer: it was now in open competition with any alternative.

Opening up the possibilities of dispute settlement did not mean that conciliation had to lose place, let alone that it became without object. Regardless of the acceptance that all disputes can in principle be submitted to a court, in fact many disputes remain excluded from the jurisdiction of any adjudicatory body.[50] Multilateral agreements frequently either do not provide for binding settlement,[51] or allow parties to exclude binding dispute settlement,[52] and therefore leave States frustrated in addressing alleged violations of other States' obligations in a legal and binding manner.[53] Moreover, it is consistently acknowledged that in many cases it is better *not* to submit a particular dispute to adjudication.[54] This may be so for instance because a Court can only deal with part of the dispute, or because the available procedure is slow, cumbersome and expensive. It may be that one or both of the parties do not want to face the prospect of losing, or that they wish to avoid the creation of precedent. They may

---

48 H. Lauterpacht, *The Function of Law in the International Community* (1933). See chapter II 1.8.

49 *Habicht* 975.

50 J.G. Merrills, 'The Optional Clause at Eighty', in N. Ando and others (eds.), *Liber Amicorum Judge Shigeru Oda* (2002) 435.

51 E.g., 1993 Convention for the Conservation of the Southern Bluefin Tuna.

52 E.g., Convention on the Law of the Sea, Arts. 297-299.

53 E.g., Arbitral Award, *Southern Bluefin Tuna* Case (*Australia and New Zealand* v. *Japan*) (*Jurisdiction and Admissibility*), (2000) 39 *ILM* 1359.

54 C. Chinkin, 'Alternative Dispute Resolution under International Law', in M. Evans (ed.), *Remedies in International Law: The Institutional Dilemma* (1998) 123; P.H. Kooijmans, 'International Arbitration in Historical Perspective: Past and Present', in A.H.A. Soons (ed.), *International Arbitration: Past and Prospects* (1990) 23; R.B. Bilder, 'The Settlement of Disputes in the Field of the International Law of the Environment', (1975) 144 *Recueil des Cours* Vol. I 139, 225-226; I. Brownlie, 'The Justiciability of Disputes and Issues in International Relations', (1967) 42 *BYIL* 123, 141; H. Lauterpacht, 'Non Liquet and the Completeness of the Law', in F.M. van Asbeck (ed.), *Symbolae Verzijl* (1958) 196, 200.

have a cultural aversion to adjudication, or distrust the available bench. They may also want to protect their frail or friendly relationship from negative decisions, or they may hold that a legal decision does not do justice to the interests at stake. It may also be that because of the number of parties involved, adjudication is unfeasible. Adjudication may also be unfeasible if one of the parties lacks the required legal standing.

These and other reasons make clear that while there are no non-justiciable disputes, there are disputes that parties will not settle judicially, at least if they can avoid it. Looked at it from the other side, many reasons can be and are often given why parties may prefer to employ a third party non-binding procedure as conciliation.[55] The review of inter-State practice supports the generally held perceptions that positive reasons for the selection of conciliation are (1) that the dispute is not of the highest importance, or (2) that no crucial issue of legal principle is involved,[56] that (3) States enjoy friendly relations, or that (4) protecting a precarious relation is judged important,[57] that (5) confidentiality is required, that (6) there is a possibility that parties may settle through negotiations, that (7) an independent investigation of the matter may help to draw out more options than are at first sight available, or (8) solutions may be preferred that cannot be offered by adjudication, such as detailed co-operation commitments, appointment of special functionaries, etc.[58]

For these reasons, alternatives to adjudication such as conciliation have retained a place in the canon of dispute settlement, and for these reasons also there continues to be further development of all kinds of diplomatic dispute settlement. A clear example of this is the recent emergence of non-compliance procedures, whose existence is often explained as a solution for disputes that are not suitable for submission to adjudication.[59] Despite the problems incurred by its two founding ideas, a conceptual basis for conciliation therefore continues to exist. The basic idea of Max Huber, that conciliation can be a desirable

---

[55] E.g., H.J. Brown and A.L. Marriott, *ADR Principles and Practice* (2nd edn. 1999) 12-15; A. Rycroft, 'The Mediation of Human Rights Disputes', (2002) *South African Journal on Human Rights* 287, 295.

[56] It is this that creates most problems in settlement attempts around the implementation of specific norms, such as demonstrate by the European Commission of Human Rights (chapter IV 3) and non-compliance procedures (chapter IV 6).

[57] E.g., the *France/Siam* Case and the *F.OABV* Case. See chapter II 1.11.

[58] E.g., the special role accorded to the OAS in the continuing negotiations between Guatemala and Belize in the Agreement on a Framework for Negotiations and Confidence Building Measures Between Belize and Guatemala (7 September 2005). See chapter II 1.15.

[59] M.A. Fitzmaurice and C. Redgwell, 'Environmental Non-compliance Procedures and International Law', (2000) 31 *NYIL* 35, 37; M. Koskenniemi, 'Breach of Treaty or Non-compliance? Reflections on the Enforcement of the Montreal Protocol', (1993) 3 *Yearbook of International Environmental Law* 123, 125-127.

alternative to adjudication, remains valid. The practice of conciliation nevertheless continued to suffer from a lack of clarity about its true identity, in particular whether it was a legal or a political method.

3.2 The judicialisation of conciliation

The conciliation provisions in the bilateral treaties concluded in the 1920s did not stipulate any basis on which the commission was to make its recommendations.[60] The 1919 Swiss report calling for conciliation also did not require application of legal principles.[61] As discussed, many even thought that for various disputes there were no international legal principles. Therefore, the initial conception was that of political conciliation. Nevertheless, as the review of practice has shown, actual cases were often assessed on a legal basis. The apparent difference is understandable in part because conciliation was a new procedure, which unlike adjudication or mediation was not based on a globally present domestic analogy or on longstanding international practice. Into the 1950s it is reported that conciliation commissions devoted their first meetings to discussing the nature of their responsibility.[62]

Further, many of the persons called to act as conciliators were lawyers. This will have exhibited the assumptions of the parties on the nature of the procedure, but also made it more likely that the procedure would develop further in the direction of what international lawyers were most familiar with, namely adjudication. In addition, it were of course mainly international lawyers who commented on the method. The judicialisation of conciliation comes out clearly in the discussions in the Institut de Droit International in 1961,[63] when François and Rolin conducted a serious debate about the place of legal conclusions in the recommendations of the report, but where the comments of others, stating that conciliation may also be of a non-legal nature, never arrived at the centre of the discussions.

This approach developed further in the adoption of conciliation as a preferred means of dispute settlement in the many multilateral treaties that were concluded under UN auspices since the 1960s. It started with the Vienna Con-

---

60 E.g., Treaty of Conciliation, Arbitration and Compulsory Adjudication (Germany-Switzerland) (adopted 3 December 1921, entered into force 25 May 1922); Treaty of Conciliation, Arbitration and Compulsory Adjudication (France-Switzerland) (signed 6 April 1925). See chapter II 1.6.

61 'Rapport du Conseil fédéral à l'Assemblée fédérale concernant les traités internationaux d'arbitrage', (1919) 71 *Feuille Fédéral Suisse* Vol. V 808, 820.

62 F.M. van Asbeck, 'La tâche et l'action d'une commission de conciliation', (1956) *NTIR* 1; H. Rolin, 'Une conciliation belgo-danoise', (1953) 57 *RGDIP* 353.

63 (1961) 49 *Annuaire de l'Institut de Droit International* Vols. I and II. See chapter III 3.

vention on the Law of Treaties. The many States involved in the drafting could not agree on adjudication as the ultimate means of dispute settlement for cases arising under the Convention, largely because many states preferred diplomatic settlement.[64] In a package deal, it was concluded that regular cases should be submitted to compulsory conciliation and therefore not to a court, but that the legal nature of conciliation should be strengthened, by providing for legally oriented conciliators and by allowing explicit legal conclusions.[65] These provisions inspired many other multilateral treaties, including the Law of the Sea Convention, which itself became a major source of guidance for subsequent multilateral treaties.[66]

None of the conciliation provisions in multilateral treaties are known to have been applied, as also since the 1960s there are no known cases of application of the provisions of the classic bilateral treaties. All conciliation cases since that time occurred on the basis of *ad hoc* agreements. It is submitted that the longstanding confusion about the identity of conciliation and the reasoning behind it hindered the practical application of conciliation, while the eventual domination of the legal conception of conciliation limited the inherent flexibility it has to offer. This did not, however, stop the proliferation of conciliation clauses, though also there tendencies toward judicialisation were noted.

3.3 The development of new procedures for conciliation

Despite the limited practice of conciliation in inter-State disputes, and despite the development of alternatives, there remains a tradition of including conciliation as a means of dispute settlement in international agreements, though often only referring to conciliation without giving procedural details.[67] When a dispute under such a basic clause arises, parties may benefit from the 1995 UN Model Rules of Conciliation[68] and the 1996 PCA Optional Conciliation Rules,[69]

---

[64] I. Sinclair, *The Vienna Convention on the Law of Treaties* (2nd edn. 1984) 226-233. See chapter III 3.2.

[65] Vienna Convention on the Law of Treaties Art. 66.

[66] E.g., the Convention on the Representation of States in Their Relations With International Organisations of a Universal Character (1975); The Vienna Convention on the Succession of States (1978); the Vienna Convention on Succession in Respect of State Property, Archives and Debts (1983); the Vienna Convention on the Law of Treaties between States and International Organisations or Between International Organisations (1986), and see the treaties following LOSC set out in chapter IV 1.

[67] E.g., Framework Convention on Tobacco Control (21 May 2003), (2003) 42 *ILM* 520 Art. 27; Agreement for the Establishment of the Indian Ocean Tuna Commission (25 November 1993), 1927 *UNTS* 330 Art. 23; Israel-Palestine Liberation Organisation Interim Agreement on the West Bank and the Gaza Strip (28 September 1995), (1997) 36 *ILM* 551. See chapter II 1.12.

[68] UNGA Res 50/50 (1995) Annex. See chapter II.2.

[69] Permanent Court of Arbitration *Basic Documents* (1998) 153. See chapter II.2.

as well as, for conciliation under multilateral environmental agreements, the 2002 PCA Optional Rules for Conciliation of Disputes Relating to Natural Resources and/or the Environment.[70] All these rules may be referred to when a case arises, and may also be used as a general reference to be included in relevant treaties. These various model rules are helpful also in offering the help of the United Nations or the Permanent Court of Arbitration in the set-up and administration of a conciliation commission.

More caution is due regarding other wide-ranging efforts to promote conciliation by creating new procedures. The many settlement options produced by the OSCE in the early 1990s make that the appeal of any is hidden in the maze,[71] and moreover create difficulties regarding the subsidiarity or exhaustion of remedies.[72] The OSCE Court of Conciliation and Arbitration, though initially an encouraging symbol of hope, has through disuse become a lonely token of remembrance.

Plans for new conciliation institutions continue to be developed, such as the 1999 proposal for a global permanent conciliation commission by Orrego Vicuña and Pinto,[73] and the 2001 suggestion by Caflisch of a global agreement on a procedure of compulsory conciliation, which states can opt into.[74] These proposals, however, fail to acknowledge important characteristics of conciliation.[75] To be effective, conciliation commissions require the confidence of the parties. To that end, they are best composed by the parties themselves. The establishment of standing bodies which may deal with any dispute does not sit well with the *ad hoc* confidence in the conciliators that cautious parties need. The lack of practice of conciliation, and therefore the risk that, like the OSCE Court of Conciliation and Arbitration, a standing body may have nothing to do for long periods of its existence, should caution against such initiatives.

On the other hand, independent of the practice of conciliation, one could also claim that the codification of conciliation in so many agreements was a success in itself. After all, since the 1920s the new method of settlement quickly spread around the world, and involved politicians and diplomats in the elaboration of a new alternative to the politics of power. It may further be argued that particularly the existence of compulsory conciliation has helped the early settle-

---

[70] (16 April 2002) <http://www.pca-cpa.org/upload/files/ENV%20CONC.pdf> (5 October 2007). See chapter II.2.

[71] See chapter II 1.14.

[72] Idem.

[73] F. Orrego Vicuña and C. Pinto, 'The Peaceful Settlement of Disputes: Prospects for the Twenty-First Century', (1999) [106]-[108] [257]-[259]. See chapter I 3.3.3.

[74] L. Caflisch, 'Cent ans de règlement pacifique des différends interétatiques', (2001) 288 *Receuil des Cours* 245, 460.

[75] See chapter I 3.3.3.

ment of disputes, even before recourse to conciliation itself was had.[76] Such a positive effect cannot, however, be seen in practice. It can certainly be assumed that there is an advantage in the fact that politicians and diplomats negotiate a project with their foreign colleagues, but the actual development of particular settlement methods has always been the responsibility of a limited number of experts. Moreover, there is no significant evidence that agreeing in principle on diplomatic dispute settlement methods has led to pre-emptive settlement. Only in 1934, in the *France/Portugal* Case, did a unilateral application under compulsory conciliation result in a settlement by negotiation even before the commission could commence its work.[77] Further, as the situation in the Americas demonstrates, the conclusion of general dispute settlement agreements has had little effect. Seemingly without appreciating the earlier commitments made, new conventions were proposed and concluded on a regular basis, presumably on the basis of a perceived need thereto, while disputes were mostly dealt with on an *ad hoc* basis.[78]

The practice of conciliation mechanisms has made clear that there is little benefit of pre-establishing commissions. Many of the bilateral dispute settlement treaties incorporating conciliation have expired, or are now forgotten. Even where the method is included in influential multilateral treaties, the conciliation provisions themselves are dormant and therefore do not merit a permanent institution. The OSCE Court of Conciliation and Arbitration remains inactive, just as the UNESCO Conciliation and Good Offices Commission on Discrimination in Education.[79] The conciliation provisions created over the years are not in proportion to their application. Applying the method on an *ad hoc* basis, on the other hand, has had a respectable measure of success. The UN and PCA Conciliation Rules are useful instruments to facilitate *ad hoc* conciliation, when States agree that conciliation may be a useful way to settle their particular dispute. The lack of application of conciliation in inter-State disputes is not due to the lack of procedures, but due to the choices made by their potential users.

---

[76] E.g., C.P.R. Romano, *The Peaceful Settlement of Environmental Disputes* (2000) 44.

[77] H. Wehberg, 'Die Vergleichskommissionen im modernen Völkerrecht', (1958) 19 *ZfAŐRV* 551. See chapter II 1.9. Further, in ICSID conciliation, in 2005 a settlement was reached before the commission was constituted in *TG World Petroleum Limited* v. *Republic of Niger* (CONC/03/1); see chapter II 1.13.1.

[78] F. Galo Leoro, 'Peaceful Settlement of Disputes – an overview', (1994) Inter-American Juridical Committee Doc 34/94; L.R. Scheman and J.W. Ford, 'The Organisation of American States as Mediator', in S. Touval and I.W. Zartman (eds.), *International Mediation in Theory and Practice* (1985) 197.

[79] Though in 2005 an attempt was made to revive it: <http://portal.unesco.org/en/file_download.php/7c7208f1c2c1c1ec4eaea00a2ffe932bCCBO+Report.pdf> (26 July 2006). See chapter I 3.3.1.

4. The Future Use of Inter-State Conciliation

In 1972 Jean-Pierre Cot found that conciliation did not live up to the expectations surrounding its creation, but noted that it had a good record of success in dealing with relatively minor disputes.[80] In 1953, Henri Rolin had noted:

> 'Or, chose curieuse, alors que la conciliation apparaît ainsi aujour d'hui dans le droit des gens positif comme une des méthodes essentielles de règlement pacifique de litiges, il semble que dans la pratique les Etats s'abstiennent d'y recourir.'[81]

More than fifty years later, conciliation is still routinely included in international agreements, but with few new cases to its record, the overall balance appears disappointing. Orrego Vicuña recently stated to expect a significant increase in the use of diplomatic dispute settlement methods including conciliation,[82] but so far that is still an expectation.

It was pointed out above that there are many reasons why parties wish to avoid adjudication in particular cases, and that there are many cases where adjudication is simply not an available option. In addition, a range of factors was given why States may make a positive decision to employ conciliation. Parties considering conciliation may further be assisted by reviewing what type of conciliation could best suit a given dispute.

4.1 When to use political conciliation

In political conciliation, the arguments on which the commission bases its recommendations may include anything it deems may facilitate settlement. Conciliation can then be a means to avoid litigation: litigation can be a source of resentment and can therefore give rise to new conflicts.[83] The articulation of the dispute in terms of the law, also in legal conciliation, can invite the escalation of differences. On the other hand, political conciliation is clearly not suited if what is desired is an outcome on legal principle. Political conciliation invites the creation of a settlement on broader, and therefore potentially more creative grounds that the application of the law. Political conciliation is best suited for disputes where parties wish to retain a large degree of control over the process,

---

[80] *Cot* 330-331.

[81] H. Rolin, 'Une conciliation belgo-danoise', (1953) 57 *RGDIP* 353, 354.

[82] F. Orrego Vicuña, *International Dispute Settlement in an Evolving Global Society* (2004) 101.

[83] 'Rapport du Conseil fédéral à l'Assemblée fédérale concernant les traités internationaux d'arbitrage', (1919) 71 *Feuille Fédéral Suisse* Vol. V 808, 820.

and when they wish to actively think along with the conciliation commission in finding possible settlements. By being allowed to maintain their righteousness in the dispute, the parties are enabled to sacrifice their practical positions to a sufficient extent to reach a settlement: 'La conciliation permet de céder tout en laissant entière la question de principe.'[84]

Political conciliation was often, and with some success, used in conciliation of disputes involving substantial national interests, particularly issues regarding borders, such as the *Chaco* Case, and between the Dominican Republic and Haiti, between France and Siam, and between Guatemala and Belize. It is arguably the clearest alternative for the many territorial disputes brought to the ICJ against reluctant neighbours in recent years.[85] Conciliation could possibly also have served to deal with the *Beagle Channel* dispute between Argentina and Chile in the 1970s and 1980s,[86] the *Ethiopia/Eritrea* border dispute[87] or the *Cameroon/Nigeria* boundary dispute,[88] all of which were submitted to adjudication. Even though these disputes then led to binding legal determinations, these themselves led to further confrontation, owing to the reluctance of the losing party to accept the result. In the *Cameroon/Nigeria* Case, for instance, problems arose regarding the demarcation of straddling villages along the line set out by the ICJ, and the argument is made that there should be scope for more leniency and possibly for cross-border co-operation.[89]

---

84 Idem, 820.

85 E.g., *Maritime Delimitation in the Black Sea* (*Romania* v. *Ukraine*), (2004) *ICJ Rep* (pending); *Territorial and Maritime Dispute* (*Nicaragua* v. *Colombia*), (2003) *ICJ Rep*; *Maritime Delimitation between Nicaragua and Honduras in the Caribbean Sea* (*Nicaragua* v. *Honduras*), (2002) *ICJ Rep*.

86 As the 1977 Arbitral Award ((1977) 52 *ILR* 93) was rejected by Argentina (Declaration of Nullity (1978) 17 *ILM* 738)), war seemed imminent, but was averted by mediation on behalf of the Pope: E. Lauterpacht, 'Whatever Happened to the Beagle Channel Award?', in *Le droit international au service de la paix, de la justice et du développement* (1991) 359.

87 Which following a war in 1998-2000, was submitted to the Eritrea-Ethiopia Boundaries Commission and to the Eritrea-Ethiopia Boundary Commission. The Boundary Commission's Decision on Delimitation of 13 April 2002 ((2002) 41 *ILM* 1057) continues to be the object of strive and the source of threats of war. Progress Report of the Secretary-General on Ethiopia and Eritrea, UN Doc S/2005/142, 7 March 2005.

88 The judgement in the *Land and Maritime Boundary between Cameroon and Nigeria* Case (Cameroon and Nigeria; Equatorial Guinea intervening) (2002 ICJ Rep 303) gave rise to objections in implementation. Following mediation by the UN Secretary-General, a 'Mixed Commission' was established to review the issues: UNSG Statement 15 November 2002 <http://www.un.org/unowa/cnmc/preleas/sgstmts.htm#3> (5 October 2007). On 20 June 2006 Nigeria and Cameroon concluded the Agreement Concerning the Modalities of Withdrawal and Transfer of Authority in the Bakassi Peninsula <http://www.un.org/unowa/cnmc/preleas/cn_agreement.pdf> (5 October 2007).

89 G. Oduntan, 'The Demarcation of Straddling Villages in Accordance with the International Court of Justice Jurisprudence: The Cameroon-Nigeria Experience', (2006) 5 *CJIL* 79, 101.

It can obviously not be ascertained whether in these particular cases conciliation would have had more success. Adjudication clearly had a significant appeal to the parties applying for it, whether it be perceived as a positive choice or as a measure of last resort. Rather than continuing to negotiate and leaving the settlement dependent on power politics and a willingness to compromise on the other side, a binding legal determination could be thought to settle the dispute once and for all, and presumably on the basis of objective standards, objectively applied. Nevertheless, in these particular cases, the legal norms themselves appear not to carry sufficient moral or other persuasive force to ensure acquiescence by the losing party. It seems fair to say that in many territorial disputes, outcomes rather than principles are of paramount importance. At least some of the parties were evidently not ready to accept negative binding legal decisions, leading to threat of armed conflict in the event of implementation of the settlement.

In such cases, it is suggested, political conciliation, though not a panacea, by allowing for more leeway and avoiding the appearance of complete loss, could possibly have made a contribution to peace and security.[90] While also providing a formal setting devoted to finding a solution to the territorial dispute, in political conciliation it would have been possible to also take account of, for instance, the economic consequences of a certain delimitation, which in most of the mentioned cases were a significant obstacle to the acceptance of a tribunal's findings.[91] It could have been agreed, for instance, that even though one State would be awarded the territory, the other would share in the benefits. Joint development zones could also be agreed to. Conciliation would further have allowed for an exchange of territory, including any that was not subject of the dispute. If, for instance, one State attaches more value to maritime areas, and the other to agricultural plains, or one desires membership of an exclusive club to which the other belongs, exchanges and deals could be conceived. Furthermore, in political conciliation it is presumably easier for conciliators and parties to take account of important details such as the interests of straddling villages and individuals working along a contested border, than it is for the ICJ to do so, particularly when the latter has to base itself on colonial maps, and not on the current political and economic situation.

Conciliation generally, including political conciliation, does have the disadvantage that it does not guarantee that a settlement will be reached: it remains

---

[90] Cf., S.R. Ratner, 'Land Feuds and their Solutions: Finding International Law beyond the Trial Chamber', (2006) 100 *AJIL* 808, 821 ff.

[91] E.g., the *Jan Mayen* conciliation case: see chapter III 3.4.1; 'Report and Recommendations of the Conciliation Commission on the Continental Shelf Area between Iceland and Jan Mayen', June 1981, (1981) 20 *ILM* 797.

non-binding. If, however, as in the cases mentioned above, it appears that a binding legal determination also does not lead to a final settlement of the dispute, this disadvantage is of less significance. One downside more particular to political conciliation can of course be its political nature; it does not represent a shield against political pressures or against undue interference of parties not formally connected to the conciliation, such as outside regional powers. This is likely to favour the party that can call on such additional resources. If for a particular party this feature of political conciliation is seen as a determining flaw, it may still consider the use of legal conciliation.

4.2 When to use legal conciliation

An advantage of legal conciliation over political conciliation is that the recommendations of the commission can gain persuasive force, provided they clarify the application of legal principles. In the view of Van Asbeck, legal conciliation can help the parties to obtain a view of a possible outcome of litigation, so that their settlement negotiations can be better informed. All the while they would not be faced with a binding and unchangeable arbitral award,[92] and therefore keep the freedom to let themselves be persuaded by legal arguments only up to a point.

Of particular interest for conciliation regarding the application of multilateral treaties, is that law-based recommendations confirm and find support in the applicable principles. Moreover, if the recommendations issued by a commission practicing legal conciliation are made public, these can help elucidate the subject-matter of the dispute also for third parties in their relations with the conciliating parties, and among each other. In addition, by interpreting and applying any multilateral treaty norms, the exercise in conciliation to some extent also takes into account the interests of the other States Parties, even if the disputants subsequently decide to deviate from the recommendations of the commission.[93]

As in the view of Van Asbeck, legal conciliation may be similar to arbitration, with an unwavering application of the law to the issues in dispute, with the only difference being that the ruling is not binding. This is the model of the *Germany/Lithuania* Case[94] and the *France/Switzerland* Case.[95] These particu-

---

[92] F.M. van Asbeck, 'La tâche et l'action d'une commission de conciliation', (1956) *NTIR* 1, 6.

[93] See chapter IV 2.

[94] See chapter II 1.9.; H. Wehberg, 'Die Vergleichskommissionen im modernen Völkerrecht', (1958) 19 *ZfAÖRV* 551, 568.

[95] See chapter II 1.11; S. Bastid, 'La commission de conciliation franco-suisse', (1956) 2 *AFDI* 436.

lar cases to some degree concerned claims to financial compensation, and their successful resolution is likely to be due also to their technical nature, and the fact that the parties were eager to settle the dispute one way or other. The option of legal conciliation appears useful when the persuasive force of the rules trumps concerns the parties could have about the outcome, such as the height of a settlement amount, or the lack of popular support for a resolution of the dispute. Legal conciliation can also be useful when the parties have a prior commitment to adopt the commission's report, and they wish to rely on the commission to the correct legal appreciation.

The strict version of legal conciliation is however not the only option. An alternative legal approach was advocated by Rolin. In this model, the matter is to be assessed on a legal basis, but the conciliation report is not a non-binding arbitral award; it does not offer substantive legal reasoning.[96] This is what occurred for instance in the *Gorm and Svava* Case[97] and in the two *Japanese Loans* Cases.[98] One option within this model is for the commission just to state its final conclusion. Another option focuses more on the procedure, and requires the commission first to regard the range of legal views in the matter, and then only consider those that attract commission members' serious support. These legal views are then to be assessed and given relative weight, without discarding any. The commission's recommendation is then a reflection of the relative weight of competing arguments. Thus, the commission can make a recommendation on the basis of legal arguments, without giving definitive pronouncements. In this case, the parties and the commission do not rely on the persuasiveness of the rules, but rather on the authority of the commission. This authority then creates the leeway either to accept the recommendation as given, or to use this as a beacon for further negotiations, without being constrained by definitive parameters, as would be given in a reasoned legal opinion. The important difference is that in this model the commission's recommendation does not present one settlement option as the 'right' one. Parties can still negotiate a different outcome, without the necessary implication that every modification from the commission's findings is a political concession by one party to the other.

To some users, an advantage of conciliation over adjudication is that the former enables them to settle a dispute without prejudice to other disputes.[99] If

---

[96] This is different from the practice of GATT panels to submit drafts of partial reports to the parties during the proceedings, particularly because these drafts only provided a description of the facts and of the arguments, but did not include a suggested basis for settlement.

[97] H. Rolin, 'Une conciliation belgo-danoise', (1953) 57 *RGDIP* 353.

[98] Involving the Japanese government and private parties: *Japanese 4% Loan* Case, (1966) 29 *ILR* 5; *Tokyo 5% Loan* Case, (1966) 29 *ILR* 11.

[99] J.G. Merrills, *International Dispute Settlement* (4th edn. 2005) 319.

the report remains confidential, any precedential value is obviously excluded. If it does not, the closer the conciliation comes to pure legal conciliation, the more basis there will be in other cases for parties to argue that there the commission's report constitutes a form of case law.[100] Parties should therefore take this aspect into account when they agree to legal conciliation and to publishing the report.

4.3 **Other conciliation options**

The *Jan Mayen* conciliation suggests that parties may develop *ad hoc* terms of reference, which allow for deviation from the law, but only in certain respects, or only for certain reasons.[101] If one party is only willing to pragmatically settle a dispute if its special principles or interests are taken into account, the other party may accommodate this while still insisting on general applicability of the law. A similar situation may exist when, as provided for in the conciliation provisions of the OSCE Court of Conciliation and Arbitration,[102] parties recognise that in addition to legal principles, they want to take into account the particular considerations and requirements existing within their international organisation. In such situations, a fine-tuned form of conciliation can find a place as a mixture of law and politics. Such compromise options are suitable when there are specific reasons why purely legal or political proceedings would not be acceptable to one or both parties, or when insistence thereon would block a settlement of the dispute. Stipulating certain parameters expressly can also help to create confidence in the proceedings, and thereby promote the chances of success.

The flexibility of conciliation also allows for the possibility that not only disputes are submitted to it, but also mere differences. This is provided for in the 2001 ICC ADR Rules, designed for private parties.[103] As argued above, whereas a dispute requires mutually exclusive claims, a difference also encompasses conflicting views.[104] In international affairs, the possibility of referring also differences to conciliation could be a useful means of preventive diplomacy. It could allow States, for instance, to address their varying interpretations of the rights of navigation before they act on the basis of their own interpretation. It could prevent the development of the difference of opinion into a dispute, and thereby prevent scope for unilateral application for international adjudication.[105]

---

[100] See chapter III 3.4.1 and 4.7.

[101] See chapter III 3.4.1.

[102] OSCE Convention Art. 24; chapter III 3.4.2.

[103] Preamble of the 2001 ICC ADR Rules.

[104] See chapter I 1.1.

[105] E.g., LOSC Art. 286, 297(1)(a), (b).

On the other hand, by granting jurisdiction for a third party procedure such as conciliation also in the case of mere differences, there would effectively no longer be a jurisdictional threshold as to the content of the case. A State may then always contend that it has a different view, and initiate proceedings. Therefore, there would be a near infinite range of cases that could be unilaterally submitted, and this could hinder the efficient operation of diplomatic relations. For that reason, it is advisable that *if* public international instruments would create the possibility for recourse to conciliation also for differences, jurisdiction of the commission would only exist by *ad hoc* mutual consent. There is no place for compulsory conciliation of differences.

4.4 Use of conciliation and norms

There is a clear development supporting the adoption of new norms to regulate the behaviour of States, but there is not always a matching willingness to adopt binding settlement methods regarding such norms. When there is no binding mechanism under which they may be held to account, States may agree to compulsory conciliation as an alternative to adjudication.[106] If the parties then still wish to ensure to the extent possible that in disputes under the treaty the treaty norms obtain the greatest regard, they should ensure that a settlement that could emerge from conciliation between two parties is closely linked to the principles of the multilateral regime.[107] To this end, most multilateral agreements incorporating conciliation include aspects of legal conciliation.[108] Legal conciliation can promote settlement on the basis of the norms, such as by (i) the inclusion of experts in the conciliation commission; (ii) the inclusion of neutral persons who may be expected to treat the dispute objectively on the basis of applicable norms, and (iii) the mentioning of the treaty norms in the terms of reference of the commission.[109] The effect of these measures is clearly assisted if the provided dispute settlement mechanism excludes recourse to other mechanisms, and if it is compulsory, meaning that unilateral application suffices to initiate proceedings.

Remarkably, multilateral agreements normally leave out any requirement to publish the commission's report, even though such could obviously contribute to restraining parties from deviating from the commission's findings and recommendations.[110] Provided that the report of the conciliation commission is

[106] E.g., the Convention on the Law of the Sea and the Vienna Convention on the Law of Treaties: chapter III 3.2.

[107] Cf., N. Klein, *Dispute Settlement in the Convention on the Law of the Sea* (2005) 52.

[108] Idem.

[109] See chapter IV 2.

[110] Idem.

not confidential, conciliation can also help the development of principles and norms by creating a mild form of precedent.[111] By prescribing that the report of the conciliation commission is made available to the other treaty parties, they can take it into account in their subsequent practice. Further, the mechanism may be so designed that an independent treaty body supervises the settlement process, and can even block settlements that in its view do not respect the norms at issue, as was the case for instance with the European Commission of Human Rights. It such a case, however, the non-binding, consensual nature of the conciliation comes into question.

Nevertheless, from the perspective of a treaty regime, even if based on the law, a conciliated compromise contains risks. Any settlement is likely to some extent to reflect the power balance between the parties, and may thereby not just entail application of the rules. Conciliation is no alternative if unqualified application of norms is what is desired. The question is however not properly whether in the absence of an alternative anything less than strict application of the norms is acceptable, but whether a negotiated settlement may be better than no settlement at all. If settlement is preferred, forms of legal conciliation constitute a better option for regime compliance than bilateral negotiation or mediation.

Stronger norm-oriented settlement forms were found in the ECHR system and in GATT. The former European Commission of Human Rights could decide to facilitate settlement between an applicant and a respondent State, and to that end offer suggestions as to the existence, in its opinion, of a violation of the Convention. In such cases, governments were encouraged to give compensation and possibly commit to legislative or administrative changes.[112] In pre-WTO GATT, panels would not give out preliminary suggestions of legal findings during their deliberations on the merits. They would not actively support any settlement efforts by the parties.[113] GATT panels would rather produce a formal non-binding legal assessment of an allegation of violation of GATT norms. By doing so in view of the likelihood that this finding would result in a binding determination, panel reports provided a solid basis on which a settlement could be negotiated between the parties.

In the ECHR system, as throughout most of the GATT years, effectiveness was high. The Commission of Human Rights, an independent treaty body, had the power to block settlements concluded by the parties on the basis that these did not respect the treaty norms. Further, if settlement efforts did not succeed or if particular offers were not acceptable, the case could be submitted to the

[111] See chapter III 4.7.
[112] See chapter IV 3.2.
[113] See chapter IV 4.2.

Court, which has the power to issue binding legal decisions. In GATT, due to a strong belief in the system and due to communal political pressure on losing parties to abide by panel rulings, the panel reports were nearly always adopted by the higher treaty body entitled to take such binding decisions. Both systems therefore created a settlement environment strongly attached to the norms, such as in legal conciliation, but with an overarching mechanism that severely limited the consensual nature of the friendly settlement option.

Even in such a system there can be widespread criticism of settlements supposedly deviating from fundamental norms. As is suggested here, however, while the criticism may be correct in itself, sometimes, as in the ECHR's inter-State Turkey case, the friendly settlement may be worth more than a Court judgement would have been.[114] Adding diplomatic leeway to a settlement process can sometimes also produce greater benefits.

A non-compliance procedure is another norm-oriented form of diplomatic dispute settlement, offering a different way of raising the concerns of individual States and the concerns of the treaty regime concerning norm violations.[115] It relies less on application of the norms than GATT Panels and the ECHR, but the settlement process itself is more formalised, as the process of offer, negotiation and acceptance is an integral part of the proceedings. NCPs are instruments of addressing alleged deviant behaviour of one party, and use the institutions and resources of the international organisation backing the relevant multilateral treaty.[116] A multilateral standing committee investigates a case of alleged violation, and discusses an amicable settlement with the supposed transgressor. The outcome of the discussions is then submitted to the regular meeting of the parties to the treaty. Like conciliation, NCPs aim to produce an amicable solution. Often the outcome consists of a threat to rescind institutional rights, coupled with an offer of assistance by the Implementation Commission or the treaty organisation to ensure future compliance with the relevant norms.[117] NCPs also rely in part on the concern that parties display for their reputation among their peers. Consequently, NCPs will be less useful if a

[114] Report of the European Commission of Human Rights, 7 December 1985, DR 44, 31; see chapter IV 3.

[115] R.R. Churchill and G. Ulfstein, 'Autonomous Institutional Arrangements in Multilateral Environmental Agreements: A little noticed phenomenon in International Law', (2000) 94 *AJIL* 623; see chapter IV 2.

[116] M. Ehrmann, 'Procedures of Compliance Control in International Environmental Treaties', (2002) 13 *Colorado Journal of International Environmental Law and Policy* 377, 390 ff.

[117] E.g., O. Yoshida, 'Soft Enforcement of Treaties: The Montreal Protocol's Noncompliance Procedure and the Functions of Internal International Institutions', (1999) 10 *Colorado Journal of International Environmental Law and Policy* 95, 133-139; M.M. Goote, 'Noncompliance Procedures', (1999) 10 *Yearbook of International Environmental Law* 155.

party does not share such concerns. In any case, the confidentiality of the report – often a part of bilateral conciliation – has no place in NCPs.

While NCPs have many elements in common with conciliation, the aim of NCP procedures is largely different: it is not primarily to find common ground between two parties, but it is to ensure compliance by one party. To that end, NCPs rely on the involvement and political pressure of a large number of parties to the multilateral agreement, to be mobilised against one deviating party. The institutions and persons involved are not independent neutrals, they are rather jointly striving towards respect for the multilateral treaty norms. Rather than aiming for a compromise solution between the parties, based on an investigation into what would be a suitable settlement, NCPs are geared towards getting a wayward party back in line with its treaty obligations. Conciliation and non-compliance procedures are therefore essentially distinct settlement methods, in the way they are set-up, in the way they operate, and in their objectives. This distinct identity is sometimes overlooked in academic and political discussion; this may be a case in which it is useful to re-emphasise existing differences.

As NCPs, included in multilateral treaties since the 1990s, commonly coexist in these treaties with conciliation provisions, they may be thought not to affect conciliation practice. However, NCPs are explicitly designed a mixture of law and politics, and a mixture of conciliation and adjudication elements, in order to provide a settlement function targeted to improve expected non-compliance with the relevant norms. NCPs therefore pose questions that affect not only recourse to adjudication, but also the employment of conciliation.[118] In this respect, and also in light of the widespread use of NCPs in environmental treaties, they can in that field be seen as effectively overtaking any alternative as the preferred diplomatic settlement method.

It has been noted that the history of conciliation shows an excessive focus the development of new mechanisms and procedural rules. It was also commented that conciliation became increasingly dominated by jurists, who then developed the method to more closely resemble adjudication. At the same time, powerful parties developed a greater interest in ensuring implementation of certain norms, leading for instance to the increasing judicialisation of dispute settlement in the 1990s in both the European Commission of Human Rights and in GATT panels. This reduced the prominence of conciliation-like settlement mechanisms.

The replacement of successful conciliation-like practices with adjudication-like practices, just as the overshadowing of unused conciliation provisions by non-compliance procedures, should not be understood to negate the usefulness

---

118 See chapter IV 6.

of conciliation as a method. There are many instances where adjudication is not preferable, or not available, just as there are various good reasons to attempt conciliation. Furthermore, as in the case of the current European Court of Human Rights, increased reliance on courts to resolve disputes frequently brings with it such a judicial workload that calls for increased friendly settlement are likely to follow.[119]

Nonetheless, to the extent that the judicialisation of the method of conciliation, or its replacement by judicial methods, is the result of a lack of understanding of the identity and distinct contributions of conciliation, this process should be stopped. Inter-State conciliation has a distinct identity, while at the same time it can take on many forms. It offers many ways to deal with norms, and offers useful building blocks for the pragmatic development of a procedure to fit the needs of parties, and to make use of the particular abilities of those called to conciliate. The limited use of inter-State conciliation is not in itself wrong. Limited use of conciliation would only be misplaced if the procedure is misunderstood, or if it is forgotten. It is hoped that this work may contribute to the continuation and proper understanding of this method of diplomatic dispute settlement.

[119] E.g., Lord Woolf and others, 'Review of the Working Methods of the European Court of Human Rights' December 2005 <http://www.echr.coe.int/ECHR/Resources/Home/LORDWOOLFREVIEWONWORKINGMETHODS.pdf> (5 October 2007); European Commission, *Green Paper on Alternative Dispute Resolution in Civil and Commercial Law* (2002) (EC Doc COM (2002) 196).

SELECTED BILBIOGRAPHY

Abbott, K.W. and others, 'The Concept of Legalization', (2000) 54 *International Organization* 401

Abi-Saab, G., *The United Nations Operation in the Congo 1960 – 1964* (1978)

Adede, A.O., *The System for Settlement of Disputes under the United Nations Convention on the Law of the Sea* (1987)

Ahooja-Patel, K., *The Greco-Bulgarian Dispute Before the League of Nations, 1925-1927* (1974)

Akehurst, M., 'Equity and General Principles of Law', (1976) 25 *ICLQ* 801

Al-Baharna, H., 'The Fact-finding Mission of the United Nations Secretary-General and the Settlement of the Bahrain-Iran Dispute, May 1970', (1973) 22 *ICLQ* 541

Alfaro, R.J., 'Signification internationale du Congrès de Panama', in H. Accioli and others, *Hommage d'une Génération de Juristes au Président Basdevant* (1960) 10

Alfredsson, G. and R. Ring (eds.), *The Inspection Panel of the World Bank* (2001)

Ang, F. and E. Bergmand, 'Friendly Settlement and Striking Out of Applications', in P. Lemmens and W. Vandenhole (eds.), *Protocol No. 14 and the Reform of the European Court of Human Rights* (2005) 89

Anghie, A., K. Highet, and G. Kahale, 'Certain Phosphate Lands in Nauru', (1993) 87 *AJIL* 282

Arbo, H., 'Le conflit entre la Bolivie et le Paraguay à propos du Chaco Boréal', (1929) 36 *RGDIP* 528

Asbeck van, F.M., 'La procédure suivi par la commission de conciliation franco-suisse', (1956) 3 *NTIR* 209

——'La tâche et l'action d'une commission de conciliation', (1956) 3 *NTIR* 1

Badinter, R., 'La cour de conciliation et d'arbitrage au sein de l'OSCE', (1999) 1 *International Law Forum* 99

Bardonnet, D. (ed.), *Le Règlement Pacifique des Differends Internationaux en Europe: Perspectives d'Avenir* (1991)

Bartels, L., 'The Separation of Powers in the WTO: How to Avoid Judicial Activism', (2004) 53 *ICLQ* 861

Bar-Yaacov, N., *The Handling of International Disputes by Means of Inquiry* (1974)

Bastid, S., 'La commission de conciliation franco-siamoise', in C. Rousseau (ed.), *La Technique et les Principes du Droit Public: Etudes en l'Honneur de Georges Scelle* (1950) 1

——'La commission de conciliation franco-suisse', (1956) 2 *AFDI* 436

——'Une nouvelle commission de conciliation?', (1964) *Mélanges Offerts à Henri Rolin* 5

Baudenbacher, C., 'Judicialization: Can the European Model Be Exported to Other Parts of the World?', (2004) 39 *Texas International Law Journal* 381

Bederman, D.J., 'The Hague Peace Conferences of 1899 and 1907', in M.W. Janis (ed.), *International Courts for the Twenty-First Century* (1992) 9

Beekhuis, L.H., 'NAI minitrage; een welkome aanvulling', (1995) 2 *Tijdschrift voor Arbitrage* 66

Bekhechi, M.A., 'Une nouvelle étappe dans le developpement du droit international de l'environnement: la convention sur la désertification', (1997) 101 *RGDIP* 5

Bensalah, T., *L'Enquête Internationale dans le Règlement des Conflits* (1976)

Bercovitch, J., and J. Fretter, *Regional Guide to International Conflict Management from 1945 to 2003* (2004)

Berger, V., 'Le règlement amiable devant la Cour européenne des droits de l'homme', in F. Matscher and H. Petzold (eds.), *Protecting Human Rights: The European Dimension* (1988) 55

Beyerlin, U., 'Pactum de Contrahendo und Pactum de Negotiando im Völkerrecht?', (1976) 36 *ZfAŐRV* 407

——, P.-T. Stoll and R. Wolfrum (eds.), *Ensuring Compliance with Multilateral Environmental Agreements: Academic Analysis and Views from Practice* (2006)

Bien, W.J., 'The Oslo Channel: Benefits of a Neutral Facilitator to Secret Negotiations', in M.C. Greenberg, J.H. Barton and M.E. McGuiness (eds.), *Words over War* (2000)

Bilder, R.B., 'The Settlement of Disputes in the Field of the International Law of the Environment', (1975) 144 *Recueil des Cours* Vol. I 139

——'International Third Party Dispute Settlement', (1989) 17 *Denver Journal of International Law and Policy* 475

——and O. Young, 'Book Review: 'The Collapse of the Kyoto Protocol and the Struggle to Slow Global Warming'', (2002) 96 *AJIL* 736

Bindschedeler, R., 'Report', in Max Planck Institut (ed.), *Judicial Settlement of International Disputes – An International Symposium* (1974)

Birnie, P.C., and A.E. Boyle, *International Law and the Environment* (2nd edn. 2002)

Blix, H., 'The Principle of Peaceful Settlement of Disputes', in M.K. Nawaz and others, *The Legal Principles Governing Friendly Relations and Co-operation Among States* (1966) 45

——*Disarming Iraq: The Search for Weapons of Mass Destruction* (2004)

Bodansky, D., J.R. Cook, and E. Brown Weiss, 'Invoking State Responsibility in the Twenty-First Century', (2002) 96 *AJIL* 798

Boeg, N.V., 'Le différend dano-belge au sujet des navires danois 'Gorm' et 'Svava'', (1953) 23 *Acta Scandinavica Juris Gentium* 48

Boisson de Chazournes, L., 'Compliance with Operational Standards: The Contribution of the Word Bank Inspection Panel', in G. Alfredsson and R. Ring (eds.), *The Inspection Panel of the World Bank* (2001) 67

——'Water and Economics: Trends in Dispute Settlement and Practice', in E. Brown Weiss, L. Boisson de Chazournes and N. Bernasconi-Osterwalder (eds.), *Fresh Water and International Economic Law* (2005) 333

Bolla, P., 'Quelques considérations sur les commissions de conciliation prévues par l'article 83 du traité de paix avec l'Italie', in F.M. van Asbeck (ed.) , *Symbolae Verzijl* (1958) 67

Bothe, M., and others (eds.), *The OSCE in the Maintenance of Peace and Security* (1997)

Bourloyannis, M.C., 'Fact-finding by the Secretary-General of the United Nations', (1990) 22 *NYUJILP* 641

Boutros Ghali, B., *An Agenda for Peace*, UN Doc A/47/277(1992)

Bowett, D.W., 'Contemporary Developments in Legal Techniques in the Settlement of Disputes', (1983) 180 *Recueil des Cours* Vol. II 169

Boyle, A.E., 'Saving the World: Implementation and Enforcement of International Environmental Law Through International Institutions', (1991) 3 *Environmental Law* 229

——'Dispute Settlement and the Law of the Sea Convention: Problems of Fragmentation and Jurisdiction', (1997) 46 *ICLQ* 37

Brehio, A., 'Good Offices of the Secretary-General as Preventive Measures', (1998) 30 *NYUJILP* 589

Breton-Jokl, M., 'La commission permanente de conciliation italo-suisse', (1957) *AFDI* 210

Brierly, J.L., 'The General Act of Geneva, 1928', (1930) 11 *BYIL* 19

Broches, A., 'The Convention on the Settlement of Investment Disputes between States and Nationals of Other States', (1972) 136 *Recueil des Cours* Vol. II 330

——'The Experience of the International Centre for the Settlement of Investment Disputes', in S. Rubin and R. Nelson (eds.), *International Investment Disputes: Avoidance and Settlement* (1985) 75

Broms, B., 'The Declaration on the Peaceful Settlement of International Disputes (Manilla)', in J. Makarczyk, *Essays in Honour of Judge Manfred Lachs* (1984) 339

Brower, C.F., 'Evidence before International Tribunals: The Need for Some Standard Rules', (1994) 28 *International Lawyer* 47

Brown, C., 'The Settlement of Disputes Arising in Flexibility Mechanism Transactions under the Kyoto Protocol', (2005) 21 *Arbitration International* 361

Brown, H.J. and A.L. Marriott, *ADR Principles and Practice* (2nd edn. 1999)

Brown Scott, J., (ed.), *The Hague Conventions and Declarations of 1899 and 1907* (1915)

——(ed.), *The Hague Court Reports* (1916)

——(ed.), *The Reports of the Hague Conferences of 1899 and 1907* (1917)

——(ed.), *The Proceedings of the Hague Peace Conferences; The Conference of 1899* (1920) 797-800

——(ed.), *Treaties for the Advancement of Peace* (1920)

——(ed.) , *The Hague Court Reports* (1932) Second Series

Brown Weiss, E. (ed.), *International Compliance with Nonbinding Accords* (1997)

——'Conclusions: Understanding Compliance with Soft Law', in D. Shelton (ed.), *Commitment and Compliance: The Role of Non-Binding Norms in the International Legal System* (2000) 535

Brownlie, I., *International Law and the Use of Force by States* (1963)

——'The Justiciability of Disputes and Issues in International Relations', (1967) 42 *BYIL* 123

——*Principles of Public International Law* (5th edn. 1998)

——'Why do States Take Disputes to the International Court?', in N. Ando and others (eds.), *Liber Amicorum Judge Shigeru Oda* (2002) 829

——*Principles of Public International Law* (6th edn. 2003)

Brus, M.M.T.A., *Third Party Dispute Settlement in an Interdependent World* (1995)

Bührig-Uhle, C., *Arbitration and Mediation in International Business* (1996)

Busch, M.L. and E. Reinhardt, 'Bargaining in the Shadow of the Law: Early Settlement in GATT/WTO Disputes', (2001) 24 *Fordham International Law Journal* 158

Butler, W.E., 'The Hague Permanent Court of Arbitration', in M.W. Janis (ed.), *International Courts for the Twenty-First Century* (1992) 43

Cabral Barretto, I., 'Le règlement amiable devant la Cour européenne des droits de l'homme', (2002) *Bulletin des Droits de l'Homme* (10) 27

Caflisch, L., 'The OSCE Court of Conciliation and Arbitration: Some Facts and Issues', in M. Bothe and others (eds.), *The OSCE in the Maintenance of Peace and Security* (1997) 381

——'La subsidiarité des méchanismes de la Convention de 1992', in L. Caflish (ed.), *The Peaceful Settlement of Disputes between States: Universal and European Perspectives* (1998) 55

——'Cent ans de règlement pacifique des différends interétatiques', (2001) 288 *Receuil des Cours* 245

Cairns, D.J.A. and I. Madalena, 'The ICC Dispute Board Rules', (2005) 8 *International Arbitration Law Review* 41

Caller, R. (ed.), *ADR and Commercial Disputes* (2002)

Cameron, J., and K. Campbell (eds.), *Dispute Resolution in the World Trade Organization* (1998)

Canal-Forgues, E., *L'Institution de la Conciliation dans le Cadre du GATT* (1990)

——and R. Ostrihansky, 'New Developments in the GATT Dispute Settlement Procedures', (1990) 24 *Journal of World Trade* (2) 67

Cassar, A., 'Introductory Note to OSPAR/UNCLOS: Mox Plant Award and Order', (2003) 42 *ILM* 1116

Chan, P.C.W., 'Acquiescence/Estoppel in International Boundaries: Temple of *Preah Vihear* Revisited', (2004) 3 *CJIL* 421

Charney, J.I. and L.M. Alexander, *International Maritime Boundaries* (1993)

——'Maritime Delimitation in the Area between Greenland and Jan Mayen', (1994) 88 *AJIL* 105

——'Progress in International Maritime Boundary Delimitation Law', (1994) 88 *AJIL* 227

——'Compliance with International Soft Law', in D. Shelton (ed.), *Commitment and Compliance: The Role of Non-Binding Norms in the International Legal System* (2000) 115

——'The Implications of Expanding International Dispute Settlement Systems: The 1982 Convention on the Law of the Sea', (1996) 90 *AJIL* 69

Charpentier, J., 'Article 2 Paragraphe 3', in J.P. Cot and A. Pellet, *La Charte des Nations Unies; Commentaire Article par Article* (1985) 103

Chayes, A. and A. Handler Chayes, *The New Sovereignty* (1995)

Cheng, B., 'Justice and Equality in International Law', (1955) 8 *Current Legal Problems* 185

Chesterman, S.A., *Just War or Just Peace?* (2000)

——*Secretary or General? The UN Secretary-General in World Politics* (2007)

Chicot, P.Y., 'L'Actualité du principe du réglement pacifique des différends: essai de contribution juridique à la notion de paix durable', (2003) *Revue Québécoise de Droit International* 5

Chigas, D., 'Negotiating Intractable Conflicts: The Contributions of Unofficial Intermediaries', in C.A. Crocker, F. Osler Hampson and P. Aall (eds.), *Grasping the Nettle: Analyzing Cases of Intractable Conflict* (2005) 123

Chinkin, C.M., 'Third Party Intervention before the International Court of Justice', (1986) 80 *AJIL* 495

——'Alternative Dispute Resolution under International Law', in M. Evans (ed.), *Remedies in International Law: The Institutional Dilemma* (1998) 123

Chroestjtsjov, N., *De Glasnost Tapes* (J.L. Schecter and V.V. Loetsjkov (eds.), Dutch trans.) (1990)

Chua, A., 'Precedent and Principles of WTO Panel Jurisprudence', (1998) 16 *Berkeley Journal of International Law* 171

Churchill R.R., 'Maritime Delimitation in the Jan Mayen Area', (1985) 9 *Marine Policy* 16

——and A.V. Lowe, *The Law of the Sea* (3rd edn. 1999)

——and G. Ulfstein, 'Autonomous Institutional Arrangements in Multilateral Environmental Agreements: A Little Noticed Phenomenon in International Law', (2000) 94 *AJIL* 623

Clark, G. and L.B. Sohn, *World Peace through World Law* (3rd edn. 1960)

Cohen, J., *Conflict Prevention in the OSCE: An Assessment of Capacities* (1999)

Collier, J.G., 'The International Court of Justice and the Peaceful Settlement of Disputes', in A.V. Lowe and M. Fitzmaurice (eds.), *Fifty Years of the International Court of Justice* (1996) 364

——and A.V. Lowe, *The Settlement of Disputes in International Law* (1999)

Colson, D.A. and P. Hoyle, 'Satisfying the Procedural Prerequisites to the Compulsory Settlement Mechanisms of the 1982 Law of the Sea Convention: Did the *Southern Bluefin Tuna* Tribunal Get it Right?', (2003) 34 *Ocean Development & International Law* 59

Conwell-Evans, T.P., *The League Council in Action* (1929)

Coombe, G.W., 'The Resolution of Transnational Commercial Disputes: A Perspective from North-America', (1999) 5 *Annual Survey of International and Comparative Law* 13

Cot, J.P., *La Conciliation Internationale* (1968)

——*International Conciliation* (English trans. 1972)

Council of Europe, *Protocole No. 11 à la Convention de Sauveguarde des Droits de l'Homme et des Libertés Fondamentales et Rapport Explicatif* [brochure] (1994)

Craig, P. and G. de Búrca, *EU Law: Text, Cases and Materials* (3rd edn. 2002)

Craik, A.N., 'Recalcitrant Reality and Chosen Ideals: The Public Function of Dispute Settlement in International Environmental Law', (1998) 210 *Georgetown International Environmental Law Review* 551

Crawford, J., J. Peel, and S. Olleson, 'The ILC's Articles on Responsibility of States for Internationally Wrongful Acts: Completion of the Second Reading', (2001) 12 *EJIL* 963

Crnic-Grotic, V., 'Object and Purpose of Treaties in the Vienna Convention on the Law of Treaties', (1997) 7 *Asian Yearbook of International Law* 141

Crocker, C., F.O. Hampson, and P. Aall (eds.), *Herding Cats: Multilateral Mediation in a Complex World* (1999)

Dalgaard-Knudsen, F., 'The Greenlandic Offshore Area', (1992) 5 *New York International Law Review* 63

Dallier, P., and A. Pellet, *Droit International Public* (1999)

Davey, W.J., 'The WTO Dispute Settlement System: The First Ten Years', (2005) 8 *Journal of International Economic Law* 17

Davies, W. and P. Fouracre (eds.), *The Settlement of Disputes in Early Mediaeval Europe* (1986)

Degan, V.D., 'International Conciliation: Its Past and Future', in P. Fischer, H.F. Köck, and A. Verdross, *Völkerrecht und Rechtsfilosofie* (1980) 261

Dholakia, A., *The Role of Mediation in Resolving India-Pakistan Conflict: Parameters and Possibilities* (2005)

Donner, R., 'The Procedure of International Conciliation: Some Historical Aspects', (1999) 1 *Journal of the History of International Law* 103

Dore, I.I., *Arbitration and Conciliation under the UNCITRAL Rules: A Textual Analysis* (1986)

——*The UNCITRAL Framework for Arbitration in Contemporary Perspective* (1993)

Downs, G.W., D.M. Rocke and P.N. Barsoom, 'Is the Good News About Compliance Good News About Cooperation?', (1996) 50 *International Organization* 379

Dreher, M.E., *Die Institution der Guten Dienste im Völkerrecht* (1980)

Drzemczewski, A., 'A Major Overhaul of the European Human Rights Convention Control Mechanism: Protocol No. 11', in Academy of European Law (ed.), 6 *Collected Courses of the Academy of European Law* (1995) Vol. 2

Dworkin, R.M., *Law's Empire* (1986)

Efremoff, J., 'La conciliation internationale', (1927) *Recueil des Cours* Vol. III 18

——'L'Organisation de la conciliation comme moyen de prevenir des guerres', (1937) 59 *RCADI* 99

Ehrmann, M., 'Procedures of Compliance Control in International Environmental Treaties', (2002) 13 *Colorado Journal of International Environmental Law and Policy* 377

Elias, T.O., 'The Commission of Mediation, Conciliation and Arbitration of the Organization of African Unity', (1964) 40 *BYIL* 336

Emory, R.W., 'Probing the Protections in the Rotterdam Convention on Prior Informed Consent', (2000) *Colorado Journal of International Environmental Law and Policy* 47

European Commission, *Green Paper on Alternative Dispute Resolution in Civil and Commercial Law* (2002)

European Bank for Reconstruction and Development, *Independent Recourse Mechanism: Guide to Making a Complaint About an EBRD-financed Project* (2004)

Evans, M.D., *Relevant Circumstances and Maritime Delimitation* (1989)

——'Case Concerning Maritime Delimitation in the Area between Greenland and Jan Mayen', (1994) 43 *ICLQ* 697

——'Less than an Ocean Apart: The St Pierre and Miquelon and Jan Mayen Islands and the Delimitation of Maritime Zones', (1994) 43 *ICLQ* 678

Evensen, J., 'La délimitation du plateau continental entre la Norvège et l'Islande dans le secteur de Jan Mayen', (1980) 26 *AFDI* 711

Eyffinger, A., *The International Court of Justice 1946-1996* (1996)

——*The 1899 Hague Peace Conference* (1999)

——'A Highly Critical Moment: Role and Record of the 1907 Hague Peace Conference', (2007) 54 *NILR* 197

Ezeizaberrana, X., 'The Role of the International Court of Environmental Arbitration and Conciliation', in M.-C. Cordonier Seggar and C.G. Weeramantry (eds.), *Sustainable Justice: Reconciling Economic, Social and Environmental Law* (2005) 506

Fawcett, L. and A. Hurrell (eds.), *Regionalism in World Politics* (1995)

Fenwick, C.G., 'Revision of the Pact of Bogotá', (1954) 48 *AJIL* 123

Fischer Williams, J., 'Justiciable and Other Disputes', (1932) 26 *AJIL* 31

Fisher, T.C., 'A Commentary on Regional Institutions in the Pacific Rim: Do APEC and ASEAN Still Matter?', (2003) 13 *Duke Journal of Comparative and International Law* 337

Fitzmaurice, M., 'Consent to Be Bound – Anything New under the Sun?', (2005) 74 *Nordic Journal of International Law* 483

——and C. Redgwell, 'Environmental Non-compliance Procedures and International Law', (2000) 31 *NYIL* 35

Footer, M.E., 'The Role of Consensus in GATT/WTO Decision Making', (1996/1997) 17 *Northwestern Journal of International Law and Business* 653

Forsythe, D.P., *United Nations Peacemaking – The Conciliation Commission for Palestine* (1972)

Francioni, F., 'International "Soft Law" a Contemporary Assessment', in V. Lowe and M. Fitzmaurice (eds.), *Fifty Years of the International Court of Justice* (1996) 161

Franck, T.M., *The Power of Legitimacy Among Nations* (1990)

——*Fairness in International Law and Institutions* (1995)

——and H.S. Fairley, 'Procedural Due Process in Human Rights Fact-Finding by International Agencies', (1980) 74 *AJIL* 308

François, J.P.A., 'La Cour Permanente d'Arbitrage', (1955) 87 *Recueil des Cours* 456

——'Le Palais de la Paix en 1956', (1957) 4 *NTIR* 69

Frowein, J.A., 'Die Verpflichtungen erga omnes im Völkerrecht und ihre Durchsetzung', in R. Bernhardt and others, (1983) *Völkerrecht als Rechtsordnung Internationale Gerichtsbarkeit Menschenrechte: Festschrift für Hermann Mosler*, 241

Frumer, P., *La Renonciation aux Droits et Libertés: La Convention Européenne des Droits de l'Homme à l'Epreuve de la Volonté Individuelle* (2001)

Fuerle, L., 'Informal Consultation: A Mechanism in Security Council Decision Making', (1985) 18 *NYUJILP* 267

Fullilove, M., 'All the Presidents' Men: The Role of Special Envoys in U.S. Foreign Policy', (2005) 84 *Foreign Affairs* (2) 12

Galo Leoro, F., 'Peaceful Settlement of Disputes – An Overview', (1994) Inter-American Juridical Committee, Doc. 34/94

Geamanu, G., 'Théorie et pratique des négociations en droit international', (1980) 166 *Receuil des Cours* 369

Gehring, T., 'International Environmental Regimes: Dynamic Sectoral Legal Systems', (1990) 1 *Yearbook of International Environmental Law* 35

Ghozali, N., 'La négociation diplomatique dans la jurisprudence internationale', (1992) *Revue Belge de Droit International* 323

Gold, J., 'Book Review', (1984) 24 *Virginia Journal of International Law* 729

Gonzalez-Calatayud, A. and G. Marceau, 'The Relationship between the Dispute-Settlement Mechanisms of MEAs and those of the WTO', (2002) 11 *RECIEL* 275

Goodrich, L.M., E. Hambro, and A.P. Simons, *Charter of the United Nations; Commentary and Documents* (3rd rev edn. 1969)

Goote, M.M., 'Non-Compliance Procedures in International Environmental Law: The Middle Way between Diplomacy and Law', (1999) 1 *International Law Forum* 82

——'Noncompliance Procedures', (1999) 10 *Yearbook of International Environmental Law* 155

Gorgé, C., 'L'Evolution de la conciliation internationale', (1927) 54 *RDILC* 58

Götzand, V., and others (eds.), *Liber Amicorum Günther Jaenicke – Zum 85. Geburtstag* (1998)

Gowlland Debbas, V., 'The Relationship between the International Court of Justice and the Security Council in the light of the Lockerbie Case', (1994) 88 *AJIL* 643

Gowlland Gualtieri, A., 'The Environmental Accountability of the World Bank to Non-State Actors: Insights from the Inspection Panel', (2001) 72 *BYIL* 213

Gray, K.R., 'Eleventh Meeting of the Conference of the Parties to the *United Nations Framework Convention on Climate Change*/First Meeting of the

Parties to the *Kyoto Protocol*', (2006) 10 *ASIL Insight* 8 (electronic, 3 April 2006)
Greenberg, M., J. Barton, and M. McGuinness (eds.), *Words over War* (2000)
Gros, A., 'Remarques sur la conciliation internationale', in *L'Evolution du Droit Public; Etudes Offertes à Achille Mestre* (1956) 279
Grotius, H., *De Jure Belli ac Pacis* (1625)
Guggenheim, P., 'Völkerrecht', (1950) 7 *ASDI* 123
——'Droit international public', (1954) 11 *ASDI* 173
Guzman, A.T., 'The Design of International Agreements', (2005) 16 *EJIL* 579
Habicht, M., *Post-War Treaties for the Pacific Settlement of International Disputes* (1931)
——*The Power of the International Judge to Give a Decision "Ex aequo et bono"* (1935)
Hackworth, G.H., *Digest of International Law* (1940-1944) Vol. I-VIII
Haersolte–Van Hof, J.J. van, 'The Revitalization of the Permanent Court of Arbitration', (2007) 54 *NILR* 395
Hafner, G., 'Bemühungen um ein gesamteuropäisches Streitbeilegungssystem im Rahmen der KSZE', in K. Böckstiegel and others (eds.), *Völkerrecht, Recht der Internationalen Organisationen, Weltwirtschaftsrecht* (1988) 147
Hamilton, P. and others (eds.), *The Permanent Court of Arbitration: International Arbitration and Dispute Resolution* (1999)
Hamilton, S., 'ICC Conciliation: A Glimpse into History', (2001) *ICC International Court of Arbitration Bulletin Special Supplement* 23
Hampson, F.O., *Multilateral Negotiations* (1995)
Hamzeh, F.S., *International Conciliation with Special Reference to the Work of the United Nations Conciliation Commission for Palestine* (1963)
——*United Nations Commission for Palestine 1949-1967* (1968)
Hanotiau, B., 'Arbitrage, médiation, conciliation: approches d'Europe continentale et de common law', (1996) 1 *Revue de Droit des Affaires Internationales* 203
Harris, D.J., M. O'Boyle, C. Warbrick, *Law of the European Convention on Human Rights* (1995)
Harris, J.W., *Legal Philosophies* (2nd edn. 1997)
Hart, H.L.A., *Concept of Law* (2nd edn. 1994)
Hermann, G., 'Commentary on the UNCITRAL Conciliation Rules', (1981) 6 *Yearbook of Commercial Arbitration* 170
Higgins, R., 'Policy Considerations and the International Judicial Process', (1968) 17 *ICLQ* 58
——'International Law and the Avoidance, Containment and Resolution of Disputes', (1991) 230 *Recueil des Cours* 9

——'Presentation of the Topic', in *United Nations International Law as a Language for International Relations* (1996) 111
Hill, C.E., *Danish Sound Dues* (1926)
Hirsch, M, *The Arbitration Mechanism of the International Centre for the Settlement of Disputes* (1993)
Hoijer, O., *La Solution Pacifique des Litiges Internationaux: Avant et Depuis la Société des Nations* (1925)
Holbrooke, R., *To End a War* (1998)
Holtzmann, H.M., 'Dispute Resolution in Europe under the UNCITRAL Conciliation Rules', in D. Bardonnet (ed.), *Le Règlement Pacifique des Differends Internationaux en Europe: Perspectives d'Avenir* (1991)
Horchani, F. (ed.), *Règlement Pacifique des Différends Internationaux* (2002)
Horlick, G.N., 'Problems with the Compliance Structure of the WTO Dispute Resolution Process', in D.L.M. Kennedy and J.D. Southwick (eds.), *The Political Economy of International Trade Law* (2002) 636
Horn, N., 'Außergerichtliche Streitbeilegung bei internationalen Finanzgeschäften. Eine Bestandsaufnahme', in K.P. Berger and others (eds.), *Festschrift für Otto Sandrock zum 70. Geburtstag* (2000) 385
Hostie, J., 'Différends justiciables et non-justiciables', 55 *RDILC* 263
Huber, K.J., 'Preventing Conflict in the New Europe The CSCE High Commissioner on National Minorities', in I.M. Cuthbertson and J. Liebowitz (eds.), *Minorities: The New Europe's Old Issue* (1993)
Hudec, R., *Enforcing International Trade Law: The Evolution of the Modern GATT Legal System* (1993)
Hudson, M.O., 'The Members of the League of Nations', (1935) 16 *BYIL* 130
——*International Tribunals: Past and Future* (1944)
Hughes, V., 'Accomplishments of the WTO Dispute Settlement Mechanism', in Y. Taniguchi, A. Yanovich and J. Bohanes, *The WTO in the Twenty-First Century* (2007) 185
Hume, C.R., *Ending Mozambique's Civil War: The Role of Mediation and Good Offices* (1994)
Hunter, D., 'Using the World Bank Inspection Panel to Defend the Interests of Project-Affected People', (2003) 4 *Chicago Journal of International Law* 201
Hurewitz, J.C., 'The United Nations Conciliation Commission for Palestine: Establishment and Definition of Functions', (1953) 7 *International Organization* 482
Hyde, C.C., 'Commissions of Conciliation and the Locarno Treaties', (1926) 20 *AJIL* 103
——'The Place of Commissions of Inquiry and Conciliation Treaties in the Peaceful Settlement of Disputes', (1929) 10 *BYIL* 96

Iklé, F.C., *How Nations Negotiate* (1964)
International Law Association, *Report on the Fifty-Third Conference* (1968)
Imobighe, T.A., *The OAU and the OAS in Regional Conflict Management: A Comparative Assessment* (2003)
Iwasawa, Y., 'Settlement of Disputes concerning the WTO Agreement: Various Means other than Panel Procedures', in M.K. Young and Y. Iwasawa (eds.), *Trilateral Perspectives on International Legal Issues* (1996) 377
Jackson, J.H., *The World Trade Organisation: Constitution and Jurisprudence* (1998)
——'The Legal Meaning of a GATT Dispute Settlement Report: Some Reflections', in N. Blokker and S. Muller (eds.), *Towards More Effective Supervision by International Organisations* 149
Jacobi, S., 'Subsidiarity and Other Obstacles to the Use for the OSCE Dispute Settlement Procedures', in M. Bothe and others (eds.), *The OSCE in the Maintenance of Peace and Security* (1997) 425
Jacquet, J.M., 'La loi-type de la CNUDCI du 24 juin 2002 sur la conciliation commerciale internationale', (2004) *Revue de l'Arbitrage* 1
Jaenicke, G., 'Dispute Settlement Under the Convention on the Law of the Sea', (1983) 43 *ZfAŐRV* 813
Janis, M., 'Equity in International Law' *Encyclopaedia of Public International Law* (1995) Vol. 2
Jenks, W., *The Prospects of International Adjudication* (1964)
Jennings, R.Y., 'Equity and Equidistance Principles' (1986), *Annuaire Suisse de Droit International* 27
——and A. Watts, *Oppenheim's International Law* (9th edn. 1992)
Kahn, P., 'Nuclear Weapons and the Rule of Law', (1999) 31 *NYUJILP* 349
Kearney, R.D. and R.E. Dalton, 'The Treaty on Treaties', (1970) 64 *AJIL* 495
Kelly, C.R., 'Enmeshment as a Theory of Compliance', (2005) 37 *NYUJILP* 303
Kelsen, H., *Reine Rechtslehre* (2nd edn. 1960)
Kennedy, R.F., *Thirteen Days* (1971)
King, H.T. and M.A. Le Forestier, 'Arbitration in Ancient Greece', (1994) 38 *Dispute Resolution Journal* 49
——and M.A. Le Forestier, 'Origins of Modern International Arbitration', (1996) 51 *Dispute Resolution Journal* 42
——and M.A. Le Forestier, 'Papal Arbitration', (1997) 52 *Dispute Resolution Journal* 74
Kingsbury, B., 'Operational Policies of International Institutions as Part of the Law-Making Process: The World Bank and Indigenous Peoples', in G. Goodwin-Gill and S. Talmon (eds.), *The Reality of International Law; Essays in Honour of Ian Brownlie* (1999) 323

Kirgis, F.L., *Prior Consultation* (1983)

Kiss, A.C., 'Conseil de l'Europe', (1955) 1 *AFDI* 425

——'Conciliation', in R. St. James Macdonald and others (eds.), *The European System for the Protection of Human Rights* (1993) 703

——and D. Shelton *International Environmental Law* (3rd edn. 2004)

Klein, N., *Dispute Settlement in the UN Convention on the Law of the Sea* (2005)

Koester, V., 'The Five Global Biodiversity-Related Conventions: A Stocktaking', (2002) 11 *Review of European Community and International Environmental Law* 96

Kolb, R., 'Note sur certaines caractéristiques du différend international', 1 *The Global Community* (2004) 227

Komuro, N., 'The WTO Dispute Settlement Mechanism – Coverage and Procedures of the WTO DSU', (1995) 29 *Journal of World Trade* (4) 5

Kooijmans, P.H., 'International Arbitration in Historical Perspective: Past and Present', in A.H.A. Soons (ed.), *International Arbitration: Past and Prospects* (1990) 23

Koopmans, S.M.G., 'The PCA in the Field of Conciliation and Mediation: New Perspectives and Approaches', in Permanent Court of Arbitration (ed.), *International Alternative Dispute Resolution: Past, Present and Future* (2000) 67

——'Minitrage: Het nut van een alternatief voor mediation en arbitrage', (2003) 78 *Nederlands Juristenblad* 1070

——'De onbekende en genereuze bescherming van Nederlandse investeringen in het buitenland', (2006) 81 *Nederlands Juristenblad* 74

Koroma, A.G., 'The Peaceful Settlement of International Disputes', (1996) 43 *NILR* 227

Koskenniemi, M., 'Breach of Treaty or Non-Compliance? Reflections on the Enforcement of the Montreal Protocol', (1993) 3 *Yearbook of International Environmental Law* 123

Kozyris, P.J., 'Lifting the Veils of Maritime Entitlements: Equidistance with Proportionality around the Islands', (1998) 26 *Denver Journal of International Law and Policy* 319

Krüger, H.C. and C.A. Nørgaard, 'Reflections Concerning Friendly Settlement under the European Convention on Human Rights', in F. Matscher and H. Petzold (eds.), *Protecting Human Rights: The European Dimension* (1988) 329

Kunz, J.L., 'International Arbitration in Pan American Developments', (1948) 27 *Texas Law Review* 182

Kusumowidagdo, J.U., *Consultation Clauses as a Means of Providing for Treaty Obedience* (1981)

Kwiatowska, B., 'The Southern Bluefin Tuna Arbitral Tribunal Did Get It Right: A Commentary and Reply to the Article by D.A. Colson and P. Hoyle', (2003) 34 *Ocean Development & International Law* 369

Lachs, M., 'International Law, Mediation, and Negotiation' *Multilateral Negotiation and Mediation: Instruments and Methods*, reprinted in M.E. O'Connell, *International Dispute Settlement* (2003) 55

Lagergren, G., 'The Taba Tribunal, 1986-89', (1989) 1 *RADIC* 525

Lall, A., *Modern International Negotiation* (1966)

Langeland, E., 'The Viability of Conciliation in International Dispute Resolution', (1995) 50 *Dispute Resolution Journal* 34

Lantané, J.H., *Development of the League of Nations Idea; Documents and Correspondence of Theodore Marburg* (1932) Vols. I, II

Lapidoth, R., 'Equity in International Law', (1987) 22 *Israel Law Review* 165

——'Some Reflections on the Taba Award', (1992) 35 *GYIL* 224

——'Dispute Settlement under the 1997 Convention on the Law of the Non-navigational Uses of International Watercourses', in M.N. Schmitt (ed.), *International Law Across the Spectrum of Conflict* (2000) 231

Lauterpacht, E., 'The Taba Case; Some Recollections and Reflections', (1989) 23 *Israel Law Review* 443

——'Whatever Happened to the Beagle Channel Award?', in *Le Droit International au Service de la Paix, de la Justice et du Développement* (1991) 359

——*Aspects of the Administration of International Justice* (1991)

Lauterpacht, H., *The Function of Law in the International Community* (1933)

——*Oppenheim's International Law* (7th edn. 1952) Vol. II

——'Non Liquet and the Completeness of the Law', in F.M. Van Asbeck (ed.), *Symbolae Verzijl* (1958) 196

Lavalle, R., 'Dispute Settlement under the Vienna Convention of Succession of States', (1979) 73 *AJIL* 407

——'The Amicable Dispute Settlement Scheme Brought to the Attention of States by the United Nations General Assembly in 1989: A Critical Commentary', (1991) 42 *Austrian Journal of Public International Law* 163

——'Conciliation under the United Nations Convention on the Law of the Sea: A Critical Overview', (1997) 2 *Austrian Review of International and European Law* 25

Leach, P., *Taking a Case to the European Court of Human Rights* (2nd edn. 2005)

Lee, J.K., 'Non-binding Dispute Resolution Process- Experience in Korea', in International Council for Commercial Arbitration *New Horizons in International Commercial Arbitration and Beyond* (2005) 430

Lee, R.S., 'Multilateral Treaty-Making and Negotiation Techniques: An Appraisal', in Cheng B. and E.D. Brown (eds.), *Contemporary Problems of International* Law (1988) 157

——'A Case for Facilitation in the Settlements of Disputes', (1991) 34 *GYIL* 138

Leitner, K., and S. Lester, 'WTO Dispute Settlement 1995-2004: A Statistical Analysis', (2005) 8 *Journal of International Economic Law* 231

Lenk, A., 'Fact-Finding as Peace Negotiation Tool – The Mitchell Report and the Israeli-Palestinian Peace Process', (2002) 24 *Loyola of Los Angeles International & Comparative Law Review* 289

Leoro, G., 'Peaceful Settlement of Disputes – An Overview', (1994) Inter-American Juridical Committee, OAS Doc CJI/SO/II doc 34.94

Lew, J.D.M., 'Multi-Institutional Conciliation and the Reconciliation of Different Legal Cultures', International Council for Commercial Arbitration, *New Horizons in International Commercial Arbitration and Beyond* (2005) 421

Leweler, J.K., 'International Commercial Arbitration as a Model for Resolving Treaty Disputes', (1989) 21 *NYUJILP* 379

Long, O., *Law and its Limitations in the GATT Multilateral Trade System* (1985)

Lowe, A.V. and C. Warbrick (eds.), *The United Nations and the Principles of Public International Law* (1994)

Lowenfeld, A.F., 'Remedies Along with Rights: Institutional Reform in the New GATT', (1994) 88 *AJIL* 477

Mackie, K.J., 'Mini-trials and Executive Tribunals in Practice', (1995) 3 *Tijdschrift voor Arbitrage* 132

MacMillan, M., *Peacemakers* (2001)

Madhava Sharma, K., 'Compliance with the Multilateral Environmental Agreements to Protect the Ozone Layer', in U. Beyerlin, P.-T. Stoll and R. Wolfrum, *Ensuring Compliance with Multilateral Environmental Agreements: Academic Analysis and Views from Practice* (2006) 25

Mandelstam, A., 'La commission internationale d'enquête', (1905) 12 *RGDIP* 161

Manga Fombad, C., 'Consultation and Negotiation in the Pacific Settlement of International Disputes', (1989) 1 *RADIC* 707

Mangoldt von, H., 'Arbitration and Conciliation', in H. Mosler and R. Bernhardt (eds.), *Judicial Settlement of International Disputes* (1974) 417

——*Die Schiedsgerichtbarkeit als Mittel internationaler Streitschlichtung* (1974)

Manning, W.O., *Arbitration Treaties Among the American Nations* (1924) 25

Marsit, M.M., 'La conciliation dans la Convention des Nations Unies sur le droit de la mer', in *Colloque International, Monaco 27-29 Mars 2003* (2004) 343

Martin Estebanez, M.A., 'The High Commission on National Minorities: Development of the Mandate', in M. Bothe and others (eds.), *The OSCE in the Maintenance of Peace and Security: Conflict Prevention, Crisis Management and Peaceful Settlement of Disputes* (1997) 123

Martin, A., 'Private Property, Rights and Interests in the Paris Peace Treaties', (1947) 24 *BYIL* 273

Maundi, M.O., et al., *Getting In: Mediator's Entry into the Settlement of African Conflicts* (2006)

McCall Smith, J., 'The Politics of Dispute Settlement Design: Explaining Legalism in Regional Trade Pacts', (2000) 54 *International Organization* 137

Meron, T., 'Norm Making and Supervision in International Human Rights: Reflections on Institutional Order', (1982) 76 *AJIL* 754

Merrills, J.G., 'The International Court of Justice and the General Act of 1928', (1980) 39 *Cambridge Law Journal* 137

——*The Development of International Law by the European Court of Human Rights* (2nd edn. 1993)

——*Human Rights in Europe* (4th edn. 2001)

——'The Belize-Guatemala Territorial Dispute and the Legal Opinion of January 2002', (2002) 2 *The Global Community* 77

——'The Optional Clause at Eighty', in N. Ando and others (eds.), *Liber Amicorum Judge Shigeru Oda* (2002) 435

——*International Dispute Settlement* (4th edn. 2005)

——'The Mosaic of International Dispute Settlement Procedures: Complementary or Contradictory?', (2007) 54 *NILR* 361.

Meth, E.M., 'Final Offer Arbitration: A Model for Dispute Resolution in Domestic and International Disputes', (1999) 10 *American Review of International Arbitration* 383

Meulen ter, J., *Der Gedanke der Internationalen Organisation in seiner Entwicklung 1300-1800* (1917)

——*Der Gedanke der Internationalen Organisation in seiner Entwicklung 1789-1889* (1929)

Miehsler, H., 'The European Convention for the Peaceful Settlement of Disputes', in H. Kipp and others (eds.), *Um Recht und Freiheit* (1977)

Miguel Diaz, L. and N.A. Oretskin, 'The US Uniform Mediation Act and the Draft UNCITRAL Model Law on International Commercial Conciliation', (2002) 670 *Practising Law Institute / Litigation and Administrative Practice Course Handbook Series* 791

Miles, E.L. and others, *Environmental Regime Effectiveness: Confronting Theory With Evidence* (2002)

Miller, D.H., *The Drafting of the Covenant* (1928) Vols. I, II

Mistelis, L.A., 'ADR in England and Wales', in J. Bell (ed.), *Studies in UK Law* (2002) 197
Mitchell, G., *Making Peace* (1999)
Mnookin, R.H., 'When Not to Negotiate: A Negotiation Imperialist Reflects on Appropriate Limits', (2003) 74 *University of Colorado Law Review* 1077
Moinuddin, H., *The Charter of the Islamic Conference* (1987)
Momtaz, D., 'Les Nations Unies et les commissions d'établissement des faits', in United Nations (ed.), *International Law as a Language for International Relations* (1996) 450
Moore, J.B., *History and Digest of International Arbitrations to which the United States has been a Party* (1898) Vol. I, V
Morgan, D.L., 'Implications of the Proliferation of International Legal Fora: The Example of the Southern Bluefin Tuna Cases', (2002) 43 *Harvard International Law Journal*
Mosler, H.W., 'The International Society as a Legal Community', (1974) 140 *Receuil des Cours* Vol. IV 1
Movsesian, M.L., 'The Sutherland Report and Dispute Settlement', (2005) 2 *IOLR* 201
Münch, F., 'Die Schweizerische Initiative zu zweiseitigen Abmachungen über die friedliche Beilegung von Streitigkeiten', (1966) 26 *ZfAŐVR* 705
Murthy, B.S., 'Diplomacy and Resolution of International Disputes', in United Nations (ed.), *International Law as a Language for International Relations* (1996) 161
Murthy, C.S.R., 'The Role of the UN Secretary-General since the End of the Cold War', (1995) 35 *IJIL* 181
Neuhold, H., *Internationale Konflikte – verbotene und erlaubte Mittel ihre Austragung* (1977)
Noel-Baker, P., *The Geneva Protocol* (1925)
Nordquist, M.H., S. Rosenne, and L.B. Sohn (eds.), *United Nations Convention on the Law of the Sea 1982: A Commentary* (1989)
Nørgaard, C.A., and H.C. Krüger, 'Article 28 § 1-b et § 2', in L.-E. Pettiti, E. Decaux and P.-H. Imbert (eds.), *La Convention Européenne des Droits de l'Homme; Commentaire Article par Article* (1999) 661
Northedge, F.S. and M.D. Donelan, *International Disputes: The Political Aspects* (1971)
Nurick, L. and S.J. Schnably, 'The First ICSID Conciliation', (1986) 1 *ICSID Rev-Foreign Investment Law Journal* 340
Nurmukhametova, E., 'Problems in Connection with the Efficiency of the World Bank Inspection Panel', (2006) 10 *Max Planck Yearbook of United Nations Law* 397

Oda, S., 'Dispute Settlement Prospects in the Law of the Sea', (1995) 44 *ICLQ* 863

Odinkalu, C.A., 'The Individual Complaints Procedure of the African Commission on Human Rights: A Preliminary Assessment', (1998) 8 *Transnational Law and Contemporary Problems* 359

Oduntan, G., 'The Demarcation of Straddling Villages in Accordance with the International Court of Justice Jurisprudence: The Cameroon-Nigeria Experience', (2006) 5 *CJIL* 79

Oellers-Frahm, K. and A. Zimmerman (eds.), *Dispute Settlement in Public International Law: Text and Materials* (2nd edn.) (2001)

——'The Mandatory Component in the CSCE Dispute Settlement System', in M.W. Janis (ed.), *International Courts for the Twenty-First Century* (1992)

Onwuamaegbu, U., 'The Role of ADR in Investor-State Dispute Settlement: The ICSID Experience', (2005) 22 *News from ICSID* (2) 12

Orakhelashvili, A., 'The World Bank Inspection Panel in Context', 1 *IOLR* (2005) 57

Orrego Vicuña, F. and C. Pinto, *The Peaceful Settlement of Disputes: Prospects for the Twenty-First Century* (1999)

——*International Dispute Settlement in an Evolving Global Society* (2004)

Oxman, B.H., 'Complementary Agreements and Compulsory Jurisdiction', (2001) 95 *AJIL* 277

Palmeter, D., and P.C. Mavroidis, 'The WTO Legal System: Sources of Law', (1998) 92 *AJIL* 398

Parra, A.R., 'ICSID and New Trends in International Dispute Settlement', (1993) 87 *ASIL Proc* 2

Pasqualucci, J.M., *The Practice and Procedure of the Inter-American Court of Human Rights* (2003)

Paulsson, J., 'Cross Enrichment of Public and Private Law Dispute Resolution Mechanisms in the International Arena', (1992) 9 *Journal of International Arbitration* 1

Pazartzis, P., *Les Engagements Internationaux en Matière de Règlement Pacifique des Différends entre Etats* (1992)

Pechota, V., 'The Quiet Approach: A Study of the Good Offices Exercised by the United Nations Secretary-General in the Cause of Peace', in K. Venkata Raman (ed.), *Dispute Settlement through the United Nations* (1977) 577

Peck, C., *The United Nations as a Dispute Settlement System. Improving Mechanisms for the Prevention and Solution of Conflict* (1996)

Pescatore, P., W.J. Davey and A.F. Lowenfeld, *Handbook of GATT/WTO Dispute Settlement* (1991)

Peter, J.T., 'Med-Arb in International Arbitration', (1997) 8 *American Review of International Arbitration* 83

Peters, A., 'International Dispute Settlement: A Network of Cooperational Duties', (2003) 14 *EJIL* 1

Petersmann, E.-U., *The GATT/WTO Dispute Settlement System: International Law, International Organization and Dispute Settlement* (1997)

——(ed.), *International Trade Law and the GATT/WTO Dispute Settlement System* (1997)

——'Alternative Dispute Resolution: What Lessons for the WTO?', in R. Briner and others (eds.), *Law of International Business and Dispute Settlement in the 21st Century* (2001) 615

——'WTO Dispute Settlement Practice 1995-2005: Lessons from the Past and Future Challenges', in Y. Taniguchi, A. Yanovich and J. Bohanes, *The WTO in the Twenty-First Century* (2007) 38

Philipse, A.H., *Le Rôle du Conseil de la Société des Nations dans le Règlement Pacifique des Différends Internationaux* (1929)

Politis, N., 'L'Avenir de la médiation', (1910) 17 *RGDIP* 136

Porges, A., *Guide to GATT Law and Practice: Analytical Index* (6th edn. 1995) Vol. II

Potter, P.B., 'The Wal Wal Arbitration', (1936) 30 *AJIL* 27

——*The Wal Wal Arbitration* (1938)

Pratap, R., 'Trade and Environment: Trends in International Dispute Settlement', (2002) 42 *IJIL* 451

Princen, T., *Intermediaries in International Conflict* (1992).

Probst, R., 'Die Schweiz und die internationale Schiedsgerischtbarkeit', (1960) 17 *Schweizerisches Jahrbuch für internationales Recht* 99

Quéneudec, J.P., 'Article 33', in J.P. Cot and A. Pellet, *La Charte des Nations Unies; Commentaire Article par Article* (1985) 567

Quoc Dinh, N., 'Les commissions de conciliation sont elles aussi des commissions d'enquête?', (1967) 71 *RGDIP* 565

Ralston, J.H., *International Arbitration from Athens to Locarno* (1929)

Randelzhofer, A., 'Article 2', in B. Simma and others (eds.), *The Charter of the United Nations; A Commentary* (1994) 74

Ratliff, D.P., 'The PCA Optional Rules for Arbitration of Disputes Relating to Natural Resources and/or the Environment', (2001) 14 *LJIL* 887

Ratner, S.R., 'Does International Law Matter in Preventing Ethnic Conflict?', (2000) 32 *NYUJILP* 591

——Land Feuds and Their Solutions: Finding International Law beyond the Trial Chamber', (2006) 100 *AJIL* 808

Raustiala, K., 'Form and Substance in International Agreements', (2005) 99 *AJIL* 581

Redgwell, C., 'Non-Compliance Procedures and the Climate Change Convention', in B. Chambers (ed.), *Inter-Linkages: The Kyoto Protocol and the International Trade and Investment Regimes* (2001) 43

Registry of the European Court of Human Rights *Survey of Activities* (2007)

Rehman, J., 'Institutions of International law and the Development of Regional Forum for Peaceful Dialogue in South Asia', (2006) 1 *Asian Journal of Comparative Law* article 16

Reif, L.C., 'Conciliation as a Mechanism for the Resolution of International Economic and Business Disputes', (1990-1991) 14 *Fordham International Law Journal* 578

Reimann, H.B., 'Le règlement pacifique des différends à l'OSCE', in M.G. Kohen (ed.), *Promoting Justice, Human Rights and Conflict Resolution through International Law* (2007) 891

Reinisch, A., 'The Use and Limits of Res Judicata and Lis Pendens as Procedural Tools to Avoid Conflicting Dispute Settlement Outcomes', (2004) 3 *The Law and Practice of International Courts and Tribunals* 37

Rehbinder, E. and D. Loperena, 'Legal Protection of Environmental Rights: The Role and Experience of the International Court of Environmental Arbitration and Conciliation', (2001) 31 *Environmental Policy and Law* 282

Reuter, P., 'Le droit au secret et les institutions internationales', (1956) 2 *AFDI* 46

——'Principes de droit public', (1961) 103 *Recueil des Cours* Vol. III 635

Richardson, E.L., 'Jan Mayen in Perspective', (1988) 82 *AJIL* 443

Riphagen, W., 'Dispute Settlement in the 1982 United Nations Convention on the Law of the Sea', in C.L. Rozakis and C.A. Stephanou (eds.), *The New Law of the Sea* (1983) 281

Ritter, J., 'La conférence et la convention sur la répresentation des Etats dans leurs rélations avec les organisations internationales', (1975) 21 *AFDI* 471

Roberts, A. and B. Kingsbury (eds.), *United Nations, Divided World* (2nd edn. 1993)

Robertson, A.H. and J.G. Merrills, *Human Rights in Europe* (3rd edn. 1993)

Robinson, M., *Arbitration and the Hague Peace Conferences* (1936)

Roelofsen, C.G., 'The Jay Treaty and All That; Some Remarks on the Role of Arbitration in European Modern History and its 'Revival', in 1794', in A.H.A. Soons (ed.), *International Arbitration: Past and Prospects* (1990) 201

Rogoff, M.A., 'The Obligation to Negotiate in International Law: Rules and Realities', (1994) 16 *Michigan Journal of International Law* 141

Rolin, H., 'Une conciliation belgo-danoise', (1953) *RGDIP* 353

——'L' Heure de la conciliation', (1957) 3 *European Yearbook* 1

Romano, C.P.R., *The Peaceful Settlement of International Environmental Disputes* (2000)

Rosenne, S., 'The Settlement of Treaty Disputes under the Vienna Convention of 1969', (1971) 31 *ZfAŐRV* 1

——*The Law and Practice of the International Court 1920-2005* (4th edn. 2006)

Rothwell, D.R., and T. Stephens, 'Dispute Resolution and the Law of the Sea: Reconciling the Interaction between the LOS Convention and Other Environmental Instruments', in A.G. Oude Elferink and D.R. Rothwell (eds.), *Oceans Management in the 21st Century: Institutional Frameworks and Responses* (2004) 209

Rousseau, C., 'Echec de la procedure d'enquête et de conciliation dans l'affaire du déroutement de l'avion transportant de Rabat a Tunis les chefs nationalistes algériens le 22 octobre 1956', (1958) 62 *RGDIP* 691

——*Droit International Public* (1983) Vol. V

Rozakis, C.L., 'Unilateral Declarations as a Means of Settling Human Rights Disputes: A New Tool for the Resolution of Disputes in the ECHR's Procedure', in M.G. Kohen (ed.), *Promoting Justice, Human Rights and Conflict Resolution through International Law* (2007) 1003

Rubino-Sammartano, M., *International Arbitration Law and Practice* (2001)

Ruda, J.M., 'Intervention before the International Court of Justice', in V. Lowe and M. Fitzmaurice, *Fifty Years of the International Court* (1996) 487

Rycroft, A., 'The Mediation of Human Rights Disputes', (2002) 18 *South African Journal on Human Rights* 287

Saiki, N., 'WTO Rules and Procedures for the Settlement of Disputes – Their Formation: A Practitioner's View', in M.K. Young and Y. Iwasawa (eds.), *Trilateral Perspectives on International Legal Issues* (1996) 403

Salvia, M. de and M.E. Villiger (eds.), *The Birth of European Human Rights Law* (1998)

Sanders, P., *Quo Vadis Arbitration* (1999)

——'The Links between Arbitration and Conciliation', in K.P. Berger and others (eds.), *Festschrift für Otto Sandrock zum 70. Geburtstag* (2000) 823

——*The Work of UNCITRAL on Arbitration and Conciliation* (2004)

Sandifer, D.V., *Evidence Before International Tribunals* (rev edn. 1975)

Sands, P., 'Non-compliance and Dispute Settlement', in U. Beyerlin, P.-T. Stoll and R. Wolfrum (eds.), *Ensuring Compliance with Multilateral Environmental Agreements: Academic Analysis and Views from Practice* (2006) 353

Sands, P. and R. MacKenzie, 'Guidelines for Negotiating and Drafting Dispute Settlement Clauses for International Environmental Agreements', in International Bureau of the Permanent Court of Arbitration (ed.), *International Investments and the Protection of the Environment* (2001) 305

Sardaro, P., 'Jus Non Dicere for Allegations of Serious Violations of Human Rights; Questionable Trends in the Recent Case Law of the Strasbourg Court', (2003) *EHRLR* 601

Sarooshi, D., 'The Future of the WTO and its Dispute Settlement System', (2005) 1 *IOLR* 151

Sayan, G., 'Arbitration, Conciliation and the Islamic Legal Tradition in Saudi Arabia', (1997) 9 *University of Pennsylvania Journal of International Business Law* 211

Scelle, G., *Théorie Juridique de la Révision des Traités* (1936)

Scheman, L.R. and J.W. Ford, 'The Organisation of American States as Mediator', in S. Touval and I.W. Zartman (eds.), *International Mediation in Theory and Practice* (1985) 197

Schindler, D., *Die Schiedsgerichtbarkeit seit 1914* (1938)

Schram Stokke, O., J. Hovi and G. Ulfstein (eds.), *Implementing the Climate Regime* (2005)

Schreuer, C.H., *The ICSID Convention: A Commentary* (2001)

Schrijver, N.J., 'De treurige lotgevallen van de pogingen tot opstelling van een multilateraal investeringsverdrag', (2001) 49 *SEW-Tijdschrift voor Europees en Economisch Recht* 7

Schücking, W., *Das Völkerrechtliche Institut der Vermittlung* (1923)

Schulte, C., *Compliance with Decisions of the International Court of Justice* (2004)

Schwartz, E.A., 'The Resolution of International Commercial Disputes under the Auspices of the ICC International Court of Arbitration', (1995) 18 *Hastings Journal of International and Comparative Law* 719

Schwebel, S.M., *The Secretary-General of the United Nations* (1952)

Seidl-Hohenfelder, I., 'General Principles of Law as Applied by the Conciliation Commissions Established under the Peace Treaty with Italy of 1947', (1959) 53 *AJIL* 853

——'Die Vergleichungskommission gemäss Art. 83 des Friedenvertrages mit Italien von 1947', (1961) *Archiv des Völkerrechts* 278

Shaw, M.N., 'Peaceful Resolution of "Political Disputes": The Desirable Parameters of ICJ Jurisdiction', in J. Dahlitz (ed.), *Peaceful Resolution of Major International Disputes* (1999) 49

Shawcross, W., *Deliver Us From Evil* (2000)

Shelton, D., 'Law, Non-law and the Problem of "Soft Law"', in D. Shelton (ed.), *Commitment and Compliance: The Role of Non-Binding Norms in the International Legal System* (2000) 1

——'The Boundaries of Human Rights Jurisdiction in Europe', (2003) 13 *Duke Journal of Comparative and International Law* 95

Shifman, B.E., 'The Revitalization of the Permanent Court of Arbitration', (1995) 23 *International Journal of Legal Information* 284

Shihata, I.F.I., 'The Settlement of Disputes regarding Foreign Investment: The Role of the World Bank, with Particular Reference to ICSID and MIGA', (1986) 1 *American University Journal of International Law and Policy* 97

——*MIGA and Foreign Investment* (1988)

——'Avoidance and Settlement of Disputes – the World Bank's Approach and Experience', (1999) 1 *International Law Forum* 90
——*The World Bank in a Changing World* (2000) Vol. III
——*The World Bank Inspection Panel in Practice* (2nd edn. 2000)
——'The World Bank Inspection Panel – Its Historical, Legal and Operational Aspects', in G. Alfredsson and R. Ring (eds.), *The Inspection Panel of the World Bank* (2001) 7
Simmonds, K.R., 'The Belize Mediation', (1968) 17 *ICLQ* 997
Simpson, J.L. and H. Fox, *International Arbitration* (1959)
Sinclair, I., *The Vienna Convention on the Law of Treaties* (2nd edn. 1984)
Sipri/UNESCO *Handbook: Peace, Security and Conflict Prevention* (1998)
Shany, Y., *The Competing Jurisdictions of International Courts and Tribunals* (2003)
Skjelsbaek, K., 'The UN Secretary-General and the Mediation of International Disputes', (1991) 28 *Journal of Peace Research* 99
——and G. Fermann, 'The UN Secretary-General and the Mediation of International Disputes', in J. Bercovitch, *Resolving International Conflict* (1996)
Slemmer-Schulte, S., 'Introductory Note to the Conclusions of the Second Review of the World Bank Inspection Panel', (2000) 39 *ILM* 243
Snow, A.H., *Judicative Conciliation* (1916)
Söderlund, C., 'Lis Pendens, Res Judicata and the Issue of Parallel Proceedings', (2005) 22 *Journal of International Arbitration* 301
Sohn, L.B., 'International Arbitration in Historical Perspective: Past and Present', in A.H.A. Soons (ed.), *International Arbitration: Past and Prospects* (1990) 9
——'Bipartite Consultative Commissions for Preventing and Resolving Disputes Relating to International Trade Treaties', in M. Rama-Montaldo (ed.), *El Derecho Internacional en un Mundo en Transformacion* (1994) Vol. II 1181
——'The Use of Consultations for Monitoring Compliance with Agreements Concluded Under the Auspices of International Organizations', in N. Blokker and S. Muller (eds.), *Towards More Effective Supervision by International Organizations* (1994) 65
——*Broadening the Role of the United Nations in Preventing, Mitigating or Ending International or Internal Conflicts that Threaten International Peace and Security* [brochure] (1997)
Steinberger, H., 'The Conciliation Procedure Established by the Convention on Conciliation and Arbitration within the OSCE', in L. Caflisch (ed.), *The Peaceful Settlement of Disputes between States: Universal and European Perspectives* (1998)
Street, L., 'Mediation', (1994) *American Review of International Arbitration* 149

Strupp, K., 'Le droit du juge international de statuer selon l'équité', (1930) 33 *Recueil des Cours* (3) 357

Stuyt, A.M., *Survey of International Arbitrations 1794 – 1989* (3rd edn. 1990)

Sugihara, T., 'The Judicial Function of the International Court of Justice with Respect to Disputes involving Highly Political Issues', in A.S. Muller, D. Raic, and J.M. Thuránsky (eds.), *The Internationl Court of Justice* (1997) 117

Talayev, A.N., 'Negotiations – Major Means of Peaceful Settlement of International Disputes', in International Law Association, *Report on the Fifty-Third Conference* (1968) 57

Tammes, A.J.P., *Internationaal Publiekrecht* (2nd edn. 1973)

Thant, U., *View from the UN* (1978)

Thomas, L., 'A Comparative Analysis of International Regimes on Ozone and Climate Change with Implications for Regime Design', (2003) 41 *Columbia Journal of Transnational Law* 795

Tigroudja, H. and I.K. Panoussis, *La Cour Interaméricaine des Droits de l'Homme* (2003)

Timsit, G., 'Le fonctionnement de la procédure d'enquête dans l'affaire du "Red Crusader"', (1963) 9 *AFDI* 460

Tomuschat, C., 'Article 2(3)', in B. Simma and others (eds.), *The Charter of the United Nations; A Commentary* (1994) 97

——'The 1928 General Act for the Pacific Settlement of Disputes Revisited', in N. Ando and others (eds.), *Liber Amicorum Judge Shigeru Oda* (2002) 977

Touval, S., 'Does the High Commissioner Mediate?', (2000) 32 *NYUJIP* 707

——and I.W. Zartman (eds.), *International Mediation in Theory and Practice* (1985)

Treves, T., '"Compulsory" Conciliation in the U.N. Law of the Sea Convention', in C. Philipp (ed.), *Liber Amicorum Günther Jaenicke – Zum 85. Geburtstag* (1999) 611

——'Dispute-Settlement in the Law of the Sea: Disorder or System?', in M.G. Kohen (ed.), *Promoting Justice, Human Rights and Conflict Resolution through International Law* (2007) 927

Trooboff, P.D., H. Ding, and S. Koenig, 'Boundary Dispute Concerning the Taba Area', (1989) 83 *AJIL* 590

Turlington, E., 'The Pact of Bogotá', (1948) 42 *AJIL* 608

Udombana, N.J., 'The Unfinished Business: Conflicts, the African Union and the New Partnership for Africa's Development', (2003) 35 *George Washington International Law Review* 55

United Nations *Systematic Survey of Treaties for the Pacific Settlement of International Disputes 1928-1948* (1948)

——*A Survey of Treaty Provisions for the Pacific Settlement of International Disputes 1949-1962* (1966)
——*Handbook on the Peaceful Settlement of Disputes between States* (1992)
UNEP *Handbook for the International Treaties for the Protection of the Ozone Layer* (6th edn. 2003)
Umbricht, V.H., 'Principles of International Mediation. The case of the East African Community', (1984) 187 *Recueil des Cours* 307
——*Multilateral Mediation – Practical Experiences and Lessons* (1989)
Unger, G., *Aristide Briand* (2005)
Urquhart, B., *Hammarskjold* (1974)
Vajic, N., 'Diplomatic Settlement or Adjudication? Advantages and Drawbacks', in L. Caflisch (ed.), *The Peaceful Settlement of Disputes Between States: Universal and European Perspectives* (1998) 17
Vattel, M. de, *Le Droit des Gens ou Principes de la Loi Naturelle* (1768)
Venkata Raman, K. (ed.), *Dispute Settlement through the United Nations* (1977)
Vera, C. de, 'Arbitrating Harmony: "Med-Arb" and the Confluence of Culture and Rule of Law in the Resolution of International Commercial Disputes in China', (2004) 18 *Columbia Journal of Asian Law* 149
Verzijl, J.H.W., 'La base des jugements internationaux au cours de l'histoire', (1955) 59 *RGDIP* 370
——*International Law in Historical Perspective* (1968) Vol. I
——*International Law in Historical Perspective* (1976) Vol. VIII
Victor, D.G., 'The Operation and Effectiveness of the Montreal Non-Compliance Procedure', in D.G. Victor, K. Raustiala and B. Skolnikoff (eds.), *The Implementation and Effectiveness of International Environmental Commitments: Theory and Practice* (1998) 137
Vignes, D.H., 'La commission de conciliation franco-italienne', (1955) 1 *AFDI* 212
Villani, U., 'Conciliation and Consensus in UNCTAD', (1976) 2 *Italian Yearbook of International Law* 61
——*La Conciliazione nelle Controversie Internazionali* (1979)
——'A New Conciliation Procedure: The Vienna Convention on the Representation of Sates in Their Relations with International Organisations of a Universal Character', (1978-1979) 4 *Italian Yearbook of International Law* 31
Visscher de, C., 'Les commissions de conciliation et la Société des Nations', (1922) 29 *RGDIP* 410
——*Théories et Réalités en Droit International Public* (4th edn. 1970)
——*De l'Equité dans le Règlement Arbitral ou Judiciaire des Litiges de Droit International Public* (1972)
Vulcan, C., *La Conciliation dans le Droit International Actuel* (1932)

Waart de, P.J.I.M., *Het Onderhandelingselement in de Vreedzame Regeling van Geschillen tussen Staten* (1971)

——*The Element of Negotiation in the Pacific Settlement of Disputes between States* (1973)

Waldock, C.H.M. and F. Vallat (eds.), *International Disputes: The Legal Aspects* (1972)

Walters, F.P., *A History of the League of Nations* (1952) Vols. I, II

Wampach, A., 'Pratiques de la commission: ses relations avec les réquerants', in M. de Salvia and M.E. Villiger (eds.), *The Birth of European Human Rights Law* (1998) 339

Wang, X. and G. Wiser, 'The Implementation and Compliance Regimes under the Climate Change Convention and its Kyoto Protocol', (2002) 11 *Review of European Community and International Environmental Law* 181

Watts, A., 'State Succession: Some Recent Practical Problems', *Liber Amicorum Günther Jaenicke Zum 85. Geburtstag* (1998) 397

——'Introductory Note to Agreement on Succession Issues between the Five Successor States of the Former State of Yugoslavia', (2002) 41 *ILM* 1

Webb, K., V. Koutrakou, and M. Walters, 'The Yugoslavian Conflict, European Mediation and the Contingency Model: A Critical Perspective', in J. Bercovitch (ed.), *Resolving International Conflict* (1996) 171

Wehberg, H., 'Le Protocol de Genève', (1925) 7 *Recueil des Cours* Vol. II 1

——'Die Vergleichskommissionen im modernen Völkerrecht', (1958) 19 *ZfAÖRV* 551

Weil, P., 'Some Observations on the Arbitral Award in the Taba Case', (1989) (1) 23 *Israel Law Review* 1

Weiler, J.H.H., 'The Rule of Lawyers and the Ethos of Diplomats; Reflections on the Internal and External Legitimacy of WTO Dispute Settlement', (2001) 35 *Journal of World Trade* 191

Weisburd, A.M., 'The Effect of Treaties and Other Formal International Acts on the Customary Law of Human Rights', (1995/1996) 25 *Georgia Journal of International and Comparative Law* 99

Wembou, D., 'A propos du nouveau méchanisme de l'OAU sur les conflits', (1993) 6 *RADIC* 723

Werksman, J., 'Compliance and the Kyoto Protocol: Building a Backbone into a "Flexible" Regime', (1998) 9 *Yearbook of International Environmental Law* 48

White, N.D., *The Law of International Organisations* (1996)

——*Keeping the Peace* (2nd edn. 1997)

Whitfield, T., 'Good Offices and "Groups of Friends"', in S. Chesterman (ed.), *Secretary or General? The UN Secretary General in World Politics* (2007) 86

Wilkenfeld, J. and others (eds.), *Mediating International Crises* (2005)
Wirth, D.A., 'The Sixth Session (part two) and Seventh Session of the Conference of the Parties to the Framework Convention on Climate Change', (2002) 96 *AJIL* 648
Woolsey, L., 'Bolivia – Paraguay Dispute', (1929) 23 *AJIL* 110
——'Bolivia – Paraguay Dispute', (1930) 24 *AJIL* 122
Wright, Q., 'The Test of Aggression in the Italo-Ethiopian War', (1936) 30 *AJIL* 45
WTO Consultative Board, *The Future of the WTO: Addressing Institutional Challenges in the New Millennium* (2005)
Wyler, E., 'Le médiateur, tiers impartial au coeur du droit', in M.G. Kohen (ed.), *Promoting Justice, Human Rights and Conflict Resolution through International Law* (2007) 973
Ye, A., 'Commentary on Integrated Dispute Resolution Systems in the PRC', International Council for Commercial Arbitration *New Horizons in International Commercial Arbitration and Beyond* (2005) 478
Yoshida, O., 'Soft Enforcement of Treaties: The Montreal Protocol's Noncompliance Procedure and the Functions of Internal International Institutions', (1999) 10 *Colorado Journal of International Environmental Law and Policy* 95
Young, O. (ed.), *The Effectiveness of International Environmental Regimes* (1999)
Zaagman, R. and H. Zaal, 'The CSCE High Commissioner on National Minorities: Prehistory and Negotiations', in A. Bloed (ed.), *The Challenges of Change* (1994) 9
——'The CSCE High Commissioner on National Minorities: An Analysis of the Mandate and the Institutional Context', in A. Bloed (ed.), *The Challenges of Change* (1994) 113
Zartman, I.W., *Ripe for Resolution: Conflict and Intervention in Africa* (1989)
Zemanek, K., 'The Legal Foundations of the International System. General Course on Public International Law', (1997) 266 *Recueil des Cours* 1
——'Is the Term "Soft Law" Convenient?', in G. Hafner and others (eds.), *Liber Amicorum Professor Ignaz Seidl-Hohenveldern* (1998) 843
Ziadé, N.G., 'ICSID Conciliation', (1996) 13 *News from ICSID* (2) 3
Žourek, J., 'Le projet du Roi tchèque George Podiebrad', (1964) *AFDI* 14

Anonymous:

——'Chronique des faits internationaux', (1958) 62 *RGDIP* 665
——'L'Affaire du F. OABV', (1958) 4 *AFDI* 282

——'The Peacemaker: An Interview with UN Under-Secretary General Alvaro de Soto', (2002) 26 *Fletcher Forum of World Affairs* 83

——'United Nations Mediation of Regional Crises', (1986) 80 *ASIL Proceedings* 135

TABLE OF CASES

Adjudication Cases and Advisory Opinions

Conciliation, Settlement and Analogous Cases

TABLE OF INTERNATIONAL AGREEMENTS

MULTILATERAL AGREEMENTS AND INSTRUMENTS

Bilateral Agreements

INDEX

www.ingramcontent.com/pod-product-compliance
Lightning Source LLC
Chambersburg PA
CBHW071240230926
51849CB00001B/167
* 9 7 8 9 0 6 7 0 4 2 6 0 4 *